WHY MACHINES WILL I RULE THE WORLD

The book's core argument is that an artificial intelligence that could equal or exceed human intelligence—sometimes called artificial *general* intelligence (AGI)—is for mathematical reasons impossible. It offers two specific reasons for this claim:

1. Human intelligence is a capability of a complex dynamic system—the human brain and central nervous system.
2. Systems of this sort cannot be modelled mathematically in a way that allows them to operate inside a computer.

In supporting their claim, the authors, Jobst Landgrebe and Barry Smith, marshal evidence from mathematics, physics, computer science, philosophy, linguistics, and biology, setting up their book around three central questions: What are the essential marks of human intelligence? What is it that researchers try to do when they attempt to achieve "artificial intelligence" (AI)? And why, after more than 50 years, are our most common interactions with AI, for example with our bank's computers, still so unsatisfactory?

Landgrebe and Smith show how a widespread fear about AI's potential to bring about radical changes in the nature of human beings and in the human social order is founded on an error. There is still, as they demonstrate in a final chapter, a great deal that AI can achieve which will benefit humanity. But these benefits will be achieved without the aid of systems that are more powerful than humans, which are as impossible as AI systems that are intrinsically "evil" or able to "will" a takeover of human society.

Jobst Landgrebe is a scientist and entrepreneur with a background in philosophy, mathematics, neuroscience, and bioinformatics. Landgrebe is also the founder of Cognotekt, a German AI company which has since 2013 provided working systems used by companies in areas such as insurance claims management, real estate management, and medical billing. After more than 10 years in the AI industry, he has developed an exceptional understanding of the limits and potential of AI in the future.

Barry Smith is one of the most widely cited contemporary philosophers. He has made influential contributions to the foundations of ontology and data science, especially in the biomedical domain. Most recently, his work has led to the creation of an international standard in the ontology field (ISO/IEC 21838), which is the first example of a piece of philosophy that has been subjected to the ISO standardization process.

'It's a highly impressive piece of work that makes a new and vital contribution to the literature on AI and AGI. The rigor and depth with which the authors make their case is compelling, and the range of disciplinary and scientific knowledge they draw upon is particularly remarkable and truly novel.'

Shannon Vallor, *Edinburgh Futures Institute,*
The University of Edinburgh

WHY MACHINES WILL NEVER RULE THE WORLD

Artificial Intelligence without Fear

Jobst Landgrebe and Barry Smith

NEW YORK AND LONDON

Cover image: © Abstract Aerial Art / Getty Images

First published 2023
by Routledge
605 Third Avenue, New York, NY 10158

and by Routledge
4 Park Square, Milton Park, Abingdon, Oxon, OX14 4RN

Routledge is an imprint of the Taylor & Francis Group, an informa business

© 2023 Jobst Landgrebe and Barry Smith

The right of Jobst Landgrebe and Barry Smith to be identified as authors of this work has been asserted in accordance with sections 77 and 78 of the Copyright, Designs and Patents Act 1988.

All rights reserved. No part of this book may be reprinted or reproduced or utilised in any form or by any electronic, mechanical, or other means, now known or hereafter invented, including photocopying and recording, or in any information storage or retrieval system, without permission in writing from the publishers.

Trademark notice: Product or corporate names may be trademarks or registered trademarks, and are used only for identification and explanation without intent to infringe.

Library of Congress Cataloging-in-Publication Data
A catalog record for this title has been requested

ISBN: 978-1-032-31516-4 (hbk)
ISBN: 978-1-032-30993-4 (pbk)
ISBN: 978-1-003-31010-5 (ebk)

DOI: 10.4324/9781003310105

Typeset in Bembo
by Apex CoVantage, LLC

CONTENTS

Foreword ix

1 Introduction 1

   1.1 The Singularity 1
   1.2 Approach 3
   1.3 Limits to the modelling of animate nature 7
   1.4 The AI hype cycle 9
   1.5 Why machines will not inherit the earth 11
   1.6 How to read this book 18

PART I
Properties of the human mind 21

2 The human mind 23

   2.1 Basic characteristics of the human mind 23
   2.2 The mind-body problem: monism and its varieties 24

3 Human and machine intelligence 37

   3.1 Capabilities and dispositions 37
   3.2 Intelligence 41
   3.3 AI and human intelligence 48

vi Contents

4 The nature of human language   63

    4.1 Why conversation matters 63
    4.2 Aspects of human language 64

5 The variance and complexity of human language   74

    5.1 Conversations: an overview 74
    5.2 Levels of language production and interpretation 77
    5.3 Conversation contexts 77
    5.4 Discourse economy: implicit meaning 82
    5.5 Structural elements of conversation 85
    5.6 How humans pass the Turing test 88

6 Social and ethical behaviour   90

    6.1 Can we engineer social capabilities? 91
    6.2 Intersubjectivity 93
    6.3 Social norms 95
    6.4 Moral norms 98
    6.5 Power 106

PART II
The limits of mathematical models   107

7 Complex systems   109

    7.1 Models 109
    7.2 Computability 115
    7.3 Systems 117
    7.4 The scope of extended Newtonian mathematics 119
    7.5 Complex systems 124
    7.6 Examples of complex systems 140

8 Mathematical models of complex systems   144

    8.1 Multivariate distributions 144
    8.2 Deterministic and stochastic computable system models 146
    8.3 Newtonian limits of stochastic models of complex systems 149
    8.4 Descriptive and interpretative models of complex systems 153
    8.5 Predictive models of complex systems 158

8.6 Naïve approaches to complex system modelling 160
8.7 Refined approaches 180
8.8 The future of complex system modelling 187

Part III
The limits and potential of AI   193

9 Why there will be no machine intelligence   195

    9.1 Brain emulation and machine evolution 195
    9.2 Intentions and drivenness 203
    9.3 Consciousness 205
    9.4 Philosophy of mind, computation, and AI 213
    9.5 Objectifying intelligence and theoretical thinking 214

10 Why machines will not master human language   217

    10.1 Language as a necessary condition for AGI 217
    10.2 Why machine language production always falls short 219
    10.3 AI conversation emulation 226
    10.4 Mathematical models of human conversations 235
    10.5 Why conversation machines are doomed to fail 242

11 Why machines will not master social interaction   245

    11.1 No AI emulation of social behaviour 245
    11.2 AI and legal norms 248
    11.3 No machine emulation of morality 250

12 Digital immortality   259

    12.1 Infinity stones 259
    12.2 What is a mind? 261
    12.3 Transhumanism 282
    12.4 Back to Bostrom 287

13 AI spring eternal   288

    13.1 AI for non-complex systems 288
    13.2 AI for complex systems 295
    13.3 AI boundaries 298
    13.4 How AI will change the world 301

Appendix: Turbulence: Mathematical details   *302*
Glossary   *304*
References   *313*
Index   *335*

FOREWORD

Rationale for this book

This book is about artificial intelligence (AI), which we conceive as the application of mathematics to the modelling (primarily) of the functions of the human brain. We focus specifically on the question of whether modelling of this sort has limits, or whether—as proposed by the advocates of what is called the 'Singularity'—AI modelling might one day lead to an irreversible and uncontrollable explosion of ever more intelligent machines.

As concerns the current state of the art, AI researchers are, for understandable reasons, immensely proud of their amazing technical discoveries. It therefore seems obvious to all that there is an almost limitless potential for further, equally significant AI discoveries in the future.

Enormous amounts of funding are accordingly being invested in advancing the frontiers of AI in medical research, national defense, and many other areas. If our arguments hold water, then a significant fraction of this funding may be money down the drain. For this reason alone, therefore, it is probably no bad thing for the assumption of limitless potential for AI progress to be subjected to the sort of critical examination that we have here attempted.

The result, we must confess, is not always easy reading. To do our job properly, we found it necessary to move to a rather drastic degree beyond the usual disciplinary borders, drawing not merely on philosophy, mathematics, and computer science, but also on linguistics, psychology, anthropology, sociology, physics, and biology. In the "Approach" section of the Introduction we provide the rationale for this methodology and, where this is needed, for our choice of literature. In the "Glossary" (pp. 304ff.) we provide what we hope are reader-friendly definitions of the technical terms used in the main text.

We raise what we believe are powerful arguments against the possibility of engineering machines that would possess an intelligence that would equal or surpass that of humans. These arguments have immediate implications for claims, such as those of Elon Musk, according to whom AI could become 'an immortal dictator from which we would never escape'. Relax. Machines will not rule the world.

At the same time, our arguments throw light on the question of which varieties of AI *are* achievable. In this respect we are fervent optimists, and one of us is indeed contributing to the creation of new AI products being applied in industry as this book is being written. In the final chapter of the book we outline some of the positive consequences of our arguments for practical applications of AI in the future.

A new *affaire Dreyfus?*

This book is concerned not with the tremendous successes of artificial intelligence along certain narrow lanes, such as text translation or image recognition. Rather, our concern is with what is called *general* AI and with the ability of computers to emulate, and indeed to go beyond, the general intelligence manifested by humans.

We will show that it is not possible (and this means: not ever) to engineer machines with a general cognitive performance even at the level of vertebrates such as crows. When we have presented our arguments in favour of this view to friendly audiences, the most common reaction has been that we are surely just repeating the mistake of earlier technology sceptics and that our arguments, too, are doomed to be refuted by the inevitable advances of AI in the future.

Hubert Dreyfus was one of the first serious critics of AI research. His book *What Computers Can't Do*, first published in 1972, explains that symbolic (logic-based) AI, which was at that time the main paradigm in AI research, was bound to fail, because the mental processes of humans do not follow a logical pattern. As Dreyfus correctly pointed out, the logical formulation of our thoughts is merely the end-product of a tiny fraction of our mental activities—an idea which seems to be undergoing a mild revival (Fjelland 2020).

In the third edition of his book, Dreyfus (1992) was still claiming that he had been right from the beginning. And so he was; though he did not provide the sorts of arguments we give in this book, which are grounded not on Heideggerian philosophy but on the mathematical implications of the theory of complex systems.

We start out from the assumption that all complex systems are such that they obey the laws of physics. However, we then show that for mathematical reasons we cannot use these laws to analyse the behaviours of complex systems because the complexity of such systems goes beyond our mathematical modelling abilities. The human brain, certainly, is a complex system of this sort; and while there are some of today's AI proponents who believe that the currently fashionable AI paradigm of 'deep neural networks'—connectionist as opposed to symbolic AI (Minsky 1991)—can mimic the way the brain functions, we will show in what follows that, again for mathematical reasons, this is not so, not only for deep neural networks but for any other type of AI software that might be invented in the future.

We define artificial general intelligence (AGI) as an AI that has a level of intelligence that is either equivalent to or greater than that of human beings or is able to cope with problems that arise in the world that surrounds human beings with a degree of adequacy at least similar to that of human beings (a precise definition of what this means is given in sections 3.3.3–3.3.4).

Our argument can be presented here in a somewhat simplified form as follows:

A1. To build an AGI we would need technology with an intelligence that is at least comparable to that of human beings (from the definition of AGI just provided).
A2. The only way to engineer such technology is to create a software emulation of the human neurocognitive system. (Alternative strategies designed to bring about an AGI without emulating human intelligence are considered and rejected in section 3.3.3 and chapter 12.)

However,

B1. To create a software emulation of the behaviour of a system we would need to create a mathematical model of this system that enables prediction of the system's behaviour.[1]
B2. It is impossible to build mathematical models of this sort for complex systems. (This is shown in sections 8.4–8.7.)
B3. The human neurocognitive system is a complex system (see chapter 7).
B4. *Therefore*, we cannot create a software emulation of the human neurocognitive system.

From (A2.) and (B4.) it now follows that:

C. An AGI is impossible.

An analogy from physics

We conceive thesis (C.) to be analogous to the thesis that it is impossible to create a perpetual motion machine.

---

1 The requirements which such predictions would need to satisfy are outlined in 3.3.4, with mathematical details in 7.1.1.4 and 8.5.

Someone might, now, argue that our current understanding of the laws of physics might one day be superseded by a new understanding, according to which a perpetual motion machine *is* possible after all.

And similarly someone might argue against the thesis of this book that our current understanding of the laws of *mathematics* might one day change. New ways of modelling complex dynamic systems may be discovered that would indeed allow the mathematical modelling of, for example, the workings of the human mind.

To see why this, too, is impossible, we show that it would have to involve discoveries even more far-reaching than the invention by Newton and Leibniz of the differential calculus. And it would require that those who have tried in the past to model complex systems mathematically, including Feynman (Feynman et al. 2010) and Heisenberg (Marshak et al. 2005, p. 76), were wrong to draw the conclusion that such an advance will never be possible. This conclusion was drawn not only by the best minds in the past. There exist also today no proposals even on the horizon of current physics or mathematics to surmount the obstacles to the modelling of complex systems identified in what follows.[2]

Acknowledgements

We thank especially Kevin Mulligan, Ingvar Johannson, and Johannes Weiß for their critical review of the manuscript. In addition, we thank Yuri Basharov, David Braun, Janna Hastings, David Hershenov, David Limbaugh, Jens Kipper, Bill Rapaport, Alan Ruttenberg, Len Talmy, Erik Thomsen, Leo Zaibert, and our anonymous reviewers for their valuable comments. We alone are responsible for any errors that remain.

The book is dedicated to our families.

---

[2] Two papers on *turbulence* written in 1941 by Kolmogorov (1941b, 1941a) raised some hopes that at least this complex system phenomenon could be understood mathematically. But these hopes, too, were abandoned, as we show in 8.7.1.1, with mathematical details provided in the Appendix.

1
INTRODUCTION

Since the research field of AI was first conceived in the late 1940s, the idea of an artificial general intelligence (AGI) has been put forward repeatedly. Advocates of AGI hold that it will one day be possible to build a computer that can emulate and indeed exceed all expressions of human-specific intelligence, including not only reasoning and memory, but also consciousness, including feelings and emotions, and even the will and moral thinking. This idea has been elaborated and cultivated in many different ways, but we note that AGI is far from being realised (Cohen et al. 2019).

Pennachin et al. (2007, p. 1) assert that 'AGI appears by all known science to be quite possible. Like nanotechnology, it is "merely an engineering problem", though certainly a very difficult one'. As we shall see, assertions of this sort are common in the literature on AGI. As the examination of this literature reveals, however, this is not because the thesis that there might be *fundamental* (which means: mathematical) obstacles to the achievement of AGI has been investigated and ruled out. Rather, it is because this possibility has simply been ignored.

1.1 The Singularity

Closely related to the concept of AGI is the idea of the 'Singularity', a term first applied in the AI field by Vinge (1993) and then popularised by Ray Kurzweil (2005), a pioneer of second generation AI. The term is used to refer to a point in time after which the development of AI technology becomes irreversible and uncontrollable,[1] with unknown consequences for the future of humanity.

---

1 See the Glossary for a definition. The decrease and increase of the values of a function close to a singularity is hyperbolic, which is why the term 'singularity' was repurposed to describe an

DOI: 10.4324/9781003310105-1

These developments are seen by Kurzweil as an inevitable consequence of the achievement of AGI, and he too believes that we are approaching ever closer to the point where AGI will in fact be achieved (Eden et al. 2012). Proponents of the Singularity idea believe that once the Singularity is reached, AGI machines will develop their own will and begin to act autonomously, potentially detaching themselves from their human creators in ways that will threaten human civilisation (Weinstein et al. 2017). The Singularity idea features widely in debates around AGI, and it has led scientists and philosophers (as well as politicians and science fiction authors) to explore the ethical implications of this idea, for instance by postulating norms and principles that would need to be somehow built into AGIs in the future in order to counteract their potentially negative effects. Visions are projected according to which AI machines, because of their superior ethical and reasoning powers, will one day supplant existing human-based institutions such as the legal system and democratic elections. Moor (2009) talks of 'full ethical agents', which are for him the highest form of machine morality, though at the same time he believes that agents of this sort will not appear any time soon.

Visions of AGI have been associated with lavishly promoted ideas according to which we are moving towards a time when it will be possible to find cures for human diseases by applying ever more powerful computers to 'big' biological data. In the wake of the successful sequencing of the human genome and the related advent of DNA microarrays and of mass spectrometry, mass cytometry, and other sophisticated methods for performing mass assays of the fundamental components of organic matter, considerable funds have been invested in big 'ome' (transcriptome, proteome, connectome) and similar projects. Yet at the same time, even after some 20 years of research (in which both of us have participated), there is a haunting awareness of the paucity of results with significant implications for human health and disease achieved along these lines.

But we already know enough from what we have learned in the foregoing that the Singularity will not arise, given that

D1. Such a Singularity would require the engineering of an AI with the capability to engineer another machine more intelligent than itself.
D2. The exercise of this capability, at least in its early stages, would require assistance from and thus persuasive communication with human beings in bringing about the realisation of a series of highly complex goals (section 12.2.5).
D3. Only an AGI could succeed in the realisation of such goals (section 3.3).
D4. Therefore, the Singularity would require an AGI.

imagined rapid realisation of 'superintelligence' once a certain point is reached in the development of AI.

Now, however, using the proposition C (from p. xi), that an AGI is impossible and (D4.) we can infer:

E. The Singularity is impossible.

1.2 Approach

In the pages that follow we will analyse the scope and potential of AI in the future and show why the dark scenarios projected by Nick Bostrom (Bostrom 2003), Elon Musk, and others will not be realised. First, however, we set forth the sources and methods we will use. The reader interested more in content than methods may accordingly skip this section and proceed directly to page 9.

1.2.1 Realism

The overarching doctrine which binds together the different parts of this book is a non-reductivist commitment to the existence of physical, biological, social, and mental reality, combined with a realist philosophy about the world of common sense or in other words the world of 'primary theory' as expounded by the anthropologist Robin Horton (1982).[2] Thus we hold that our common-sense beliefs—to the effect that we are conscious, have minds and a will, and that we have access through perception to objects in reality—are both true and consistent with the thesis that everything in reality is subject to the laws of physics. To understand how scientific realism and common-sense realism can be reconciled, we need to take careful account of the way in which systems are determined according to the granularity of their elements. (This book is essentially a book about systems, and about how systems can be modelled scientifically.)

Central components of our realist view include the following:[3]

1. The universe consists of matter, which is made of elementary particles: quarks, leptons, and bosons.[4] Entities of various supernumerary sorts exist in

---

2 Those parts of primary theory which concern human mental activities—for example thinking, believing, wanting—correspond to what elsewhere in this book we refer to as the common-sense ontology of the mental, and which is (sometimes disparagingly) referred to by analytic philosophers as 'folk psychology'.
3 The view in question is inspired by Johansson's 'irreductive materialism' (Johansson 2012). It is similar also to the liberal naturalism expounded by De Caro (2015), which attempts 'to reconcile common sense and scientific realism in a non-Cartesian pluralist ontological perspective' and which explicitly includes as first-class entities not only material things such as you and me but also entities, such as debts, that have a history and yet are non-physical. See also Haack (2011).
4 This is the current view, which is likely to change as physics progresses. Changes on this level will not affect any of the arguments in this book.

those parts of the universe where animals and human beings congregate. (See item 6 in this list.)
2. All interactions of matter are governed by the four fundamental forces (interactions) described by physics (electromagnetism, gravity, the strong interaction, the weak interaction), yielding all of the phenomena of nature that we perceive, including conscious human beings.
3. Fundamental entities should not be multiplied without necessity.[5] No counterpart of this maxim applies, however, to the vast realms of entities created as the products of human action and of human convention. The kilometre exists; but so also does the Arabic mile, the Burmese league, and the Mesopotamian cubit—and so do all the 'ordinary objects' discussed by Lowe (2005).
4. We thus hold that the totality of what exists can be viewed from multiple different, mutually consistent granular perspectives. From one perspective, this totality includes quarks, leptons, and the like. From another perspective it includes organisms, portions of inorganic matter, and (almost) empty space.[6]
5. At all levels we can distinguish both types and instances of these types. In addition we can distinguish at all levels continuants (such as molecules) and occurrents (such as protein folding processes).
6. Some organisms, for instance we ourselves and (we presume) you also, dear reader, are conscious. Conscious processes, which always involve an observer, are what we shall call emanations from complex systems (specifically: from organisms).[7] When viewed from the outside, they can be observed only indirectly (they can, though, be viewed directly via introspection).
7. In the world made by conscious organisms, there exist not only tapestries and cathedrals, dollar bills and drivers' licenses, but also social norms, poems, nation states, cryptocurrencies, Olympic records, mathematical equations, and data.

1.2.2 General remarks on methods

To answer the question of whether AGI is possible, we draw on results from a wide range of disciplines, in particular on technical results of mathematics and theoretical physics, on empirical results from molecular biology and other hard science domains, and (to illustrate the implications for AI of our views when

---

5 This is Schaffer's Laser (Schaffer 2015).
6 On the underlying theory of granular partitions see Bittner et al. (2001, 2003).
7 We adapt the term 'emanation' from its usage in physics to mean any type of electromagnetic radiation, for example, thermal radiation, or other form of energy propagation (for example, sound), which is observable, but which is produced by a system process which is hidden (Parzen 2015) (cannot be observed); for a detailed definition see 2.1.

applied to the phenomenon of human conversation) on descriptive results from linguistics. In addition to the standard peer-reviewed literature, our sources in these fields include authoritative textbooks—above all the *Introduction to the Theory of Complex Systems* by Thurner et al. (2018)—and salient writings of Alan Turing, Jürgen Schmidhuber, and other leaders of AI research.

We also deal with contributions to the Singularity debate made by contemporary philosophers, above all David Chalmers (see section 9.1), and—by way of light relief—on the writings of the so-called transhumanists on the prospects for what they call 'digital immortality' (chapter 12).

1.2.3 Formal and material ontology

For reasons set forth in (Smith 2005), most leading figures in the early phases of the development of analytic philosophy adhered to an overly simplistic view of the world, which left no room for entities of many different sorts. Thus they developed assays of reality which left no room for, *inter alia*, norms, beliefs, feelings, values, claims, obligations, intentions, dispositions, capabilities, communities, societies, organisations, authority, energy, works of music, scientific theories, physical systems, events, natural kinds, and entities of many other sorts. Many analytic philosophers embraced further an overly simplistic view of the mind/brain, often taking the form of an assertion to the effect that the mind operates like (or indeed that it is itself) a computer. Computer scientists often think the opposite, namely that a computer 'acts' like the human brain and that the differences between these two types of machines will one day be overcome with the development of AGI.[8] But a computer does not *act*, and the human brain is not a machine, as we shall see in the course of this book.

In recent years, on the other hand, analytic philosophers have made considerable strides in expanding the coverage domain of their ontologies, in many cases by rediscovering ideas that had been advanced already in other traditions, as, for example, in phenomenology. They continue still, however, to resist the idea of a comprehensive realist approach to ontology. This reflects a more general view, shared by almost all analytic philosophers, to the effect that philosophy should not seek the sort of systematic and all-encompassing coverage that is characteristic of science, but rather seek point solutions to certain sorts of puzzles, often based on 'reduction' of one type of entity to another (Mulligan et al. 2006).

There is however one group of philosophers—forming what we can call the school of realist phenomenologists (Smith 1997)—who embraced this sort of comprehensive realist approach to ontology, starting out from the methodological guidelines sketched by Husserl in his *Logical Investigations* (Husserl 2000).

---

8 Mathematicians who have to deal with computers take the view that computers are mere servants (*Rechenknechte*) which exist merely to perform calculations.

Like Frege, and in contrast to, for example, Heidegger or Derrida, the principal members of this school employed a clear and systematic style. This is especially true of Adolf Reinach, who anticipated in his masterwork of 1913—'The *A Priori* Foundations of the Civil Law' (Reinach 2012)—major elements of the theory of speech acts reintroduced by Austin and Searle in the 1960s.[9] Husserl's method was applied by Reinach to the ontology of law, by Roman Ingarden to the ontology of literature and music, and to the realm of human values in general (Ingarden 1986, 1973, 2013, 2019).[10]

Two other important figures of the first generation of realist phenomenologists were Max Scheler and Edith Stein, who applied this same method, respectively, to ethics and anthropology on the one hand, and to social and political ontology on the other. Ingarden is of interest also because he established a branch of realist phenomenology in Poland.[11]

The most salient members of the second generation of this school were Nicolai Hartmann, whose systematisation of Scheler's ideas on the ontology of value will concern us in chapter 6, and Arnold Gehlen, a philosopher, sociologist, and anthropologist working in the tradition of the German school of philosophical anthropology founded by Scheler.[12]

For questions of perception, person, act, will, intention, obligation, sociality, and value, accordingly, we draw on the accounts of the realist phenomenologists, especially Reinach, Scheler, and Hartmann. This is both because their ideas were groundbreaking and because their central findings remain valid today. For questions relating to human nature, psychology, and language, we use Scheler and Gehlen, though extended by the writings of J. J. Gibson and of the ecological school in psychology which he founded.

1.2.3.1 An ecological approach to mental processing

A subsidiary goal of this book is to show the relevance of environments (settings, contexts) to the understanding of human and machine behaviour, and in this we are inspired by another, less familiar branch of the already mentioned ecological

---

9 (Smith 1990; Mulligan 1987) It is significant that Reinach was one of the first German philosophers to take notice, in 1914, of the work of Frege (Reinach 1969).
10 Ingarden's massive three-volume work on formal, existential, and material ontology is only now being translated into English. This work, along with Husserl's *Logical Investigations*, provides the foundation for our treatment of the principal ontological categories (such as continuant, occurrent, role, function, and disposition) that are used in this book.
11 One prominent member of the latter was Karol Wojtyła, himself an expert on the ethics and anthropology of Scheler (Wojtyła 1979), and it is an interesting feature of the school of phenomenological realists, perhaps especially so when we come to gauge the value of its contribution to ethics, that two of its members—namely Stein (St. Teresa Benedicta of the Cross) and Wojtyła (St. John Paul II)—were canonised.
12 Gehlen was one of the first to explore theoretically the question of the nature and function of human language from the evolutionary perspective in his main work *Man. His Nature and Place in the World* (Gehlen 1988), first published in German in 1940 (Gehlen, 1993 [1940]).

school in psychology, which gave rise to a remarkable volume entitled *One Boy's Day: A Specimen Record of Behavior* by Barker et al. (1951). This documents over some 450 pages all the natural and social environments[13] occupied by Raymond, a typical 7-year-old schoolboy on a typical day (April 26, 1949) in a typical small Kansas town.

Barker shows how each of the acts, including the mental acts, performed by Raymond in the course of the day is tied to some specific environment, and he reminds us thereby that any system designed to emulate human mental activity inside the machine will have to include a subsystem (or better: systems) dealing with the vast and ever-changing totality of environments within which such activity may take place.

1.2.3.2 Sociology and social ontology

A further feature of the analytic tradition in philosophy was its neglect of sociality and of social interaction as a topic of philosophical concern. Matters began to change with the rediscovery of speech acts in the 1960s by Austin and Searle, a development which has in recent years given rise to a whole new sub-discipline of analytic social ontology, focusing on topics such as 'shared' or 'collective agency' (Ziv Konzelmann 2013). Many 20th-century analytic philosophers, however, have adopted an overly simplistic approach also to the phenomena of sociology and social ontology[14], and to counteract this we move once again outside the analytic mainstream, drawing first on the classical works of Max Weber and Talcott Parsons, on the writings on sociality of Gibson and his school (Heft 2017), and also on contemporary anthropologists, especially those in the tradition of Richerson et al. (2005).

1.3 Limits to the modelling of animate nature

It is well known that the utility of science depends (in increasing order) on its ability to *describe*, *explain*, and *predict* natural processes. We can *describe* the foraging behaviour of a parrot, for example, by using simple English. But to *explain* the parrot's behaviour we need something more (defined in section 7.1.1.4). And for *prediction* we need causal models, and these causal models must be mathematical.

---

13 These are called 'settings' in Barker's terminology (Barker 1968), (Smith 2000). Schoggen (1989) gives an overview of the work of Barker and his school, and Heft (2001) describes the philosophical background to Barker's work and his relations to the broader community of ecological psychologists.

14 The legal philosopher Scott Shapiro points to two major limitations of much current work on shared agency by analytic philosophers: 'first, that it applies only to ventures characterised by a rough equality of power and second, that it applies only to small-scale projects among similarly committed individuals' (Shapiro 2014). Examples mentioned by Shapiro are: singing a duet and painting a house together.

For this reason, however, it will prove that the lack of success in creating a general AI is not, as some claim, something that can and will be overcome by increasing the processing power and memory size of computers. Rather, this lack of success flows not only from a lack of understanding of many biological matters, but also from an inability to create mathematical models of how brains and other organic systems work.

In biology, valid mathematical models aiming at system explanation are hard or impossible to obtain, because there are in almost every case very large numbers of causal factors involved, making it well-nigh impossible to create models that would be predictive.[15] The lack of models is most striking in neuroscience, which is the science dealing with the physical explanation of how the brain functions in giving rise not only to consciousness, intelligence, language and social behaviour but also to neurological disorders such as dementia, schizophrenia, and autism.

The achievement of AGI would require models whose construction would presuppose solutions of some of the most intractable problems in all of science (see sections 8.5 to 8.8). It is thus disconcerting that optimism as concerns the potential of AI has been most vigorous precisely in the promotion of visions relating to enhancement, extension, and even total emulation of the human brain. We will see that such optimism rests in part on the tenacity of the view according to which the human brain is a type of computer (a view still embraced explicitly by some of our best philosophers), which on closer analysis betrays ignorance not only of the biology of the brain but also of the nature of computers. And for a further part it rests on naïve views as to the presumed powers of deep neural networks to deal with emanations from complex systems in ways which go beyond what is possible for traditional mathematical models.

1.3.1 Impossibility

Throughout this book, we will defend the thesis that it is impossible to obtain what we shall call *synoptic* and *adequate* mathematical models of complex systems, which means: models that would allow us to engineer AI systems that can fulfill the requirements such systems must satisfy if they are to emulate intelligence.

Because the proper understanding of the term *impossible* as it is used in this sentence is so important to all that follows, we start with an elucidation of how we are using it. First, we use the term in three different senses, which we refer to as *technical*, *physical*, and *mathematical* impossibility, respectively.

To say that something is *technically impossible*—for example, controlled nuclear fusion with a positive energy output—is to draw attention to the fact that it is

---

15 There are important exceptions in some specific subfields, for example models of certain features of monogenetic and of infectious diseases, or of the pharmacodynamics of antibiotics. See 8.4.

impossible *given the technology we have today*. We find it useful to document the technically impossible here only where (as is all too often) proponents of transhumanist and similar concepts seek to promote their ideas on the basis of claims which are, and may for all time remain, technically impossible.[16]

To say that something is *physically impossible* is to say that it is impossible because it would contravene the laws of physics. To give an example: in highly viscous fluids (low Reynolds numbers), no type of swimming object can achieve net displacement (this is the scallop theorem [Purcell 1977]).[17]

To speak of *mathematical impossibility*, finally, is to assert that a solution to some mathematically specified problem—for example, an analytical solution of the n-body problem (see p. 189) or an algorithmic solution of the halting problem (see section 7.2)—cannot be found; not because of any shortcomings in the data or hardware or software or human brains, but rather for *a priori* reasons of mathematics. This is the primary sense in which we use the term *impossible* in this book.

1.4 The AI hype cycle

Despite the lack of success in brain modelling, and fired by a naïve understanding of human brain functioning, optimism as to future advances in AI feeds most conspicuously into what is now called 'transhumanism', the idea that technologies to enhance human capabilities will lead to the emergence of new 'posthuman' beings. On one scenario, humans themselves will become immortal because they will be able to abandon their current biological bodies and live on, forever, in digital form. On another scenario, machines will develop their own will and subdue mankind into slavery with their superintelligence while they draw on their immortality to go forth into the galaxy and colonise space.

Speculations such as this are at the same time fascinating and disturbing. But we believe that, like some earlier pronouncements from the AI community, they must be taken with a heavy pillar of salt, for they reflect enthusiasm triggered by successes of AI research that does not factor in the fact that these successes have been achieved only along certain tightly defined paths.

In 2016 it became known that the company DeepMind had used AI in their AlphaGo automaton to partially solve the game of Go.[18] Given the complexity of the game, this must be recognised as a stunning achievement. But it is an achievement whose underlying methodology can be applied only to a narrow set of problems. What it shows is that, in certain completely rule-determined

---

16 For example: 'Twenty-first-century software makes it technologically possible to separate our minds from our biological bodies.' (Rothblatt 2013, p. 317). We return to this example in chapter 11.
17 We return to this example in section 12.3.3.1.
18 Solving a game *fully* means 'determining the final result in a game with no mistakes made by either player'. This has been achieved for some games, but not for either chess or GO (Schaeffer et al. 2007).

confined settings with a low-dimensional phase space such as abstract games, a variant of machine learning known as reinforcement learning (see 8.6.7.3) can be used to create algorithms that outperform humans. Importantly, this is done in ways that do not rely on any knowledge on the part of the machine of the rules of the games involved. This does not, however, mean that Deep-Mind can 'discover' the rules governing just *any* kind of activity. DeepMind's engineers provided the software with carefully packaged examples of activity satisfying just this set of rules and allowed it to implicitly generate new playing strategies not present in the supplied examples by using purely computational adversarial settings (two algorithms playing against each other).[19] The software is not in a position to go out and identify packages of this sort on its own behalf. It is cognizant neither of the rules nor of the new strategies which we, its human observers, conceive it to be applying.

Yet the successes of DeepMind and of other AI engineering virtuosi have led once again to over-generalised claims on behalf of the machine learning approach, which gave new energy to the idea of an AI that would be *general* in the same sort of way that human intelligence is general, to the extent that it could go forth into the world unsupervised and achieve ever more startling results.

Parallel bursts of enthusiasm have arisen also in connection with the great strides made in recent years in the field of image recognition. But there are already signs that there, too, the potential of AI technology has once again been overestimated (Marcus 2018; Landgrebe et al. 2021).

Why is this so? Why, in other words, is AI once again facing a wave of dampening enthusiasm[20] representing the third major AI sobering episode after the mid-1970s and late 1980s, both of which ended in AI winters? There are, certainly, many reasons for this cyclical phenomenon. One such reason is that genuine advances in AI fall from public view as they become embedded in innumerable everyday products and services. Many contributions of working (narrow) AI are thereby hidden. But a further reason is the weak foundation of AI enthusiasm itself, which involves in each cycle an initial exaggeration of the potential of AI under the assumption that impressive success along a single front will be generalisable into diverse unrelated fields (taking us, for instance, from *Jeopardy!* to curing cancer [Strickland 2019]).[21]

---

19 This is an excellent example of the use of synthetic data which is appropriate and adequate to the problem at hand.
20 This is not yet so visible in academia and in the public prints; but it is well established among potential commercial users, for example Bloomberg is clearly indicating this in fall 2021 (https://www.bloomberg.com/opinion/articles/2021-10-04/artificial-intelligence-ain-t-that-smart-look-at-tesla-facebook-healthcare). Further documentation of a breakdown in AI enthusiasm is provided by Larson (2021, pp. 74ff.).
21 The consequences of this assumption are thoroughly documented by Larson (2021), who explains why it is so difficult to re-engineer AI systems built for one purpose to address a different purpose.

Assumptions of this sort are made, we believe, because AI enthusiasts often do not have the interdisciplinary scientific knowledge that is needed to recognise the obstacles that will stand in the way of envisaged new AI applications. It is part of our aim here to show that crucial lessons concerning both the limits and the potential of AI can be learned through application of the right sort of interdisciplinary knowledge.

1.5 Why machines will not inherit the earth

In this book, we will argue that it is not an accident that so little progress has been made towards AGI over successive cycles of AI research. The lack of progress reflects, rather, certain narrow, structural limits to what can be achieved in this field, limits which we document in detail.

The human tendency to anthropomorphise is very powerful (Ekbia 2008). When our computer pauses while executing some especially complicated operation, we are tempted to say, 'it's thinking'. But it is not so. The processes inside the computer are physical through and through and, as we shall see in section 7.2, limited to certain narrowly defined operations defined in the 1930s by Turing and Church. The fact that we describe them in mental terms turns on the fact that the computer has been built to imitate (*inter alia*) operations that human beings would perform by using their minds. We thus impute the corresponding mental capabilities to the machine itself, as we impute happiness to a cartoon clown.

As Searle (1992) argued, computation has a physical, but no mental, reality because the significance that we impute to what the computer does (what we perceive as its mental reality) is observer dependent. If we take away all observers, then only the physical dimensions of its operations would remain. To see what is involved here, compare the difference between a dollar bill as a piece of paper and a dollar bill as money. If we take away all observers, then only the former would remain, because the latter is, again, 'observer dependent'. While we *impute* consciousness to computers, we ourselves *are* conscious.

Computers also will not be able to *gain* consciousness in the future, since as we will show, whatever remarkable feats they might be engineered to perform, the aspect of those feats we are referring to when we ascribe consciousness or mentality to the computer will remain forever a product of observer dependence.

As we discuss in more detail in chapter 9, any process that machines can execute in order to *emulate* consciousness would have to be such that the feature of consciousness that is imputed to it would be observer dependent. From the fact that a certain green piece of paper is imputed to have the observer-dependent value of one dollar, we can infer with high likelihood that this piece of paper has the value of one dollar. As we will show in chapter 9, no analogous inference is possible from the fact that a process in a machine is imputed to have the feature of consciousness (or awareness, or excitedness, or happiness, or wariness, or desire). And thus we will never be able to create an AI with the faculty of consciousness in the sense in which we understand this term when referring to humans or animals.

But if we cannot *create* consciousness in the machine, the machine might still surely be able to *emulate* consciousness? This, and the related question of the limits of computer emulation of human *intelligence*, is one of the main questions addressed in this book.

1.5.1 The nature of the human mind

As mentioned earlier, in the eyes of many philosophers working in the theory of mind, the mind works like a universal Turing machine: it takes sensory inputs and processes these to yield some behavioural output. But how does it do this? When it comes to answering this question, there are three major schools: connectionists (Elman et al. 1996), computationalists (Fodor et al. 1988), and the defenders of hybrid approaches (Garson 2018). All of them think that the mind works like a machine. Connectionists believe that the mind works like a neural network as we know it from what is called 'artificial neural network' research.[22] Computationalists believe that the mind operates by performing purely formal operations on symbols.[23]

Most important for us here are the hybrid approaches as pioneered by Smolensky (1990), which seek to reconcile both schools by proposing that neural networks can themselves be implemented by universal Turing machines, an idea that was indeed technically realised in 2014 by Graves et al. (2014), who used a neural network to implement a classical von Neumann architecture. Their result proves that the initial dispute between connectionists and computationalists was mathematically nonsensical, because it shows that a universal Turing machine can implement *both* connectionist *and* symbolic logic. In other words, both types of computational procedures can be expressed using the basic recursive functions defined by Alonzo Church (1936). That both symbolic and perceptron (neural network) logic are Turing-computable has been known to mathematicians and computer scientists since the 1950s, and this makes the whole debate look naïve at best.

However there is a deeper problem with all ideas according to which the functioning of the mind (or brain) can be understood and modelled as the functioning of one or other type of machine, namely that such ideas are completely detached from the standpoint of biology and physics.[24] We will show that the

---

22 An artificial neural network is an implicit mathematical model generated by constraining an optimisation algorithm using training data and optimisation parameters; see further in chapter 8.
23 The relation between these two schools from an AI research perspective is summarised by Minsky (1991), who made important contributions to connectionist AI.
24 We shall see in detail why this is so in chapter 2 and section 9.4 and 12.2.

mentioned alternatives fail, because the mind (or brain) does not operate like a machine, and those who propose that it does do not acknowledge the results of neuroscience. For while we do not know how the mind works exactly, what we do know from neuroscience is that the workings of the mind resist mathematical modelling.[25] Therefore, we cannot emulate the mind using a machine, nor can we engineer other non-machine kinds of complex systems to obtain so-far undescribed kinds of non-human intelligence, and we will understand why in the course of this book.

1.5.2 There will be no AGI

The aim of AGI research, and of those who fund it, is to obtain something useful, and this will imply that an AGI needs to fulfill certain requirements—broadly, that it is able to cope with the reality in which humans live with a level of competence that is at least equivalent to that of human beings (see sections 3.3.3 and 3.3.4). We show that this is not possible, because there is an upper bound to what can be processed by machines. This boundary is set, not by technical limitations of computers, but rather by the limits on the possibilities for mathematical modelling.

There can be no 'artificial general intelligence', and therefore no 'Singularity' and no 'full ethical agents', because all of these would lie way beyond the boundary of what is even in principle achievable by means of a machine.

As we show at length in chapters 7 and 8, this upper bound is not a matter of computer storage or processing speed—factors which may perhaps continue to advance impressively from generation to generation. Rather, it is a matter of mathematics, at least given the presupposition that the aim is to realise AGI using computers.[26] For every computational AI is, after all, just a set of Turing-computable mathematical models taking input and computing output in a deterministic manner. Even 'self-learning' stochastic models behave deterministically once they have been trained and deployed to operate in a computer.

We shall deal in this book with all types of models that can currently be used to create computer-based AI systems, and we present each in great detail in chapter 8. Our arguments are completely general; they apply to all these types of models in the same way, and we are confident that these same arguments will apply also to any new types of models that will be developed in the future. At the same time, however, we note that these arguments potentially provide a boon to our adversaries, who can use them as a guide to the sorts of obstacles that would need to be overcome in order to engineer an AI that is both more useful than what we already have, and feasible from the point of view of engineering.

---

25 The 1,696 pages of *Principles of Neural Science* by Kandel et al. (2021), which is the gold standard textbook in the field and summarises some 100 years of neuroscientific research, contain almost no mathematics. And this is not about to change.

26 Other approaches, for example resting on the surgical enhancement of human brains, are considered in section 12.2.4.

1.5.3 Prior arguments against artificial human-level intelligence

We are not alone in believing that the idea of AGI, and of the Singularity which will follow in its wake, is at least to some degree a reflection of overconfidence among some members of the AI research community, and a number of AI proponents have expressed views which anticipate at least part of what we have to say here. For example, and most usefully, Walsh (2017). Walsh does indeed believe that AI with human-level intelligence will be achieved within the next 30–40 years; but he holds at the same time that there are a number of reasons why the Singularity will not arise:

1. intelligence is much more than thinking faster,
2. humans may not be intelligent enough to design superintelligence,
3. there is no evidence at all that an ML (machine learning) algorithm which achieves human level intelligence would thereby somehow proceed to becoming *more* intelligent (what David Chalmers [2010] calls 'AI+'),
4. there are diminishing returns from AI performance, so that performance improvements to the level of a Singularity may be stymied,
5. systems have physical limits, and there are 'empirical laws that can be observed emerging out of complex systems'. Intelligence itself as 'a complex phenomenon may also have such limits that emerge from this complexity. Any improvements in machine intelligence, whether it runs away or happens more slowly, may run into such limits' (op. cit., p. 61)[27],
6. the computational complexity required to go beyond human level intelligence may not be physically realisable.

Other important reservations concerning the possibility of the Singularity and the limits of AI in general have been brought forward by:

- Yann LeCun, who addresses the claims made by some researchers concerning an anticipated exponential growth in the powers of AI and points out that,

    the first part of a sigmoid looks a lot like an exponential. It's another way of saying that what currently looks like exponential progress is very likely to hit some limit—physical, economical, societal—then go

---

[27] We note in passing that this may be one reason for the apparent contradiction between the lack of evidence for extraterrestrial civilisations and various high estimates for their probability (Fermi's paradox). Why do we see no evidence of alien superintelligences? Because the same limits to the increase in power of AI would (we believe) apply also to any technology developed by other intelligent life forms. This has implications also for the idea, favoured by Elon Musk, according to which the world in which we live is a simulation.

through an inflection point, and then saturate. I'm an optimist, but I'm also a realist.

(LeCun 2015)

- Yoshua Bengio, who makes the point that it is impossible to teach machines moral judgement: 'People need to understand that current AI—and the AI that we can foresee in the reasonable future—does not, and will not, have a moral sense or moral understanding of what is right and what is wrong' (Ford 2018, p. 31).
- Judea Pearl, who emphasises that the currently fashionable stochastics-based 'opaque learning machines' (Pearl 2020) lack an important feature of human-level intelligence in that they cannot answer questions related to causality and thus they cannot develop understanding about how things work. Pearl does not exclude the possibility of creating an AGI. He insists only that 'human-level AI cannot emerge solely from model-blind learning machines; it requires the symbiotic collaboration of data and models'.[28]
- Brian Cantwell Smith (2019), who states that

  > neither deep learning nor other forms of second-wave AI, nor any proposals yet advanced for third-wave, will lead to genuine intelligence. Systems currently being imagined will achieve formidable reckoning prowess, but human-level intelligence and judgment, honed over millennia, is of a different order.
  >
  > (*The Promise of Artificial Intelligence*, Introduction)

- For Shannon Vallor:

  > Those who are predicting an imminent 'rise of the robots' or an 'AI singularity,' in which artificially intelligent beings decide to dispense with humanity or enslave us, in my view serve as an unhelpful distraction from the far more plausible but less cinematic dangers of artificial intelligence. These mostly involve unexpected interactions between people and software systems that aren't smart enough to avoid wreaking havoc on complex human institutions, rather than robot overlords with 'superintelligence' dwarfing our own.
  >
  > (Vallor 2016, p. 250)

- Steven Pinker argues that the threats to freedom in the future lie not so much in the advent of any putative Singularity, but rather in the way

---

[28] We shall see what this means in chapter 8; essentially, that the AI we can realise is determined by us.

societies choose to use technology. He draws what we shall recognise later as the crucial distinction between intelligence and motivation. And while he is ready to accept that we might technically realise something like the former, he points out that 'there is no law of complex systems that says that intelligent agents must turn into ruthless megalomaniacs'. He also clearly sees that intelligence is not a boundless continuum with no limits to its potency (a point which we discuss in chapter 12); he recognises that stochastic models do not create knowledge and that AI is just a technology like any other, which is 'constantly tweaked for efficacy and safety' (Pinker 2020).

- Darwiche stated in (2018) that

   what just happened in AI is nothing close to a breakthrough that justifies worrying about doomsday scenarios.... The current negative discussions by the public on the AI Singularity, also called super intelligence, can only be attributed to the lack of accurate ... characterisations of recent progress.
   (p. 66)

Although such expressions of AGI pessimism are rarely encountered in the public prints, we suspect that the passages just cited in fact represent the views of a majority of AI experts. But they are all arguments to the effect that the Singularity *might not happen*. Here, in contrast, we will present arguments to the effect that already the creation of AI with an intelligence comparable to that of a human being is *impossible to achieve*, and thus that the Singularity, too, *will never happen*.

One notable exception is François Chollet, who argues that the idea of an 'intelligence explosion comes from a profound misunderstanding of both the nature of intelligence and the behavior of recursively self-augmenting systems'.[29] His main hypotheses are:

- that AGI theorists employ an erroneous definition of intelligence,
- that human intelligence depends on innate dispositions, on interaction with the environment (sensorimotor affordances), and on socialisation; it can be exemplified only by a human being who is part of a society,
- that complex real-world systems cannot be modelled using the Markov assumption.

Chollet points out further that the 'no free lunch theorem' (8.6.6.3) implies that if 'intelligence is a problem-solving algorithm, then it can only be understood with respect to a specific problem'. In sum, Chollett defends a view of AGI very much in the spirit of this book, but he provides only limited arguments on behalf of this view, as contrasted with the sort of detailed discussion that we present in

---

29 Retrieved at https://medium.com/@francois.chollet/the-impossibility-of-intelligence-explosion-5be4a9eda6ec

chapters 7 and 8. For we will demonstrate that it is impossible to create the sorts of mathematical models even of vertebrate intelligence that would be needed in order to engineer its counterpart in a computer.

1.5.3.1 On abduction

A more recent, and for our purposes more significant, contribution to the debate on AGI is the book by Larson (2021). Larson hedges his bets as to whether human-level AI will or will not be achieved in the future, though he points out that 'no one has the slightest clue how to build an artificial general intelligence' (p. 275). But he emphasises that we do not have today, even on the horizon, anything like human-level AI. This is so, he argues, because of the current dominance of the assumption that the arrival of AGI is only a matter of time, because 'we have already embarked on the path that will lead to human-level AI, and then superintelligence'. He calls this assumption 'the myth of AI', arguing that the assumption of inevitability is so deeply entrenched that—as we ourselves have discovered in many of our encounters with AI scientists—arguing against it is taken as a form of Luddism. Larson points out in this connection that there are after all strong incentives for proponents of AI to keep its limitations in the dark, where a healthy culture for innovation 'emphasises exploring unknowns, not hyping extensions of existing methods—especially when these methods have been shown to be inadequate to take us much further'.

As we shall see in great detail in what follows, human and machine intelligence are radically different. The myth of AI insists that the differences are only temporary, in the sense that, step-by-step, more powerful AI systems will erase them. Yet, as Larson points out, the success achieved by focusing on narrow AI applications such as game-playing or protein folding 'gets us not one step closer to general intelligence. ... No algorithm exists for general intelligence. And we have good reason to be skeptical that such an algorithm will emerge through further efforts on deep learning systems or any other approach popular today'. To identify one potential alternative approach, Larson points to what he sees as the three different types of inference: *deduction*, which is explored by classic symbolic AI; *induction*, which he classifies as the province of modern stochastic AI[30]; and a third type which, following the American pragmatist philosopher Peirce, he calls *abduction*. Peirce's term is nowadays used in different contexts as another word for 'hypothesis formation' or also just plain 'guessing'.[31]

---

30 This is not correct, as we shall see in chapter 8.6.6.1. Machines do not engage in inductive reasoning; they rather compute local minima for loss functions, which can be seen as a very primitive emulation of induction from data because a functional is indeed obtained from observations (individual data). However, machines do not perform the induction themselves; they merely compute human-designed optimisation algorithms which emulate a narrow form of human induction.
31 For an account of problems we might face in formalising Peirce's notion, see Frankfurt (1958).

It is abduction, Larson argues, which is at the core of human intelligence, and thus engineering a counterpart of abduction—a combination of intuition and guessing—would be needed for human-level AI. His book provides a thorough and convincing account of why this is so. Yet at the same time he complains that 'no one is working on it—at all'.

His explanation for this lack of interest is that the myth of AI is holding back AI researchers. Yet this surely underestimates the degree to which the AI field is and has always been unrestrainedly opportunistic. For if modeling abduction truly provided even the beginnings of a feasible path toward modeling human-level intelligence, would there not be contrarian AI researchers who would have started off already down this path?

The fact, if it is a fact, that there is no one who is exploring a strategy along these lines leads us to postulate that this is not for reasons having to do with the culture of AI research. Rather, it is because attempts to engineer the types of abductive inference characteristic of human reasoning have in every case failed to reach even first base. The reasons for this are explored in what follows. For where, already on the first page of his book, Larson asserts that 'the future of AI is a scientific unknown', we show that there are in fact many things that we know about the future of AI, all of which derive from the premise that any AI algorithm must be Church-Turing computable.

1.6 How to read this book

If you have not done so already, please go back and read the Foreword. This provides an account of how the AGI scepticism defended in this, book differs from earlier varieties of scepticism, in that it is based in mathematics, physics, and biology.

For those who want to go straight to the technical details of our argument against the possibility of AGI, read chapters 7 and 8 first. The earlier chapters are there to set the scene, especially as concerns the reasons why human dialogue and human ethics cannot be modelled in a neural network because of the impossibility of collecting representative samples that can be used for training.

For everyone else: read chapter 2 to understand our view of the relationship between the mental and the physical: mental events are a special type of physical event in the brain and are subject to the same laws. We argue that this view is consistent with a common-sense understanding of human mental activity (of how it feels from the inside to be a conscious human being).

Read chapter 3 to understand what the 'intelligence' is that AI researchers are seeking to emulate. We introduce a distinction between two types of intelligence: the basic kind, which we share with higher animals; and the type of intelligence that is unique to humans and is closely associated with our ability to use language. We then examine the definition of 'intelligence' used by AI researchers and show that this definition does justice to neither of these.

Read chapters 4 to 6 to get an idea of the complex systems formed when human beings interact. These chapters survey our social capabilities as humans, including our capability to use language, to follow social (including ethical) norms, and to engage in social interactions. Human languages and human societies are complex systems—in fact they are complex systems of complex systems.

Read chapters 7 and 8 to understand what complex systems are and why their behaviour cannot be modelled mathematically and therefore cannot be emulated by using computers. We survey attempts to model complex systems in medicine, psychology, and economics. We survey the entire mathematical repertoire of available approaches to the emulation of complex systems, from recursive neural networks through evolutionary process models to entropy models. And we show why they all fail.

Read chapter 9 to find out how the results obtained so far throw light on philosophers' attempts to demonstrate that an AGI, and with it the 'Singularity', can be achieved 'before long'. We focus especially on the attempts by David Chalmers to show how the Singularity might be achieved, either by emulating human intelligence in a machine or by creating a machine intelligence that would emulate the entire course of evolution.

Read chapters 10 and 11 to find out why machines cannot emulate human conversation or moral behaviour. We cover in detail why machines will neither conduct conversations nor interpret text as humans can for a variety of reasons again having to do with the properties of complex systems. We then show why this same complexity rules out the possibility of an AI ethics.

Read chapter 12 if you are interested in 'transhumanism' and in what some are pleased to call 'digital immortality'. Here we address some of the more outlandish speculations that have grown up in the hinterlands of the Singularity. We demonstrate that we can neither create a machine emulation of anything like the human mind nor transcend our human condition as mortal organisms with organic bodies in order to enjoy immortal life in digital form. We also show, along the way, that there will be no AGI, and no Singularity.

Read chapter 13 if you are interested in what can still be achieved by AI in the future, even after taking account of the limits identified in this book. For there are still many grounds for optimism as concerns the potential uses of AI. This chapter is entitled 'AI spring eternal', and it describes how narrow AI will intensify and further broaden the technosphere that mankind has been creating since the beginning of urbanisation and the advent of the first high cultures. Even though there will be no AGI, and no Singularity, AI in the narrow sense will prove itself able to bring about new and still unconceived enhancements and extensions to the texture of our industrialised societies.

PART I
Properties of the human mind

2
THE HUMAN MIND

Any discussion of artificial intelligence (AI) must begin with a definition of intelligence *simpliciter*. What is it that the Artificial Intelligence engineer is supposed to be engineering?

Before we address this question, we discuss some basic properties of the human mind.

2.1 Basic characteristics of the human mind

The human mind is an integral part of the human body (or of what we shall later call the human mind-body continuum). There is no separation of mind and body; there is only one whole. Mental processes are physical processes. But how then do mental processes differ from the non-mental processes occurring in the brain? Our answer to this question is similar to that proposed by Silberstein et al. (2012), who see cognitive systems as 'non-linearly coupled brain–body–niche systems'.

Conscious mental processes (including remembered dreams and similar phenomena bordering on consciousness) are what we shall call *emanations* of the non-mental processes occurring in the brain. Here we adapt the term 'emanation' from physics, where it was used originally to designate the release of material in non-solid form from mostly solid starting compounds. For example, the isotope ^{222}Rn (radon), a gaseous product of the decay of the alkaline earth metal radium, is said to *emanate* from the latter. We use the term here more generally to describe any type of electromagnetic radiation or composite form of energy propagation (for example, of sound).[1]

---

[1] Energy propagation comprises not only physical movement in the sense of classical mechanics, but also for example propagation of sound, heat, or radiation which can be directly observed but which

The movements of the nematode *C. elegans* are emanations, as also are the speech acts performed by humans. In both cases they are physiological emanations of complex neurophysiological processes occurring in an organism. Just as there are physical processes in external nature that have emanations, for example the snapping sound when a twig in the forest breaks, so there are physical processes in the brain that have emanations, which are observable through that kind of observing process we call introspection. The act of perceiving the snapping sound is in a sense a double observation, involving both *our awareness of the sound* and *our simultaneous awareness of this awareness of the sound*.

Our subjective sensations of pain, hunger, euphoria, grim determination, and so forth, are emanations in the sense defined. When we experience such sensations, we do not observe the physical processes which cause them. The emanations themselves are observable, but the neuronal processes are not. An example of an emanation from an inanimate complex system is the wind in Chicago. The wind itself is observable. But the precipitating processes are not—what *can* be measured here are changes in air pressure, which serve as local proxies for the workings of the earth's global climate system.

2.2 The mind-body problem: monism and its varieties

2.2.1 The role of physics

If we are to understand how human intelligence works, then we will need to understand how those experiences we call mental are related to processes in the realm of physics. We therefore attempt to clarify in what follows our position on the old question of the relationship between mind and body, and show how it differs from standard alternative positions.

We start, first of all, from the hypothesis that all mental processes are physical processes. The brain, the physical location of mental processes, is made of matter and is subject through and through to the laws of physics. The mental realm is thus a part of physical reality, and we have experiences of processes in this part of physical reality that are no less robust than our experiences of external nature.

Mental processes occur, in the simplest case, because they are caused by other physical processes. There is thus a bridge between the mental and the (rest of the) physical. Consider, for example, what happens when I perceive one frame (a very short fragment) of some visual sensory input without any motor activity on my part. The action potentials thereby generated in my retina lead (via several synapses) to signals in my occipital brain, which lead in turn to my

---

are produced by processes which are either not observable or observable only indirectly (for example by using proxies, or via indirect observations using measuring instruments).

conscious apprehension of what is depicted in the frame.[2] The visual system and the optic tract can thus be seen as a bridge between visual input and its conscious perception, and both are quite well understood (Kandel et al. 2021, chapters 21–25). Yet we cannot represent the events occurring during this process in a synoptic mathematical model, in other words a model of the sort that would allow us, for example, to engineer the replacement of neuronal parts of the optical tract in a way that would rectify a visual impairment.

2.2.2 Materialistic monism

The view that all mental processes are physical processes is one variant of a more general family of monistic views, which are defined in contrast to the dualist views of, for example, Descartes, who held that mind and body are two entirely different kinds of substance. We are interested here only in those versions of monism which are materialistic. Thus we do not discuss the idealistic monisms proposed for example by Leibniz, Berkeley, or Hegel, though we do discuss the popular semi-idealistic view of 'naturalistic dualism' that has been proposed in our own day by David Chalmers.

We first of all distinguish the two main branches of materialistic monism, with their major subtypes, which are distinguished according to whether they hold that mental entities can or cannot be 'reduced' to physical entities, where one type of entity is said to be reduced to a second kind of entity when talk about the former can be shown to be logically equivalent to talk about the latter.

1. Reductive physicalism:

    - mechanical monism,
    - type-type identity theory,
    - behaviourism,
    - functionalism.

2. Non-reductive physicalism:

    - emergentism,
    - eliminativism,
    - biological naturalism,
    - anomalous monism à la Davidson.

Reductive physicalism is a family of doctrines according to which all mental processes can be identified as belonging to the domain of physiology and

---

2 This is a very simple case. Visual perception in the more normal case is more complex than this static example would suggest, as is shown for example by Gibson (2015).

ultimately of physics (Hempel 1969). All assertions about putative mental properties can on this view be translated logically into assertions of physics.

Mechanical monism was first proposed by Julien Offray de La Mettrie in the middle of the 18th century (La Mettrie 1748). La Mettrie believed that the higher capabilities of humans (as compared to other animals) result from the complexity of their brains, and that the human mind works like a complicated machine. Mental experiences are the workings of this machine.³

Type-type identity theory holds that every 'mental property is identical with some physical property' (Stoljar 2017). This view is close to ours, but we think that mental types are complex physical types—complex because they arise where physical entities are related to each other to form a complex system of the sort defined in chapter 7. The type-type theories proposed by analytical philosophers typically view mental and physical properties through the simplifying lens of predicate logic (Smith 2005).

Behaviourism is the doctrine according to which all that there is to mental processes is observable behaviour. On one 'logical' version, behaviourism asserts that 'any proposition about a mental state could be converted, without loss of meaning, into a proposition about behavior'. On another 'ontological' version, behaviourism explicitly denies that 'there are any "inner" mental states' (Mills 2012). But in all its variants, behaviourism fails to do justice to our (first-person) mental experience, and its main theses, for example concerning learning via stimulus response, have fared badly when tested empirically.

Functionalism is, as Ned Block has shown, 'a new incarnation of behaviourism' (Block 1978, p. 262) which tries to re-interpret the language we use to describe mental experiences by using functional relations between inputs and outputs. We can see how this view works, on one incarnation, by considering a sample sentence from a psychological theory T, of the form:

$$T(p, s_1 \ldots s_n, i_1 \ldots i_k, o_1 \ldots o_m). \tag{2.1}$$

This sentence states of some person p, and of some mental states s_j, that they relate certain given inputs i_j to outputs o_j (Block 1978, pp. 269f). The expression 2.1 might, for example, be interpreted as an assertion to the effect that *person p is in pain*, where the inputs i_j might be sensory afferences, the s_j states of the conscious mind, and the outputs expressions of pain in terms of vocalisations or facial expressions.

What, now, is the functionalist reading of sentence (2.1)? How, in other words, are we to understand the references to mental entities (the mental

---

3 A version of mechanical monism is embraced by many contemporary philosophers who hold that the mind works like a Turing machine—for example Fodor et al. (1988). However, there is also the following much later remark by Fodor: 'So, how does the mind work? I don't know. You don't know. Pinker doesn't know. And, I rather suspect, such is the current state of the art, that if God were to tell us, we wouldn't understand' (Fodor 2005).

states s_j) which it seems to contain? One strategy popular among analytic philosophers involves applying what is called Ramseyfication to the propositions of a scientific theory in order to reveal what terms found in that theory really mean (Ramsey 1931). The result of applying this strategy to sentence (2.1) is a new sentence:

$$\lambda y \exists x_1 \ldots x_m, x_n [T(y, x_1 \ldots x_m, i_i \ldots i_k, o_1 \ldots o_m) \wedge h(y, x_n)], n > m. \qquad (2.2)$$

Here h denotes the predicate 'have', x_n is a functional variable denoting 'being-in-pain'. The x_i, $i = 1\ldots m$ are *bound* in sentence (2.2) by the functional abstraction operator λ, which we can think of here as a set abstractor (Gamut 1991b, chapter 4.4), since we are reading this sentence as defining a set of entities y which have the properties listed in the brackets after the $\exists$ quantifier. λy in other words denotes the set of pain-affected entities (a certain subset of people). And then, as Block writes of sentence (2.2): 'This expression contains input and output terms, but no mental terms'. The resulting version of functionalism, accordingly, could 'be said to reduce mentality to input-output structures' (Block 1978, p. 270).

Non-reductive physicalism, the second family of materialist monist positions, holds that, even though the brain generates our mental experiences, we cannot logically reduce the propositions which we use to describe mental processes to the propositions of physics. Major subtypes of this view are:

Emergentism, which states that mental and physical properties are metaphysically distinct, but yet necessarily connected (Stoljar 2017). A classical emergentist view was formulated by Samuel Alexander in 1920:

> The higher quality emerges from the lower level of existence and has its roots therein, but it emerges therefrom, and it does not belong to that level, but constitutes in its possessor a new order of existent with its special laws of behaviour. The existence of emergent qualities thus described … admits no explanation.
>
> (Alexander 2004)

Eliminativism holds that reductionism fails because our ordinary, commonsense understanding of the mind is deeply wrong and that some or all of the mental states posited by common sense do not actually exist (Ramsey 2019). Propositions about the mental have no referents. Churchland, a proponent of this view, holds that 'folk psychology', which uses concepts such as *will*, *belief* or *desire*, is a false theory that will be eliminated by neuroscience (Churchland 1981), just as the concept of 'ether' was eliminated by modern physics.

Biological naturalism, proposed by Searle (2002), holds on the one hand that mental phenomena are biological processes in the brain (they are what he calls 'features' of the brain), while on the other hand insisting that the mental is 'ontologically irreducible'. Searle derives this irreducibility from the fact that mental processes are experienced by the subject and are therefore a matter of what he calls 'first-person ontology'. This implies, in his eyes, that they cannot be reduced to 'third-person ontology'. From our point of view, however, the difference between what is experienced in the first- and third-person is merely a matter of epistemology. All processes belong equally to the same third-person ontology which we call physics, though as we shall see, this does not mean that we can quite so easily state the physical equations which govern those processes which we experience as mental.

Naturalistic dualism, proposed by David Chalmers (1996), is 'naturalistic' in that it purports that mental states supervene 'naturally' on physical systems such as brains (McLaughlin et al. 2018). But it is at the same time dualist, because Chalmers believes that mental states are ontologically distinct from and not reducible to physical states. Chalmers (1996, p. xi) affirms that 'We have good reason to believe that consciousness arises from physical systems such as brains, but we have little idea how it arises, or why it exists at all'. In some phases of his thinking Chalmers has toyed with the idea that consciousness may be a fundamental ingredient of reality, which means an entity of a type not capable of being explained in terms of anything simpler. On one reading—under which 'explained' means 'mathematically modelled'—we agree with Chalmers here. But we reject any reading which draws from this the conclusion that mental entities have a special, non-physical status.

2.2.2.1 Nomological monism

Our own position can be called a 'no layers' approach in that it embraces a materialistic monist view according to which mental processes are physical processes. It stands apart from the versions of materialistic monism listed earlier in its acceptance of the following theses:

1. there are no layers in the human mind-body continuum—thus no underlying neurophysiological substrate—but rather a continuum of physical processes which we can view at different levels of resolution;
2. mental processes are *emanations* of complex physical processes which we can describe in combination mereological and causal chains down to the four basic interactions of matter[4] at what, given current-day physics, is the fundamental granular level of microparticles;

---

4 More specifically, of matter in the brain.

3. mental processes are themselves identical with processes which conform to the laws of physics, but, for reasons which will become clear, we have no way of describing, explaining, or predicting mental processes in terms of physical laws;
4. we can observe, for instance by using brain imaging devices, only certain aspects of how mental processes are produced;
5. we can observe, for instance through introspection, certain aspects of how mental processes are arranged in a continuous temporal sequence called 'consciousness'; the terminology of the common-sense ontology of the mental is thus a serviceable framework through which to view the various types of mental entity.

This position holds that all mental experiences are processes subject to the laws of physics, and in this respect the monism that we defend is *nomological*. We accept, of course, that we can describe mental processes in physical terms only in very general ways. The description of the brain in terms of physics is, for these purposes, underdeveloped, and we will show in chapters 8 and 12 that it will remain underdeveloped. We can, however, provide very detailed accounts of mental experiences when we use the terminology of psychology. Indeed, when it comes to many of their features, we cannot think and speak of our mental experiences in any other way.

Mental processes can, like all other processes, be described in terms of partitions at different granular levels. This means that the entities recognised at any given granular level are linked mereologically (which means: they are *parts of*) the entities at the next coarser granular level. The entire edifice of physical processes can thus be described on our view using a combination of mereological and causal chains down to particle physics and the four fundamental interactions at the finest granular levels.

What is described here is not 'layered' in the sense that there would be more or less independent levels or strata of the sort conceived, for example, by defenders of emergentist doctrines. Rather, we hold that organisms are made of cells, cells are made of molecules, and so on all the way down to the fundamental particles. The matter of the human mind-body continuum[5] can be partitioned, depending on our scientific perspective, into atoms, molecules, cell components, cells, portions of tissue, organs, organisms, organisations, populations, etc. All of these partitions select elements joined together in various systems.

Analogous partitions can be drawn also along the process axis. At the coarsest grain we have the partition which picks out only one process, for example

---

5 We use this expression in order to make clear that mental processes may extend to include also bodily processes outside the brain. When I have a pain in my foot, for example, my pain sensation is a mental process caused, in the typical case, by tissue damage that is localised in the foot. It is one process of the mind-body continuum which we experience as pain.

(depending on the selected object-granularity) the entire history of one single molecule, or of the entire universe. At finer process granularities we can pick out processes such as, for example, your adolescence or my spell in the Navy. Such process partitions are themselves coarse-grained partitions relative to the finest-grained process partition at the granular level of the interactions of the four fundamental forces.[6]

A mental process, now, is a process in the brain and, depending on the chosen level of object granularity, it can be seen as a process in an aggregate of neurons, of molecules, of atoms, and so forth. Depending on the chosen level of process granularity it may be seen as a sequence of steps in processes leading, for example, to the movement of an arm, or involving a neuronal action potential, or the phosphorylation of ion channels. And for each and every one of the mentioned granular partitions, the items selected for are physical in nature and are subject to the same laws of physics.

To express the matter in a slightly different way, the granular levels of neuroscience from brain to neuron to molecules to atoms, and so on, are merely reflections of different scientific models of a single, highly complex physical process. And whether it is dealing with psychological processes in some single brain, or with psychological processes in general, or with natural processes of any sort, science has to work with systems of entities at different levels of granularity in order to describe and (potentially) explain and predict the processes identified.

We can now see that our talk of 'emanations' does not imply that mental experiences emerge, in any sense, out of an underlying layer of physics. Rather an emanation *is* a physical process. It stands apart from other physical processes in that we can experience it—as we experience a pain, for example—where we cannot experience the molecular changes in our neurons, which occur at too fine a grain for them to be observable by organisms like us. At the granularity of the fundamental forces, they occur as different combinations of these forces. Our mental (introspective) experience and our overt physical behaviour are all emanations from the complex system which is the human mind-body continuum. But due to their nature as processes of a complex system, we are unable to model these processes mathematically, and so we cannot causally explain them at the fine level of granularity that would be needed to answer questions such as: which cells and molecules are involved in what way to generate a certain memory recall or a certain emotional nuance?

Multiple realisability This has implications, now, for the doctrine of what is called 'multiple realisability'. According to this doctrine, a mental process of a single type can be realised in a variety of processes of distinct physical types.

---

6 The strong and the weak force have a range of only 2×10^{-15}m and 2×10^{-18}m respectively, while the range of the electromagnetic interaction and of gravitation are unlimited.

For example, a psychological process type such as pain might be realised by different states of your brain, but also by mechanical states of an appropriately programmed digital computer.[7] The premise of multiple realisability is often used in arguments against the sort of nomological variant of physicalism that we are here defending. For if a given mental process (type) *m* can be caused by processes of different physical types, then it seems hard to conceive the process *m* as being physical in nature. Rather, it seems to imply that the former belong to a different, and in some sense higher, level, as on the emergentist doctrine or on one or other doctrine of supervenience (Kim 1984).

To understand what is going on here, let's look at some examples. Pain is often used by proponents of multiple realisability as something that can be realised by multiple physical processes. At a first glance, this seems to be true. A causalgia in the foot (a pain that feels like a burning) can be felt either after an acute burning, or in the course of a case of complex regional pain syndrome (CRPS) (also termed 'reflex sympathetic dystrophy'), or as a type of phantom limb pain after the loss of the foot. Although these pains may *feel* the same, they are nonetheless of different pathological kinds, and they are therefore also of different physical kinds, as can be detected by medical examination.

The defenders of multiple realisability might now argue that it is the same pain qua feeling that is realised by each of these three different physical processes. But to say that one pain feels to be of the same type as another and must therefore be of the same mental type contradicts the assumption that all mental processes are physical in nature. Pains caused by different pathological sources may feel the same to an individual due to the *lack of resolution of the faculty of inner perception* so that we cannot feel the detailed physics of the pain processes, even though they are physically different. But if we could measure these processes at a sufficiently fine granularity (exact neuronal excitation patterns, ion flows, protein conformation changes, alterations of protein phosphorylation, etc.), then we would see that these are processes of different types with different molecular properties.

We can create a formally identical argument against apparent cases of multiple realisability also in the realm of physical processes where we can prove the difference of apparently identical physical process types, and therefore also of their instances. Consider for example the following scenario: two sound waves of the same type, i.e. of a choir singing the 'Hallelujah Chorus', are quite possibly emanations of completely different types of physical events, for example a real choir, or a digital recording playing via a mobile phone connecting to wireless earphones, or a vinyl recording playing via an old-fashioned vacuum-tube amplifier connection to magnetic-coil speakers using copper cables.

7 Bickle (2020); see also 8.3.3.

That a live voice and its recording are physical processes of quite different types is easily shown for example, using a Fourier transformation, which will reveal (potentially inaudible) differences made apparent by their respective mathematical signatures. The sound waves are in this sense not of the same type. However, when viewed at a certain level of granularity (the level of resolution which humans use to distinguish melodies, chords, voices, and so forth), then a certain common pattern becomes evident, parallel in some ways to the common pattern that we can recognise between two different stars with similar light intensity and distance from the earth on a cloudless night. In the case of the 'Hallelujah Chorus', the common pattern results from the fact that the compared sound processes have a common etiology in that they are all live or recorded performances of the same musical work, the instructions for performing which were laid down by Händel in 1741.

Anomalous monism There is much that our nomological monism shares with the doctrine of anomalous monism introduced by Donald Davidson in his paper 'Mental Events' (Davidson 1970). First, there is the thesis that physical events are governed by physical laws. Second is the thesis that every mental event is identical to some physical event. For Davidson, however, this identity relation holds only as it pertains to *instances*. When it comes to *types* of mental and physical events, Davidson would have it that there are, as he puts it 'no "strict" laws' governing the relations between them (roughly, laws of the form: P_i entails M_i) as a result of what he sees as the 'lawlessness of the mental'.

The relations between the mental and the physical at the level of types are in this sense 'anomalous'.

Thus, on Davidson's account, there is no law which allows us to draw, from the fact that a mental process of a given type occurs, any inference to the effect that a physical process of some corresponding type occurs. This follows in part from Davidson's externalist view of mental content, which holds that someone can have the belief, for example, that Aristotle was a philosopher only if there is something like a causal chain that links the pertinent belief state to Aristotle rather than to some other ancient philosopher. Whether a person has a mental process of this or that kind can thereby depend on an unlimited number of relations that the person has to external things (Davidson 1987). On the other hand, Davidson concedes that we are able to make psychological generalisations, for example when we apply the rule that someone who does not eat for a long time will experience hunger. Unfortunately, however, to subscribe to the 'no strict laws' thesis is to assert that there are physical processes for which the laws of nature are invalid. Mental processes are certainly of a special nature, because it is through them that we experience ourselves and the world. But this special nature must, for us as for Davidson, be compatible with the processes in question being through and through physical.

We are puzzled, not least, by the fact that Davidson holds that there is identity between every mental process instance and the corresponding physical process instance. For of course, from an ontological point of view, identical instances are also identical at the level of types, by a simple application of Leibniz's law.

The difference between our two sets of views can, however, be easily resolved if we take account of the fact that we hold different views of what a law of physics is. For Davidson, laws are linguistic in nature, so that he can assert that 'events can instantiate laws, [and] hence be explained and predicted in the light of laws, *only as those events are described*' (Davidson 1970, emphasis added). On the view we defend, in contrast, the laws of physics obtain independently of whatever descriptions, terminologies, or theories humans might have developed at any given point in history. These laws were, after all, in force some billions of years before humans, or theories, or terminologies existed.

We are in some cases able to express these laws using linguistic (including mathematical) formulations. But when a process occurs, it is conformant to these laws whether or not we can formulate the latter in the form of equations. Explanation and prediction do of course require linguistic expression, but only in the trivial sense that we cannot make assertions of any sort without using language.[8]

Davidson's anomalism is based, therefore, not on some anomaly at the level of laws, but rather only on an incompatibility as between the predicates of the common-sense ontology of the mental and the predicates of whatever physics we are currently able to formulate.

As he formulates the matter, 'we may say that an event is mental if and only if it has a mental description', while physical events 'are those picked out by descriptions or open sentences that contain only the physical vocabulary essentially' (Davidson 1970).

We infer from this that Davidson's anomalist position is based on the following theses:

1. that there are causal relations between mental and physical events which obtain in virtue of the *physical* properties of the mental events involved (a thesis which has left Davidson open to the charge that he is embracing a species of epiphenomenalism [Robinson 2019]),
2. that it is the mental verbs we use in describing mental processes that are determinative of the types they instantiate, and not the underlying processes themselves.

---

8 We take Davidson literally here and assume that when he refers to how events are 'described' he means *described by people using language*. He may conceivably avoid our charge of triviality if by 'described' he means something like *described by propositions in some ideal realm*. A view along these lines is however ruled out by Davidson's account of truth as belonging not to propositions in the logical sense, but to sentences or statements (see (Davidson 2009)).

34 Properties of the human mind

These theses entail a nominalist position which, for mental phenomena at least, rejects the existence of types in reality. The laws of nature, in Davidson's world, do not apply to mental entities at the level of types even in spite of the fact that they apply in every case to mental entities at the level of instances. For us, in contrast, there may very well be laws of psychophysics, and even laws of psychology; these would be physical laws of immense complexity, impossible to formulate in mathematical form given the resources available to human beings, but laws nonetheless. They would relate to the kinds of entities recognised by the commonsense ontology of the mental (beliefs, desires, and so forth), but the latter would be defined in physical terms in highly complex ways.

2.2.3 An analogy with social facts

A usefully illustrative analogy to the situation with mental facts can be obtained by means of the following comparison.

There is a social fact F_0, one of many instances of fact type F, to the effect that the value of the Euro at noon in London on January 24, 2020, was USD 0.90. F_0 obtains in virtue of a huge number of more basic facts. But we cannot know the nature of the relations between F_0 and the many fine-grained explanatory facts in virtue of which F_0 obtains, and this for several reasons:

1. Because we cannot collect adequate data.
   a. Because we do not know which data to collect (and the relevant data are constantly changing, often in ways which are causally unconnected to the data supporting the immediately preceding counterpart facts [in this case the preceding London valuations of the Euro in terms of US dollars]).
   b. Because a large fraction of the data would be implicit (that is, it would be in the minds of the valuing subjects) and thus inaccessible.
   c. Because the process which creates instances of F is a non-Markovian erratic emanation of a complex system.[9] This means that we cannot obtain a representative sample of explanatory facts that would allow us to model the relationship between these facts and any given instance of F. Therefore, every time we attempt to create such a model, we do so on the basis of a non-representative data sample, so that the next time we try to predict F from a later set of data, our model will fail the test for being a good model because the predictions generated will with high likelihood fail.
2. Because, even if we *could* collect all the data about all the relevant facts, we still could not use these data to model mathematically how these lower-level facts yield any given instance of F which depends on them; for as we shall see

---

[9] We explain at length in chapters 7 and 8 the thesis presented here and the terms it contains.

in chapters 7 and 8, the involved variables and their relationships have properties that prevent mathematical modelling.

Could we perhaps collect just a useful fraction of the data, and use this fraction to provide a stochastic explanation of the relations between the independent lower-level facts and F_0? For the reasons listed under 1., this, too, would be impossible. We would never gain access to a sufficiently representative sample of lower-level facts of the sort that would be needed to generate even a stochastic model that would yield F_0 as output. Something along these lines is indeed attempted on a daily basis in parts of the Fintech industry, though on the basis of econometric high-level facts (so-called macroeconomic indicators). This yields good *descriptive* results, but without any *predictive* success over time, for reasons explained in section 8.4.3.

What, now, is the analogy between facts of type F and the fine-granularity facts pertaining to the human brain and its output in the form of human behaviour? *First*, we cannot measure the molecular properties of the brain at a sufficient level of detail. But *second*, and more importantly, even if we could assemble the needed body of granular facts, *we still could not use these data to engineer an AGI*. For there is no way to obtain on their basis a mathematical model of the relationship between the molecular events inside the brain and the associated mental experiences and observed behaviours that is of the sort that would enable such engineering. To underpin this thesis is the aim of this book.

2.2.4 The human mind-body continuum

The mental events we experience unfold in accordance with physical laws, but in ways which are far too complex (thus in ways involving far too many variables) to allow descriptive or explanatory modelling. The complex system—or rather, the system of complex systems—in which such events occur is what we call the human mind-body continuum. The interactions of the central nervous system with the other organs of the body cause what we experience as the mind—the material of the body is in this sense the physical carrier of our mental experience, which is itself physical (a matter of physical processes). It is now inevitable that the way in which the mind is related to the body varies between individuals, so that, while some fundamental relation types are indeed shared among human beings (this is the medieval *quidditas*), others (the *haecceitas*) are specific to individuals and dependent on their genetic endowment and their socialisation, as also on other, random factors. Otherwise we would have no way of accounting for the differences between human beings.

To understand this relationship at the level of detail which would enable explanation or prediction, however, we would have to understand the functions of all the cells and of all the cell constituents which contribute to consciousness and to the mental phenomena based thereon, including self-consciousness, perception, emotions, language, and so on. Moreover, given the inter-individual variance[10], we would have to do this at the level of instances (individual human beings) rather than at the level of general types. We would also have to understand the functions of neuronal cells during periods of non-consciousness (for example sleep or hypnosis). In other words, we would have to understand, *inter alia*, the molecular configurations of all neurons with sufficient detail to allow us to understand how their dynamic interactions create the subjective experience side of mental processes.[11]

Our view thus comes close to that of Schaffer, for whom

> minds are natural dynamical structures. Minds are not quite like the mousetraps or Coke dispensers commonly invoked in the literature (e.g. Fodor (1981, p. 120)), for those are artefacts, and artefact kinds are determined in part by the intentions of their artificer. Rather minds are more like ecosystems, holistic and dynamic structures of interacting components enacted in nature. For instance, what makes a given ecosystem feature a nutrient cycle is that the system dances out an abstract and multiply realisable loop, seen in the way water on earth precipitates down from the sky and then evaporates back up.
> (Schaffer 2021).

As we shall see in the course of this book, even if we could, by some miracle, collect all the needed data, we still could not even come close to modelling a system like this. We also cannot emulate those processes in the body which produce what we call the mind, because the mind is connected both in its structure and in its functions to trillions of molecular components of the body, not only of the central nervous system, but also of the peripheral endocrine, proprioceptive, and nociceptive systems (Damasio 1999).

---

10 We define 'variance' in the stochastic sense as the degree of dispersion from the centre of a uni- or multivariate distribution (see Glossary).
11 The knowledge of neuroscience we have today is mostly qualitative and descriptive. Even in spite of the many advances for example in brain imaging technologies, we still see few significant steps towards a comprehensive understanding of how the brain works; see on this also 12.2.3.

3
HUMAN AND MACHINE INTELLIGENCE

In 1921 the psychologist William Stern defined intelligence: as the ability to adapt to new situations.[1] The current consensus view is captured by Gottfredson (1997) in a more recent definition of intelligence: 'A very general mental capability that, among other things, involves the ability to reason, plan, solve problems, think abstractly, comprehend complex ideas, learn quickly, and learn from experience'.

3.1 Capabilities and dispositions

Common to both definitions is the use of the term 'capability' (or some cognate term such as 'ability' or *'Fähigkeit'*[2]). Capabilities in general and mental capabilities in particular did not fare well under the various forms of empiricism, behaviourism, materialism, and anti-mentalism that dominated philosophical thinking for much of the last century.[3] However, starting with the book *Causal Powers* by Harré et al. (1975), realist theories of dispositions began to be accepted by

---

1 We translate the original text at (Stern 1920, pp. 2–3) as: 'Intelligence is the general capability of an individual consciously to adjust his thinking to new requirements; it is general mental adaptability to new problems and conditions of life'.
2 In German the term 'mental faculty' is translated as *'geistige Fähigkeit'*.
3 To recycle an argument from Mackie: if there were mental capabilities, 'then they would be entities or qualities or relations of a very strange sort, utterly different from anything else in the universe'. Correspondingly, if we were aware of them, it would have to be by some special faculty of 'perception or intuition, utterly different from our ordinary ways of knowing everything else' (Mackie 1977, p. 38). In similar vein, Quine, in his 'Natural Kinds' (Quine 1969) claimed that 'dispensing with disposition terms, such as "intelligent" or even "water-soluble", is a mark of the maturity of a branch of science'.

DOI: 10.4324/9781003310105-4

metaphysicians and philosophers of science,[4] and this meant that capabilities, too, acquired an incipient ontological respectability (Maier 2020). Interest in intelligence as a mental capability then received an additional impulse with the growth of research on AI.

Here we view *capability* as one species of the genus *disposition*, with *instinctive reaction tendency* and *intention* among its sibling species. A capability is, roughly, a disposition which some entity possesses, and which is such that the bearer, or the bearer's wider community (or, in the case of an artefact, its user or creator or owner) has an *interest* in its realisation (Merrell et al. 2021). This interest may be biological—every living organism has an interest in its own survival and reproduction—or it may relate to human intentions which go beyond the biological, for example in the case of interests of a scientific or aesthetic or pecuniary nature.

Dispositions in general and capabilities in particular are, on the view we are here defending, real entities which serve as the truthmakers for assertions of real possibility, as when we refer to the disposition of a glass vase to shatter when hit with a hammer (Borghini et al. 2008). Every disposition is rooted in the physical makeup of its bearer. Dispositions are further associated with two sets of processes, called triggers and realisations. The processes of *watering* serve as trigger, and the processes of *germination* serve as realisation, of the disposition of a seed to *form a new plant*. But not all dispositions require triggers. And (because some seeds fall on stony ground) not all dispositions are realised.

3.1.1 Human identity

All human activities take place against an enduring, and typically slowly changing, background, consisting of the evolving intentions[5] of the persons involved and of their respective personalities, habits, capabilities, beliefs, and other attributes drawn from their personal biographies. These form what we shall call the 'identity' of a human being, by which we mean that highly complex individual pattern of dispositions, among which the most important are (in ascending order) the visceral, motor, affective, and cognitive dispositions—thus also including the intelligence—that determine a person's possibilities of reaction to internal or external stimuli.[6]

---

4 We take the term 'disposition' from Basic Formal Ontology (BFO), where it is defined as: a realisable entity that is rooted in the physical makeup of its bearer. Subtypes of disposition include capabilities and functions. BFO is an upper level ontology that is the subject of international standard ISO/IEC 21838-2. It is used as common architecture for some hundreds of formalised domain ontologies applied in bioinformatics, digital manufacturing, defense intelligence analysis, and other information-driven fields. See https://www.iso.org/standard/74572.html and (Arp et al. 2015; Smith et al. 2010; Smith et al. 2007). On AI applications see Smaili et al. (2019).
5 Note that the intention to do X, while it is a disposition, is a disposition to do X only in those cases where the bearer of the intention is capable of doing X (Merrell et al. 2021).
6 The underlying account of dispositions is sketched in (Hastings et al. 2011; Spear et al. 2016).

Your identity, in this sense, results from the combination of genotypic and environmental influences which affect your brain as it develops through time.[7]

We can distinguish three broad families of dispositions through the realisation of which our identity is manifested:

1. habits, tendencies, personality traits (for example tendencies to stutter, to fret, to avoid commitment, to behave politely, to behave honestly, ...[8])
2. capabilities (to speak a language, to play the piano, to manage complex activities, to do long division, to play championship tennis, to practice law, ...)
3. intentions, goals, objectives (to pass this or that exam, to marry Jack, to impress Jack's mother, to lose weight, to heal the rift with your brother, ...)

Our intentions carry the goals and motives of our behaviour and are typically short-lived. Our habits and capabilities are longer lasting. They provide the frame within which our intentions develop and how (and whether) they are realised. But where does the *drive* that is manifested in our behaviour, thus in the *realisation* of our intentions, come from?

3.1.2 Human excess drive

To answer this question we introduce a notion which will be important for our treatment of the feasibility of AI in chapter 9, namely *human excess drive*. Humans, like all living organisms, are *driven* to preserve their life and to reproduce. But unlike animal drive, which is of a quantity just adequate to their survival and reproduction[9], humans have a degree of surplus drive; their drive is never fully satisfiable (Russell 1938, p. 1).[10] This surplus drive[11] dominates our conscious life and manifests itself in the form of goals, desires, and intentions that go beyond the merely biological. It leads both to positive achievements and in some cases also to self-damaging behaviour, as in the case of some devotees of extreme sports or of those who engage in psychotropic substance abuse.

---

7 Our 'identity' thus comes close to what Searle calls 'The Background' (Searle 1978), of which Searle himself says that it is at one and the same time (i) 'derived from the entire congeries of relations which each biological-social being has to the world around itself' and (ii) purely a matter of that being's neurophysiology (Searle 1983, p.154).
8 The disposition we call memory also falls under this heading.
9 This is true at the level of the individual animal. Under certain environmental conditions, animals can reproduce to the disadvantage of their host population, for example in predator overpopulation scenarios. Animals also play and perform other complex acts, but they have no excess drive.
10 For the definition of what it is to be driven, and our treatment of drivenness in general, see 7.5.2.5.
11 The German term '*Triebüberschuss*' is translated in Gehlen (1988) as 'impulse excess' or 'over drive'. The topic is discussed by Gehlen especially in chapter 42 of this work.

Gehlen describes several aspects of this excess drive:

1. The human ability to view our environment in an unengaged, abstracted fashion, thereby both freeing ourselves from the burden of responding continuously to external stimuli and also enabling planning for the future. This is enabled by the human-specific ability to postpone the fulfilment of an intention and the achievement of rewards.
2. The massive diminution of the role of instincts[12] in human behaviour. According to Gehlen, because human behaviour is instinct-driven to a much lesser degree than that of animals, humans need a surplus of drive to compensate for this loss. The nature of human sexuality, which preserves instinctive aspects in the sexual act itself but leads to many forms of non-instinct-based sexualised human behaviour alien to that of animals, is a good example for this.
3. The chronic nature of the human excess drive. Vertebrates still follow instinctive behaviour patterns specialised to match their environments. In his essay 'Notes on the Evolution of Systems of Rules of Conduct' (Hayek 1967), Hayek points to cases of animal behavior which involve adoption of 'spatial models' of action while on the move or during defense or hunting activities carried out by groups: 'The arrow formation of migrating wild geese, the defensive ring of the buffaloes, or the manner in which lionesses drive the prey towards the male for the kill'. Lorini (2018) argues that these are cases not of instinctive behaviour but rather of the sort of rule-following that enables animals to co-ordinate the actions of multiple individuals. But they enhance these behaviour patterns by exercising what we shall come to recognise as their primal intelligence capabilities, and this combination of instinct and intelligence is of critical importance for the survival especially of higher animals. Humans, in contrast, are non-specialised, and thus they need to constantly adapt to new and sometimes alien environments.[13] This requires a much more powerful drive than is manifested in animals, one consequence of which is the creation of a huge infrastructure of what we can think of as cultural environments.

Human drive is the source of our intentions and of our realisation of our intentions. It is the source of our ambition. It is therefore also the source of the constant expansion of the sphere of culture which—starting with the temporary

---

12 We define an instinct (innate behaviour) as a hard-wired complex behavioural reaction mechanism, which responds to an internal or external stimulus of a given type in a way that leaves no alternatives to its bearer in how it reacts.
13 This may involve technical equipment such as submarines or spaceships to enable survival in an environment outside of the narrow range necessary for the maintenance of homeostasis.

shelters in the palaeolithic—has enabled human beings to survive despite the fact that, unlike animals, we do not have an adaptation to a specific habitat.[14]

3.2 Intelligence

3.2.1 Primal intelligence

Clearly, the Stern definition of intelligence as the ability to adapt to new situations can be applied not only to humans but also to organisms in general; not, however, the Gottfredson definition, which refers to capabilities such as reasoning, planning, and abstract thinking. For clarity's sake we therefore distinguish between two aspects of intelligence, which we shall call 'primal' and 'objectifying' intelligence, respectively.[15] Humans, of course, have only one type of intelligence, which is a fusion of both.

The idea of what we are here calling 'primal intelligence' was introduced by the philosopher Max Scheler as what he called 'practical intelligence'[16]. Scheler used this term to refer to the sort of intelligence that is shared by humans and other higher animals, and which he summarised as 'the power of making a meaningful response in the face of a new situation' (Scheler 1961, p. 30, our translation).

Scheler emphasises in his account that primal intelligence is not the result of learning. Rather, it *enables* learning, because learning involves being confronted with new situations. He asserts in addition that, to be a marker for intelligence, the response to the new situation must be *immediate*.[17] Primal intelligence is also 'organically bound', by which Scheler means that the process that the organism executes in responding to the new situation is in the service of an instinctive

---

14 Gehlen sees a greater gulf between human and animal behaviour than is warranted by more recent ethological research (for a survey see Bekoff et al. (2002) and our further discussion of animals in this chapter). Gehlen's ideas will nonetheless prove fruitful in our discussions of the qualities of human intelligence in what follows. Animals do not engineer systems.
15 Note (i.) that what we shall define as 'primal intelligence' is found in higher animals such as mammals and birds, and it may be present in other species also. Fish do not seem to display it, but currently it is not known where the exact evolutionary boundary lies (Aellen et al. 2021). Note also (ii.) that primal and objectifying intelligence (defined in 3.2.3) are both correlated with the so-called 'g factor' (Jensen 1998).
16 Scheler (1961, p. 82) is here perhaps echoing views of pragmatist philosophers such as James or Peirce. Scheler was one of the first German philosophers to discuss the American pragmatist movement (Davis 2017).
17 The relevant passage from Scheler is as follows: 'Ein Lebewesen verhält sich *intelligent*, wenn es ohne Probierversuche ein sinngemäßes Verhalten neuen, weder art noch individualtypischen Situationen gegenüber vollzieht, und zwar *plötzlich*, und vor allem unabhängig von der *Anzahl* der vorher gemachten Versuche, eine triebhaft bestimmte Aufgabe zu lösen'. This we translate as: 'A living organism behaves *intelligently* when, without trial-attempts, it behaves in a meaningful, appropriate way in relation to a situation that is novel, typical neither for an organism of this species nor for this individual organism, and does this *suddenly* and above all independently of the *number* of its prior attempts to solve a problem whose solution is determined instinctively' (Scheler 1961, p. 29).

42 Properties of the human mind

behavioural urge.[18] Primal intelligence is realised in non-human organisms always in an action through which the organism aims to fulfil a biological need such as drinking, eating, or life preservation through flight or fight.[19] Animals (by which we mean in all that follows non-human animals) always live to fulfil immediate goals; they cannot create complex long-term plans.[20] They live in the present situation and cannot abstract away from what holds only of their survival or, in higher species, the survival of their offspring.[21] Animal perception is structurally restricted (for an example from rodents, which are higher animals, see King et al. 2015). Animals are blind to stimuli that are not related to the fulfilment of their immediate biological needs, which means that their worldview is highly restricted. Sensual clues that do not belong to the environment to which they have been adapted by evolution are ignored in something like the way that we humans, in normal circumstances, ignore ultraviolet light or radioactivity. Primal intelligence thus satisfies the following criteria:

1. it is a disposition (a capability) of a higher animal to adapt to new situations that is enabled by the organism's physical makeup;
2. it is a capability whose realisation is sudden—springs suddenly forth—which means that it can happen at any time;
3. it is realised in actions which are

   a. meaningful, or in other words: appropriate to the situation, in the sense that they serve the achievement by the acting organism of its instinctive goals;
   b. not primed by prior experiences; thus they are untrained, and not a product of repeated attempts involving trial and error;
   c. from the perspective of the acting organism, novel.[22]

---

18 Both instinct and intention are sources of actions, but instinctive actions are pre-determined by the types of environmental stimuli in relation to which they evolved, and instances of which now serve as their triggers. Intentions, in contrast, can target goals beyond what is biologically pre-determined. Note that humans are distinguished from animals by their ability to overcome the mentioned behavioural urge on a consistent basis.
19 Primal intelligence is manifested in non-human organisms also when they engage in play and mock fights to exercise their developing motor apparatus. Note, however, that as this and similar behaviour occurs in humans, it is not a straightforward example of primal intelligence. In humans it involves ingredients also of the second type of intelligence treated in 3.2.3.
20 The sorts of extended-term planning we find in migrating birds is determined by innate structures of their brains (Mouritsen et al. 2016).
21 The behaviour of trained circus animals is not a counterexample to this rule, since it is reward-conditioned and vanishes without food rewards and human monitoring and correction.
22 This means either that the animal has never before experienced a situation of this sort, or that it has completely forgotten earlier encounters.

3.2.2 Intelligence and culture

Parrots, dolphins, and chimpanzees are long-lived and highly social vertebrates. Their most important daily task is foraging to obtain food (parrots and chimps are plant-eaters; dolphins are predatory piscivores). In their foraging behaviour, all display an intelligence that satisfies all of the given criteria in the ways they search for and identify new food sources, communicate via calls or physical displays to fellow group members, and fight competitors from rival groups for food sources. Food sources change over short intervals because foraging animals very quickly exhaust the plant and animal resources within any given area and because prey animals flee from their predators. Hence there is a constant need for forager groups to seek out new environments, and some animals can make use of a rudimentary understanding of causation under certain circumstances (Jelbert et al. 2014). All these capabilities are used in narrow contexts such as foraging and not in the way humans adapt the world to their ends via technology.

Foraging behaviour of this sort can be found in both mammals and non-mammalian vertebrates such as parrots. It is instinctive behaviour in which genetically encoded activity patterns are triggered by sensory stimuli. But higher animals also transmit knowledge to their offspring about food sources and search strategies (Milton 2000). This means that higher animals can indeed transmit learned knowledge from one generation to the next and thus that they can engage in what can properly be called elementary cultural behaviour.[23]

Many varieties of animals have rudimentary culture in this sense; that is, they have non-genetically transmitted knowledge. What they do not have is *cumulative cultural evolution* (Boyd et al. 1996), which occurs when such learned content acquires greater complexity, power, and reach through processes analogous to those which take place on the level of the genome in the course of biological evolution. Such processes arise only among humans, and they depend essentially on at least oral, and, for high cultures, written language, and also on the ability to pursue long-term goals. These processes allow humans to adapt in a much more radical way than animals and to create the imposing man-made environments (the technosphere) that enable them not only to survive but also to express their objectifying intelligence in ever new ways.

Culture evolves in a target-oriented fashion (Sperber et al. 2008), where the targets are dictated, not by immediate instinctive needs, but rather by individual human intentions whose consequences may aggregate in impressive fashion over time. It is this sort of cumulative evolution of human culture that explains the gigantic successes achieved by humans over some thousands of years in all areas of culture, from techniques for social interaction to scientific knowledge and technology.

---

23 Following Richerson et al. (2005, p. 5), we use the word *culture* to refer to information capable of affecting individuals' behavior that they 'acquire from other members of their species through teaching, imitation, and other forms of social transmission.'

44 Properties of the human mind

Humans stand out also in their ability to shape the natural environment in discretionary fashion in order to make it fit their own needs and desires (Gehlen 1988, ch. 9). Animals, in contrast, even when engaging in what we can recognise as cultural activities, always remain tied to the natural habitat to which they are adapted.[24] To understand this thesis, however, we must take care to do justice to the distinction between habitat types and habitat instances.[25] We can then identify a number of different possibilities:

1. The habitat type to which an animal is adapted may change because the animal itself changes, for instance as a result of growth and development (for many types of animals the habitat of infants is tightly constrained around the mother).
2. Successive generations of animals may be subjected over long periods of time to incremental changes in virtue of which later generations are adapted to a new type of habitat, as for example when rat or bird species became adapted over time to city life. However, these species had a huge global adaptation sphere already before the Industrial Revolution. Humans select some of these species for domestication—those seen as providing some kind of utility—while others are regarded as vermin or plagues.
3. The specific geospatial habitat of an animal at one time may itself change, so that the animal is forced to seek another habitat. Winter habitats may for this reason be different from summer habitats. But the habitat types to which the animal is genetically adapted do not themselves change. In all such cases the animal (or, of course more typically, packs of animals) will be forced to move from one geospatial location to another, thereby spending periods of time during which they are in what we might call a *transition* or—in the case where a new habitat has to be sought out—an *exploratory* habitat, which has to have a large degree of matching with the genetically determined adaptations of the animal.[26]
4. Further complications are introduced by the fact that, for domesticated animals such as dogs and cats, some of the adaptation is lost by domestication. Hence the ability of homeless dogs and cats to take care of themselves

---

24 Rats and the common fly are found around the world; but they are still adapted to a niche, their behaviour is the same everywhere.
25 We must take account also of the relation between 'habitat' as referring on the other hand to a *site* in the geospatial sense of this term (Smith et al. 1999) and on the other hand to a *niche* in the sense of Hutchinson (1957), or in other words to a specific constellation of environmental factors (pertaining to temperature, availability of food, presence of predators, and so forth).
26 (Smith and Varzi 2002). Sometimes the association between instinctive behaviour and habitat is highly complex. For example the breeding behaviour of penguins stretches over weeks or months and extends geographically over large distances, which is the result of adaptation to the extremely harsh conditions of their environment. Without the contribution of both parents in incubating the egg, the brooding animal would die because energy consumption in the cold is so high. The parents therefore have to take turns in their respective incubating/hunting behaviours so that they can alternate in replenishing their fat reservoirs. This behaviour is programmed by the amounts of fat remaining at any given time and is highly instinctive.

when they revert to the feral state, but only for so long as they remain in their adaptive environment.
5. And finally, animals may also change their environments, for example when beavers build dams. Here they are indeed shaping their natural environment. But what they do is a case of primal intelligence nonetheless, because it is instinctive; it does not create anything new, since both beaver dams and the activity of building beaver dams are, after all, part of the beavers' adaptation to its natural environment. Male bower birds similarly create highly elaborate displays around their nesting places in order to attract females. But these, too, are a matter of primal intelligence; they are an expression of the hard-wired evolutionary adaptation of these animals to their habitat. The male bird knows by instinct what kind of visual display can trigger the interest of the female (for instance because of its similarity to flowers).

But on every single one of these scenarios, the species-normal individuals in any given generation are still subject to the law that they are tied to the natural habitat to which they and their generational cohorts are at that stage adapted.

3.2.3 Objectifying intelligence: what sets humans apart

If beavers or bower birds are removed from their habitat, they cannot survive unaided. Humans, by contrast, have an intelligence that comprises, in addition to the spectrum of capabilities of primal intelligence, also the ability to conceive, and then deliberately plan and build, artefacts that will enable them to survive even where there is no life at all—in polar barrens in the high arctic, for example, or in submarines, or in outer space. This is achieved by modifying these environments not only in ways that will ensure the preservation of homeostasis as concerns the availability of ambient temperature, a breathable (adequately oxygenated and non-toxic) gas mix, water, and comestibles as well as waste disposal necessities but also in such a way that entirely new goals can be realised. They do this, again, via cumulative cultural evolution. Complex and powerful artefacts of the given kinds evolved across many generations from earlier, simpler, and less powerful artefacts, where each step towards something new involved some human being electing to shape the natural environment by making a new artefact or modifying some existing artefact in a way that would fit new sets of self-determined goals. This recalls Searle's idea of a *world-to-mind direction of fit*; we change the world in order to make it fit what we have in our minds (Searle 1975).

For the intelligence specific to our species[27], we adopt the term 'objectifying intelligence', drawing from the work of Husserl, who used the term 'objectifying'

---

27 Turing and others conceive the specific kind of intelligence which sets humans apart from other animals as 'the ability to use language' (Turing 1950). While of course language use is the hallmark capability of objectifying intelligence, it is itself a special form of intelligence.

for those mental and linguistic acts which involve *consciousness of* or *directedness towards* some target (Schuhmann et al. 1987). The simplest examples of objectification occur in acts of perception or judgement—as contrasted with feelings, desires, or acts of will, which gain their intentional directedness by inheritance from some underlying act of perception or judgement. The exercise of this objectifying capability in making judgements can clearly go beyond what is instinctive, and indeed beyond all biological needs. Objectifying acts of these sorts are found when, for example, a mother conceives how she will divide the available food to leave enough also for those of her children who will return home only later. But they are found just as much in, for example, mathematical reasoning, or in reasoning about astrobotany, or about aleatoric music. It is the exercise of the capability of objectifying intelligence as it relates to the world through intelligence-guided and language-dependent actions that enables the sort of cumulative cultural evolution that is needed to create complex artefacts such as the Large Hadron Collider or the Kaleshwaram Lift Irrigation Project.

3.2.3.1 Features of objectifying intelligence

Where non-human vertebrates and all lower organisms relate to their environment in a pre-determined set of ways, objectifying intelligence allows *homo sapiens* to disengage himself from his environment in a way that allows him to see himself, other human beings, and the elements of this environment (both biological and non-biological) as objects, each with its own trajectory and its own array of properties and causal powers. This capability is manifested already in early infancy and is rooted in categorical thinking[28], for example when a small child categorises every flying object she sees as 'fly' or when an adult categorises tiny flying animals with which she is unfamiliar under 'insect' and draws thereby on her human ability to infer properties and causal powers of objects from their categories and to infer how they will relate to other objects (and most importantly, to human beings).

We can characterise the capability of objectifying intelligence as involving:

- the ability to objectify both the person's environment and her own self; each person can serve as target not only of her own but also of the others' conscious acts; and each person is aware that they can themselves become the target of the conscious acts of others;
- the ability to focus on and to track objects through time in a way that enables both short- and longterm planning (potentially extending across multiple

---

28 (Kim et al. 1999). Organisms possessing primal intelligence are capable of categorical perception, for example, chinchillas can categorically perceive speech sounds (Green et al. 2020). Animals have a capability to perceive and exploit the usage of categorical patterns, as is evident from their ability to use affordances (Gibson 2015) in a manner similar to humans. But this capability is not derived from thinking about the world in terms of general kinds and classes and the relations between them.

generations), including the setting aside of resources for the future; investment in the creation of enduring physical artefacts (churches, factories, roads, theatres) and institutions (governments, legal and financial systems, religions);
- the ability to make sense of the world in terms of causality and teleology; to understand object persistence for different categories of object; to associate specific categories of processes, dispositions, capabilities, and functions with specific categories of objects; and to differentially and consciously value objects (including other persons) in light of their different contributions to the realisation of one's goals;
- the power of language, including the ability to think of and to categorise objects under universals and to exploit such linguistically mediated categorisations to enable more complex activities, including activities involving shared agency;
- a heightened degree of independence (relative to what is the case for lower animals) from immediate organic necessities, which manifests itself in having and realising intentions of new sorts, including intentions belonging to cultural worlds;
- self-distancing, which means the ability to stand outside natural life also in the sense that we are able to reflect upon ourselves as taking the point of view of an observer in relation to other objects in the world;
- distance from the world: this means that humans have a wide range of choices as to which parts of reality they will direct their attention and interests, where animals are restricted to modes of interaction with the world that are optimised to the environmental niche into which they have evolved;
- the ability to modify our directedness towards targets by cancelling the belief-moment.[29] It is this which allows all forms of imaginative directedness towards objects, in the literary and visual arts as well as in planning for the future and in all forms of speculation and hypothetical reasoning. The ability to direct one's thinking to entirely new kinds of objects is a characteristic feature of human creativity.

Our genetic disposition for objectifying intelligence arose in tandem with the degeneration of our biological adaptation to the natural world (Scheler 1961; Gehlen 1988). As *homo sapiens* lost the specialisation to natural environments which higher non-human mammals still enjoy, our species acquired—slowly, over millions of years of evolution—the general purpose adaptation which we are calling objectifying intelligence, and this capability has in modern times enabled humans to create their own environments: nurseries, schools, zoos, planetaria, cinemas, hospitals, airports; as well as dwelling places incorporating air conditioning and wireless networks allowing instantaneous communication across the entire planet. In sum: the contemporary technosphere.

---

29 (Husserl 2000, p. 180), (Schuhmann et al. 1987)

In humans, as we pointed out, primal and objectifying intelligence are fused. Let's look at two examples at different points on a scale of mixture. At the one extreme, consider a small child trying to build a simple structure with wooden bricks. We assume that the child tries this for the first time, so that it performs what is from her own perspective novel behaviour, and she obviously uses primal intelligence to achieve her goals. However, these goals go beyond meeting merely biological needs. In addition, the child already has a notion of the objects she is dealing with and of the categories under which they fall[30], and she draws on her objectifying intelligence to use this categorical knowledge—in combination with primal intelligence—to achieve her goals.

At the other extreme, consider a mathematician creating a novel proof of some algebraic theorem. All the structures she is dealing with are highly abstract and may have no counterparts in external physical reality. Her thinking is seemingly dominated by objectifying intelligence. It may involve exploring new domains of objects, which she herself has postulated. Yet the basic structural approach she adopts—the same one that she employs in all novel problem-solving situations—is provided by her primal intelligence. She takes step after step to reach a solution, following her will to solve the problem in a way analogous to but also different from the way non-human vertebrates solve a problem. For the latter follow their instincts. Their primal intelligence does not allow them to explore in a novel way, to take entirely new kinds of steps, break through into entirely new types of environments. The analogies lie in the directedness of the problem-solving process and the trial-and-error steps involved. The differences consist of the sometimes highly abstract content of the steps involved and in their detachment from the immediate needs of survival or reproduction.

3.3 AI and human intelligence

But in a book concerned with demonstrating the limits of machine intelligence, should we really be focusing in this way on *human* intelligence? AI proponents since Turing have after all often argued that the goal of AI research should be, not to recreate *human* intelligence, but rather to create a different kind of intelligence, a machine intelligence. They claim that using human intelligence as the goal of AI engineering suffers from what they see as the defect of anthropomorphism (Bostrom 2003; Yudkowsky 2001b; Muehlhauser et al. 2012a). They then reinforce this narrative by admitting that an AI would certainly have an 'alien intelligence', but that this is something with which the rest of us would just have to learn how to cope (Yudkowsky 2001b, pp. 24f).

---

30 (Medin et al. January 1989; Solomon et al. 1999; Gelman et al. 1991)

3.3.1 Definitions of machine intelligence in the AGI community

But what, then, do they mean by 'intelligence', whether of the machine or of human beings?

To answer this question we first examine representative definitions of this term provided by the leading proponents of AI, and specifically of AGI, starting with what is in the AGI community the most influential and still the most widely accepted definition, which was put forward by Legg and Hutter in a paper entitled 'Universal Intelligence: A Definition of Machine Intelligence' published in 2007.

The definition proffered in this paper reads as follows: 'Intelligence measures an agent's ability to achieve goals in a wide range of environments'. Here *agent* signifies an AI algorithm running on a universal Turing machine (Legg et al. 2007, p. 15), which can run inside a data centre or inside a (possibly mobile) robot, for example an assembly line robot, a self-driving car, or a mechanical traffic police officer.

Based on this verbal definition, Legg and Hutter develop a mathematical definition of 'achieving goals'[31] for such an agent by means of a series of steps, based on the following utility function:

$$V_\mu^\pi := \mathbf{E}\left(\sum_{i=1}^{\infty} r_i\right) \leq 1 \tag{3.1}$$

where the utility V_μ of the agent π depends on μ, which is the minimal binary description of an environment of the agent.[32] This environment may be a fiat, abstract structure that is manipulated inside the computer (for example in a theorem prover scenario); or it may relate to something in the physical world (for example in a nuclear power debris clean-up scenario). Its description is in either case a binary string, and it is this *description* which plays the role of environment in the Hutter model (since only something like a description can serve as input to a computer).[33] $\mathbf{E}$, here, is the expectation over the sum of the rewards r_i which the algorithm receives upon *each step i* it undertakes.

---

31 We will analyse what 'goal' could mean in this context in chapter 6 and section 12.2.7.
32 A binary description is a Turing-computable representation of some entity using a binary vector, which is a set of numbers expressed as binary digits ordered in a linear fashion. For example, the binary vector ⟨10100, 1000110⟩ of length two could store measurements of the inches of rain collected on a given day in a rain gauge and the average temperature during that day in Fahrenheit (in this case, 20 inches and 70°, respectively).
33 Initially, Legg and Hutter define μ as a probability measure of an observation-reward tuple $o_k r_k$ conditioned on past tuples of observations, actions and rewards: $\mu(o_k r_k | o_1 r_1 a_1 ... o_{k-1} r_{k-1} a_{k-1})$ (Legg et al. 2007, p. 409). However, they state that 'each environment μ_i is described by a minimal length program that is a binary string' (p. 23). The place of environments in their model is thus taken by input data represented by means of binary strings, which are what the authors designate as 'environment descriptions'. We interpret this as implying that the variable μ ranges over descriptions of this sort.

Unfortunately, the definition given by Legg and Hutter in equation (3.1) is mathematically faulty. This is because the standard definition of 'expectation' or 'expected value' of a random variable in probability theory is the *weighted* average of its possible values, where the weight assigned to each possible value is the probability that the variable takes that value.[34] The expectation operator **E** should thus not be applied to the sum of the values of a random variable, but rather directly to these values themselves, in order to take account of the norming denominator p_i (the probability) for each r_i. Ignoring this issue with the definition, however, equation (3.1) states (in simplified terms) that an agent π reacting to an environment description μ obtains a finite reward which corresponds to the expectation of rewards it achieves over all the steps it undertakes.

Based on such a valuation function, mainstream authors in the world of AGI (including Schmidhuber (2007) and Pennachin et al. (2007)) derive a utility function-based definition of the intelligence Υ of an agent π, which is structured as follows (Legg et al. 2007, p. 23):

$$\Upsilon(\pi) := \sum_{\mu \in \mathbf{U}} 2^{-K(\mu)} V_\mu^\pi \qquad (3.2)$$

Here K is the Kolmogorov complexity function (indicating the length of the shortest algorithm needed to computationally represent the environment description μ of the agent π, also designated as the algorithmic complexity of the executed program), **U** is the set of environment descriptions with which the agent can cope[35], and V_μ^π is the utility achieved by the agent π for a given environment description $\mu \in \mathbf{U}$, as defined in equation (3.1). The first factor of the product, the 'algorithmic probability distribution over the space of [environment descriptions]', serves to penalise the complexity of the algorithm executed by agent π—that is, it will assign a lower utility to a more complex algorithm. The definition of Υ is chosen to yield the most efficient possible algorithm.[36] Leaving aside the unclear definition of **E** in equation (3.1), the result is a statistically reliable measure of the intelligence-surrogate which its authors use as a tool for optimising the behaviour of an agent that is biased towards effectiveness at low cost. The definition of intelligence given in (3.2), which yields what we shall call the Hutter-set of AI algorithms, provides on this basis a good initial

---

34 Thus, $\mathbf{E}(r_i) = \Sigma_{i \in I} r_i p_i$, where the probability of each step is designated by p_i, $\forall i: 0 \leq p_i \leq 1$ and I is the countable (possibly infinite) index set.
35 **U** depends on the type of agent. For AlphaZero, for example, **U** is the set of environments (board positions, opponent activities, etc.) occurring in games it can play (Silver et al. 2018). For a putative universal agent, of course, all possible environments would have to be taken into account.
36 Note that the summation over all environment descriptions $\mu \in \mathbf{U}$ prevents the sort of random hit which arises when some given μ_i yields an exceptionally high V^π from distorting the quantification of Υ.

demarcation of the space of candidate realisations of 'machine intelligence' as conceived by the leading figures in the AI field.

3.3.2 The Hutter definition and its shortcomings

But now, consider again the basic verbal definition of intelligence provided by Legg et al. (2007), which underlies their claim to have defined what they are pleased to call 'universal intelligence': 'Intelligence measures an agent's ability to achieve goals in a wide range of environments'. Even when applied narrowly to the field of machine intelligence, this definition is too restrictive if (as its authors—and other advocates of AGI—presuppose) the intelligent machine is to achieve, or indeed exceed, the cognitive capabilities of humans. Indeed, the definition captures just one part—adapting to new environments—of Scheler's definition of *primal* intelligence. It lacks the three further constitutive properties of suddenness, untrainedness, and novelty. And at the same time the Hutter verbal definition is also too broad, since it allows that *C. elegans*, a nematode (worm) of length one millimeter with 1000 cells and only 302 neurons, would be intelligent, because it can forage and reproduce in a range of complex environments[37] (fruit, vegetable, mushroom compost, temperate soil, including using snails and slugs as migration vectors). Even a slime mold or an amoeba (single-celled eukaryote) is intelligent, according to this definition.[38]

3.3.2.1 Perception

The mathematical definition of intelligence by Hutter brings three additional problems.

First, its proposed 'measure of the complexity of environments' presupposes that the environment can be represented by using a binary vector. We do indeed accept that, given enough sensors and a specific, appropriately defined problem, it is possible to capture many of the problem-relevant external raw data relating to a given environment in a form that can be expressed as a binary vector.[39]

---

37 Of course, nematodes, like any other animal, have only limited adaptation capabilities and cannot survive in entirely novel environments that go beyond their genetically programmed adaptation.
38 Hutter's definition provides an example of what, already in 1976, Drew McDermott called 'wishful mnemonics' (McDermott 1976). This is the tendency of those working with computers to designate what the computer or the algorithm is doing by using labels (such as 'understanding' or 'memory' or 'problem-solving') referring to human cognitive traits. Larson (2021, p. 4), too, argues forcefully against this tendency, which he sees as part of the wider phenomenon whereby AI researchers propagate a simplified view of the world, where what he calls cheap imitations block the way to deeper ideas.
39 Data pertaining to the mental contents of the (conscious and unconscious) memories, feelings, and beliefs which humans use all the time as co-variables of their perception are of course not accessible via sensors.

But sensors enable only *passive impressions*. In mammals, a sensory impression takes the form of a burst of raw (which means: unprocessed) stimuli (Kandel et al. 2021, chapter 17) which results when an input is received by competent sensor cells that create the initial electric coding which reaches the CNS at its first synapse (via bone marrow or the brain directly). Examples of impressions are: the electric signals generated by the photoreceptor cells upon looking at a luminescent watch at night or the signals generated when one stretches one's thumb from the Golgi organs in its tendons. In the context of machines, impressions in this sense are electric signals of the same unprocessed form, but they are generated by sensors which have been engineered with a specific target type, span, and resolution.

Clearly, in order to have a machine substitute for the ways human beings experience what is going on in their environments, the restriction to binary vectors representing passive impressions makes the Hutter approach deficient along a number of dimensions. We focus here on just one of these dimensions, which relates to the problems caused by the fact that many of the signals humans need to deal with emanate from complex systems such as the natural environment, including other humans. They therefore require interactive interpretation and re-assessment.[40] This means that it does not suffice for a human to merely passively measure the data, as is done, for example, with a rain gauge. To emulate the perception of a mammal using a computer, the types of measurements performed at each stage would need to be continuously re-adjusted to take account of the interpretation of the measurement result obtained at each prior stage. As we shall see in chapter 5, this interpretation massively depends on typed, implicit mental material on the part of the observer.[41] In the course of an ambush, for example, a predator continuously adapts its observations as prey and predator move around in the environment. The predator makes not only new observations, but new actively determined types of observations.

The experiences of humans are constantly evolving in a similar way as they interact with their environment, as was recognised in the middle of the 20th century by both Gehlen (1988) and Merleau-Ponty (2012). Both describe perception as a dynamic process of constant iterative feedback loops between sensory and motor neuronal circuits. Gibson especially has contributed to our understanding of perception as an exploratory activity that is directed towards invariants in the environment: 'The normal activity of perception is to explore the world' (Gibson 1963). As we do so, we alter the perspectives which are available to us—or events alter them for us—so that now this side of an object is available, now that side. 'What exploration does is to isolate the invariants. The sensory system can separate the permanence from the change only if

---

40 The entire set of problems is described in more detail in 11.3.1.2.
41 Where the types used by animals are mostly fixed, the repertoire of types used by humans is highly variable (and the types themselves may be highly abstract).

there is change'. This is why 'we strive to get new perspectives on an object in order to perceive it properly'. Gibson's theory thus relies on

> the existence of certain types of permanence underlying change. These invariants ... are facts of stimulus ecology, independent of the observer although dependent upon his exploratory isolation of them. This kind of order in stimulation is not created by the observer ... [but is discovered] by the attentive adjustments of his sense organs and by the education of his attention.
> (Gibson 1963)

The infant learns to perceive 'precisely by exploring with eyes, hands, mouth, and all of his organs, extending and refining his dimensions of sensitivity. He has to separate what comes from the world and what comes from himself'. (Gibson 1963). But the infant does not have to learn to convert sensations into perceptions: our sensory systems have evolved to pick up the information in our environment directly. Gibson liked to use in this connection the metaphor of the radio, which does not *interpret* the electromagnetic waves it receives, but rather picks them up directly and 'resonates' with them: 'A perceiver is a self-tuning system' (Gibson 1963, p. 271). The infant can also be *taught* to perceive in the sense that 'the adult who talks to a child can educate his attention to certain differences instead of others. ... Perceiving helps talking, and talking fixes the gains of perceiving' (Gibson 1963). And once the word is a part of his growing vocabulary, 'when a child talks to himself he may enhance the tuning of his perception to certain differences rather than others' (p. 282).

Perception depends, therefore, on more than just sensory stimulus. It requires the observer's purposeful activity, including direct manipulation of the objects in its environment and an innate or acquired knowledge of the expected patterns of reality. Compare the way in which humans, in grasping an object, adapt the force of their hand's grip to the consistency of the object which is to be grasped. As O'Regan et al. (2001, p. 940) put it, visual perception is a 'mode of exploration of the world that is mediated by knowledge of what we call sensorimotor contingencies'. And these ideas have been recently much further elaborated, for example, in the hypothetical theory of predictive coding (Rao et al. 1999)[42] and in the view of the mind as an error-minimising mechanism (Hohwy 2013).[43]

Perception becomes even more demanding when its objects are animate organisms, because the behaviour of the latter is harder to perceive and interpret than the behaviour of inanimate nature. For example, it is easier to interpret a falling rock as a threat than an approaching wild sow that is known to be

---

42 The reader should note that as Friston (2018) points out, the theory of predictive coding as a hypothesis pertaining to message-passing in cortical hierarchies has not as yet been empirically confirmed.
43 These developments confirm and expand the view of sensorimotor-perception first advanced by Peirce and James (Mulligan 2018).

dangerous only if in company of her offspring. And the sow again is easier to perceive as a threat than is a subtle change in the social order occurring over long stretches of time and space (Gibson 1966), (Heft 2017, p. 134).

We could capture some of these changes by means of carefully positioned and carefully calibrated sensors. But these would need to be repositioned and recalibrated as the environment changes, and potentially augmented with entirely new types of sensors. And all such changes would need to be carried out under the guidance of human beings who are actively *perceiving* the environment in the ways described—ways beyond the reach of anything like the Legg-Hutter set of algorithms.[44]

3.3.2.2 Motion as sensorimotor activity

The second problem generated by Hutter's mathematical definition of intelligence relates to the fact that the human motor activity that is engaged both in bodily motion and in the performance of speech acts is not a linear sequence of motor-neuron efferences. Rather, it is a loop involving motor activity closely coupled with both proprioception and outer sensation. When we move, this stimulates proprioceptors which measure the movements of all our skeletal muscles. Tactile and proprioceptive sensations occur, for example, when we use our fingers in grasping, caressing, or writing, when we simultaneously feel what they touch and correct their motion based on this feedback. When we walk, we feel our feet touching the ground. When I walk towards a woman on the deck of a swaying ship and reach out to shake her hand, then the feeling I have of my own steps makes me adjust my movements, including the way I extend my hand, to the movement of the ship and of the other person. The sensory stimuli involved in directed motion, as well as the outer sensations and proprioception are all experienced as inseparable parts of all sensorimotor activity.

Thus both perception and motor action require sensorimotor activity. Jean Piaget (in his work on infant development published in the 1930s) and Arnold Gehlen (in his work on anthropology from the 1930s and 1940s) were among the first to describe this interaction of sensory and motor activity as forming a continuum (Gehlen 1988, ch. 23). The crucial point, made again in our own day by Degenaar et al. (2015) and by many others, is that without sensorimotor activity there is no conscious relationship to the world. Perception and motor activity (including speech) are the two fundamental functions of behaviour, and all human behaviour requires the integration of the two.

---

44 Note that we cannot save Hutter's definition by imputing to him the view that the only environments that matter to him and his collaborators are the environments inside computers. For they refer continuously to 'real-world environments'. To build computer applications that can function in such environments is the very point of AGI. The problem is that many in the AGI community do not see a big difference between 'world' and 'model of the world inside the computer'.

Where the steps of the utility function described by the Hutter definition of intelligence constitute a linear sequence of discrete actions characteristic of the behaviour of machines, human motor acts require fast and fine-tuned interaction of perception and motor activity that involves at every stage a dense synergism of multiple body systems at multiple levels of granularity, the details of which remain largely unknown and to a large extent not understood. This interaction could potentially be described at one level as a linear sequence of efferent, afferent, and intra-CNS neuronal signalling events; but the coupling of such a sequence to any sort of reward à la Hutter is at best very indirect, so that, as we will see in the next section, conceiving the sequence in reward terms would not even come close to providing a model of its underlying mechanism.

3.3.2.3 Reward, environment, and goal

Third, Hutter's definition is drastically narrower than that of Scheler, because it restricts the meaning of intelligence to those cases that involve the summation of a series of rewards obtained in discrete steps. This, however, does not do justice even to how animals use their primal intelligence.

Unlike vertebrates, a machine realising the putative 'universal intelligence' defined by Legg and Hutter is in one sense not intelligent at all, because it relies on some human AI engineer who defines the reward for the system, as was done for example in engineering the AI that was able to defeat humans in the game of Go.[45] In this respect a system satisfying the Hutter definition will always be environment-specific—it will work only in those contexts where a human has already been at work in calibrating appropriate rewards—and thus not 'general' or 'universal' at all.

This is because the mathematical definition provided by Hutter requires that the environment **U** must be matched quite narrowly to the reward r_i—it is not possible to define an r that works for all environments.[46] A further problem then arises in that the assumption is made that all rewards r must be of the same fixed type for every step under a given environment μ.

It has recently been shown that the nematode *C. elegans*, a primitive organism, indeed maximises utility in a way that can be modelled using a utility function

---

45 See section 10.3 for our discussion of DeepMind's strategy.
46 Many situations require complex reward sequences where the reward sequence is mathematically speaking itself the trace of a complex system process, as described in detail in section 8.6.7.4. If the reward type could change at each step, the representation of its proper handling would require a notation of the form rig_i, where the functional g might yield a different reward type for each step i. But this, depending on the nature of the functional g, might make the utility function uncomputable. This is the reason why the Hutter definition restricts itself to the use of a fixed reward type r_i, which depends solely on the tuple $\langle \mu, \pi \rangle$ formed by environment and agent, but can take different values at each step i.

from microeconomics[47] which describes the preference involved in choosing between two goods (Katzen et al. 2021):

$$U(q_H, q_M) = \left(\beta q_H^\rho + (1-\beta)q_M^\rho\right)^{\frac{1}{\rho}},$$

where U is utility, q_H and q_M are quantities of unequal food sources, β is the choice partition between the sources, and ρ the diminishing marginal utility parameter (the additional utility of a good declines with each unit already consumed). This result shows that the worm is able to make choices between two non-equal food sources q_H, q_M in a way that is also used to model demand in microeconomics. While the authors seem to imply that utility maximisation in making the choice between two goods is conserved in evolution from nematodes to humans, this does not mean that humans and animals have reward types that can be modelled deterministically (which is what the Hutter AGI definition implies).

Rather, they work with multiple different reward types (and combinations thereof) even in the same environment. Moreover, their actions often involve many different reward types from one moment to the next, since the way the subject interacts with the environment may change with each act of the subject, even if it is just an act of perception, since the latter will have an effect on the subject. Hutter's $\mu \in \mathbf{U}$ is a mere binary string. This means that it is a static environment of a type which does not exist for intelligent organisms. The latter, rather, face the world always in terms of *situations* in which certain entities—typically other organisms, but also tools, food, doors—form the 'figures' against an indeterminate 'ground' running on behind them (Smith 1999; Kogo et al. 2014). The environment of the organism is organised around a continuous sequence of such situations, characterised by determinate boundaries on the part of their constituent figures, which are related to each other and to the ground running on behind them in the sorts of complex ways we will describe in 5.3.1.

Hutter's concept cannot capture any of this.

Moreover, when we examine chains of animal behaviour at the fine-grained level, we find that the reward not only varies wildly from step to step but is even for long periods completely absent. Even if—as in most behaviouristic experiments—the reward is some dopamine-triggering event (food or drug intake), the behavioural chain that the animal must perform to achieve its goal and to obtain the reward is extended in time, and many steps must be taken which yield no reward at all, or even the opposite of a reward.[48]

---

47 The constant elasticity of substitution utility function (McFadden 1963).
48 Consider for example the cocaine self-administration experiment with self-inflicted damage, in which rats, to obtain doses of cocaine, have to step onto a heated plate causing burn wounds to their feet (Roberts et al. 2007).

This means that higher animals have a certain attention interval in which they can act to realise a goal in the expectation of a reward but with no reward actually being achieved.[49] However, the Hutter utility model assumes that each step of the algorithm μ has a reward r_i, where i is the index indicating the step of the algorithm and each step corresponds to a behavioural step on the part of the agent. Moreover, it assumes that all r_i are of the same fixed type. Of course, since the valuation function sums over all the steps, the system could in principle deal with zero-value, and indeed with negative, rewards. But in complicated real-world settings it is very often impossible to define the reward value of such intermediate steps, and an adequate mathematical specification of the reward becomes harder with each increase in complexity of the setting and length of the behavioural chain.

There are, certainly, situations in which a reward function yielding discrete numbers of reward points is readily available for every step—for example, again, in a game of Go. But given the non-linearity and the many non-rewarded steps in vertebrate behaviour (see footnote 26), it is hard to see how this idea could ever be applied to intelligence of the sort that is manifested in complex behavioural patterns such as we find in organic nature or in human societies. Indeed, there are no examples of end-to-end deep neural networks (dNNs) exhibiting complex behaviour in novel environments that can match any type of complex behaviour we find even on the part of vertebrates, let alone of human beings.[50]

That said, a system that is externally configured with a reward r to find the shortest possible algorithm that can be used to solve all problems in a given space with the highest total utility would indeed be very useful. But only for certain problems. It would work, for example, in solving the problem of cleaning radioactive waste in a simple static environment, or of driving an autonomous vehicle on a highway without lane changes, or of identifying targets in a military defense system (where a reward-based approach of this type is already implemented). But it has nothing to do with human, or indeed primal, intelligence and, as we shall see, it will fail in situations involving complex systems because *the space of solutions to the Hutter equation is inadequate to the modelling of such systems.*

A machine that could achieve just primal intelligence would need to be able to master behavioural accomplishments as complex as those achieved by higher animals such as parrots. There is, however, not the slightest connection between the stepwise utility function of the Hutter definition (which is still the intelligence definition used in mainstream AGI research) and the intelligence achieved

---

49 For humans this interval may span great lengths of time—as for example in the planning and realisation of cathedrals in the middle ages or of the International Space Station in our own day.
50 Of course, a dNN is just one example of an output of an optimisation procedure, but we will see in later chapters that optimisation procedures in general are not able to cope with situations created by the interactions of complex systems.

by higher animals. And the remoteness from objectifying intelligence of the sort realised by humans—of what is described as 'universal intelligence'—is staggering to a degree we find difficult to fathom.

Perhaps another influential example along the same lines can bring us further. This is the definition of intelligence presupposed—though not formulated explicitly—by Jürgen Schmidhuber, one of the most creative and effective contemporary AI scientists and the inventor of LSTM neural networks (see p. 171). Schmidhuber proposes Gödel machines as his weapon to 'attack this "Grand Problem of Artificial Intelligence"' (Schmidhuber 2007), namely the problem of achieving AGI. The sort of Gödel machine he has in mind is a type of automatic problem solver that can

> rewrite any part of its own code as soon as it has found a proof that the rewrite is useful, where the problem-dependent utility function and the hardware and the entire initial code are described by axioms encoded in an initial proof searcher which is also part of the initial code.
>
> (op. cit., p. 210)

Here Schmidhuber implicitly defines intelligence as the ability to rewrite code according to a problem-dependent utility function. This definition yields what we can call the Schmidhuber set of AI algorithms. Unfortunately, this does not bring us any further forward, since it is isomorphic to the Hutter set referred to already. This is because it, too, relies on the specification of a utility function with a problem-specific reward defined by its human engineers, who are needed, again, to define the reward system in each separate case.[51]

The definition given by Yudkowsky (2008b) modifies the Hutter definition of 'intelligence' (which, to avoid the term 'intelligence', he calls 'optimisation power') by introducing a norming denominator which describes the (computational) resources used to achieve the intelligence $Y(\pi)$ (see equation (3.2)). This yields the ratio

$$\frac{\text{Hutter intelligence}}{\text{resources used}},$$

which is comparable to the concept of power in physics (defined as energy per unit time). Unfortunately, however, this norming denominator does not change the nature of the Hutter definition.

Muehlhauser et al. (2012b, p. 27) provide another, purportedly alternative definition of machine intelligence. According to these authors, 'Intelligence

---

51 It is becoming obvious to the AI community that the lack of adequate strategies for specifying and computing rewards is a major problem for machine learning. The proposed approaches to solving this problem all fail to take account of the fact that, when dealing with agent-environment interactions, the reward sequence itself is the emanation of a complex system (Leike et al. 2018)—an issue we return to in 12.2.5.3.

measures an agent's capacity for efficient cross-domain optimisation of the world according to the agent's preferences'. On close inspection, however, this is isomorphic to Yudkowski's definition, because 'cross-domain optimisation' means again 'ability to achieve goals in a wide range of environments', and 'capacity' is just the norming factor once again. So all the major proponents of machine intelligence reviewed here use an isomorphic definition, of which we have seen that it cannot provide a convincing characterisation of anything that might properly be called *intelligence*, whether on the part of a machine or of any other sort of entity.

An environment-based utility model More recently, Hibbard (2012) has proposed a new utility-based model of intelligence in order to overcome some of the problems of Hutter-style approaches, all of which make utility depend on the agent's *observations*. For Hibbard, in contrast, utility functions are 'defined in terms of a model of the environment that the agent must learn via its interactions with that environment' (op. cit, p. 2). His motivation here is the observation that artificial agents may be subject to what he calls 'self-delusions'—the assignment of rewards based on false interpretations of the environment—which create only a pseudo-utility. However, while Hibbard's approach may avoid the self-delusion problem (though Hibbard does not give a general proof that this is so), it still suffers from the problems involved in creating adequate environment models which we addressed (see p. 52). And still more importantly, it faces a new set of difficulties, which arise where the reward path is itself a complex system emanation. For this, though, the reader will have to wait until chapter 8 (section 8.6.7.4).

Taken together, all the AI definitions we have looked at try to claim that there can be machine intelligence, but only by using thereby an *Ersatz*-definition of what the word *intelligence* means.[52] As we have seen, however, this strategy will never lead us to the conclusion that there is machine *intelligence* in any commonly accepted meaning of this term. It is comparable, rather, to defining flying as 'moving in the air', and then jumping up and down and shouting: 'See, I am flying'.

3.3.3 Other potential alternative AI definitions

Let us suppose that many more AI definitions and implementations will be developed in the future. What will be their common characteristic? All of them will have to define AI in such a way that the AI agent will be able to interact with an open environment, namely the world that surrounds us. Rodney Brooks (1991) recognised this already 30 years ago, when he described his goal of building robots that can 'move around in dynamic environments, sensing the surroundings

---

52 For more on this argumentation strategy see 9.3.3.3 and the discussion of 'persuasive definition' in (Stevenson 1938).

to a degree sufficient to achieve the necessary maintenance of life and reproduction' (Brooks 1991, 140). Recently, this view of AI has led to the definition of a method to measure the performance of AI agents through systematic comparison of machine performance with primal intelligence (Crosby et al. 2019). If performed properly, such comparisons would reveal that machines fail to reach the intelligence level of higher animals. The problem is that our world is shaped by complex systems, some of them inanimate, such as the weather, the tides, or the movements caused by the earth's seismic system; and some of them animate, in particular all the behaviour of humans and other animals. Each AI agent, no matter how it is defined, will therefore have to cope with a complex-system-generated environment.

3.3.4 Defining useful machine intelligence

How, then, to obtain a definition of AI that is applicable in real user settings? For this we need to think backwards from the end result that we are seeking. Why do we want to create AI? As with any technology, the goal is to have something (some piece of equipment) that will at least increase the degree to which our needs are reliably fulfilled. What are the requirements that a machine or algorithm would have to satisfy in order to count as an AI that would fulfil this purpose?

The forms of intelligence we know and find useful are illustrated, first, in our use of animals to provide companionship, or in tasks such as searching, guarding, defending, guiding, hunting, riding, moving, pulling, or ploughing. And second, we benefit from the intelligence of our fellow humans when we interact with them, for example as friends, employees, colleagues, police officers, teachers, students, pupils, parents, children, customers, accomplices, agents, or principals. An 'alternative' general machine intelligence that cannot at least achieve the level of the primal intelligence achieved by domesticated animals is, when seen in this light, useless for human beings.

Human beings have always sought inventions that will increase their background fulfilment: clothing, fire for cooking and to provide heat, the wheel, and the combustion engine to enable easier transport, the technologies of writing, printing, and computers to store and disseminate thoughts.

Already today we have a huge amount of hidden, specialised AI that contributes to an improved background fulfillment on all of these fronts in ways that benefit large numbers of human beings, for example in automated manufacturing or in supply chain optimisation.

So our first requirement for useful AI is: to advance to a higher level, we would need autonomous agents endowed with an AI with at least primal intelligence. Otherwise, we just have an Analytical Engine. This is the machine built by Charles Babbage which, as Turing points out (Turing 1950), is Turing-complete. But an Analytical Engine, according to Ada Lovelace, has no pretensions to originate anything. 'It can do [only] whatever we know how to order it to perform' (Lovelace et al. 1843). It might be argued that AlphaGo is an exception to this rule, since it is said to have taught Go masters new moves.[53] But what AlphaGo does is to calculate, using calculus, the maximum of a gain function that its human creators have defined. This maximum is better than the maximum discoverable by humans because AlphaGo can take into account more states than humans. But AlphaGo does not fulfil the criteria even of primal intelligence, because it does not adapt to new situations. On the contrary: it went through trillions of very similar situations in order to be able to compute this maximum. Change one Go rule, and it loses immediately. Thus AlphaGo did not 'teach the master new moves'. What really happened is that the (human) master observed the emanation from the implicit gain-maximising model set up by AlphaGo's (human) creators (namely, the moves it played against him), and he used this to adapt his strategy.

But if we are talking of AGI, then we would want a machine with objectifying intelligence. For example, a robot with the ability to engage in conversations with humans in which it would be perceived as a useful interlocutor because it has, for example, the ability to understand an ambiguous order (such as: 'Give me the bottle', where there are multiple bottles standing on the shelf), disambiguate the order by asking clarificatory questions, and execute the order by moving over to the shelf and reaching out with its robot arm. Objectifying intelligence is required for this purpose because, as we will see in our discussion of human language, execution of the order presupposes an objectification of reality analogous to that performed by humans.

Thus *our second requirement for useful AI is:* objectifying intelligence—including self-objectification—which would in any case be required for all purposes in which the artificial agent is required to move freely among and interact with humans. For the agent would need to move and behave in a way that is compatible with the ways humans move and behave in relation to each other in real environments and thus in a way that would make the agent, too, a part of what we can think of as the human world.

3.3.4.1 AI definitions measured against these requirements

We believe that the definitions of intelligence based on utility functions proposed by the AGI community (see 3.3.1) throw no light at all on human intelligence in either of its two aspects of primal and objectifying. Thus they do not yield machines that can fulfill the two just specified requirements.

And neither will they yield machines that will have the capacity to go significantly beyond traditional 'narrow' AI such as the logic-based GOF-AI (good old-fashioned AI) of Newell et al. (1976). For what these definitions do is to identify the intelligence of a machine on the basis of the fact that the machine

---

53 'Humans Mourn Loss After Google Is Unmasked as China's Go Master'. *Wall Street Journal,* January 5, 2017.

62 Properties of the human mind

is endowed with an optimisation framework for obtaining some extremum for a high-dimensional functional for which derivatives can be calculated. This formulation is just an alternative way of stating that, as on all connectivist approaches to AI, they obtain a model which is defined via a loss function, or in other words that they execute a recipe found using optimisation (see 8.6.6). This brings one advantage over AI based on symbolic logic (GOF-AI), namely that the connectionist AI algorithms can be generated automatically, where GOF-AI requires algorithms that are designed explicitly. In this way, the new utility-based AI yields an approach that can scale to apply in areas where we have to deal with very large bodies of data with a certain degree of variance. But it is an approach which works only where we can assemble training samples with a variance which is *representative* of the variance in the target data. And as will become clear, this is possible only along certain very narrow lanes.

We have also seen (in section 3.3.3) that alternative definitions of intelligence are unlikely to yield anything that can fulfill the requirements described earlier. For no matter how we generate an alternative AI, it will have to emulate what we shall call a 'logic system', which is a system such as a simple device engineered in such a way that its behaviour can be predicted using the equations of physics and the rules of logic.

We will therefore proceed in what follows by using our account of human intelligence to throw light in the reverse direction—on what AI research itself has really achieved and will be able to continue to achieve in the future—using primal and human intelligence as our benchmark.

4
THE NATURE OF HUMAN LANGUAGE

The most striking capability which distinguishes human beings from other animals is our ability to speak, and more specifically to conduct conversations. Language is the most important observable expression of our objectifying intelligence. Animals have no language, and they have no non-verbal abstract symbols such as badges or insignia, no ability to manipulate numbers, and no objectifying intelligence.

This and the next chapter lay out the role that language plays for humans and describes language complexity in order to let us appreciate the challenge that lies in the attempt to mathematically model language in a way that would be required to create an AI. These chapters thereby describe the requirements for an AI that would master language.

4.1 Why conversation matters

Conversation is important for our purposes here because the ability to conduct conversations is critical for many of the intended practical applications of AGI, for example in a business enterprise or in government. How would we want to use AGI, if we had it? What type of work could an AGI machine perform that could not be performed either by human beings or by machines possessing one or other of the sorts of narrow AI that we already have at our disposal?

We consider the possible answers to this question under four headings: (a) mobile physical work; (b) intellectual work that does not involve engaging in dialogue; (c) work primarily involving communication; and (d) planning and activities, such as command and control, related to the implementation of plans.

a. Machines (robots) possessing AGI could use their intelligence to interact in a flexible and responsive manner with dynamically changing, highly complex

DOI: 10.4324/9781003310105-5

environments. Even if the work they were doing was entirely physical, for example transporting goods or disposing of waste, they would still have to be able to react to many different kinds of environmental signals, among which human utterances are the most important. The utility of such machines would thus be greatly increased were they able to understand and follow instructions issued by humans, even if they could only respond with stereotypical utterances such as "Yes, ma'am" or "I am sorry, master". The machines would also need to be able to react to human warnings and to understand suggestions from humans concerning better ways to do things. In other words, the ability to correctly interpret complex human utterances would still be required.
b. Machines performing intellectual work of the sort that does not involve spoken dialogue with humans—for example clerical work, such as loan application or insurance claim processing—would of necessity need to understand text, because the material they have to process is primarily provided in this form. Such work does not, in the normal case, require dialogue. But to process such documents with an error rate no worse than that of human beings, machines would need to understand the meanings of the texts they process.
c. Machines performing activities involving communication with human beings, for example IM-chat or telephone banking, would need to be able to conduct such dialogues in a way that, at a minimum, allows the human user to achieve her goals in an effective and efficient manner. And in order to justify a claim that a machine engaged in such activities possessed AGI, we would need to show that the machine has the ability to engage in dialogues with humans in a way that does not require the human to make extra efforts to accommodate the fact that they are dealing with a machine.
d. Machines performing planning and command and control tasks fully autonomously, for example in transportation and logistics would again be required to have the ability to engage in dialogues with humans to guide them in the proper understanding of the plan, to receive their input to the plan, and to guide their implementation, not least in those cases where implementation fails.

We note that in all four sorts of cases the AGI involved would need to demonstrate an ability to use language in communicating with humans in a variety of sometimes highly complex ways and reflecting what we shall discover to be highly complex and continuously changing contextual dependencies.

4.2 Aspects of human language

Following in the footsteps of Aristotle, most philosophers have viewed language as fulfilling an essentially descriptive function and have neglected the complex variety of other forms of language use. Some of the features contributing to this complexity were indeed recognised by philosophers, starting as early as Thomas Reid[1], and then above all in the 1960s by Austin and Searle.[2]

Already in 1913 Reinach anticipated Austin with his discovery of what Reinach called the theory of 'social acts'. As Mulligan (1987) makes clear, both Reinach and Austin shared the same primary objective, namely to

> bring into focus, and fully describe, a phenomenon of which promising is their favourite example. Other social acts dealt with in some detail by Reinach are requesting, questioning, ordering, imparting information, accepting a promise and legal enactment, which—except for the last two—are all at least touched on by Austin. In all these social acts we have 'acts of the mind' which do not have in words and the like their accidental additional expression. Rather, they 'are performed in the very act of speaking'. These cases of doing something by saying something are, and give rise to, changes in the world. They are associated with a variety of different effects.

One example of this effectivity of social acts are the obligations and claims to which promises and orders give rise. Another example are the behaviours brought about by social acts. These can be both linguistic—when a question gives rise to an answer—and non-linguistic, for example as a result of a warning of imminent danger, which gives rise simultaneously to an experience of feeling afraid, to the release of stress hormones such as adrenaline and cortisol, and to aversive action. Social acts provide an interface between what goes on in our minds and the world of collective actions, and it is not an accident that Reinach's discovery of social acts is presented in a monograph on the ontology of law (Reinach 2012).

Another interesting figure in this development is Karl Bühler, teacher *inter alia* of Karl Popper and Konrad Lorenz. Bühler places one of the main features of language, the following of linguistic rules, firmly in the context of other types of human behaviour, both innate and acquired, and most importantly including perception, behaviour, and instinct: 'all concrete speech is in vital union [*im Lebensverbande*] with the rest of a person's meaningful behaviour; it is among actions and is itself an action' (Bühler 1990, p. 51). Natural perception and natural language are, for Bühler as for Scheler, the two central components of the one and only human form of life, namely the natural attitude of common sense.

---

1 Schuhmann et al. (1990) provide a list illustrating the variety of uses of language discussed by Reid, including: questioning (asking for information or advice), providing testimony, commanding, promising, accepting or refusing (a bribe, testimony, an apology), contracting, threatening, supplicating, bargaining, declaring, and not least plighting (one's faith, one's veracity, one's fidelity).
2 See (Austin 1962; Searle 1969).

More familiar, and more influential, are the post-war contributions of philosophers in Anglo-Saxon countries, beginning above all with Wittgenstein, whose *Philosophical Investigations* (Wittgenstein 2003) was especially influential in advancing the new understanding of how (especially spoken) language works, an understanding further refined by the contributions of philosophers such as Anscombe and Grice. The results of the work of these and other philosophers have since been consolidated in a huge body of research by linguists working in areas such as discourse linguistics, and we rely on this work in what follows.

4.2.1 Language and evolution

The brain's system for production and interpretation of language is highly complex. It has evolved in humanoids over some 4 million years, starting with the use of gestures, for example the male beating of the chest, by apes (Hobaiter et al. 2014).[3] The ability of humans to generate and interpret language is part of an essential survival strategy for *Homo sapiens*, and the huge landscape of variance in natural language usage (which we will describe in chapter 5) has as its basis a variance in the languages spoken by the members of different language groups (see section 4.2.5). The latter is in turn a cumulative effect of gene flow, non-random mating, and natural selection processes operating in each generation. As human populations spread across vast areas of the planet, fissions occurred which can be traced in the evolutionary trees of both genes and languages. These phylogenetic and phylocultural trees are remarkably highly correlated, though the correlation is decreased for example through the phenomenon of language replacement occurring when one group is conquered by another (Cavalli-Sforza 2000).

Gehlen, again, was one of the first to offer a view of language as a capability that arose in the evolution of our species as a vehicle for a certain sort of controlled interaction with our environment that served as a replacement for the instinctive behaviours of our non-human ancestors. Because the latter react on the basis of their instincts and their primal intelligence, they react only to what is concretely given in their environment of the moment. They are thus able to survive only in environments which lie within the narrow bands determined by their repertoire of innate behaviours, environments to which their behavioural patterns are tuned. Nothing is neutral in this sort of environment. Everything that is experienced by the animal has a typically immediate salience for survival and, potentially, reproduction, though in some cases the scope of this salience may extend over weeks, such as in the breading of eggs by birds, and in what may be very complex ways (for example in penguins). But then it is always

---

3 In his *Inquiry into the Human Mind* (1764), Reid argued that spoken language must itself have arisen against the background of a 'natural language' consisting of 'modulations of the voice, gestures, and [for example facial] features'. On this idea, see Nyíri (2014).

still instincts that are being expressed, whether in the play of pups or in animals performing elaborate courtship displays (Fuxjager et al. 2015).

Humans, in contrast, act in non-instinctive ways, and they are able to confront the things they see in a variety of ways. We thereby do not simply *see* the objects in our environment; we also *touch* what we see, *handle* what is graspable, and so forth. We address the objects that we encounter, often by using words, as we become aware of our possible ways of making use of their properties as we 'integrate them into our activities' using 'the specific structure of human senses and movements' (Gehlen 1988, p. 162). Our language capability plays an essential role in this process of objectification. Language allows us to engage with the objects (including other persons) in our environments in a way which allows us to draw them from one sphere into another, to manipulate them in our minds and in our conversations with others, considering them under different headings and in different scenarios.

Language is not only what enables us to extend the reach of our experience in these and many other ways. It provides us also with the means to cope with the resultant massive variability in our experiences. One simple example is the way language allows us to condense what is common in a variety of actions and experiences into simple rituals such as are involved in greeting or promising or apologising or warning. The use of common nouns, too, provides us with a simple way to capture complex phenomena that appear repeatedly—for example instances of a specific type of noise, or tree, or particle accelerator—thereby also allowing a highly functional linguistic division of labour (see 5.4.2). Language condenses the complexity of real-world phenomena down to an abstract linguistic plane, encompassing just the level of detail that is needed for the specific goals in hand.

And much of this takes place unconsciously. As Whitehead remarks:

> It is a profoundly erroneous truism, repeated by all copy-books and by eminent people when they are making speeches, that we should cultivate the habit of thinking what we are doing. The precise opposite is the case. Civilisation advances by extending the number of important operations which we can perform without thinking about them.
>
> (Whitehead 1911, chapter 5)

This is a statement not only about the power of language, but more generally about the power of the human mind (or, better, of the human mind-body continuum) to take actions that at first require careful thought and careful bodily movement but then through practice become automatic (Dreyfus et al. 2000).

4.2.2 Language and intentions

Where animal behaviour is mainly instinctive, human behaviour is mainly steered by intentions, including both short-term intentions of the moment and long-term intentions flowing from past decisions and spanning both the emotional and the intellectual dimensions of the human mind. Our use of language, too, is the expression of our intentions in interacting both with the physical world around us and with other human beings. Both our production and our interpretation of language are determined by these intentions, which are the dispositions of our mind to achieve certain goals.

At the simplest level, we realise our everyday intentions—such as obtaining food, achieving agreement with a colleague, giving orders, and so forth—via spoken language, which is much more effective than the simple cries of vertebrate foragers because it allows us to encode more complex meanings, for example allowing conditionality of instructions (do this if that occurs). Language enhances the ways in which simple intentions of single individuals are realised by allowing coordination of the intentions of multiple individuals—it allows us to achieve what Searle (1990) calls 'collective intentionality', which is the capability of minds to be jointly directed towards objects, events, goals, whether this be hunting an animal or building the pyramids of Gizeh.

One of the earliest to draw attention to the role of intentions in our use of language was Karl Bühler, who focused especially on the role of mutual steering or guidance (*Steuerung*) in conversation. In every case, when I engage in conversation with other persons, there is a sense in which I want something from those other persons, and thus a sense in which I am engaged in steering them to give me what I want—even if this is only that they should understand what I have to say or that they should realise that I have understood what they have to say.

For Bühler, all understanding is based on steering of this sort, and to illustrate how this works he discusses three simple scenarios. The first is one in which a dialogue partner (A) understands what dialogue partner (B) is saying (or intending) because A perceives the steering effects B begets. The second is one in which party A understands how her dialogue partner B is understanding what she is saying because A perceives the steering effects that she is having on B. The third, and most complex scenario, is one in which these simple modes of gaining understanding break down. This occurs when what Bühler calls 'an ominous third party' enters into the scene. Now, all three persons must attempt to gauge not only what steering effects already obtain but also how they are being changed under this new scenario. And as Bühler points out (in a remark of some considerable significance for what follows in this book):

> The psychological theoretician will find this three-person triangle just as interesting—and affording just as many difficulties—as the three-body problem causes for the physicist.
>
> (Bühler 1927, pp. 94f.).

4.2.3 Speech as sensorimotor activity

Considered at the most basic level, speech is a sensorimotor activity closely related to the hand movements and associated sensory perceptions involved when we grasp an object.[4] When we perform motor activities, we simultaneously perform an action and obtain propriosensory feedback from the performance itself. In the case of the hand movement for grasping, proprioception is augmented by a second sort of feedback deriving from the object as we touch it, feedback which confirms that we have achieved our grasping intentions. These two sorts of feedback—on the one hand from our body itself, and on the other hand from our environment via our sensory system—allow us to continuously adjust our intentions. These same two sorts of feedback occur also in the case of spoken language as used in dialogue. First, we hear our own words as we are speaking. But this first type of feedback is then augmented by the feedback we receive from our interlocutor—for example in the form of facial expressions, gestures, as well as further speech. We continuously use this feedback to adjust not just what we say and the way we speak but also the intentions we are seeking to realise by engaging in dialogue with our interlocutor (Gehlen 1988, chapter 33). This makes our use of spoken language a more powerful type of sensorimotor activity than all the others.

4.2.4 Language functions

Humans are able to deal freely with the full range of their sensory inputs and to explore (and indeed to create) new environments, including new *types* of environments (consider: casinos, spas, zoos, boxing rings, chatrooms). In this sense, and in distinction to other animals, we live in what we can think of as an open world (Scheler 2008). This is, on the one hand, a defect. For it means that humans do not have at their disposal the sorts of instinctive routines that would make them well adapted to their natural environments. But on the other hand, it is a benefit, for it means that humans are adaptable to ever new environments through use not only of their mental capacities but also of tools (including language). This adaptability is seemingly without limits. Hence *general intelligence*.

At any given moment, humans are choosing from an immensely broad and ever-changing repertoire of environmental inputs—both material and symbolic—that would in principle be available to them for objectification. Already from early infancy we apply objectification strategies which enable us to avoid being overwhelmed by sensory stimuli. These are based on our capability to apprehend our environment not as some meaningless mosaic of sensations, but rather as a world of enduring objects (including persons) located in different places and divided into different kinds (for example animate and inanimate), linked by

---

4 These similarities were documented comprehensively from a philosophical point of view already by Gehlen (1988, chapters 13, 19). For a contemporary treatment, see Gómez-Vilda et al. (2013).

causal relations, and manifesting characteristic functions and rule-governed behaviours.

All of these belong to what Spelke refers to as the infant's *core knowledge* (Spelke et al. 1996; Spelke 2000; Spelke et al. 2007). As Keil noted, when such fundamental concepts are learned, 'people do not simply note feature frequencies and feature correlations; they have strong intuitions about which frequencies and correlations are reasonable ones to link together in larger structures and which are not' (Keil 1994). Without such intuitions, or more precisely: without some pre-given repertoire of the sorts of entities they will encounter in the world, people could not learn the corresponding concepts, since they would have no way to select from the potentially infinite number of feature correlations by which they are confronted in their day-to-day lives (Spelke 1990).[5]

In realising our capability to use language, we build upon this core knowledge as we acquire the general terms used in describing both inner and outer reality. Our acquisition of such general terms has its foundation in our physical experience. We learn to use 'bitter' and 'sweet' by registering (unconsciously) that contexts in which we experience how tastes of corresponding sorts go hand in hand with contexts in which people use these words.

From the very beginning, infants apprehend a subset of the behaviours of their fellow human beings—including gestures and expressions of what they will later learn to call 'pleasure' and 'pain'—as being of special significance. With increasing sophistication, they will begin to use language in ways which enhance their already inborn tendencies to recognise classificatory hierarchies and causal and functional and behavioural patterns in the world. For example, they learn to identify a certain sort of wooden stick as a pencil, and thus as a tool for writing. Simultaneously they learn to use general expressions such as 'pencil' or 'purple' or 'pain' or 'pig-headed' to describe both the things in the world to which our experiences are directed and the sensations and emotions (and associated moral appraisals) with which they are associated. They also learn to exploit the ways in which language can be used to distance ourselves from our immediate experience of what is particular in external reality and from our spontaneous emotional reactions (Gehlen 1988, chapter 28) (Kross et al. 2011).

Language extends our ability to identify, to track, and to categorise, by providing us with a publicly shareable means to represent objects, both present and absent, and a vehicle for communication which serves at the same time to enable the transmission of knowledge, our mutual collaboration, as a locus and medium for control and sanction, and as a vehicle for transforming what is transient into what is permanent and evaluable (Eisenstein 1980).

---

5 See also (Keil 1989; Gopnik et al. 1997; Horton 1982; Gopnik et al. 1997). For philosophical background on these ideas, which are related not only to what is called 'folk psychology' but also to the ontology of common sense more generally, see (Forguson et al. 1988; Forguson 1989; Smith 1995).

Language-enhanced object tracking as applied to the human beings with whom we engage may extend across many years and involve multiple different types of roles these human beings play, such as: baby, child, friend, mother, coach, boss, ... Language-enhanced tracking in the small occurs continuously in every dialogue, as we use pronouns to refer to ourselves and to address our interlocutors. We refer to what they are doing or did at some point in the past, or plan to do in the future; we refer to others not present, again assigning to them multiple different roles, as persons who deserve respect or disdain, or as persons who might approve or not approve of something we are doing or planning to do in the future (Carey et al. 2001).

Science We are interested here primarily in spoken language. However both the Anscombe-Searle example of the list (Smith 2003), and Schopenhauer's reference to the 'storing up of experience' (Schopenhauer 1986) point to the ways in which written (and printed) language expands the reach of our objectifying intelligence along myriad dimensions, not the least of which was through that product of cumulative cultural evolution we call science.

The domain of science is one of a series of new sorts of man-made cultural-symbolic environments—alongside the law, politics, prices, markets, mathematics, or computer games—which exist only through the exercise of our powers of symbolic creation. Analogous powers are exercised also by historians, who are able to move in the world formed by our past environments, where perceptual access to events is replaced with access via language (Smith 2021).

Planning Language allows individuals not only to consciously plan their own actions but also to engage with others, both known and unknown, in the achievement of complex goals. It allows delegation of responsibility and authority, so that ever more complex plans can be realised through modularisation of control at successive levels. Written and printed documents enable new forms of human coordination. Wills and testaments allow individuals to extend the reach of their intentions in such a way that they are able to control activities which will occur only in a time when they no longer exist. The institution of contracts allows ordinary humans to make agreements between each other that are legally enforceable. Stocks and bonds allow humans to pool their resources (for example through pension funds) in order to enjoy the returns from undertakings which are orders of magnitude more ambitious than what they could achieve on their own. Insurance policies allow individuals to benefit from the law of large numbers to purchase safeguards against major losses that would, again, be out of reach for individuals working on their own. In each case it is processes involving documents that make these achievements possible.[6]

---

6 (De Soto 2000; Smith 2008, 2013). Other sorts of linguistic artefacts allow more routine sorts of coordination of human intentions to take place automatically. Theatre or plane tickets, for

The standard documents and document templates created by legal and commercial systems expand the reach of these effects by encapsulating lessons learned from document-driven processes of different types (for instance in creating wills, contracts, licenses, warranties), and thereby allowing individuals and groups to engage with each other in successively more ambitious ways. In complex plan-driven human activities such as building a house, written documents and spoken dialogues involving customers, developers, and those engaged in building the house are combined to foster not only the correct interpretation of the various instructions they have to follow but also the acceptable deviations from these instructions. Building the house will involve not only physical labour but also the labour of architecting and planning, financial labour (for instance, of securing a loan), administrative labour (of acquiring necessary licenses and approvals), and legal labour (of securing a title, drawing up contracts).

4.2.5 Inexhaustible variance in language use

In these and other ways language serves to magnify, often in unpredictable ways, the powers of human beings to realise their intentions in collaborative ventures of increasing size and complexity. What this means, however, is that the resultant interplay of human beings, and thus of the intentions of human beings, in so many different kinds of contexts, implies *a potentially infinite variance and complexity in the ways language is used*.

The factors magnifying linguistic variance are magnified still further in virtue of the fact that language evolves with time. This phenomenon is typically ignored by philosophers of language, who tend to focus on simple, everyday exchanges between members of a single and homogeneous linguistic community, and to see in such exchanges support for a view of language as a relatively stable system of rules analogous, say, to the rules of chess.

It is in particular often tacitly assumed that, when two speakers engage in dialogue, they are each following (in close approximation) the *same set of rules*.

To see why this is very often not the case, and to do justice thereby to the pervasive phenomenon of *language change*, we shall adopt a view of each language—focusing now exclusively on spoken language—as the totality of the capabilities of each one of its speakers, where a capability is, again, a disposition (tendency, potential, competence) of its bearer (here, a person)—that reflects a combination of innate and acquired aspects of a person's neurophysiology. We focus, in other words, on *competence*, and only secondarily on *performance*, and more specifically we focus on the instance-level capabilities of individual speakers of the language, as contrasted with the type-level (idealised) competence postulated by Chomsky and his followers.

example, are not just a way of allowing rights to be exercised, but also a way of coordinating the plans of many people by ensuring that seats are still available when they arrive (Smith et al. 2020).

From this perspective, the linguistic capabilities which define any given language have a very wide scope. They range from the early infant to the highly literate adult, and they are not restricted to the capabilities of native speakers only. This means also that the boundaries of the aggregate of capabilities which we call 'English' will be vague along a number of dimensions. What this means is that for many examples of language production—from the langwedge and the thinkamalinks of *Finnegans Wake* to the broken English and broken pidgin English described by Görlach (1996)—there will be no answer to the question 'is this English?'[7]

Among the capabilities which form a given language, some will be primitive; they will be of the sort associated with beginning speakers, or with those learning a new language. Some will be both grammatically and lexically highly developed. Some will be realised in ways that deviate from normal speech, for example on the part of those with speech or hearing disorders, or of those with specific accents.

4.2.6 Languages and dialects

Our view of a language as a totality of capabilities can very easily be extended to the understanding of the relation between a language and its dialects. The latter are, simply, parts (sub-totalities) of the former. Speakers of a Manchester dialect are *ipso facto* speakers of English and are realising their capabilities for speaking English *by* speaking a Manchester dialect.

The geographical boundaries between dialects are of course often vague. Dialects change and spread continuously, driven, for example, by the desire of potential speakers to gain acceptance in a new group. Dialect distinctions trace not merely geography, but also age cohorts, class distinctions, and behaviour, as discussed at greater length in the next chapter.

The relevance of these phenomena—which imply that not only dialects but also the languages of which they form a part *are changing all the time* – will also become clear in the next chapter, where we deal with how they amplify the massive amount of variance in language use associated with the phenomenon of conversation. In chapter 10, we will see how this complexity prevents the realisation in the machine of language capabilities equivalent to those of humans.

---

[7] Languages and all similar cultural phenomena have vague boundaries in the sense outlined for example in Smith et al. (2000).

5
THE VARIANCE AND COMPLEXITY OF HUMAN LANGUAGE

Humans produce meaningful language and assign meaning to the language produced by others in a dynamic process. In this chapter we summarise the current view of language production and interpretation on the part of philosophers of language and of linguists. The result will then be used as basis for understanding our argument in later chapters to the effect that it is impossible to model mathematically either of these capabilities of the human mind in a way that is adequate in the sense that it is able to generate the sorts of predictions (see section 7.1) needed to support machine emulation of human language use.

5.1 Conversations: an overview

We engage in *conversations* in order to interact with other people to achieve certain goals (berating, guiding, learning, persuading, socialising, coaching, and many more). As our interlocutor responds, we take what we hear and view it, typically spontaneously and unconsciously, in light of our current intentions and also in light of what we have experienced in previous encounters. We thereby use language to condense environmental inputs and background presuppositions down to just what is needed to enable understanding.

Conversations are dynamic processes. Utterances and interpretations take place in time and (more or less) in sequence. Both rest on short- and long-term intentions and on the making of conscious and unconscious choices on the part of those involved in the conversation. These intentions and choices are in every case *implicit* in the sense that they are accessible to other parties—including any external human or machine observers—at best indirectly, for example via facial expressions or via the utterances to which they give rise.

DOI: 10.4324/9781003310105-6

```
Anne:       Why're you amazed
            (2.0)
Dick:       She was [a    wastrel] from w–]                        [Su:re
Deb:               [you ssssqu]a: : : n]dered money like th[at– [
Anne:                                                          [ I [didn't=
            =squander money=it shows you when I didn't =
            = ha[ve it I didn't sp]end it  ]
Dick:          [   sh : : : ]e was a] wastrel from [ way ba]ck.
Anne:                                              [I: : :–] spent
            it because I had the money an I eh::: =
Dick:       =Dontchu believe it. She didn't buy no [six    pairs  of  (shoes)]
Anne:                                              [ WHY DONTCHU SHU]SH
            UP [en STOP SAYING [THAT, DI:::CK,
Dick:          [heh            [°hh!
Dick:       Cuz I know the kinda home you came from.=your mother wouldn't
            let you spend [(six)
Anne:                     [Is that so::. My mother had nothing t'do with it.
```

FIGURE 5.1 Controversial conversation between three adult interlocutors. Overlapping utterance fragments are shown using brackets, upper case letters indicate shouting (from Schegloff (2000)).

Our intentions interact with the intentions of our interlocutors as the conversation proceeds through successive cycles of turn-taking,[1] a phenomenon which seems to be found in all human cultures (Schegloff 2017; Stivers et al. 2009).

Yet while, in a prototypical conversation, the interlocutors take turns, clean and regular turn taking is rather exception than rule (Schegloff 2000). In actually occurring spoken conversations there are frequent deviations from this ideal, as shown in Figure 5.1.

The utterer may pause or hesitate or stutter, create false starts, make mistakes, interrupt herself or try to add retrospective corrections to what she has said earlier, or suddenly change the subject of the conversation entirely. The interpreter may seize the speaker role by forcing a role switch before the utterer has finished her statement. If the utterer does not yield to the interruption, this leads to utterances occurring simultaneously, so that the flow of meaning transmission breaks. Sometimes, the interpreter anticipates the next statement of the utterer and takes a turn before the latter has finished. All these deviations increase the complexity of the role context and add to the pressures on the conversation participants both in forming and in interpreting conversation utterances. They often go hand in hand with emotional layers to the conversation flow, which support specific sorts of interpretation of conversation utterances, for example where one conversation partner seeks to influence the other by (as we say) playing on his emotions.

---

1 Turn-taking is guided by rules and also by what Sacks et al. (1974) call turn-constructional units, an important subtype of which are 'possible completion points', which are signals in the conversation that indicate the opportunity for a role switch.

But no matter how conversations evolve—whether smoothly, with proper role-switches, or awkwardly, with interruptions—interpreters and utterers mutually contextualise and influence each other's interpretations and utterance formations; for the conversation is in every case the interaction of two or more systems.

Moreover, for all participants of a conversation, each cycle is motivated by their respective intentions—the goals they each want to achieve by means of their utterances (Grice 1957; Austin 1962; Searle 1983). If a conversation arises spontaneously, for example when a stranger initiates a dialogue with someone on a railway platform, only the initiator may have a relevant intention; but the interpreter will very quickly form intentions of her own as soon as she is addressed, including the intention to refuse engagement in a dialogue.

When it is Mary's turn to speak in a dialogue with Jack, she tries to fulfil her intentions by conveying content meaningful to Jack in a way that Jack will find persuasive. To give some initial idea of the complexity that can arise in such cases: Mary may find that the most effective way to fulfil her intentions in communicating with Jack is to lead him to believe that she is not interested at all in fulfilling any of her intentions by communicating with Jack. As Mary tries to influence Jack, so she in turn will be influenced by the ways in which Jack responds, or fails to respond. In this way, a conversation will typically bring about changes in the intentions of its participants. A speaker may foresee the reactions of her interlocutor to her utterances and consciously or unconsciously plan out the conversation flow in advance. Creating such a plan is sometimes even the explicit intent of the conversation, as when people sit down together to reach higher-level decisions about how to synchronise their lower-level intentions.[2]

Realisations of our linguistic dispositions are triggered in conversation in various ways, including by the utterances of our conversation partners. Sometimes, such realisations may involve conscious choices, for instance the choice of whether to adopt a retaliatory, conciliatory, or even pejorative tone[3] in response to a threatening utterance, or the choice of which answer to give to a difficult (perhaps a trick) question. Selection often takes place spontaneously and unconsciously. It occurs, moreover, on a number of different levels, affecting both verbal and non-verbal aspects of communication, and we document in what follows the huge variance involved in the different sorts and features of utterance structures that can be produced in the course of a conversation.

We shall see that matters are made still more complicated by the fact that a decisive role in the formation of both utterances and interpretations is played by the *contexts* in which communicative acts take place (Fetzer 2017). We show that there is a vast range of multiple types and levels of such contexts.

---

2 Of course, other scenarios of intention-synchronisation are possible, for example in an altruistic interaction.
3 Pejorative tone can strongly influence the interpretation of an utterance (Lepore et al. 2018).

And, to make matters worse, the range of possible choices is not static or stable (Verschueren 1999, p. 59).

5.2 Levels of language production and interpretation

To document this complexity, we describe in detail the different levels on which the context and structure of a conversation and the form of its dynamic interaction processes are determined. First, we distinguish five levels of *language production and interpretation*, namely:

1. context,
2. language economics (deixis and implicit meaning),
3. conversation structure (words, sentences, sound structure, gestures ...),[4]
4. force/modality,
5. conversation dynamics.

When humans engage in conversation, all of these levels interact. Their separate treatment here is necessary merely in order to enable systematic description; in reality they can never be properly spliced apart.

Each of these levels listed has been discussed not only by classical analytical philosophy in the 1930s to 1960s and by the various linguists we cite in the following sections, but also in the more recent work in formal semantics and in the philosophy of language, for example by Williamson (2005), Stalnaker (2012), Rothschild et al. (2017), and Millikan (2018). We do not discuss the latter here, however, since our intent is not to create a survey of contemporary philosophy of language but to provide an overview of the language capabilities of humans in order to support our argument in chapter 10 that they cannot be emulated using AI.

5.3 Conversation contexts

The *conversation context* is a 'setting', where this term is to be understood in a broad sense to embrace, for instance: one's place at the dinner table, one's place in society, a geographical place, the time of day at which a conversation occurs, and many more (Barker 1968; Schoggen 1989). In each case the context is determined by an interplay between the wider environment and the mental attitudes and capabilities and current intentions of the parties involved.

There is, as we shall see, a veritable ocean of conversation contexts, and human competence in using language consists not least in the ability to navigate

---

4 We follow (Verschueren 1999), from whom our list of levels is derived, in using the term 'structure' to designate what might otherwise be referred to as 'content' or 'material'. Utterance structure can be both verbal and non-verbal (for example when it involves use of gestures).

this ocean from one wave of conversation inputs to the next. The Turing test is, from this point of view, almost infinitely removed from what would qualify as a test of this ability, since it abstracts away from features of context.

5.3.1 The conversation horizon

Conversation contexts are marked not by sharp boundaries but by what is called a 'horizon' of possibilities. The horizon of a spatial context, for example, might include the possibility of your leaving through the back door; the horizon of a temporal context that one's husband may return at any moment. For any given conversation at any given stage multiple horizons may be at work—our dialogue, for example, might suddenly be affected by my awareness of the possibility that you are lying or intending to report our conversation to your superiors.

For each interlocutor, the conversation context is in some ways analogous to the visual field of an individual subject (Werner 2020; Smith 1999). There, too, there is no sharp boundary separating what is within from what is without the visual field. Rather, there is a fading off that is difficult to specify and which changes from moment to moment as we move our eyes and head so that now those, now these things fall within its compass.[5] Consider, for example, how facial expressions become apparent as we move closer to persons in our visual field, and how these facial expressions themselves bring to light new potentialities, for example for greeting and embracing.

In each conversation, each participant will have at any given stage her own *conversation horizon*, which results from the combined effects of all her salient conversation contexts at that stage. This conversation horizon encompasses all possibilities that fall within the scope of what is relevant to her, as determined not only by her identity[6] and by her intentions of the moment, but also by the social and cultural setting of the conversation and by other contextual factors. As she shifts intentions in the course of the conversation this will also alter her conversation horizon, which in turn will determine how she perceives new utterance material, which will then have a dynamic effect leading to further new intentions, which will once again alter her conversation horizon and thereby influence the way new speech acts are formed and new contexts for interpretation are created.[7]

---

5 Compare Husserl (1989, pp. 142, 149): 'The world is pregiven to us, the waking, always somehow practically interested subjects, not occasionally but always and necessarily as universal field of all actual and possible practice, as horizon.'
6 See section 3.1.1, where we define the 'identity' of a person as the combination of personality traits, capabilities and long-term intentions.
7 David Lewis (1979) tries to capture something of what is involved here with his notion of conversational scorekeeping. The dynamic interaction between the conversation contents and its context is, he points out, analogous to the interaction between the score in a baseball game at any given stage and the way the game subsequently develops.

5.3.2 Social and documentary contexts

Social and cultural context is the social setting of the conversation (Hanks 1996), for example the context of a family outing, of two strangers bumping into each other in a bar, of a teacher berating a failing student, of a session in parliament. As the latter cases make clear, a social context may include institutional dimensions, and in such cases we can refer also to an *institutional context*. The social context exists in virtue of the fact that the participants in the conversation have formally or informally defined roles in virtue of which they are subject to certain norms. The potential social and institutional rewards and sanctions associated with these norms then form part of the conversation horizon. They influence not only what the conversation partners say (and what they do not say), but also the *ways* they speak and act.

Cultural context is a sub-type of social context created by those socialisation patterns which come into play where the participants in a conversation draw on a common cultural background passed on from one generation to the next. The cultural context is thus determined by those habits and values which result from similar types of upbringing, education, and so forth.

Documentary context is a sub-type of social context created where the conversation is generated around one or more documents to which the parties in the conversation repeatedly refer, possibly making amendments to these documents or themselves generating new documents along the way, as for example in securities litigation, military planning, or negotiations over building permits (Smith 2013). Other kinds of extra-conversational entities, too, can serve to shape the context of a conversation, and here again the example of a court of law illustrates the sort of unrepeatable complexity that may then arise.

Mixed conversation contexts There are many sorts of cases in which no single context can be established—where for example parties to a conversation differ in their cultural backgrounds, so that the speech of one party causes difficulties for another party already in the very act of listening. Similar problems arise where different parties are invested to different degrees in a positive outcome of the conversation. Consider the following fragment of dialogue from Harold Pinter's play *The Birthday Party*, which consists entirely of questions:

GOLDBERG: Webber, what were you doing yesterday?
STANLEY: Yesterday?
GOLDBERG: And the day before. What did you do the day before that?
STANLEY: What do you mean?
GOLDBERG: Why are you wasting everybody's time, Webber? Why are you
    getting in every body's way?
STANLEY: Me?

Each one of these questions opens up a new context. First, we have temporal contexts; then the dialogue itself becomes its own context; then the dialogue concludes with a case in which the anticipations forming the horizon of the context created by the pronoun *you* are frustrated by a deliberate misunderstanding on the part of one of the parties to the conversation.

Multiple connected social contexts can be in play also diachronically, where conversations form overlapping threads. Imagine a gang of building workers engaged in a conversation with the foreman about the day's tasks. The job of the foreman is to coordinate the workers' activities while overseeing quality and to liaise with management concerning progress and budget. In his conversations on site the foreman will adopt the style and tone of the workers; back in the office he will adopt the management style and tone. But then a union protest meeting is called, at which both groups are present, and the foreman is required to mediate between workers and management. How his style and tone will now be determined may depend on any number of factors, including on what he personally wants to achieve in this confrontational setting and on what he perceives to be his own standing relative to the power relations between the two groups. Such mixed conversation contexts are present also at a level above that of a single conversation, for example when one conversation is embedded as a side-conversation inside another, or when succeeding conversations are entangled with each other, as in a court case, where the content of earlier conversations may be inserted into the present conversation context in the form of written documentation.

5.3.3 Spatial and temporal contexts

Spatial context is the *site* of the conversation, formed by the physical place (the park bench, spaceship, bus, hospital, pub, bed, and so on) in which the conversation takes place. Temporal context is the *time* (day of the year, time of day, October 12, 1998, Christmas 2019, dusk, tea break) in which the conversation takes place. Both temporal and spatial context can include (at several levels) other spaces and times nested within them, for instance when a conversation relating to the food on the dinner table suddenly switches its context as the diners become aware that someone is banging hard on the front door, or when a conversation happens at one time but the interlocutors speak about other times and about their temporal order. Consider a conversation between a police officer and the various parties, including witnesses, involved in a car accident. Consider such a conversation where, among the various parties, there are some who speak different languages.

The environmental contexts of participants in a conversation may differ, as for example when Mary is driving and Jack, sitting next to her, is navigating. Here the two environmental contexts share in common the car interior, the road, the route ahead, and they share arrival at the same destination as part of their conversation horizon. Jack's environmental context includes in addition the map he is using to navigate. Mary's environmental context includes the set of driver affordances making up the car cockpit. But those parts of the environmental context which Jack and Mary share in common will be experienced by each of them in different ways. That conversations of this sort so often go wrong rests in part on the fact that there are different ways in which space itself is demarcated in different registers (Matthiessen et al. 2014).

Relations between environmental contexts may involve also factors of territoriality, for example when Jack seeks to engage Mary in dialogue by inserting himself into her personal space through displays of dominance or enticement. Environmental context also comprises those environments where power is projected (Popitz 2017a), such as the layout of a prison in which an overseer can interact via intercom with the prison inmates. Here the environmental context of the overseer comprehends multiple prison security, video surveillance, and communication systems extending across the entire prison and its surroundings; the environmental context of the inmate extends hardly beyond the walls of her cell.

The conversation is its own context at all levels of language production and interpretation. What this means is that, just as the constituents of a sentence contextualise each other, so do the successive sentences themselves. Each utterance is contextualised by its preceding utterances, and its potential future utterances form part of the context horizon of each present utterance. A question creates the context for a responding answer, and the answer (whatever the answer might be) is part of the horizon of the context from out of which the question arises. The degree to which a preceding statement influences the interpretation of the current statement is called the *contextual weight* of that statement. In prototypical conversations this weight decreases over time, so that the immediately preceding utterance has the strongest weight and more remote utterances have less as they fall away into the background. There are however cases where interlocutors can suddenly reach back to utterances made much earlier in the conversation and bring them once more into the foreground. As we shall see in more detail in chapter 10, such discontinuities in the conversation are from the mathematical point of view erratic (non-Markov).

Misunderstandings One important family of cases of this sort results from misunderstandings. Our acts of choosing how to respond to a conversation utterance are implicit. The same applies also to the interpretation of an utterance on the part of its receiver. The latter is observable only indirectly, for example by inference from the utterances the interpreter produces after a role switch between the interlocutors has occurred. This means that the continuous feedback which we rely on to adjust our intentions during conversation gives us only a partial picture of how our interlocutor is responding to our utterances. This in turn leads to misunderstandings, which may remain undetected through the entire length of the conversation. Where they are detected, this will often force an utterer to revise a statement from further back in the conversation when she realises, on the basis of how her interlocutor is now responding, that she has been misunderstood. Misunderstandings are more pervasive in conversation than may be credited by those wanting to adopt a rule-governed approach to human language. In many conversations misunderstandings—arising through mishearings or mispronunciations or ambiguity or failures of attention—are simply passed over in silence, yielding what would be an unsalvageably ragged and fragmented logical structure of any eventual transcript. But human interlocutors can deal with these problems—often unconsciously—by guessing the meaning or by deciding that the point is not worth further debate or questioning, and thereby moving on to a new topic.

5.4 Discourse economy: implicit meaning

It is part of the power of language that it enables us to condense environmental and background inputs down to just the bare bones of what is needed in a given context. Such condensation is indispensable if we are to avoid lengthy and unnecessarily explicit enumerations of all salient aspects of a conversation's context. Each party to the conversation simply assumes that the others know what she knows when she starts talking about, for example, the weather, or the political situation in Pyongyang. Such condensation is the ubiquitous and indeed obligatory phenomenon of *discourse economy*, which occurs because, in every conversation, the bearer of the interpreter role at any given stage needs to rely on a shared context for his interpretation of what has been said. This is because, for every utterance, the intended meaning must remain to some degree implicit.[8]

This reliance on shared context is normally something that comes about unconsciously, because parties to a conversation simply take for granted that they share sufficient general as well as context-specific knowledge to allow each of them to contextualise successfully the utterances of the other. Thus, they can still effectuate an adequate interpretation, even though not everything is said explicitly. This is of importance not least because it reflects the way in which the structure of the conversation is influenced by interactions between the respective identities of its participants, above all by which intentions and background (linguistic and other) capabilities they share.

The need for economy in use of language turns also on the fact that each speaker will in normal circumstances want to obtain from her speech acts the maximal effect in a limited time, and implicitness at the right level allows her

---

8 Verschueren (1999, p. 26) gives an example of our almost universal reliance on discourse economy by describing his attempt to make fully explicit the colloquial statement: 'Go anywhere today?' This resulted in a text of 15 lines that still does not achieve full explicitness.

to pass over details that would otherwise disturb the conversational flow or be boring to her interlocutor. Avoiding explicitness can also be used as a conversational tactic, for example to maintain politeness, or mask deception, or generate an impression of aloofness or efficiency.

To achieve a conversation that is productive on both sides, the preponderance of implicit meaning on the side of what is communicated by the utterer must still allow its understanding by the interpreter in a way that is close to the utterer's intention. In his *Studies in the Way of Words*, Grice (1989) formulates in this connection what he calls the 'Cooperative Principle', in which he recognises not only the need for discourse economy but also its two-sided nature. For cooperativeness, as Grice understands it, incorporates both a maxim of *quantity*—be as informative as you possibly can, and give as much information as is needed—and a maxim of *manner*—be as clear, as brief, and as orderly as you can in what you say, and avoid ambiguity. These requirements are clearly in competition with each other. If brevity is taken too far, for example, then the interlocutors will typically later require more explicitness in order to resolve potential misunderstandings.

5.4.1 Deixis

The most important form of implicit meaning is deixis, which is the use of language whose reference is determined by some feature of the context of utterance that is in the scope of awareness of the conversation partners. To interpret deictic expressions such as *him*, *next week*, *there*, the receiver needs to advert to features of this sort. Four important forms of deixis are: person deixis, temporal deixis, spatial deixis, and discourse deixis. Other variants of deixis identified by Talmy (2018) include *path* (the gunman rode off that way), *manner* (I will teach you to write like that), *quality* (I've never before seen such a sunset; the cell phone I buy will be this light), and *degree of social remove* (*Du räumst das Geschirr auf und Sie können den Wein öffnen* [you (informal) clear away the dishes and you (polite) can open the wine]).

Person deixis means references to a person, where who the person is can be inferred only if contextual information is available (Meibauer 2001; Sidnell et al. 2017). The utterer knows who he himself is, and in the setting of a face-to-face communication the interpreter knows who the utterer is, and is thus able to resolve the deictic pronouns *I* and *you*. Deixis often relies on pointing, as in 'that sheep is more expensive than that sheep'.

Spatial deixis is a phenomenon arising when reference to space requires for disambiguation spatial features that are themselves parts of or are anchored to the context (Lyons 1977). It can be seen at work in the use of prepositions such as *in*, *out*, *below*; of adverbs such as *here*, *there*; and of demonstrative pronouns such as *these* and *those*. It appears also in certain uses of verbs such as *enter, go, leave*. For example, the utterance 'Let's go downtown' when uttered in Berlin needs context to be disambiguated, since *downtown* can mean (at least) Berlin Zoologischer Garten and Berlin Mitte. Between 1961 and 1990 the term *Berlin* itself needed context for disambiguation.

Temporal deixis is the analogous phenomenon involving reference to time (Lyons 1977). To resolve the meaning of utterances like 'Yesterday Trump met Kim' or 'Next February I will travel to Rome' there are three elements—*event time point, time point of utterance*, and *reference time scale*—which need to be applied in disambiguation (Thomsen et al. 2018). The need to keep track of temporal order inside a conversation is illustrated by a statement such as 'After Paris we need to get to Abbeville before nightfall.' This involves four temporal references, one (implicit) present, and three (explicit) in successive futures, as well as three spatial references: present location at time of utterance (implicit), Paris and Abbeville (explicit). We can use this example to illustrate how the context and horizon of a conversation influence each other mutually. On the one hand, if the sentence is used in a conversation between two British tourists planning a trip from Paris to Normandy, the horizon might include potential closing times on Somme battlefield memorial sites. If, on the other hand, it is used in a conversation between two Oklahoma truck drivers, then it might include potential traffic holdups on Interstate 49 on the way from Paris, Texas, to Abbeville, Louisiana.

Discourse deixis is the use of an utterance in a conversation to refer to this utterance itself or to previous or future parts of the conversation (Levinson 1983). Examples are: 'What you just said contradicts your previous statements' or 'So what does it feel like, getting caught up in a conversation like this one?' Or again: 'This conversation must stop immediately!' Or: 'I contest the legitimacy of these entire proceedings!' While change in conversation horizon normally takes place gradually and without being noticed, the employment of discourse deixis brings the ongoing dynamics of horizon change into the foreground. Discourse deixis is often used for meta-discourse, for example when three persons leave the room, and then one of the remaining interlocutors says: 'That was a strange conversation.' Other forms of implicit meaning include non-deictic reference (Abbott 2017), presupposition and implicature (Huang 2017).

5.4.2 The linguistic division of labour

Not all implicit or ambiguous lexemes or phrases have to be interpreted or disambiguated by every utterer or recipient of an utterance, for this is not always required to realise their intentions. Hillary Putnam gives an important example of the interaction of utterance and intention in his paper on what he calls the 'linguistic division of labour' (Putnam 1975, p. 144). As he points out, there are many lexemes which are used by speakers without their full understanding. This phenomenon allows speakers and recipients to both tacitly use a lexeme while leaving its full understanding and definition to experts on which they rely, as when two politicians talk about nuclear power generation on TV. Both tacitly agree that they do not understand how nuclear power works, but they use the term nonetheless in order to sharpen their political profiles. When such tacit understanding is undermined by someone with genuine expertise, this may lead to confusion and anger, for it will add a new and potentially undesired seam of interpretation to the conversation in a way that disturbs the initial intentions of those involved.

5.5 Structural elements of conversation

When a human subject initiates a conversation, she can draw, first, on multiple sets of options at many levels of *language production*, starting with: which language to use (for example when travelling in a foreign country); the topic to be addressed; intonation, pitch, syntax, vocabulary, volume, as well as code and style of language (brazen, cautious, elegant, pious, rough, wistful, ironic); and so on. Second, she can draw on a wide repertoire of *non-verbal utterance accompaniments*, such as gesture, mimicry, gaze, posture. These factors (later documented in detail) evince (or mask) underlying intentions of the speaker, which can be argumentative, jocular, overbearing, serious, submissive, supplicative, teasing, threatening, and so forth. According to her intentions of the moment, the utterer can use different combinations as she adjusts to the responses of the recipient in accordance with the physical (temporal, spatial) and social and conversational context within which the conversation takes place. The recipient of an utterance will similarly face many options on the basis of which he can attribute meaning to what he hears. He can be suspicious, trusting, fully or only partially attentive, and so on. Which options are engaged on either side may of course change as the conversation unfolds, either for reasons internal to the content of the conversation itself or because the interlocutors are influenced by external factors such as effects of alcohol, or inclement weather, or discovering that it is your future boss who joined the conversation some minutes earlier, or indeed for no discernible reason at all. Conversations often involve random changes of subject matter, of tone, register, loudness, and so forth.

All the units that allow speakers to express their intentions are defined as structural[9] language units (Verschueren 1999). They, too, appear on a number of different levels, which are, from the coarse to the fine-grained:

---

9 Non-structural language units are the meanings of utterances that are acquired through context, including through composition with other utterances. This includes meanings both as intended by the utterer and as interpreted by the speaker, which are almost never fully congruent. See also note 8.

1. non-verbal level: including facial expression, gestures, and body language,
2. whole language level: including language choice, language code, and language style,
3. level of single conversation contributions: sentential and suprasentential utterance units,
4. level of morphemes and words,
5. level of sound structures.[10]

5.5.1 Non-verbal structural conversation units

Facial expression, glances, gestures, and body language are important ways in which uses of language are supported by non-verbal structures (Verschueren 1999, pp. 100ff.). All of them can potentially transform the sense of a verbal utterance, so that even a statement of condolence can be accompanied by facial expressions that make it appear cynical to the interpreter. In negotiations (and negotiation-based games such as poker) body language and facial impression may be indispensable to obtaining the desired results. It has been shown that their effect on the interpretation of situations, and even of the personality of the interlocutor, is quite strong (Ambady et al. 1992). The ability to perform quick and expert reading of intentions in others has played an essential role in the evolution of human social behavior, and this includes the deep-rooted cheater-detection mechanisms that have evolved in human beings to deal especially with social interactions involving exchange (Cosmides et al. 2005).

5.5.2 Language code and style

Code—also called 'register'—is a matter of the language choices systematically made by a social group, such as the inhabitants of an area or the members of a social class or profession, who are then said to speak a common *sociolect*. Sociolects arise from shared patterns of socialisation whose results are manifested in certain marked (for example 'posh' or 'rough') patterns of speech. Conversation participants under these circumstances are sometimes able to switch codes, for example, to communicate mockery or deference.

Age cohorts also have sociolects, as do members of specific criminal gangs. A *dialect* is a sociolect of those language users who share a social background that is regionally determined. A *cognolect* reflects the constraints imposed on an utterer

---

10 Ingarden (1973, pp. 29f.) identifies a similar pattern of what he calls 'strata' in his analysis of the ontology of the literary work of art, and points out how each can contribute to the aesthetic quality of the work as a whole. He emphasises that, despite the heterogeneous character of these strata, the work nonetheless constitutes an organic unity, since the strata are unified unproblematically by the reader in virtue of the dimension of meaning which runs through them all. Something similar applies in the dialogue case, though here there are two—potentially conflicting—chains of meaning which unify the strata, one for each of the two conversation partners.

by her intellectual abilities and education level, which may include a common professional or disciplinary socialisation in, for example, architecture or rap music.

Style concerns the level of *formality* of language use (Verschueren 1999); a speaker may switch, for example, to a more aggressive style in order to intimidate or punish his conversation partner. Both code and style are important dimensions of variance in utterance formation and interpretation.

Sociolects and degrees of formality in use of language reflect specifically linguistic social norms, which we will encounter again in chapter 6. The way speakers make use of language is an expression of these norms. Thus the degree to which following the norms of, for example, good grammar is accepted as an obligation (and the degree to which deviation from such norms is sanctioned) varies from one social group to another. The norms accepted in a given community of language users determine the meanings of the expressions used in that community.

5.5.3 Lying and deception

Lying and deception are frequent phenomena in language-mediated human interaction.[11] Their source is the desire to achieve one's goals and intentions without the knowledge of the interlocutor or against her will. Lying changes the entire meaning of a conversation both for the deceiver and, in the case that she becomes aware of the deception, for the deceived. Sometimes the deception may be made explicit by its target ('You must be lying to me because at that time you could not have been at home!'); but otherwise it remains implicit because the deceiver will have no motive to reveal it. It is generally therefore not possible to model lying and deception using only what is observable in a conversation.

5.5.4 Lexemes

Lexemes are the carriers of the minimal units of linguistic meaning—for example *run* or *hat*. The building blocks of sentences are lexemes in their inflected forms, which are called wordforms—for example *runs, ran, running* or *hats, hat's, behatted* (wordforms are derived by combining morphemes, which are the smallest meaningful units of language, as in *out-run* or *hat-pin-s*). For any given language there is a relatively small set of lexemes that has to cover a very wide range of possible topics. This is because it is not possible to have an exact word for each and every aspect of reality if the size of the lexicon is to be kept small enough that it can be managed by a single human being. Lexemes are therefore prototypes (Rosch 1975). They obtain part of their meaning from the context created by the other lexemes they are used with in a sentence, working together with all

---

11 Nietzsche (1980) even sees them as an essential part of our use of language; see also Gilman et al. (1990).

the other contextual dimensions identified earlier. For example, the lexeme *freedom* has a very different meaning in 1. and 2.

1. Do not clutter my desk with stuff; I need freedom to move.
2. We want freedom of speech!

5.6 How humans pass the Turing test

We invite the reader to note not merely the many *levels of conversation variance* distinguished in such examples but also the degree to which this practically infinite variance depends on multiple factors (indeed on multiple levels of multiple factors), both inside and outside the conversation itself. Such factors can extend to include almost any matter within the biographies and within the scope of the knowledge and interests of the conversation partners (or within the scope of an internet search engine one of them might access on her phone while speaking). We note further the degree to which many of these factors are a matter of continuous variation, in the sense that the range of options forms a continuum, as for example between speaking with a soft and a loud voice, or with a calm and an angry voice. Movements along multiple such continua may take place within a single conversation, and when such movements are effected by one conversation partner they will often call forth some concordant or countervailing movement on the side of her interlocutors. In all respects, indeed, preserving the flow of a conversation rests on the capacity of humans to adjust their contributions to fit those of their conversation partners and thereby to adjust their respective intentions.

The variance of language at the morphological and syntactic level is huge, and the variance at the semantic and pragmatic level is infinite. This does not mean that a computer could not in principle be built that could deal with one or other of these types of variance in such a way that it could generate responses to utterances which would be, for example, of an appropriate tone, or on an appropriate topic, or such as to demonstrate an appropriate amount of knowledge about or interest in or disdain for the political situation in Pyongyang. The problem is that the appropriate response in any given case will rest on a one-off combination of many such factors, so that it would be impossible to even begin to collect the gigantic amounts of data that would be needed to train a neural network that could generate responses that are appropriate to any given conversation when taken as a whole.

And we could not solve this problem, either, by continually updating a neural network with new training material taking account of new, or newly fashionable, conversation topics or ways of speaking. For still the same problem would remain: we could never collect enough language use data at any given stage because there is no distribution to sample from (see 8.1). Even a network repeatedly re-trained with samples from these data will fail to keep pace for example with the sorts of abrupt changes of context documented in the foregoing.

How, then, do *humans* cope with this enormous degree of variance?

First, they share linguistic capabilities and a common ground of shared knowledge. Second, language itself serves to constrain the space through which a hearer must search to determine the target intended by the speaker (Talmy 2018, §7.1.6). And then third, each speaker is able to actively form and interpret utterances based on his own intentions of the moment. These intentions further reduce the space in which choices have to be made; they provide keys to interpretation (whether correct or incorrect), and they work against the background of all those acquired capabilities and intentions that form a human identity.

Two humans will interpret the very same utterance differently and form different intentions on its basis, depending on their respective personalities and goals. Yet humans are nonetheless able in the vast majority of cases to create the level of agreement about interpretations that is needed to realise their respective intentions in the course of a conversation. Thus when it becomes clear to one party of the conversation that he is being misunderstood, he will modify his subsequent contributions to the exchange—including associated gestures, pace, and so forth—in such a way as to maximise the likelihood that he will achieve his goals in an iterative process that, as the other party becomes involved, may take on the character of a negotiation.

When a conversation occurs between human beings, multiple complex systems, each with its own evolving sets of intentions and realising its own sets of capabilities, are interacting with each other. Interactions of this sort are analogous to those which occur when other sorts of complex systems interact—for instance when the earth's tidal system interacts with the ecological systems of coastal wetlands. We can *describe* and *explain* some of what occurs in the course of such interactions; but we cannot build mathematical models that will enable us to *predict* what will occur. The two sorts of systems simply interact. That is what they do. And so, too, in the case of many sorts of interactions, both linguistic and non-linguistic, involving humans: humans do not consciously or unconsciously compute these interactions (because the human mind-body continuum is not any sort of computer[12]). Rather, they simply interact in a way that involves, at the level of ultimate physics, a constantly self-adjusting sequence of interactions between the different sets of fundamental forces deriving from the different human beings involved.

---

12 A computer is a machine that deterministically creates a numerical output based on some numerical input using a mathematical model (Turing 1937; Rojas 1997). As we will see in chapters 7 and 8, the human brain and the human mind-body continuum are not machines of this kind. Indeed, they are not machines of any kind.

6
SOCIAL AND ETHICAL BEHAVIOUR

We will show in chapter 11 that we will never be able to engineer machines with the social and ethical capabilities of human beings. In preparation for this we need to understand what these capabilities are, and to this end we will engage in an accelerated grand tour through sociology and social ontology. We focus on three sets of issues, relating to

- social behaviour in communities, societies, and institutions,
- perspective-taking and intersubjectivity, and
- social norms, including legal and moral norms.

We start with social behaviour, which occurs when two or more organisms of the same species interact.[1] Elementary social behaviour is to be found already in the prokaryotes, the most primitive of living organisms, who associate in groups to improve their chances of survival and reproduction. Bacteria form biofilms on human tissue (for example on the endocardium) in order to increase their chances of survival and reproduction by evading the immune mechanisms of their hosts (Percival et al. 2011). Ants, which are invertebrate arthropods, display a complex form of social behaviour, involving territorial demarcation and defence (Adams 2016). Higher animals have even more sophisticated forms of group behaviour, and in mammals we find social groups whose members coordinate their activities and interact not only in cooperative ways but also in ways that involve the exercise of violence.

1 We ignore here interactions between humans and, for instance, their dogs (Wilson 2000).

Our focus here is on social behaviour among humans, and in this we follow a long tradition in the social sciences of distinguishing between *communities* and *societies*. Both are social groupings with *lasting* relationships between individuals, and are thus distinguished from queues and other transient social groupings in which persistent relationships are not formed.

A 'community' is a small group of humans who associate on the basis of direct personal acquaintance, including in interactions that involve the use of language. The basic mode of interaction is what Scheler calls 'unfounded trust'.[2] Examples are: a family, a tribe, a small village comprising just a few families.

A 'society' is a larger and more formalised grouping of humans involving anonymous, non-personal interactions among its members, based on contracts (explicit reciprocal agreements) and social institutions. Here the basic mode of interaction is 'primary mistrust'[3]. For hominids and *Homo sapiens* the community was for millions of years the only form of social association. Only with urbanisation some 5000 years ago did humans begin to form societies, followed by the appearance of a series of novel forms of social behaviour now manifested within social institutions such as the state, the military, and the law (Weber 1976, § 9), (Holton et al. 2010). As Weber emphasised, most social interactions today contain elements of both community and society, and thus display aspects of human social behaviour characteristic of each. It is, for example, a part of the context horizon of the mother nurturing her child through an illness that she can call on a doctor if needed.

6.1 Can we engineer social capabilities?

Engineering a counterpart of human social behaviour is crucial for any treatment of AGI. This is because, to perform effectively in the human social world, AGI agents would need to display social capabilities of the sort that humans possess.

Humans are genetically endowed with a huge number of such social capabilities, falling under a range of different types. Examples are: to *engage* with others, for example in a conversation; to *understand* or *grasp* the intentions, emotions, and behaviour of others; to *exercise* and to *follow* authority; and to *learn* from others (including to learn a language).

Of these, learning from others may be the most important, not only because (as we saw in 3.2.2) learning is the root of all culture, but also because it is via learning—initially as a by-product of other forms of socialisation—that our generic innate social capabilities are transmuted into the sorts of specific social capabilities that can be realised in behaviour.

---

2 *Grundloses Vertrauen* (Scheler 1973, chapter VI.B.4.4)
3 *Primäres Mißtrauen* (Scheler 1973, chapter VI.B.4.4)

6.1.1 Socialisation

'Socialisation' is the process through which an individual learns to behave in a way that is acceptable to a group (community or society) to which she belongs. Since humans typically belong to multiple social groups, they will typically be subjected to multiple different sorts of socialisation, though the primary socialisation in the family is by far the most important.[4]

It is through such socialisation that humans acquire capabilities, for example, to collaborate, and to follow social (including moral) norms (Weber (1976, I §9), Berger et al. (1966, III.1)).

Such capabilities contribute to making it possible for individuals

1. to participate in the social life of their primary community,
2. to integrate themselves into secondary communities such as playgroups, school and college classes, sports teams, social clubs, and parish choirs, and
3. to participate in social institutions.

To understand what social institutions are, we draw on Talcott Parsons' masterpiece *The Social System*, which provides a widely accepted explication, starting out from the process of institutionalisation. This Parsons sees as giving rise in its subjects to the acceptance of certain values as governing their actions—a phenomenon which he illustrates by pointing to the way in which the Puritan orientation around the values of honesty, responsibility, hard work, and self-control became institutionalised in Britain in the period leading up to the Glorious Revolution of 1688 (Parsons 1949).

6.1.2 Social institutions

A *social institution* is now defined by Parsons as 'a complex of institutionalised role integrates which is of strategic structural significance in the social system in question'. Institutions are 'governed' by specific values and norms, but 'only insofar as they are "implemented" by particular collectivities and roles'. The values and norms themselves thereby become 'institutionalised' (Parsons 1971, p. 8).

An institution as thus defined is not itself a society. Rather, we can think of it as a network of relationships by which members of a society are linked together. The idea is that one and the same society can accommodate multiple institutions; one and the same human being can occupy multiple different roles in different institutions; and one and the same institutional role can be occupied by different human beings at different times.

---

4 Other environments of primary socialisation are orphanages and kibbutzim (Horgan et al. 2017).

6.2 Intersubjectivity

Parsons' *Social System* launched also the modern treatment of the topic of social interaction with the introduction of what he calls 'the problem of double contingency' (Parsons 1951, p. 10). Under this heading Parsons is referring to the fact that, when an encounter occurs between two strangers, each has to assume that the other may be, on the one hand, potentially dangerous, but also—because the encounter may lead to fruitful cooperation—potentially benign (Vanderstraeten 2002). What follows the initial encounter is said to be *doubly* contingent, because each party to the interaction has freedom of choice in how it will proceed.

Note that the double contingency scenario is hardly relevant to encounters in traditional (small) communities, where everyone is familiar with everyone else from birth. For such communities, encounters with strangers will be rare. Where, however, they do occur—for example after dark—there is a risk that they will end in violence.

With the advent of urbanisation, interactions between members of societies governed by distrust or between members of different communities becomes ever more commonplace both within and without the city walls, and the need for structured, reliable ways to address the double contingency problem begins to make itself felt.

How, then, do humans who interact with each other solve this problem? How, in other words, do humans succeed in engaging with their fellow human beings, including strangers, where any encounter may turn out to be inauspicious? Parsons' answer, which we adopt here, has two parts, based, respectively, on (i) intersubjectivity and (ii) social norms (Parsons 1968).

6.2.1 Intersubjectivity: a brief history

6.2.1.1 Phenomenology

We start with the basic human capability of taking another's perspective, of imagining oneself in someone else's shoes. This can happen on the basis of purely linguistic input; it often happens, for example, when we read a novel or a work of history. However, because language can easily be used in social interactions for dishonest purposes, it has low reliability when taken alone as a signal of the intentions of one's interlocutor. Language-based perspective taking is thus of uncertain utility in just those sorts of interactions where it is of vital importance. We can however draw on other sorts of input in face-to-face interactions. These include inputs deriving from our experience of the environment of the interaction. But more importantly they include also our experience of the other's behaviour and bodily expressions. For these, as Scheler recognised, provide a key to the other's emotions:

> we certainly believe ourselves to be immediately acquainted with another person's joy in his laughter, with his sorrow and pain in his tears, with his

shame in his blushing, with his entreaty in his outstretched hands, with his love in his look of affection, with his rage in the gnashing of his teeth, with his threats in the clenching of his fist, and with the tenor of his thoughts in the sound of his words. (Scheler 2008, p. 260) (quoted according to the translation in.

(Schlossberger 2016))

Such direct perception is at the basis of all face-to-face perspective taking[5], for we can *take* the perspective of our interlocutor only if we have some idea of the emotions they are experiencing. Like all other forms of perception, so also the perception of another's emotions can rest on error. That is, it can deviate from reality. In cases of fraud and deception, erroneous perceptions of this sort are deliberately engendered in order to instill in the deceived an ungrounded perspective of trust in the deceiver. It is at this point that the relevance of perspective taking to the issue of double contingency becomes clear.

6.2.1.2 Sociology

The phenomenon of intersubjectivity, now, emerges where perspective taking takes a quite specific sort of reciprocal form. As Parsons (1968) expressed it, face-to-face interactions normally involve a 'complementarity of expectations'—'the interaction of ego and alter is dependent on the integration of the mutual expectations of both actors' (Parsons 1951, pp. 35ff.).[6] To achieve such an integration, both alter and ego must attempt to grasp the pattern of the other's intentions—of why the other is engaging in this interaction and of what she is intending to do—in such a way that each can understand how this pattern is or can become interrelated with the pattern of their own intentions.

It is in our addressing this need that there arises the phenomenon of intersubjectivity, which combines mental experiences on the part of (in almost all cases just) two subjects, which involve on both sides perspective taking together with salient perceptions of the other's emotions, bodily postures, facial expressions, gestures, and so forth, but in such a way that these experiences are in a sense fused together.

6.2.2 Definition of intersubjectivity

In more detail, intersubjectivity obtains where:

---

5 Vetter (2020) offers a parallel framework in support of the idea that we can perceive Gibsonian affordances, and Brogaard (Brogaard 2017, 2019) presents a convincing set of arguments for the existence of a parallel ability to *perceive meanings*, for example when we interact with someone in dialogue.

6 This aspect of reciprocality, too, has been studied by philosophers, especially by phenomenologists such as Husserl, Schütz, and Sartre. Reich (2010) seeks to reconcile their competing approaches to intersubjectivity with those of Parsons and other sociologists.

- two parties encounter each other and register this encounter mutually, paradigmatically through eye contact or through some mutual touching signal or verbal greeting that is immediately acknowledged,[7]
- both parties engage in Schelerian direct perception of the other (which means that they each consciously or unconsciously take into account the other's emotions), and
- thereby engage in reciprocal perspective taking—they consciously or unconsciously create in their minds an evolving understanding of (what they take to be) the pattern of emotions and intentions of the other party.

This must then occur in such a way that both parties experience in the course of the encounter the belief/feeling that their own emotions and intentions as presented in the encounter have been understood and acknowledged also by the other party.

And in what we can think of as the ideal case of intersubjectivity, it will further be the case that the intentions each party brings to the interaction are also *accepted* by the other party (as occurs, for example, when someone makes a promise to do something and the latter simultaneously accepts the promise (Mulligan 1987)).

Intersubjectivity is maintained over time as alter and ego each unconsciously adapt their own inner lives and intentions as their understanding of the other's mental dispositions develops. The processes involved can be indefinitely nested, as when I adjust my emotions and intentions to what I think are the emotions and intentions of my interlocutor who has himself adjusted his emotions and intentions to what he thinks is going on with me.

6.3 Social norms

We now look into the second major aspect of social behaviour, which pertains to the relations between socialisation and social norms. We hereby prepare the ground for a discussion of what would be needed on the part of the machine in a society involving AGI agents if the latter were to be able to adhere to the sorts of social norms which are effective in human societies as we know them today.

6.3.1 Social norms as constraints on interactions

Social norms are built out of simple behavioural rules which apply when we interact with others, for example: do not start a conversation by yelling; respond when someone greets you; do not initiate violence; keep your

---

7 An analogue of eye contact can thereby in some cases be obtained through a medium such as phone or video which enables synchronous communication.

promises. Such norms are followed not only in everyday activities such as crossing the road and mowing the lawn and in organised social events such as weddings and funerals; they are manifested also in the numberless occasions where humans engage in semi-ritualised behaviours, as in greeting, congratulating, forgiving, cursing, apologising, bidding farewell, and the like. To see how this works, consider that almost every non-intimate situation is immediately and unconsciously recognised as such, and thereby restrains its participants from removing their clothes.

The dimension of social norms arises against the background of the sort of intersubjectivity we find in existing *communities* to allow successful functioning of human beings at the level of *societies*. Social norms arise because the general problem of double contingency takes a quite different form in those cases where strangers meet who belong to the same culture from the form it takes in encounters involving persons from different cultures. This is because, in the former case, strangers can be assumed, other things being equal, to follow the same social norms.

Social norms are behavioural constraints which enable collaboration among individuals. They are generative rules for expected behaviour in recurrent interaction situations, which means that they are rules with the ability to generate behaviour, effectively by providing attractors toward which behaviour is steered, for example because following such a rule yields rewards or avoids punishments.

They have evolved spontaneously over time (Gavrilets et al. 2017) and are continuously refined in *ad hoc* ways, as individuals experiment in determining which sorts of behaviour are permitted and which are sanctioned. They are thus a product of spontaneous order and do not form a logically structured system. They are constantly evolving, though there is no equilibrium towards which they are evolving.

Initially, social norms are a matter of local customs, passed on from generation to generation through informal means. Over time, many such norms begin to be formulated explicitly, as is recorded for example in the legend of how Moses on Mount Sinai received the Ten Commandments (*Exodus* 19). Over time, also, violations of such norms begin to be penalised through the formalised machinery of the law. There still remain at every stage, however, many social norms that are informal and become apparent only through social processes in which their violation is informally sanctioned, either through the application of physical violence or restraint or through processes such as shunning or the spreading of rumours.

Social norms have the function of *enhancing reciprocal predictability*, increasing social reliability and promoting the establishment of intersubjectivity between those who come from different communities. When humans act in a social context into which they have been socialised, then—leaving aside exceptional behaviour due, for example, to the influence of alcohol—they are consciously or unconsciously following the norms associated with that context. Popitz

(2017b) provides a useful list of central features of social norms, including the reasons why they come to be followed by the members of the groups in which they arise, which we can summarise as follows:

1. Social norms are always coupled with the situation types in which they apply (their scope). A norm is a set of behavioural rules which applies to a given type of human being in a given type of situation. A human being of the relevant type and in an appropriate situation is able, first, to consciously or unconsciously recognise what type of situation she is in and what type of role she has in that situation. And second, she is able to rely on the fact that the same norms will to a large degree also guide the behaviour of others of her type in this situation. Social norms thus serve to constrain the repertoire of available, repeating patterns of behaviour, and thereby promote the likelihood that humans will behave in conformance with them and that behaviour not in conformity will be more easily detected.
2. Because adult human beings are in almost all cases members of multiple social groups, conflicts or mismatches between the norms implied by these different groups are frequent even in very homogenous societies. A *father* may also be a *taxi driver*, and he must adhere to quite different sets of norms in each role.
3. Social norms are 'valid' where their transgression is liable to be sanctioned by the wider society.[8] What the norms prescribe becomes manifest over time through the precedents set by punishments of prior violations.

6.3.2 Legal norms

Like other social norms, legal norms serve to promote predictability and coordination of behaviour, but they do this through what we can call 'formalisation'. Legal norms stand out from social and moral norms in that they are the products of *enactments*, through which the norms governing our behaviour are changed in certain deliberate ways.

Our understanding of enactments and their consequences—which shape almost every aspect of the social world in which we live—draws heavily on the views of the realist phenomenologist Adolf Reinach, to whom we turn also in dealing in section 6.4.3.1 with the relation between law and morality.

In the beginning, all social norms were a matter of local custom. Little by little, however, such customary norms have to a large extent been replaced with a set of more precisely defined legal norms, which allow more consistent and predictable identification and sanctioning of transgressions. For these norms to prevail requires legal institutions, whose purpose is to ensure

---

8 Recent research has confirmed the traditional view that punishment of violators is essential to the upholding of social norms (Mathew et al. 2011).

adherence. These legal institutions and the associated legal norms must be grounded in turn in the expression of the political will of the holders of power in a society.

A theory of legal norms would be required for the programming of machines to be used in legal deliberation or in law enforcement. However, it will become clear in chapter 11 that the scope for AI in this area is very limited.

6.4 Moral norms

Not all social norms are ethical norms. There are social norms pertaining to ethically neutral behaviour (such as driving on the left), and also perverted social norms (and even perverted legal norms) that require people to commit morally evil acts, such as spying on neighbours (in wartime France) and on parents (in East Germany), or denouncing communists (in Germany from 1933 to 1945) or Jews (Germany from 1941 to 1945) for deportation to death camps.

Moral norms are (roughly) those social norms that define which actions are acceptable when viewed under the traditional ethical categories of *good* and *bad* (virtues and vices) as applied to human behaviour.

One can act in accordance with a social norm while violating a moral norm, for example when lying in public following the orders of one's superior. Many non-formalised moral norms have a scope shared in common with formalised legal norms, especially in criminal law. Murder is bad, both morally and legally. Coveting your neighbour's wife is bad only morally.

We shall return to the relation between law and morality later. For the moment we note only that morality is not subject to human contrivance; unlike the law, which is subject, as we have seen, to modification through a variety of different sorts of enactments. Morality is in this sense more fundamental than law.

6.4.1 Who or what is subject to moral norms?

We presuppose in what follows the axiom shared by all ethical theories since Kant (1998, 1991) onwards:

> Only entities with the ability to grasp moral norms and the ability to behave intentionally can engage in behaviour that is evaluable as moral or immoral.

The only entities that we know of with these abilities are humans.[9]

---

9 In higher animals, social norms relate almost exclusively to kin selection and kin altruism, which is social behaviour that is explained by assuming that the animal is acting to promote the preservation of its own genes (offspring) or at least the genes of closely related animals (Wilson 2000).

What, now, of machines?

We will show in later chapters that machines cannot have intentions, and they therefore also cannot be said to *behave* either morally or immorally. Machines like guns and cars can, certainly, do significant damage to human beings; yet we talk not of 'gun' or 'car ethics', but rather of 'ethics' for the people who use them. This is, again, because machines cannot have intentions.

Why, then, do we talk of an ethics of AI? We will address this question in chapter 11, where we investigate whether we can at least *emulate* ethical behaviour in an artificially intelligent machine. For the moment we note only that, to achieve such an emulation, we would need, first, to formulate a theory of the ethical behaviour that we are familiar with already in persons, and then show how this theory might be implemented in a context where machines are involved. A theory of the needed sort should therefore not be anything new. Rather, since (for the foreseeable future, at least) artificially intelligent machines would need to work primarily with and for humans, it is the moral theories with which we are already familiar that must serve as our starting point.[10]

6.4.2 Utilitarianism

Utilitarianism is a theory of ethics which postulates that the criterion for judging human behaviour from an ethical point of view is its utility, or in other words its ability to generate happiness (Mill 1863). We can sum up the most basic form of the utilitarian doctrine as the view that the morally right action in any given situation is that which would contribute maximal happiness (yield the greatest happiness for the greatest number of people) given that situation. One of the many problems facing a view of this sort is the problem of measuring happiness according to a common scale (referred to in the literature as the 'problem of interpersonal utility comparisons' (Nozick 1985)). A second problem is that of specifying what is meant by 'situation', and in particular what the spatial and temporal boundaries of a situation might be (for instance: how far into the future should our utility calculation reach?) (Chatterjee 2003).

For our purposes here, however, the major problem is that of comparing on a single scale different *kinds* of happiness (and including unhappiness/pain, on the negative side of the ledger). Mill himself distinguished between what he called lower and higher pleasures, and he took great pains to prevent utilitarianism from implying a stance which would optimise only pleasures at the lower end of the scale. In *Utilitarianism*, Mill (1863, chapter 2) identifies three factors to which one can appeal in responding to the question 'which is the best worth

---

10 We will for obvious reasons focus solely on approaches to morality which would seem to allow the sort of moral calculation that an AI ethics would require. Thus we ignore those approaches which deny the possibility of universal moral principles, as for example in Williams (1985), or (in application to legal norms) Zaibert (2018, chapter 6). As will become clear, however, we are in fact sympathetic to such approaches.

having of two pleasures, or which of two modes of existence is the most grateful to the feelings?':

1. the moral attributes associated with each alternative,
2. the consequences which would flow from choosing one or other alternative,
3. the judgement of those who are qualified by knowledge of both, or, if they differ, that of the majority among them.

Mill's reference to 'moral attributes' here and in other passages is significant, because it implies that, as he himself points out, utilitarianism rests on an implicit reference to *values* as a background for the moral judgements that underlie our actions:

> there is no known Epicurean theory of life which does not assign to the pleasures of the intellect, of the feelings and imagination, and of the moral sentiments, *a much higher value* as pleasures than to those of mere sensation.
> (Mill 1863, chapter 2, emphasis added)

To provide an adequate model of human ethical behaviour, therefore, utilitarianism must be supplemented by some broader framework.

6.4.3 Value ethics

We propose here a standard strategy for addressing this problem based on what is called 'value ethics', which rests on the idea that humans can have recourse to specifically *ethical* values, to ways of applying value terms such as 'good' or 'bad', which are distinct from and independent of their application to the value of usefulness (for example of a *good hand drill*) and to economic value (of a *good deal*, measured for instance in money prices).

The term 'value' (*Wert*) was introduced into philosophy as a technical term only in the 19th century by Hermann Lotze (1841, pp. 4ff., 323ff.), Frege's teacher at the University of Göttingen. However, it was Scheler (see 3.2.1) who was the first to develop a truly comprehensive value-based ethical theory in his *Formalism in Ethics and Material Value Ethics* (Scheler 1973), and we will draw in what follows on Scheler's ideas in this work as also on the three volumes of the *Ethics* of Nicolai Hartmann (Hartmann 2014), which systematise and also in some cases improve upon these ideas.

Scheler, first of all, identifies what he considered to be a type of experience, different from intellectual and sensual experience, consisting in what he calls 'value feelings' (*Wertfühlen*), here echoing Adam Smith's use of the term 'moral sentiments'. Among the values which are the targets of such value feelings there is a subclass of what Scheler calls 'moral values', which provide the ground for moral judgements. An example is the feeling of guilt which may be engendered when we perform an action which we know to be morally bad. (Scheler is not hereby claiming that we can use our feelings in order to make *judgements* of innocence or guilt. Rather he is simply pointing to the fact that we can *feel guilty*.)

Consider, as another example, our feeling of distress when we engage in a heated argument with someone we love. Such a feeling does not occur in isolation. Rather it exists as just one thread bound together with other experiences, including our awareness of (1) our own intentions and our sensorimotor awareness of our body; of (2) the other person or persons involved; and of (3) our environment.

Some value feelings involve also the experience of a certain sort of demand. When we see someone collapse in the middle of the street, our value feeling influences our behaviour by making us feel the demand to go out and help. When we see someone taking pleasure in torturing a child, then we experience anger and other value feelings to the effect that the torturer is doing something wrong, and these feelings, too, may go hand in hand with the experience of the demand that we go out and stop him.

6.4.3.1 Human behaviour through the lens of value ethics

Recall that our goal here is to identify an ethical theory that might reasonably be applied to support emulation in a machine of the ethical dimension of human behaviour. We should want an AGI-driven machine of the future that is tasked, for example, with looking after our children, to be able to emulate all of the appropriate demand-experiences of the just-mentioned sort and to act appropriately on this basis. This, crucially, does not mean to *act* in every case. The AGI must also be able to emulate the processes by which humans weigh alternative courses not only of action but also of non-action in any given situation.

It is in this respect that our value-based approach brings an advantage over the more familiar virtue ethics approach, which is oriented around the cultivation of virtuous behaviour on the part of human beings. When, for example, Hagendorff (2020) considers how virtue ethics should be applied to the problem of AI ethics, he sees a need to bring value ethics into play.

Some authors in AI ethics do indeed recognise the importance of values. Dignum, for examine, argues that 'AI reasoning should be able to take into account societal values, moral and ethical considerations; weigh the respective priorities of values held by different stakeholders in various multicultural contexts' (Dignum 2018). There exists also a literature on what are called 'value aligned' AI systems, for example in Osoba et al. (2020) and Gabriel (2020), where the value of fairness[11] plays in both cases a central role. However, we know of no work in the AI ethics field which attempts to deal systematically

---

11 Not a value in the traditional sense, but rather a term related to the semantic field of the value of justice (δικαιοσύνη).

with the domain of value theory of the sort we outline here. This is in part a consequence of the fact that the discipline of AI ethics has been pursued primarily by philosophers in the analytic tradition, while the main work in value theory, as we shall see, derives from the tradition of the realist phenomenologists.

Now if we take value ethics as our candidate basis for this emulation, then we must first address how this theory models the sources of moral behaviour in humans.

First, value ethics presupposes that human beings are capable of both moral and immoral actions and capable also of recognising their own and other's actions as being either moral or immoral. Not all humans, not even all mature humans, possess this capability to an equal degree—and there are some who manifest what Scheler and Hartmann (and after them many others (Larsen 2020)) call 'moral-' or 'value-blindness'.

Second, while we can teach our children to behave in a way that respects ethical values, their ability to grasp what we teach them must have what Scheler refers to as an '*a priori*' foundation in values which are what he calls 'objective' or 'absolute' and 'universal'.[12] This means that they are experienced by mature human beings as rising above the subjective decisions of individuals and as being universally applicable. It is for this reason that values can be used to account for the fact that specific human actions—even the actions of entire societies—can be counted as good or evil independently of whether the relevant actors perceive them as such.

For the utilitarian, what is *a priori*, in the sense of intrinsically intelligible and therefore unlearned, is the infant's ability to distinguish between pleasure and pain and to grasp their respective positive and negative valence. For Hartmann the domain of what is unlearned extends much further, including:

- the predisposition to identify, among the larger body of actions, those which are carriers of moral value or disvalue;
- the predisposition to distinguish positively from negatively valued actions; and
- the predisposition to experience the demand character of certain moral values.

Against this background the infant is able to handle a progressively larger repertoire of values as she moves through different stages of development.

6.4.3.2 The space of moral values

According to Hartmann (2014), moral values can be classified into two groups: (I.) Fundamental values: goodness, nobility, abundance, purity; (II.) Special values, which he subdivides by era of first formulation: (i.) Antiquity: justice,

---

12 Scheler and Hartmann here use the same terminology in talking about values as that used by Reinach in his treatment of *a priori* legal structures (Reinach 1989, p. 142) (Smith 1992).

wisdom, courage, self-control; (ii.) Middle Ages: altruism, truthfulness, fidelity, humility; (iii.) Modern Age: love of the remote, donating virtue (*schenkende Tugend*), authenticity, love.[13]

We will not analyse this classification here.[14] It suffices to note that Hartmann seems to have come close to achieving his own goal of providing a catalogue of values that is complete in the sense that it takes account of all moral values so far described in the history of philosophy (Hartmann 2014, chapter 55e-f.) Like Scheler, Hartmann distinguishes *moral* values both from aesthetic values (such as beauty and ugliness) and from a range of other positively valued goods, such as: being alive, being conscious, being free, having power, and being lucky (εὐτυχία). Moral values are related always to persons and can only be realised by acts of persons (Hartmann 2014, chapters 15, 26).

Hartmann proposes methods of ranking moral values (op. cit., chapters 27–30) and also provides a review of anti-values such as evil, impurity, and injustice, and of how these relate to values proper. But for our purposes here, it suffices to recognise that he does indeed provide a value catalogue that is probably exhaustive enough to program a value system inside a machine. If indeed that would be possible at all.

6.4.3.3 The demand character of values

It is crucial for Hartmann—and also for an understanding of the way values work in human societies—that the values themselves can be apprehended as having a *validity* that is independent of persons or circumstances, where by 'validity' here—as contrasted with validity for social norms in general—is meant that they yield (i) principles of behaviour, which are (ii) binding (even though not always followed), and (iii) mind- and thus subject-independent.

This validity of moral values is based on their demand character, which is divided by Hartmann into what he refers to as the 'ought-to-be' and the 'ought-to-do', respectively. Values are, in Hartmann's words, potential principles of moral acts (Hartmann 2014, chapter 17), by which he means that they point to something that *ought-to-be*.[15] An ought-to-be can exist without an associated ought-to-*do* on the part of some subject. For example, global peace as a value is an ought-to-be, but not necessarily an ought-to-do for any given individual. However, when a delimited sphere of physical reality is in conflict with an ought-to-be, then the latter can become transformed into an ought-to-do. For example, the abstract value of the preservation of life becomes an ought-to-do when someone sees a child drowning in a pond. Here we have an example of a *world-to-value* direction of fit.

---

13 Morgenstern (1997, p. 136) provides a useful tabulation.
14 The interested reader can refer to the comprehensive description in chapters 38 to 58 of (Hartmann 2014).
15 *Seinsollen*: see (Hartmann 2014, chapter 18).

104 Properties of the human mind

The identification, by a subject who perceives the discrepancy between an ought-to-be and reality, of a means whereby reality can be changed (namely, by saving the drowning child) transforms the ought-to-be into an ought-to-do (Hartmann 2014, chapter 19). However, values have no deterministic power over reality. The subject witnessing the drowning child may find it too risky to dive into the pond to save it, and walk away. But what we call conscience, duty, urge to act, feeling of responsibility, or feeling of guilt, are expressions of our ability to *feel* values, to feel their absence or presence, and to act according to the perceived discrepancy between ought-to-be and reality by realising an ought-to-do.

In all such circumstances actors act in accordance with a certain value mix, reflecting their individual value feelings and their value ranking of the moment. Where one might show courage by plunging into icy water to save a child, another might emphasise prudence and call an ambulance, while yet another might place the highest value on his own personal safety and withdraw from the scene entirely, possibly with a feeling of shame—a sign that one or more higher values has been felt but subordinated to a lower value (in this case, altruism and courage subordinated to safety).

6.4.3.4 A priori structures in the realm of values

It is useful to compare the realm of values as demarcated by Scheler and Hartmann to another realm of structures in which certain essential relations hold, namely the world of geometric shapes. Two features of geometric shapes are:

i. they have a relationship to reality: the circles and triangles as described by geometry are the shapes, respectively, of steering wheels and traffic warning signs that we recognise in our everyday experience;

ii. they are the subject of universal propositions whose truth is not a matter of empirical evidence but of laws that we can discover by reasoning, for example, that every point on the circumference of a circle is equidistant from its centre or that the interior angles of a triangle sum up to $180°$.

There is, however, an ontological difference between values and geometrical shapes. For when we observe the morally relevant behaviour of others, we do not perceive *instances* of corresponding value universals (which is what we experience when we see a drawing of a circle or a triangle).

When a value is realised by some act (when an ought-to-be has become an ought-to-do), this is not a relation like that between a universal and its instances. Certainly, the value is general in nature, while the act that fulfils it is particular. But the latter is not an instance of the former. Rather the value is, again, a potential principle of a moral act. We have seen that the realisation of values depends on the subject's decision to realise an ought-to-be in the face of a discrepancy with reality by making the associated ought-to-do the principle of his act. Doing this leads to the fulfilment of the value by the act of the subject.[16] Values can not only be *fulfilled* in value-consistent behaviour; they can also *fail to be fulfilled* in behaviour that involves a value conflict (Hartmann 2014, chapter 17).

Of course, our actions are often in contradiction with concomitant values, either because we suffer under value blindness or because our concern to act in accordance with values competes with other motives. This explains why someone may decide not to help a person he sees fainting in the street and why a child in a grocer's shop may decide to steal. An immoral act occurs because the actor is value blind or because she chooses to follow lower-ranked values.

A further distinction between the realm of geometrical shapes and the realm of values turns on the fact that it is possible to define the former on the basis of just a handful of basic primitives, where the idea of providing a set of definitions and basic axioms in this way for the realm of values seems to be excluded.

6.4.4 Non-legal and non-moral social norms

Many social norms are neither legal nor moral, but nonetheless of high importance for the functioning of communities and societies. These are norms such as courtesy, politeness, and other norms of appropriate behaviour in given sorts of social situations. Such norms are sometimes explicitly taught; but they are mostly unconsciously absorbed by individuals into their behavioural repertoires in the course of socialisation (Conerton 1979).

A social AGI would have to master norms of this sort also, because acceptance by humans of social robots would depend to a high degree on adequate social behaviour. This becomes visible in the way in which the fictive social behaviour of speaking droids in the *Star Wars* series is imagined to be of high conformity with the non-legal and non-moral social norms to which humans adhere. The authors of these stories could not imagine that such robots would otherwise have been adopted for use in human societies.

Because norms of this sort are complied with (if they are complied with at all) spontaneously and unconsciously, it is hard to list them, though of course there are famous attempts to do so, mostly in guides to those interested in rising in society. The most famous examples are Castiglione's *Il Libro del Cortegiano*, about the unwritten rules of the court of the Duchy of Urbino, and Adolph Freiherr Knigge's *Über den Umgang mit Menschen*, about the norms of the nobility and bourgeoisie in Germany towards the end of the 18th century. We will see that behavioural rules of this sort, too, are such that we cannot teach them to machines.

---

16 Compare the treatment of 'appropriate emotional responses' in Mulligan (1998).

6.5 Power

We can now further refine our earlier treatment of intersubjectivity to take account of social norms in general, now including both moral and legal norms. We introduce also the ingredient of power relationships, which are an important co-variable in shaping social behaviour because they constrain which of their intentions individuals can express in their encounters with others.

As Adam Smith was the first to recognise, in all social interactions—from shaking hands in order to seal a deal, to assisting in someone's suicide, to the public dialogue between magistrate and thief that precedes the thief's being condemned to the stocks—a successful outcome requires that all parties have been able to use their social capabilities to understand the situation they are in and the norms thereby entailed. It requires also that they each use these same capabilities to understand the intentions of the other parties, and the power gradients that obtain between them (Smith 1790, I.i.1.3).

Value consciousness and the ability to integrate social norms, intersubjectivity, and power relationships consciously into a coherent, deliberate form of behaviour is a capability exclusive to humans. Animals can recognise very simple value differentials (for example between pleasure and pain) and perform elementary integrations of social norms and social rank; but they do not have the capability to apprehend values of higher order or to perform the conscious integration of values, feelings, and intentions that humans are capable of. We address in chapter 11 the implications of this for the possibility of emulating ethics in the machine.

PART II
The limits of mathematical models

7
COMPLEX SYSTEMS

Artificial intelligence agents are computable algorithms engineered to model some aspect of the behaviour that emanates from the human brain[1] or to model a functionality that might be able to cope in some way useful to humans in different sorts of environments.[2] To understand an agent of this sort, we need to understand models, computable algorithms, and complex systems. We start with models.

7.1 Models

Throughout this book we use the noun *model* and the verb *to model* in the strictly scientific sense, according to which a model is a representation of an aspect of reality that uses abstract symbols (such as mathematical equations, or drawings or sketches, or physical structures such as an orrery or an architect's physical model of a building) in order to describe, explain, or predict the aspect of reality in question (Hesse 1963). The model is not exactly isomorphic to the aspect of reality it represents. Rather it is made through a process of conscious selection from a slice of reality by using abstraction. Most models are not about the individuals which make up the relevant slice of reality, but rather about the corresponding universals. For example, a model of gravitation is not about the fall of this particular apple. It is about the force which two material bodies exert upon each other. The abstraction used in creating models

---

1 This is in some cases a very small subset of such emanations, for example those involved in playing the game of Go or a first-person-shooter videogame, or in validating an insurance claim; but it may also be the emulation of primal or objectifying intelligence.
2 See 3.3.3 and 8.8.1. We refer here to artificial intelligence as something that is realised by means of computers. Other, more esoteric ideas on how artificial intelligence might be obtained, are discussed in section 12.2.4.

DOI: 10.4324/9781003310105-9

means that they represent idealisations of reality. This does not, however, invalidate models. On the contrary, their validity—and thus their usefulness—rests precisely on their ability to abstract. This abstraction reveals aspects of reality subject to universally valid laws. The validity of mathematical models is experienced in everyday life whenever we use an electric appliance such as a toaster, a mobile phone, or a car. The best models we have are indeed those of engineered artefacts designed and made by humans, and in the course of this chapter we will understand why this is the case. Such models are called 'predictive'. For mathematical models *predict* is not restricted in its meaning to the prediction of future events (as in weather forecasting). Rather, it is used more generally to denote the calculation or computation of model output from some model input. For example, in a spam detection algorithm, the identification of a piece of spam among a body of regular email is a *prediction* in the language of mathematical modelling.[3] And similarly, in a language generation algorithm—for example a bank's computerised customer response system—the generation of an adequate response by the computer is a *prediction* in this same sense.

There can, for a number of reasons, be multiple models for any given slice of reality. First, this may be because each models a different aspect of the reality in question. Second, it may be that models contradict each other, in which case at least one of the models is invalid. Or third it may be because the models themselves have different qualities, for instance, following Hertz (1899), the qualities of utility and simplicity. A model M_1 has higher utility than model M_2 (in relation to the same slice of reality) if it 'captures more essential relations between the entities it describes'. It is simpler if it 'contains fewer empty or superfluous relations' (Hertz, op. cit., p. 39). All scientific models are models of reality. Models are representations of selected aspects of reality using symbolic elements such as sentences and equations (propositions) or other types of symbols (for example drawings, sketches) used to describe, explain, or predict aspects of reality. An orrery is a three-dimensional model of the solar system, but this system can also be described using equations.

Some models can include representations of hypothetical entities which are needed in order to maintain the coherence of the model. For example, until recently, the Higgs boson was postulated as an elementary particle type but not yet shown to exist. Other hypothetical entities, however, were eventually rejected. For example, ether as the medium of wave propagation was included in 19th-century models of physical reality.

There are also models related to works of fiction, such as a model of Arthurian legend providing interpretations of its meaning.

---

3 In artificial dialogue systems, the computation of a machine utterance based on the utterance of a human being is also a prediction from the perspective of mathematics; from a user perspective, however, it is rather simply a succeeding utterance.

7.1.1 Types of models

There are three types of models: *descriptive*, *explanatory*, and *predictive* (Weber 1988, pp. 542f.), (Hesse 1980, p. 11). Examples are: for a descriptive model, a map of a town; for an explanatory model, the pharmacodynamic model of the effect of insulin on cells; for a predictive model, a differential equation which allows us to calculate the trajectory of a missile. Each of these model types has both quantitative and qualitative subtypes. A map of a town is a qualitative descriptive model, a database listing the sizes of all vertebrate species populations living in or by a lake is a quantitative descriptive model. An interpretation of the novel *Moby Dick* is a qualitative explanatory model, Newton's laws of motion yield a quantitative predictive model of the motions of the planets.

7.1.1.1 Description

Descriptive models are often qualitative. Classical examples are Aristotle's *De motu animalorum* and Brehm's *Life of Animals*. The *Merck Manual of Diagnosis and Therapy* is another example, but the latter also has quantitative aspects (laboratory parameters, pharmacological doses). There are also exact quantitative descriptive models, such as those created through X-ray crystallography of biomolecules, or the many, many quantitative descriptive models in geology and chemistry.

7.1.1.2 Explanation

There are two types of explanations:

1. Interpretative explanation of effects of certain types, in which important causes of the effect types can be listed and the relationship between cause and effect types can be qualitatively described.
2. Full causal explanation, in which the physically relevant types of causes and their effects can be enumerated and their relationships can be modelled quantitatively and exactly using an equation or a set of equations.[4]

7.1.1.3 Prediction

Prediction refers to those cases where we can model the behaviour of a system in such a way that we have an assurance that, given an input of the sort for which the model is designed, the model will yield an output (a prediction) that is in accordance with the behaviour of the modelled system.[5] Predictive models

---

4 Note that such models also enable very exact prediction if the initial conditions can be measured with sufficient precision and the elements are observable (counterexamples are deterministic chaos and quantum phenomena).
5 In the last century, the idea of a naïve or qualitative physics was advanced as an avenue by which robots could be programmed to possess a counterpart of the commonsensical physical knowledge possessed by human beings (Hayes 1985; Smith et al. 1994; Petitot et al. 1990). This idea was

can be exact (such as the earlier differential equation example) or approximative. In the latter case they are stochastic, where a simple example is a model of the outcome of throwing a dice. All stochastic AI models, such as classical statistical learning models or deep neural networks, are of this approximatively predictive type. It is exact models that enable strict scientific knowledge, including both exact causal explanatory and exact predictive models. This is the sort of knowledge that we can obtain in physics, in chemistry, and in certain areas of biology. It is illustrated for example by the Maxwell equations, a set of coupled partial differential equations formulated on the basis of observations. Taken together with the Lorentz force law, they define the models used in classical electromagnetism, classical optics, and electric circuits.

7.1.1.4 Synoptic and adequate models

The engineered technology which surrounds us consists of systems which were designed and built on the basis of a range of different kinds of mathematical models which enable reliable engineering via predictions that are more or less exact over different temporal ranges, and therefore also more or less adequate to addressing different sorts of needs.

To enable a classification of such models according to their utility[6], we introduce the notions of *synoptic* and *adequate* models. A *synoptic* model is a model that can be used either

1. to engineer a system or system component of a specified sort (for example, a combustion engine or an artificial heart), or
2. to emulate the behaviour of a system or system component (for example, the behaviour of a tiger as emulated in a computer game, or the behaviour of a clerk in a travel agency using a chatbot).

A model is *adequate* relative to some set of specified requirements if it can be used to engineer an artefact, or to create an emulation, that satisfies all the requirements of that set.[7]

An adequate model can be either

> associated with the thesis according to which the ability of humans and animals to navigate the physical world rests not on quantitative calculations, but rather on what we can think of as a qualitative prediction—prediction of types of patterns—along the lines proposed indeed already by Turing (1952). We believe that this sort of qualitative pattern prediction is of importance, but it has no significance for our present concerns, which relate to the sorts of predictions that can be generated in the context of connectionist AI, which are in every case of a quantitative nature (based on mathematical models).

6 Of course there are considerable bodies of technology, for example in medicine and in agriculture, that are not based on mathematical models. But the bulk of the infrastructure of modern societies and all technical devices are based on such models.
7 The requirements for AI systems are described in 3.3.4.

i. almost exact, where any deviation from its predictions is so small that it is not measurable in experiments; this degree of exactitude is essential for the fulfilment of the requirements of many technical systems, such as cellphones, airplanes, cars, and so forth; or
ii. approximative, but where the deviation of the model from reality is irrelevant to the fulfilment of the requirements for the satisfaction of which the model was constructed, for example in the prediction of the efficacy of an antibiotic.

Importantly, whether a model is adequate in either of these two senses is something that can be *verified using experiments*, a property which non-predictive scientific models (produced only for purposes of description or interpretative explanation) lack.

Models are never fully exact, but many are purposefully approximative, as in statistical models used in medicine, for example of the growth and development of an infant, election polling, harvest prediction, or financial price modelling. Each of these shows a high degree of deviation of the model's predictions from the observed behaviour, and so incorporates wide error margins in its outputs.[8] That many approximative models can still be adequate to their purposes is seen in the example of the short-term weather forecast. Even though marked by significant error margins, this is still in many cases of considerable utility in addressing our needs of the moment. Long-term weather forecasts are, in contrast, in almost every case inadequate, for reasons explained later in this chapter.[9]

7.1.1.5 Comprehensive and partial models

No model of a real system is ever complete. But there are synoptic models for many logic systems, which include not only engineered devices but also natural phenomena such as the movement of the planets around the sun under the force of gravity. Such comprehensive models can explain and predict the behaviour of an entire system. On the other hand, there are many partial models of systems which try to explain or predict only certain deliberately selected aspects of the system. Models of insulin secretion by Beta cells of the pancreatic islets are one of the many such models we have. For complex systems, as we shall see in chapter 8 (sections 8.4f.), we have in most cases only partial models.

---

8 The deviations are due to the fundamentally inadequate character of the models given the complex nature of the processes they represent.
9 Another example of successful just-in-time modelling is a self-balancing robot, which achieves adequacy not by computing long-term predictions, but rather through just-in-time calculations of movements based on immediately preceding measurements. Robots of this sort use Newtonian mathematics in the broadest sense. See (Chan et al. 2013).

7.1.1.6 Explicit and implicit models

Models created by humans using symbols are explicit, and the vast majority of scientific and technical models is of this nature. But models can also be generated automatically by an algorithm, for example using mechanical theorem provers (Robinson et al. 2001), inductive logic programming (Nienhuys-Cheng et al. 2008), or statistical learning (Hastie et al. 2008). Such inductive models result from the application of an optimisation algorithm to an appropriately formulated Turing-computable problem. They can be inspected, but often not understood.[10]

7.1.2 Simulation and emulation

In the context of models, the terms *simulation* and *emulation* are often used. A *simulation* is a model of a process which imitates the unfolding of the process over time in such a way that, if data about the initial state of the process are entered as input, then data about the terminal state of the process can be inferred. Each simulation reflects the choice of certain model parameters. The aim of a simulation is to understand how changes in inputs or in model parameters change the output of the modeled system. Examples are: traffic flow simulations used to optimise the settings of traffic lights or simulations of oil flow in pipelines and refineries used to maximise capacity utilisation.

An *emulation* is the imitation of the behaviour of an entity (for example a brain, an organism, a river) by means of another entity (in the context of this book often an emulation of some human behaviour by means of a computer program or a robot). The emulation is in other words a model that behaves in response to given inputs in ways which mimic the way the emulated entity would behave in response to analogous inputs. The aim of an emulation is thus to mimic behaviour. For example, the purpose of a chatbot is to emulate the conversation behaviour of a human; the purpose of an ATM is to emulate the cash-dispensing behaviour of a traditional teller.

We now turn to the Turing machine, one of the most famous scientific models of the 20th century, which—in the version described by Turing himself (Turing 1937)—uses binary digits as symbols to abstractly model a computational machine. A 'universal Turing machine', which is a Turing machine that simulates a Turing machine on arbitrary input, is Turing-complete, which means that it can compute every Turing-computable function. What this means will be defined in greater detail in the next section.

---

10 We deal with the case of statistical learning and the problem of 'explainability' of stochastic models at 8.6.6.

7.2 Computability

When models are run on computers, they take the form of algorithms. To be executable by a computer, an algorithm must be computable. We shall see that the set of computable algorithms is a subset of all the algorithms that can be formulated in mathematical terms. But what does it mean to say that an algorithm is 'computable'? On the intuitive meaning of this term it means that the algorithm can be applied to an input to yield an output *effectively*, which means automatically, without any contribution—decision, intention, insight, intuition, ingenuity, fiddling about—from a human being. It is this interpretation of computability that is relevant to the issue of the possibility of general AI.

A general AI would not merely *supplement* or *amplify* what can be achieved by humans (so that it would be able to perform its functions only with some human in the loop). It would, rather, *replace* some activities of humans: it would then perform the relevant functions all by itself.

How, then, are we to provide a precise formal characterisation of what it is to be computable in this intuitive sense? This question was answered more than 80 years ago by Alonzo Church and Alan Turing (Church 1936; Turing 1937). Working independently, they formulated their respective definitions using different terms and methods. These definitions were, however, subsequently proved to be mathematically equivalent, and the resultant Church-Turing thesis, which has remained unchallenged ever since, states that only algorithms that can be formulated as a sequence of elementary recursive functions[11] are computable (Enderton 2010).

The most important example of non-computability in elementary mathematics was given by Turing in his very first paper on what we now call Turing machines (Turing 1937). He was addressing in this paper the problem of whether there are any purely mathematical yes-no questions that can *never* be answered by computation (the halting problem[12]), which is equivalent to the *Entscheidungsproblem* described by Church (1936). Turing proved that this problem cannot be solved when 'by computation' is taken as meaning 'by a universal computation machine' (which is modelled by what we call today the universal Turing machine). This means that there is no general possibility to determine whether a syntactically well-formed mathematical proposition can be proven or falsified.

---

11 These are: the constant, successor, and identity functions as well as the composition operator and primitive recursion.
12 This term is used to refer to the fact that, when asked to answer a question of the given sort, the computer never reaches a conclusion (so that if it was left to itself it would perform an infinite series of computations). Examples of non-decidable problems are: type inference in second-order lambda calculus, Rice's theorem, the mortal matrix problem, the group isomorphism problem, and Hilbert's tenth problem. An overview is provided at https://en.wikipedia.org/wiki/List_of_undecidable_problems

From this it follows, for example, that first-order logic is not decidable[13]—that is, a universal Turing machine cannot in general decide for a given formula of first-order logic whether it is provable or not. In theory, there are *countably many* ($\aleph_0$) Turing-computable functions, but *uncountably many* ($2^{\aleph_0}$) non-Turing-computable functions. Regularly (for example in Siegelmann et al. (1994)), claims are made that algorithms can be imagined that would allow the computation of non-Turing-computable functions and thus exceed the power of a universal Turing machine. However, for reasons which we will appreciate in a later chapter (section 12.2.2), attempts have failed even to describe how such "hypercomputation" might be realised in real-world implementations.

It follows that artificial intelligence, no matter to what problems it is applied, would have to reach its solutions by executing a set of mathematical functions that are each computable in the Church-Turing sense. This places a restriction on the sorts of programs that can be executed by a computer: they must be based on some mathematical model whose outputs are computable (Turing-computable) from their inputs. By 'mathematical model', here, we mean a model in the sense defined previously, and thus a representation of an aspect of reality that uses mathematical operations to realise some goal (the goal of its creator), often to simulate or predict the ways in which some real-world system operates.

It is important to note that *any mathematical model that runs on a Turing machine can only model comprehensively and adequately what we have called logic systems.* This is because to be computable it must be isomorphic to an algorithm which can be expressed using the basic recursive Church functions. Each model consisting of a combination of these functions is always a model of a logic system, even if the latter is used to approximate a complex system. When such a model is executed on a computer, it becomes a process of the logic system which is the computer itself, which is realised in the way the binary logic of the microprocessors and the other components of the computer operate. But this system is not a subsystem of the complex system it approximates. Rather it creates an image (in the mathematical sense), which is a function mapping from the complex system space to a logic system space.

The mathematical model predicts the behaviour of the complex system by modelling the objects and relations the creator or user of the model is interested in by means of a mathematical representation using operators applied to variables. The targets of such models range over a wide variety of phenomena as diverse as: the path of a guided missile, the movement of planets in the solar system, or the optimal slope of a roller-coaster. When such models are run inside the computer,

---

13 Note that it is semi-decidable, which means that the operations needed to assign a truth-value to a first-order logic formula can be executed on a universal Turing machine because it is complete and compact, but not decidable, because the algorithm may run into the halting problem. In practice, the resulting unterminable computations can be avoided by setting time-outs on mechanical theorem provers.

the variables are instantiated by numbers (represented as bits in the computer) and the operations described by the model are executed on these numbers to yield further numbers as outputs.[14] Note that the vast majority of useful applications of mathematics can be formulated as Turing-computable algorithms—but not all of them can.[15]

7.3 Systems

We define a *system* as a totality of dynamically interrelated elements. Every system is thus associated with some process—the system's behaviour—in virtue of which there obtains the *dynamic* interrelatedness of its elements. This process may or may not be observable, but it has in every case a directly or indirectly (via measuring instruments) observable consequence.[16] The observability of process and of result are independent of one another. The observation of the result is often designated as 'outcome' in probability theory.[17] Where dynamically interrelated entities exist, there is typically a large number of ways their behaviours can be focused on—for example depending on our interests and on the resolution of our measuring instruments. To define a system of interest we accordingly use delimitation, which is a complex process involving selection of an aggregate of elements,[18] of element types and element interactions, and of types of observable outcomes. Delimitation thereby determines the system boundaries and also the levels of granularity of the system. Once a system is delimited, further delimitations may determine also its subsystems, which are systems whose total behaviour (that is, behaviour conceived independently of delimitation) is a proper part of the total behaviour of the circumcluding system.

All of this does not, however, mean that the delimiter *creates* the system. This is seen for example in the fact that a system's elements may change their types and yet the system in question remains one and the same system. It is seen also in the fact that some systems (namely those with evolutionary properties—see 7.5.2.1)

---

14 The reason why numbers are used is because, whenever any sort of computer executes any sort of software, it always employs numbers in their binary representation. As displayed to the user, of course, the outputs can also be represented in other forms, for instance as pixels on a screen or as sound from a speaker. In the reverse direction, non-numeric inputs can of course also be turned into numbers.
15 Though, as we have seen, full first-order logic (FOL) (and higher-order logic) models are not computationally decidable, both of these are essential in mathematics and useful in philosophy, linguistics, and other areas. Most mathematical proofs cannot be stated without first-order logic.
16 As we will see later, systems are always delimited by some observer, or scientist, or other person or group interested in certain behaviours of certain elements. Therefore, there can be no system without behaviour and result.
17 Here 'observable' means perceivable directly or using measuring instruments. Some non-observable processes, such as the sensory detection of serum hormone levels in the arcuate nucleus of the hypothalamus, have outcomes which can be measured.
18 This creates what is referred to as a 'granular partition' in section 2.2.2.1.

can survive the addition or removal of elements. Rather, the delimiter chooses only how the system is delimited. *A system is in this sense a fiat entity*, comparable in this respect to postal districts or to labeled regions of the brain (Smith 1994). Where we draw its boundaries depends on our intentions and on the perspectives they determine (Johansson 1998; Smith 1994; Vogt et al. 2012). Each such delimited system can be seen as part of a larger system and as itself containing smaller subsystems, so that it is as if we can move up and down the lattice of systems until our understanding comes to an end. (At the lower end are the elementary particles; at the upper end is the entire universe.) For example, in considering the behaviour of a cell, one may see the lysosome as the subsystem in which one is interested; but one can take as one's system of interest also the entire subsystem that is responsible for the removal of cellular debris, of which the lysosome is only one element.

All systems are built out of physical elements, which can be delimited at every conceivable level of granularity, from microphysical particles to the level of entire galaxies (both of which can be observed only indirectly and by using appropriate equipment). The Milan subway system consists of elements which are its tracks, trains, ticket machines, computers, human beings (employees and passengers). Each of these elements has its own set of capabilities in virtue of which the system as a whole is able to realise its function. Some elements are realising their capabilities continuously, some only at certain times of day or night. The system elements are subject to a process of constant change: new stations may open, other stations may close, different passengers use the system, new trains are added and old trains removed. And again: within each of these elements we can potentially identify further systems, down to the level of physical particles. The behaviour of the latter, however, is not salient to our understanding of the workings of the subway, and so the system we call 'Milan subway system' is delimited in a way that leaves them out of account (Smith et al. 2002a).

In the case of the solar system, the planets and their satellites are its elements and their movements its behaviour. One sort of outcome from this behaviour takes the form of a constantly updated set of measurements resulting from observations of the constellation of these elements at given points in time; another takes the form of a single image obtained by telescope; yet another the form of a continuous stream of speech as a human observer reports what is happening in the course of a solar eclipse. The outcomes most salient for our purposes here are modelled as data, more specifically as uni- or multivariate distributions based on, for example, outputs from sensors.

An interesting family of examples of delimitation are those based on the emanations which we observe in our mental experience. It is possible to delimit the human neurophysiological system by using the granular partition that is obtained when we view this system through the lens of the common-sense ontology of the mental that is part of our shared primary theory. This delimitation picks out elements according to their involvement in mental processes such as perception, whose emanations are experiences of vision, hearing, smell, and so on, and nociceptive processes, whose emanations are pain experiences. This delimitation, however, yields a neurophysiological system for which, as we shall see, we cannot obtain models that would be adequate, for example, to replacing neuronal parts of these systems artificially at the functional level of a healthy subject.

Based on the observability of system process and outcome, we can now distinguish four types of cases:

1. Process and outcome are both directly observable: for example, when looking at a French roulette wheel.
2. Process not observable, outcome directly observable: for example, the reaction of a pocket calculator to the command 1 + 3 =.
3. Process observable, outcome indirectly observable: for example, the act of mating and the resulting initiation of pregnancy through the fertilisation of an oocyte, which at first can be observed only indirectly using serum hormone tests.
4. Process not observable, outcome indirectly observable: for example, an acid-base titration which is observed indirectly through the use of an indicator substance such as phenolphthalein.

7.4 The scope of extended Newtonian mathematics

Most processes in nature, even many seemingly simple inanimate processes, cannot be modelled mathematically. We cannot write down or automatically generate equations which describe, explain, or predict such processes accurately. For example, there is no mathematical model for true random number sequences, which is why hardware random number generators transducing a physical process are needed to generate such sequences.

The class of problems in relation to which mathematical modelling has been singularly successful in generating exact or almost exact predictions belongs to the domain of physics. Only what we shall call 'extended Newtonian mathematics'—by which we mean the classical differential calculus as supplemented by fields such as statistical mechanics, differential geometry and its applications (complemented by the general theory of relativity, as well as by certain methods used in AI such as propositional and predicate logic and graph theory[19])—can yield exact predictions. In short, extended Newtonian mathematics comprises the entirety of those mathematical resources that have the

---

19 Note that quantum mechanics is not included in this list, since it cannot yield exact point predictions as outputs, but only distributions.

sort of predictive power first unleashed by the invention by Newton and Leibniz of the differential calculus.

Initially, mathematical modelling methods taken from classical geometry were successfully applied to the prediction of astronomical phenomena. When considered from the perspective of present-day mathematics, however, these early achievements appear trivial. It was with Newton and Leibniz in the 17th century that the enormous potential of mathematics for the explanation and prediction of physical events, including the exact prediction of astronomical events, first began to be revealed. Working independently, both Newton and Leibniz developed the method of differential equations and showed that this method could be used to create a type of quantitative apparatus that was capable not merely of describing but also of explaining and predicting physical phenomena—namely those physical phenomena relating to continuous motion of bodies along straight lines or smooth curves (McCauley 1993, p. 7).

Where Leibniz developed the calculus from the perspective of a pure mathematician, establishing the rudiments of both the integral and the differential calculus, Newton was interested in applications, and out of practical interest in the laws of nature he showed how the effect of gravitation on a material body can be fully modelled (described, explained, and predicted) using a solvable differential equation. Predictions can be made on this basis of the time it will take for a falling body to reach the earth or of whether a small body moving in a continuous line through space will be captured by the gravitational field of a second, much larger body.

For differential equations to be solvable, two conditions must be satisfied:

1. the phenomena they represent must be *continuous*, in other words they must be phenomena that can be graphed as progressing along straight lines, smooth curves or as manifolds. (For example: the trajectory of a missile, the ideal flight route of a plane given the curvature if the earth, the propagation of heat in a homogeneous material.[20])
2. there must be a *limited number of interacting variables* in the phenomena they model.

Physical systems described with ordinary differential equations involve only one variable. Systems described with partial differential equations involve two, or at most very few, variables.[21]

An example of a law of nature that can be expressed as an ordinary differential equation is Newton's second law of motion, which describes the movement of a

---

20 In this case we have propagating manifolds of continuously increasing sise, where the manifolds are smoothly curved two-dimensional surfaces. Manifolds may also be of higher dimensions, as in the case of the general theory of relativity.
21 Solvable partial differential equations rarely involve more than 4 to 5 variables (Nandakumaran et al. 2020).

particle under constant force:

$$F = m\frac{dv}{dt} \tag{7.1}$$

where F is force, m mass, v velocity, and t time.

An example of a partial differential equation is the so-called heat equation developed by Fourier in 1822, which describes the distribution of a quantity in a solid body along a gradient, as for example when heat propagates through a metal cube:

$$\frac{\partial u}{\partial t} = \alpha \left(\frac{\partial^2 u}{\partial x^2} + \frac{\partial^2 u}{\partial y^2} + \frac{\partial^2 u}{\partial z^2} \right) \tag{7.2}$$

Here $u(x, y, z, t)$ is the heat at a point defined by the three spatial coordinates x, y, and z; t is time; and α is the diffusivity of the medium. This equation can be solved analytically (using Fourier series or fundamental solutions) due to its mathematical properties. Other important examples of differential equations are the Maxwell equations, which model classical electromagnetic fields. They are used in many applications of such fields, for example in wireless communication via mobile phone.

A large part of the body of technically useful applied mathematics (physics, chemistry[22], engineering) is based on the use of such equations, which yield an incredibly powerful tool for modelling phenomena in the inanimate parts of nature. This paradigm has changed our world and created the technosphere in which we live today. We rely on the differential calculus for the design and control of all pumps, drains, dams, and all water and heat and air conditioning supply systems that sustain our lives. It is only with the help of the differential calculus that we can now not only predict the motions of heavenly bodies but also design and control space vehicles that fly under our direction through the cosmos on the basis of calculations of thrust that we make by using the ideal rocket equation (Perko 2013).

7.4.1 Applicability of the differential calculus

Some differential equations can be solved exactly using standard methods from calculus. But many cannot. Using computers, however, a subset of these can be solved via very good approximations (which yield predictions accurate enough that they can be used reliably in practical applications). The solutions are then 'almost exact' in the sense defined in section 7.1.1.4.

Such solutions are obtained, for example, by representing the interval on which the solution is sought as a discrete grid in such a way that the needed smooth

---

22 Chemistry, of course, also operates with the laws of physics.

progressions can be approximated to each cell of the grid. The differential function is then represented using finite difference equations which approximate the derivatives in each cell. Together, they yield a system of equations which can be solved using standard linear algebra on matrices or numerical procedures. All these steps can be formulated as Turing-computable recursive functions. Where analytical solutions which can be obtained by applying the laws of calculus yield exact predictions, numerical solutions are not exact, but they are often still predictive in the sense of Weber (because they are, again, 'almost exact').

Only certain sorts of systems allow the models that can predict their behaviour almost exactly. We refer to such systems as *logic systems* because they can be successfully modelled using propositions of mathematics linked together by logical relations. Such systems satisfy the following four conditions[23] (Thurner et al. 2018, pp. 2f.):

- The system behaviour can be explained by reference only to one of the four fundamental interactions of *gravity*, *electromagnetic force*, and the *weak* and *strong nuclear force*.
- The system behaviour of interest is dominated by a single homogeneous and isotropic force in such a way that the effects of the other interactions are so small, in the context of the modelled aspect, that they can be neglected.[24] If there is more than one relevant force in a system, for example gravity and electromagnetic force, their effects can be modelled separately, given that each force dominates relative to its effects on corresponding separate aspects of the system's behaviour. The interaction with other forces can be neglected (Thurner et al. 2018, pp. 2f).
- In each system there are groups consisting of elements of the same type. The elements of each such group interact with each other in an identical manner, and they also interact with the elements of other such groups again in an identical manner (which may be different for different groups). All interaction patterns are in this sense homogeneous. For example, in the solar system, the sun and the planets can be seen as a group of elements (of type: lump of matter) which interact via gravitation. But the sun is a star and the earth, Mars, as well as the other satellites of the sun are planets, and the sun (seen as a star) also interacts with these satellites through its electromagnetic radiation.
- The boundary conditions of the system can be assumed to be fixed without invalidating the model, so that the system can be considered to be context-

---

23 Note that this class consists of systems at different granularity levels including many composed of entire subsystems that can be modelled separately. For example, the solar system is a gravitation system, but the gravitational field of the earth with its natural and artificial satellites, is a more fine-grained sub-system of the former.
24 A force is homogeneous if it acts everywhere and at every time in the same way. A force is isotropic if it is uniform in all orientations.

free, and thus the context in which the system is embedded can be abstracted away without detriment to the predictive power of the model.

Even given the vast range of successful applications of the differential calculus in physics and engineering, the class of logic systems with all four of these properties is rather small.[25] The overwhelming majority of systems in the universe, and even of the systems that we encounter in our daily lives, are what we shall learn to identify as *complex systems*.[26] The predictive power of physics manifests itself in the realm of what we called *technically useful applied mathematics* (physics, chemistry, and engineering). It is this that has enabled the creation of composite systems, such as aircraft, made up of many subsystems, most of which—including all of those related to the process of flight itself[27]—are modelled exactly to yield the overall reliability that we have come to expect of all modern vehicles.

Clearly, however, very many of the systems we encounter in nature, including the global climate and plate tectonic systems, and almost all the systems we encounter in the realm of living organisms, are complex. This means that *they cannot be modelled in a way that would yield the sorts of mathematical predictions that can be reliably used in technological applications* (Thurner et al. 2018, p. 5). This applies not merely to the many single-organism systems inside your body and to multi-organism systems such as an ant colony or a troop of monkeys. It applies also to hybrid human-technology systems such as the New York Stock Exchange. Consider, now, the case of models for self-driving cars. Algorithms used here are adequate where the software is able to model the sensory input deriving from traffic events through sensors (camera, radar, lidar, sonar) in such a way that it reacts to this input, given the destination, at least as well as (or, realistically, better than) the average human; otherwise self-driving cars will cause more accidents than cars driven by humans, and this will be deemed unacceptable.

Sensors react to changing physical conditions by relaying electrical signals that carry information about the environment. A characteristic feature of the sensors and other engineering components embedded in the car is that they have been thoroughly tested in experiments. On the basis of these experiments the manufacturer guarantees that the sensor realises a mathematical model enabling it to detect physical changes of given types and relay corresponding information to the user with a certain specified (high) degree of reliability and accuracy. To say that the sensor-input processing model is *adequate* means that it has

---

25 Note that the general theory of relativity and the Schrödinger equation also model such systems.
26 Introductions to complex systems from the perspective of physics are given in: (Thurner et al. 2018; Fieguth 2017).
27 Non-core systems, such as the climatisation unit, may be modelled with less care.

been tested and validated to yield output to the degree of reliability and accuracy specified for the purpose for which it is used.

Something similar holds if, for example, we want to automate the processing of business documents, another AI task. Here, we need a model which can interpret the meaning of the text in order to apply to it the appropriate business logic; otherwise payments may be misrouted and customers lost. For example, the sentence "I withdraw herewith yesterday's cancellation of the contract" should not be interpreted as a cancellation. Here, too, we want our model to be exactly predictive, and thus the model must be mathematical in nature (very roughly: it will assign numerical values to features of the textual units that are being processed). For any given type of document we can predict, from the structure of the model, which interpretation it will assign to which sentences in the document. The relevant laboratory test in this case is to run the software on a representative sample of documents and verify manually that it is performing correct assignments of meaning. Only then will we deploy the model in a real-world business environment.

And similarly in medicine. If we want to use AI, for example for therapeutic decision support, then inaccurate modelling may harm or kill patients. The models must accordingly output treatment recommendations that are at least as accurate as those made by the best physicians in any given discipline, and the relevant test is to run the software on a sample of phenotypic inputs and verify manually that it is producing on this basis outputs of acceptable accuracy.

It must be noted that even adequate models may deviate from reality. Even if the model gives a full account of the patterns of behaviour of the system, the starting conditions—the variables that get plugged into the equations—are not exactly measured and the measurement error may multiply as we apply a sequence of differential equations. This is the reason why we cannot model a double pendulum (an example of what is called 'deterministic chaos' to which we shall return in 7.5.2.7).

7.5 Complex systems

For general AI, the goal is to create a computable model of the behaviour of important aspects of the human mind-body continuum (or perhaps better: of the human mind-body-environment continuum[28]), thereby enabling an emulation of intelligent human behaviour. But the mind-body continuum is a complex system (it is indeed a complex system of complex systems, at many levels). Thus, if our ability to create mathematical models of complex systems is severely limited, then so also is our ability to create the computable models that would be needed to create general AI.

---

28 This is an example of the intricacies involved in the setting of system boundaries (see 7.3).

Consider, for instance, the realm of dialogue engines. If our goal is to create a chatbot that will provide a pleasant diversion to its users in the manner of Xiaoice (see section 10.4.1), then we can dispense with exact computable models of the sort described. If, however we wish to build a general AI that can be incorporated into technological artefacts—for example into a medical device or an autonomous jet fighter or a free-moving factory robot—then the exactness achieved by predictive mathematical models is indispensable. This holds, where the AI is to be incorporated into a sociotechnical artefact such as a surgical theatre or a nuclear power station. And it holds, *a fortiori*, where the artefact we have in mind is the sort of digital continuation of a human being which transhumanists have in mind when they talk of 'digital immortality'.

7.5.1 History of the concept of complex systems

One of the first to argue that for all animate systems we are unable to create predictive models was Henri Bergson in 1907.[29] In part under Bergson's influence, the mathematics of complex systems was pioneered by Ilya Prigogine in his work on what he called 'dissipative structures', specifically in his *Introduction to Thermodynamics of Irreversible Processes* (Prigogine 1955).[30] Prigogine identified many mathematical properties of complex systems, for example relating to the ways in which such systems exhibit processes which involve a constant passage away from equilibrium, which we address in the following sections. These processes are illustrated everywhere in biology, for example during the early stages of differentiation in embryogenesis, where they give rise to the structures responsible for the realisation of all the functions of the organism (Prigogine et al. 1973).

We note in passing that complex systems are of considerable interest from the perspective of the philosophy of science, and have accordingly received a good deal of attention from philosophers, and this has resulted in interesting insights

---

29 Bergson writes: 'The intellect is characterised by a natural inability to comprehend life. ... It treats everything mechanically' (Bergson 1911, p. 182).

30 As Gunter (1991, p. 121) points out, Bergson's metaphysics rests on a duality between 'life' and 'matter'. For Bergson, life is headed towards ever higher levels of development while matter becomes increasingly degraded. Bergson hereby reveals his adherence to the classical concept of entropy employed by Boltzmann. For Prigogine, in contrast, 'real creativity' (the sort of spontaneity that is found far from equilibrium) has been found in nature, or, rather, in matter. In a letter to Gunter from May 1, 1989, Prigogine states:

> In short, Bergson's direction of thought was to oppose life and matter. My view is that life is deeply rooted in matter whenever the instability of dynamical systems and, closely related to this, autocatalytic reactions are taken into account.

We therefore find in Prigogine's work, what Gunter refers to as a 'naturalised' variant of Bergson's metaphysics, in which we can postulate a 'creative evolution' ('évolution créatrice' in Bergson's words) without recourse to agencies outside of physical and chemical nature.

into various aspects of these systems.[31] Here, however, we concentrate on complex systems theory from the perspective of physics, because the central question of this book is the possibility of the emulation of the most complex single-organism complex system on earth, namely the human mind-body continuum.

7.5.2 Properties of complex systems

We are now in a position where we can identify the precise challenges involved in the modelling of complex systems that would be needed to fulfil the purposes of AGI. We do this by

a. identifying what is characteristic of *complex systems* using the definition of 'system' given in 7.3,
b. reviewing the models that are available for the mathematical representation of such systems, and
c. identifying the limitations of such representations for AGI purposes.

Starting with (a), the properties characteristic of complex systems can be described as follows.

7.5.2.1 Change and evolutionary character

The logic systems addressed in 7.4.1—for example, engineered artefacts or simple physical systems such as the solar system—are referred to by physicists as 'simple dynamical systems' (Thurner et al. 2018, pp. 5f.). The types of relations among the elements of such systems do not change over time, and so the types of behaviours manifested by these elements are given and fixed.

In complex systems, in contrast, *the types of inter-element relations can change from one time to the next as a consequence of the workings of the system.* One feature of complex systems is thus that they are systems whose elements can, over time, change their behaviour in the strong sense that they change the *types* of their behaviour (Thurner et al. 2018, p. 7f.).

This is due to the evolutionary character of complex systems.

As Thurner et al. (Thurner et al. 2018) point out, the process of evolution has three steps:

> 1. A new thing comes into existence within a given environment. 2. The new thing has the chance to interact with its environment. The result of this interaction is that it gets selected (survives) or is destroyed. 3. If the

---

31 Overviews are provided in Haugeland (1993), Wimsatt (1994), Mitchell (2009), and Ladyman et al. (2013), and there are attempts to define a 'theory of complexity' from a philosophical perspective; see Chu et al. (2003) as an example.

new thing gets selected in the environment, it becomes part of this environment (boundary) and thus transforms the old environment into a new one. New and arriving things in the future will experience the new environment.
(Thurner et al. 2018, pp. 14f.)

Many complex systems have evolutionary properties in this sense: they are evolutionary systems. A system is delimited by its boundaries, which are located at the interface between each last element belonging to the system and the corresponding part of its surrounding environment.[32] For example, a vinegar fly *(Drosophila melanogaster)* is a complex system at various levels of granularity, and its boundary is the limit of its body.[33]

Evolutionary systems are adaptive and robust at the same time, a phenomenon that is very hard to model because robustness requires lack of divergence from a fixed set of states while adaptation requires the exploration of new phase spaces. Evolutionary systems are also such as to manifest path-dependence in their development and thus show a strong and long-lasting memory (in the sense that the relation of their present to their past cannot be captured using Markov models). Such systems are therefore both *non-ergodic* (they cannot be modelled by averaging over space and time without losing information) and *non-Markovian* (their behaviour depends not just on one or two immediately preceding steps). The lack of ergodicity is, as we shall see, one of the chief obstacles to using stochastic AI for complex systems.

Note that systems with evolutionary properties keep their identity when they lose or gain an element. For example, neither the loss of a kidney nor the gain of an organ graft need affect the continued existence of the human being involved. Such systems are identity invariant over element change. Their elements do not form a *set*, which is not identity invariant against element change, but rather a totality (or what in Basic Formal Ontology is called an *object aggregate* (Arp et al. 2015)).

The human organism is a complex system that is made up of many, many complex systems at successively lower levels of granularity. As the philosopher Roman Ingarden, a member of the school of realist phenomenologists referred to already in chapter 1, expressed the matter, each multi-cellular organism is a relatively isolated system of a very high order, containing many, likewise relatively isolated, systems of lower and lower levels, which are hierarchically ordered and variously situated within the organism, and are at the same time both partially interconnected and also partially segregated. As a consequence, each system at each granularity level can exercise its specific functions

---

32 This also applies to alien systems that exist inside other host systems. For example, the cyst in the liver caused by the parasite *echinococcus granulosus* is delimited by the host's liver tissue.
33 When a technical system is embedded inside a complex system, for example a combined pacemaker defibrillator that can transmit electromagnetic waves to some external receiver (alerting system) is inserted into a human body, this does not change the boundaries of the host system.

relatively undisturbed and at the same time regulate its behaviour in tandem with the behaviour of the systems with which it is laterally associated (Ingarden 1983).

In particular, the human cognitive system comprises billions of elements (neurons) each made up of hundreds of thousands of molecular elements that are distinguished further for example by their glycosylation and phosphorylation states. A typical neuron contains some 100 trillion atoms forming some 100 thousand different types of RNA molecules (Wu et al. 2014). New element types in the nervous system arise when novel types of memories are stored, and new element combinations and relations arise when new synapses are formed. All of these elements have their own complex system-specific properties, which provide the material basis for the gamut of human behavioural and cognitive dispositions that are realised in human cognitive activity.

And to make things worse, this activity takes place in very many cases in a social context, thereby forming even more complex *social* systems, whose elements are single human beings interacting with each other. When a human being evolves new properties, for example by learning a new skill, this may lead to a change in the social system of which this human is an element. The evolutionary property of the social system is thereby also reflected in changes in the contexts of its constituent human elements.

In contrast to this, consider the case of the solar system,[34] when an asteroid is caught by the gravitational pull of a planet and starts to orbit around it. The system would thereby gain a new element. But it would gain no new element type, no new interaction types, and undergo no change in its context-independence.

7.5.2.2 Element-dependent interaction

When bodies are related to each other in the sorts of logic systems described in classical physics, for example through the force of gravitation, their interaction is homogeneous and not specifically related to the bodies involved—it depends only on the mass of the bodies and on the distance between them. In contrast to this, the elements of complex systems have relations specific to their nature, the interaction types are dependent on the types of the elements they relate.

Examples from biology   Consider, for example, the protein phosphorylation system, which is of central importance in biology since it is the major mechanism by which protein functioning in the cell is regulated. This regulation occurs in response to internal and external signals of many different kinds, deriving (for example) from hormones, light, or the chemicals that transmit messages between neurons and from neurons to muscles. Simplifying somewhat, the

---

34 When seen as a gravitational system, this is a natural logic system.

phosphorylation system has three elements: a kinase, a protein, and a compound called ATP.[35] The system operates when the kinase uses ATP to add a phosphate group to a hydrogen site of the protein, thereby transforming the protein's biochemical properties, for example allowing it to modify the behaviour of an ion channel. And to give an example from pathophysiology: mis-phosphorylation of the proteins which regulate the cell cycle can lead to cancer.

As a second example of a system of biological interactions consider the myocyte, a type of cell that makes up the bulk of our muscles. The myocyte is related inside the organism to many different types of cells through both hormonal and electro-chemical signals. After a meal, for example, myocytes receive chemical signals in the form of insulin molecules synthesised by the beta cells in the pancreas. When a myocyte receives such a signal, this brings about the transport of glucose from the blood into the cytosol inside the myocyte.

Most interesting for our purposes here is the role played by myocytes as elements in the body's kinetic system. When, for example, we are typing on a keyboard, myocytes in different parts of our body receive electrochemical signals from motor neurons. This creates the patterns which direct the muscles of the shoulders, arms, and fingers to contract and relax in those specific ways which lead to our exerting pressure on corresponding sequences of keys.

The digestive and kinetic cases each gives rise to a set of interaction types that are highly specific for the myocyte; other cells cannot react to the hormonal or electrochemical signals myocytes are sensitive to. The myocyte itself undergoes internal reorganisation depending on the environment it is in. For example, when it undergoes regular phases of insufficient oxygen supply, the myocyte will alter itself by building up more mitochondria and more myoglobin as a means of storing oxygen in readiness for energy production peaks. This process can be seen as a form of training of the myocyte, and it does indeed often occur—in the form of increased muscle strength—as a consequence of physical training activities of the entire body.

We see from these and many similar examples that complex biological systems may display many different interaction types, even for one and the same system element.

Whether a model is valid is established by determining its ability to predict the outcomes of controlled experiments on systems of a given type. We can make no exact models of this sort for most aspects of biological systems—in contrast to what is the case for logic systems, that is, of those systems which can be predictively modelled using the laws of physics—because biological systems are complex systems.

---

35 Adenosine triphosphate is a universal energy carrier of cells. In some processes guanosine triphosphate (GTP) and flavin adenine dinucleotide (FAD(H$_2$)) are also used as energy sources; the latter is an electron source in many redox reactions.

Functional change in complex systems In complex systems such as we find in biology, the function of a system element can change[36] and interact with its state. To understand what this means, we need to define what is meant by the *state* of a system.

First, we note that we can divide the properties of systems and system elements into two groups; those that are invariant, and those that change over time. *A state of a system element at a given time is the set of measurable values of the non-invariant properties of the system at that time.* A state is thus a vector instance of measurable values. For example, in classical mechanics, the state of a centre of mass of a body is given by its location and momentum. In this context, the shape of the body is invariant. In quantum mechanics (where the system elements can only be observed as probabilities), the state of a physical system is given by the corresponding normed state vector in Hilbert space.

Importantly, in a logic system, whether natural or artificial, an element can change its state but not its type. For example, the gravitational force a planet exerts on other bodies depends solely on its mass, no matter which state of matter it is in. As we saw, however, in the sorts of complex systems we find in biology *elements can dynamically change their function*, and when such changes occur this interacts with their state. What this means is that when the function of an element, for example a membrane protein of a myocyte, changes due to phosphorylation, then this brings about changes in the set of its measurable non-invariant property values. It can acquire new states due to the functional change. The former are dynamically dependent on the latter. There is no way to model this sort of change mathematically for many elements and states at the same time, which is why models of complex systems can model, at best, only certain narrow aspects of a system's behaviour (see 8.7).

7.5.2.3 Force overlay

All system behaviour, including the behaviour of complex systems, is the result of the four basic physical interactions (electromagnetic, gravitational, strong, and weak). But these forces interact with each other and are overlaid upon each other in such a complicated way in complex systems that it is impossible to model how the observed behaviour of such systems is generated. This is already the case for the biomolecules (proteins) of the simplest (and oldest) single-celled organisms, namely the prokaryotic archaea. With these proteins, they are able, for example, to autonomously create energy from matter via biochemical reactions such as methanogenesis (Conrad 1999). Using all that we know about the four interactions and about the amino acid sequences of the constituent proteins of these organisms, we

---

36 We define the function of an element as a disposition to realise processes whose realisation provides the reason for the existence of the element. In the case of living systems this means: properties that have arisen through evolution. In the case of engineered logic systems (artefacts) it means: properties that are essential to the artefact's design (Spear et al. 2016).

can indeed describe and (to some extent) explain what happens when these proteins are folded and modified. But we can predict neither when nor how these processes will occur nor how the resultant modified proteins will behave (Li et al. 2018).

What we are describing here is *force overlay*, a phenomenon that is present in all animate (but not in all inanimate[37]) complex systems. Consider the New York Stock Exchange (NYSE), a complex system made up of humans and physical (including digital) infrastructure, which is connected to the entire world via the events which influence the prices of stocks. Information generated in the NYSE is rendered on computer screens and is perceived by humans. Humans use their fingers and keyboards to initiate further processes (buying and selling), resulting in changes in what appears on computer screens, which are perceived and cognitively processed by other humans in successive cycles.

Since all system elements are made of matter, so all interactions of these elements are ultimately governed by the four fundamental interactions. This is also true for those legal entities, such as collateralised loan obligations and other securities, which are not made of matter but which exist as *bona fide* social entities because there exist associated physical artefacts (paper, contracts, computer files, database entries), which are created and maintained by humans. But more trivially, the buying and selling processes include, among much else, fingers depressing keys. These processes result from fundamental forces acting where a fingertip meets the key surface. The electromagnetic forces that are at work where light waves (from computer screens) trigger the brain activity in the minds of the floor brokers, which then leads to ion fluxes and protein conformation changes in their neurons and, ultimately, to selling or buying decisions. All these activities are governed by the four forces. But we have no idea how this happens. Billions of variables are involved even in the brain of a single broker and the forces involved are continuously overlaid. Worse than that, the brokers interact not only with the information they receive but also with each other. And yet more overlaying forces derive from their interactions with their families, their friends and enemies, the weather, the traffic on their daily commute, and many more. There is no way to model mathematically what is going on here in any exact way.

7.5.2.4 Complex phase space

We have defined a state of a system as the measurable values of its non-invariant properties at a given point in time. System elements instantiate types (element types). For example, in the system 'ampul of pure water', the elements are water molecules and we view the element type *molecule of water* as a universal. Each element type has its own specific state (an electron, for instance, has a state differing from that of a blood cell or of a planet). The state of a given element type forms the basis of the phase space for that type (which is a vector space). This

---

37 See section 7.5.2.5.

space has as many dimensions as the number of distinct state variables an element of the space can have. For example, the ideal (simple gravity) pendulum has a two-dimensional phase space with the two state variables *angle* and *angular velocity*. Each element of this space (each ideal pendulum) can be represented with a vector of state scalar instances of those variables, the latter changing as the pendulum moves. The variables in this space are determined by the way the system is modelled mathematically, and thus in any given case it consists of a finite set of measurable values.

Complex systems have a rich phase space, which is to say that the set of all elements and their states that would be needed to describe the entire workings of the system is very large. Some directly observable macrostates such as temperature, pressure, or density are explainable exhaustively from microstates at lower granular levels (for example, from states of molecules in Brownian motion). The former, in other words, can be predicted from the latter. In complex systems, however, we observe macrostates that emerge in a fashion that cannot be predicted or derived from knowledge about the microstates which compose them. For example, we cannot adequately model regional or global average temperatures (a macrostate) from the microstates of the earth's climate system in the case where adequacy would mean that the model could predict the temperature time series with good accuracy over decades.

7.5.2.5 Drivenness

Complex systems are often *driven* in the technical sense that is defined in physics (more precisely in statistical mechanics). Driven systems undergo a flow of energy, which prevents them from converging or moving to an equilibrium; the energy flow pushes them ever onward from one state to the next.

A classical equilibrium system is the chemical equilibrium achieved immediately when, for example, chloride gas is dissolved in water to yield hydrochloric acid:

$$HCl + H_2O \rightleftharpoons H_3O^+ + Cl^- \tag{7.3}$$

The left hand side of the equation shows the hydrogenated acid and water molecules, which are in equilibrium with the right hand side—the reactants, namely H_3O^+ kations (positively charged ions) and the Cl^- anions (negatively charged ions).[38]

The fact that the logic system is in a state of equilibrium means that there is *no energy gradient* between the two sides of the equation and that the stochiometry will stay as it is in the absence of further external effects. An example of a non-

---

38 The stochiometry of the molecules and ions in equilibrium (how many molecules and ions of which kinds there are) depends on the acid dissociation constant

$$K_a = \frac{[Cl^-][H^+]}{[HCl]} \tag{7.4}$$

driven system converging to equilibrium is a natural pendulum (such as a child swinging on a swing), which stops swinging after a while, thereby reaching its equilibrium (when it is standing still) unless some external momentum is exerted, which might be an adult pushing the swing.

In contrast to this, systems which are out of equilibrium display 'flows of energy through [them which] make these systems do things they would never do in equilibrium, such as produce convective currents or turbulence'. (Thurner et al. 2018, p. 86). And further: 'Complex systems are often so-called driven systems, where the system is driven away from its equilibrium states. ... The mathematical difficulties in dealing with out-of-equilibrium or non-equilibrium systems are tremendous and beyond analytical reach'.

Therefore, driven systems do not reach an equilibrium but consume energy to move through a series of states in a process which ends only when their (external or internal) sources of energy run dry.[39]

Driven systems in the sense of statistical mechanics are characterised by the energy flowing through them: if one process (the energy source) 'charges' the system and another (the energy sink) 'discharges' it, it is called driven (Thurner et al. 2018). Such systems are dissipative, which means that there is inside them a process that distributes energy.[40] Thurner, et al. summarise as follows:

> With the exception of a few physical phenomena, virtually all processes that take place on this planet, including the entire biosphere and the anthroposphere, are driven non-equilibrium processes. Systems in equilibrium are the exception in nature and exist practically only in laboratories or for systems at relatively short timescales. Any machine, say an electric drill, is a driven dissipative system. ... The energy fed into the system will eventually be converted to work and heat, which dissipate into the environment. The energy source of the earth is the sun, and its energy sink is the approximately 3° Kelvin background radiation of the universe.
>
> (Thurner et al. 2018, p. 86)

Minimally complex systems To illustrate drivenness, Thurner et al. provide the example of a steam engine as a complex system with this feature. The engineer does not describe the workings of a steam engine by using differential equations to describe the motions of each one of its many different sorts of parts. Rather, he provides

---

39 It is due to this lack of convergence to equilibrium that the fixed-point equations used in chemistry for equilibrium (logic) (such as equation (7.4) in footnote 38) cannot be used to model complex systems.

40 When in equilibrium, such systems (which are 'logic systems' in the terminology we proposed earlier) obey the fluctuation-dissipation theorem from quantum mechanics (Band et al. 2012). This states that the reaction of a system in thermal equilibrium to a very small external disturbance is identical to a spontaneous fluctuation, where the dissipating (energy-distributing) effect of this reaction is directly proportional to the fluctuation. This theorem does not hold of driven systems.

a list of rules regarding how the dynamics of the system updates its states and future interactions, which then lead to new constraints on the dynamics at the next time step. First, pressure builds up here, then a valve opens there, vapour pushes this piston, then this valve closes and opens another one, driving the piston back, and so on.

(Thurner et al. 2018, p. 7)

The steam engine, however, though it is a complex system, is a complex system of a very basic sort because it operates with a fixed set of elements (its component parts), which remain always of the same type, and it has fixed inputs of water and coal. Thus it is a merely dissipative system, though one that is driven by an external force (of heat, gained in traditional steam engines from burning coal). Its dissipation does not affect its function, which can be modelled abstractly as a logic system with a strictly mechanical behaviour using Newtonian mathematics. But this is to leave out of account the way in which energy dissipates in the system, which creates entropy by reducing the level of organisation of the coal and water that is consumed, in a process that cannot be predictively modelled at the level of the molecules involved.

Similar remarks hold for the *computer*, another energy-dissipating system. As Landauer showed in 1961, the erasure of memory contents in computers requires heat dissipation, which makes the process logically irreversible (Landauer 1961).[41] Computers are driven devices which consume energy needed for their functioning and thereby dissipate heat. However, if they are sufficiently cooled, this dissipation does not impede their function. Ladyman et al. (2007) confirmed Landauer's results 50 years later by showing that the logical irreversibility of logical transformations 'implies thermodynamic irreversibility of every corresponding machine' that performs such transformations.

We now look in more detail at more examples of driven systems in animate and inanimate nature.

Driven animate systems In inanimate driven systems, the energy comes from an external source—for example, the aforementioned swing is driven only so long as the child or adult uses energy to exert force to keep it in motion. In animate systems, this energy is produced by the organism itself by *actively exploiting* external sources of energy.[42] Aristotle was perhaps the first to observe this fundamental difference between inanimate and living nature, and he called it entelechy (ἐντελεξία), which can be translated as 'inner drive',

---

41 He concluded: 'Actual devices which are far from minimal in size and operate at high speeds will be likely to require a much larger energy dissipation to serve the purpose of erasing the unnecessary details of the computer's past history'. Indeed, the cooling of a typical larger data centre today continually consumes 40–50 MW per hour Werner 2017.
42 For details see 9.1.1.1.

something which in his view is always directed towards some ideal goal (τέλος).[43] On the modern view of drivenness, in contrast, the sole goals to the attainment of which the organism strives are: (a) to maintain itself in existence over its own limited lifespan and (b) to maintain certain of its molecules in existence thereafter—namely those whose structure is *inheritable* (its DNA)—in new organisms of the same type as themselves.[44]

In both of these cases, the drive is not towards an equilibrium, but rather towards the maintenance of a specific order between the organism and its environment—the order in which life is maintained through survival and reproduction. In the case of human beings, this drive manifests itself in excess drivenness, which ultimately (as a result of a complicated chain of neurophysiological processes) manifests itself in the form of intentions. This is a feature exclusive to humans which has evolved to fill the gap opened by the much lower level of instinctive behaviour on our part as compared to all other organisms.

So long as the organism lives, its inner drive works counter to the second law of thermodynamics (to the effect that the entropy of a system increases over time). As Mora (1963, p. 216) puts it: 'Living processes persist to a degree improbable in a physical system. ... They *draw negative entropy from their environment* consistently' (emphasis added).[45] Once life has ceased, however, the organism degrades down to its chemical components as a result of the impacts of physical forces, including those exerted via other life forms such as bacteria, fungi, worms, and insects.

The drivenness of living organisms is *essential*; it is inherent to our form of existence. It manifests itself in the organism as a whole, but also in its parts, for example in the drive of spermatogonia to generate spermatocytes, in the permanent, survival-critical generation of replacement cells in the bone marrow, the skin and the endothelia, and in the constant activity of the respiratory system and the heart. It can also be pathological, as in the case of a cancer growing inside someone's body, where the criteria of essential, animate drivenness (ATP synthesis from matter for survival) are also satisfied.

The human central nervous system is the most complex single-organism-based animate system on earth. Its workings are complex in something like the way in which the processes of water flowing in a brook are complex, where the water, its solutes, and its dispersed substances never stop moving.[46] But in the brain what is flowing are molecules with electrochemical properties, and these, too, never stop moving. And the brook in which they flow is a

---

43 The molecular biologist Mora (1963) refers to drivenness in animate systems using the term 'urge' (which he derives from Spinoza's *conatus*)
44 Note that all animate systems have drivenness, but only humans have excess drive (3.1.2).
45 By 'physical system' Mora means what in our terminology is called a logic system.
46 The system to which the water flowing in the brook belongs is driven as well, but by an external force, gravitation.

gigantic interwoven mesh of billions of molecules that are themselves constantly in flux as ever new experiences lay down new connections between them and introduce new and dispersed molecules into the flow.

Driven inanimate systems Living organisms (and societies and organised collections of living organisms) are not the sole driven complex systems. Drivenness in also found in inanimate complex systems, where it takes two forms: *natural* and *artificial*.

In the *first category*, we find the earth's water cycle (rain → percolation → water source → evaporation → rain) and the perpetual activity of winds, both of which are driven by solar energy. Another important example is the geothermal system of the earth, which is driven by the energy remaining from the original formation of the planet combined with the energy resulting from the radioactive decay of long-lived radionuclides (Gando et al. 2011). Such systems receive energy from the outside, which flows through them and is then dissipated into the external environment thereby, again, creating entropy (Thurner et al. 2018, 2.5.4). Most processes in nature display energy gradients of this sort between what is inside and what is outside the relevant system. This holds for example of processes of glacier formation, and of all other weather processes such as cloud or hurricane formation. It holds, too, of the formation of subterranean water reservoirs, the flow of water into which eventually yields pressure which manifests itself in the emergence of river headwaters.

To the *second category* (that of artificial drivenness) belong the water evaporation pattern of a steam engine, which is driven by the energy deriving from burning coal; the fuel-burning pattern in an internal combustion engine; or the chain reaction in a nuclear reactor. This drivenness is *accidental*, because it exists only for as long as there is human supplied fuel and human maintenance. Each such system ceases to be driven when this energy is used up or its maintenance ceases and the machine breaks down.[47]

Such driven systems, as they unfurl, display chaotic phenomena such as convection currents or turbulence. A water molecule from a rain drop which percolates into a subterranean water reservoir may stay there for a long, long time, until the chaotic turbulences in the reservoir determine that it will rise once more to the surface and evaporate. Such systems also lack the Markov property, as their behaviour at any given time point t_i cannot be *modelled* as depending merely upon one or a few earlier observations.

---

47 For inanimate systems, the distinction between natural and artificial may seem somewhat arbitrary, because after all the sun, too, will one day run out of fuel. But (1.) for human purposes there is quite a difference between the remaining lifetime of the sun and the reach of a tank of gas. And (2.) more importantly, driven machines are man-made and depend on human maintenance, while natural drivenness in inanimate nature does not—a difference to which we will return in chapter 9.1.

7.5.2.6 No fixed boundaries

We stated earlier that complex systems are often evolutionary and typically function in a larger environment. In complex systems, the boundary conditions at the interface between system and environment are constantly changing. This is why a complex system cannot be modelled by assuming that its boundary conditions (formed by the elements at the boundary) are fixed: doing this would create an invalid model. In other words, one cannot abstract from this environment without fundamentally mismodelling the behaviour of the systems it contains. When dealing with logic systems, in contrast, one can abstract from the context; the boundary conditions of the system can be assumed to be fixed, and the system itself is in this sense context-free.

Because complex systems are context-dependent; their boundary conditions massively determine how they work. For example, consider what happens in the food-energy-water system of a small farm on the verge of transition from subsistence to surplus production. When the farm begins to pump water for irrigation, this brings about transitions at lower ecosystem levels leading to enhanced crop growth but also increased energy consumption. This in turn can bring about also progressively larger changes in the entire landscape of the farm and its surroundings, impacting local social systems and producing new types of interaction over multiple scales, for example when other farm-holders introduce irrigation systems of their own in imitation of the initial success, thereby leading to drastically increased pressure on energy availability (Babaie et al. 2019).

7.5.2.7 Chaotic nature

Chaotic behaviour results from the dependence of a system on its starting conditions and is referred to as *deterministic chaos* in physics. It arises not only in complex systems, but also in simple systems, for which it was first described. In such systems, we know exactly which laws govern a physical process and can model it with a number of variables that is sufficiently small to allow us, in principle, to obtain a predictive model. However we fail to do so because we are unable to measure the starting conditions with sufficient exactness (Schuster et al. 2005).

Consider as an example the movement of a double pendulum, that is, a pendulum with another pendulum attached to its end. This is a logic system, but it shows a rich dynamic behavior with a strong sensitivity to its initial conditions. Although this system is simple and the physical laws determining its behaviour are known, its movements cannot be predicted because the system is completely chaotic.

Another example is behaviour of the molecules of water in a steam engine, which is a complex system due to its drivenness (energy gradient). This behaviour, too, is chaotic in the sense that, while we know that any given molecule of water will evaporate through the exhaust at some point in time, we cannot

138   The limits of mathematical models

calculate when and along which path in the system this evaporation will occur (McCauley 1993).

No matter which type of system we are dealing with, chaos cannot be predictively modelled—the divergence from the real outcome may sometimes be low over very short observation intervals, but it increases exponentially over time. While there are non-chaotic simple (Newtonian) systems, complex systems are in every case chaotic.

7.5.3 Summary of the seven properties of complex systems

To summarise, complex systems are marked by the following seven properties:

Property 1: Change and evolutionary character—sudden continuous and potentially non-differentiable or non-continuous changes of element types and element (type) combinations, which include changing behaviours on the part of all instances of a type. The system has a creative character, which means that it can at any time create new elements and new patterns of interaction.

Property 2: Element-dependent interactions—which lead to irregularity and non-repeatability. Irregularity means that the system does not behave in a way that can be formalised using equations. Non-repeatability signifies a behaviour that cannot be reproduced experimentally.

Property 3: Force overlay—several forces acting at the same time and thereby potentially interacting. This property is often correlated with anisotropy (which means that the effect resulting from force overlay *does not propagate with the same magnitude in all directions*).[48]

Property 4: Non-ergodic phase spaces—which cannot be predicted from the system elements and lead to time-irreversibility. A time-irreversible process is a process which cannot be described by equations which are invariant or symmetrical under a change in the sign of time.[49]

Property 5: Drivenness—either involving some external energy force or resulting from some sort of inner drive; drivenness implies the lack of an

---

48 Wood, for example, the product of an animate complex system, is anisotropic with regard to cleavability, elasticity, and length alterations under dryness and heat.

49 Mathematically speaking, time invariance can be expressed using the following temporal evolution operator equation: $O-t=\pi Ot\pi$, where π is an involution that allows the mapping between the time-reversed evolution $O-t$ of any state to the forward-time evolution Ot. In stochastics, a process is time-reversible if the joint probabilities of the forward and reverse state sequences are identical for all time increments (Leff et al. 2002).

equilibrium state to which the system would constantly be converging. This lack of equilibrium is caused by an energy gradient and results in energy dissipation.

Property 6: Context-dependence—non-fixable boundary conditions and embeddedness in one or more wider environments.

Property 7: Chaos—inability to predict system behaviour due to inability to obtain exact measurements of starting conditions.

7.5.3.1 The passing of time in complex systems

When time passes, the behaviour of complex systems becomes unpredictable. Why is this so? Prediction always starts from an initial time point t_0 which is arbitrarily chosen by the observer of the system. If we truly do have a predictive model of a system, then that model should work whatever is the value of t_0 that we choose. But because most of the properties identified here imply that there will be changes to the system conditions over time, this leads to the failure of those mathematical models which aim at prediction. Changing element and interaction types and the evolutionary character of the system can induce a change in the composition of the system and in the relations between its elements. All mathematical models, however, require a fixed set of elements with fixed relation types to produce meaningful results (in other words, to output numbers which correspond to the measurements of the events they are aiming to model).[50] The non-ergodic character of complex systems makes it impossible to model how and where in the system its elements distribute and makes the passage of time irreversible (see Property 4). This means that there is no way to transform a future state back into a previous state mathematically and vice versa. And finally, the context-dependence of complex systems causes an erratic behaviour over time. The chaotic nature of such systems makes it impossible even to model the passing of time in a comprehensive manner (something which holds even for simple systems, such as simple energy flows through liquid).

Let's briefly look at two examples, one animate and one inanimate. If we set a ladybug on a leaf at time t_0, we cannot predict when it will start to forage for the aphids from which it feeds and in what direction it will move when its foraging starts. If we observe a waterfall at another initial time point t'_0, we cannot predict from its shape at that moment the exact future shape of the falling water at any future time or the trajectory of a water molecule within the stream. In both cases, such predictions would be impossible, and this is so even if we could measure the exact location of all the molecules of the bug or of the waterfall at their corresponding initial timepoints t_0 and t'_0.

---

50 Some methods discussed in 8.6 offer more flexibility, but we will see that they, too, are unable to model time in complex systems.

TABLE 7.1 Some examples of systems and their properties

System	Property						
	1	2	3	4	5	6	7
Solar system[a]	0	0	0	0	0	0	0
Steam engine	0	0	0	0	1	0	1
Prion[b]	0	0	1	1	0	1	1
Turbulent flow[c]	0	1	1	1	1	0	1
Virus	1	1	1	1	0	1	1
C. elegans[d]	1	1	1	1	1	1	1
Traffic system[e]	1	1	1	1	1	1	1
New York Stock Exchange[e]	1	1	1	1	1	1	1
Global climate	1	1	1	1	1	1	1
Human language system	1	1	1	1	1	1	1

[a]The solar system seen as gravitational system. It has some deterministic chaos, but its extent is negligible over very long time periods.

[b]A prion is not a living organism, but an infectious protein causing neurodegenerative diseases such as the Creutzfeldt-Jakob disease. Prions can be transmitted by food intake.

[c]Turbulent flow is a system of water, smoke, or gas manifesting an energy gradient. It is discussed in section 8.7.1.1.

[d]As a living organism, *C. elegans* (which can autonomously generate energy from matter) has all seven properties. Its elements are its organs and its cells, which are both also systems at a more fine-grained level.

[e]The traffic system and the New York Stock Exchange are hybrid systems, involving both natural and artificial components. These may be animate-driven, for example humans, inanimate-driven, for example the weather, or non-driven, for example road surfaces. Artificial systems are provided, maintained, and used by interacting animate complex systems. In the case of the traffic system it is not only the participating humans, but also animals, plants, and inanimate-driven systems (rainstorms, earthquakes, floods, and so on) that interfere with the behaviour of the system by disturbing traffic or eroding infrastructure.

7.6 Examples of complex systems

In Table 7.1 we provide some examples of systems, classified according to the presence or absence the just-listed properties.

7.6.1 Animals and human beings as complex systems

We already saw that the human mind-body continuum is a complex system. To see what this means for science, it is useful to look at the results of research on human non-Mendelian diseases, which means: diseases caused by mutations in multiple gene loci and potentially involving also interaction between innate (gene-based) properties and the subject's environment. All major diseases—above all, coronary heart disease, arterial hypertension, and cancer—belong in this group. Indeed, the vast majority of human traits, including body height, facial traits, and all personality traits such as agreeableness and conscientiousness, as well as intelligence in the sense defined in chapter 3, show a non-Mendelian inheritance pattern (Strachan et al. 2018).

The methods used to identify genetic variants associated with such complex traits and diseases are genome-wide association studies (GWAS), which are used to advance understanding of disease and trait causation by identifying novel susceptibility genes and associated biological pathways. To determine whether there is some genetic variant associated with a particular phenotype (a disease or personality trait), a GWAS compares the genomes of two groups, one with and one without the phenotype. For each genetic variant identified in such a comparison, a test is then performed to determine whether it varies in a statistically significant way between the groups. Because the non-Mendelian disease and personality traits studied are genetic in nature, this means that they are inheritable. The variants identified through GWAS thus far, however, can be seen to confer only relatively small increments of risk, and this means that, even when taken together, they explain only a small fraction of the observed familial clustering. In other words, the GWAS results cannot, as yet, explain the observed inheritance patterns for complex traits (Manolio et al. 2009; Tam et al. 2019), though geneticists hope that gene-gene and gene-environment interactions will be found that will explain some of the missing heritability.

A further problem is that GWAS are not able to find many of the variant loci that play a causal role in giving rise to the phenotype in question.

It seems that as many as 90,000–100,000 variant loci may be needed to explain 80% of the heritability of the comparably simple human trait of body height.[51] Boyle et al. (2017) postulate in light of this and similar results that a substantial fraction of *all* genes may be contributing to the variation in complex traits, and they thus propose an *omnigenic model* according to which gene regulatory networks are interconnected to an extent that all the genes expressed in trait-determining cells contribute to the observed phenotype. Most of the heritability would then be explained by the effects of genes lying outside those core pathways on which research on model organisms such as mouse, fly, and yeast has been based thus far.

Support for this hypothesis is provided by discoveries pertaining to the closely related phenomenon of epistasis, in which the effect of a gene mutation is dependent on the presence or absence of mutations in one (or more) other modifier genes. Although we know of many occurrences of epistasis from research on model organisms, we cannot identify the phenomenon in humans with genetic methods—probably, because the human population variance is too high or because we are not able to set up adequate control groups.

---

51 Other traits, such as facial morphology or personality traits, for example, the level of sexual desire, are much more complex.

Even more soberingly: for most complex traits, the use of identified single nucleotide polymorphisms (SNPs) aggregated together to serve as predictors leads to poor performance in discriminating between individuals with and without the disease, even though the separate SNPs were identified by comparing such groups at the individual level (Tam et al. 2019).[52]

The explanation for such problems is, on our view, that the human organism, like any animate organism, is a complex system. If up to 100 thousand genetic loci are needed to account for 80% of the heritability of body height, then it is likely that even more widely dispersed and significant fractions of the genome are contributing to mental traits such as intelligence or to traits associated with moral (or immoral) behaviour.

As we will see in the next chapter, we are not able to model this type of complexity, even in a way that would lead to explanations of a seemingly uni-dimensional human trait such as height. Furthermore, these results make it clear why we find it so difficult to answer the question of the degree of innateness versus socialisation and learning that are involved in giving rise to complex mental traits such as intelligence. It is likely that the answers to such questions will always remain subject to speculation. This will also prevent us from bringing about any artificial changes in complex traits via genetic engineering of the human embryo—even height and strength.

However, this does not mean that no modelling at all is possible. In the field of precision medicine, for example, important new discoveries are made on the basis of interdisciplinary efforts involving analysis of large quantities of heterogeneous data. Luo et al. (2020b), for example, describe the identification of a new subtype of autism which is associated with dyslipidemia. To achieve this, phenotypic data from multiple sources were combined: whole-exome genetic sequences, gene expression patterns, health records, and healthcare insurance claims. Using unsupervised learning[53] as well as hypothesis-testing methods on

---

52 This insight is not called into question by results from the use of SNPs to discriminate individuals in forensics. For example, it has been reported that 41 SNPs can be used to predict eye, hair, and skin colour from DNA samples (Chaitanyaa et al. 2018). But how good are the predictions? The prediction performance metrics are not reported in the cited paper, but can be found on the associated website (https://hirisplex.erasmusmc.nl/). Sensitivity (for three eye, four hair, and five skin colours) ranges from 0 (intermediate eye colour) to 93% (blue eye colour), while specificity ranges from 65 to 99%, but the latter is only achieved with 0% sensitivity (intermediate eye colour). These metrics are not obtained by a separate validation set, but rather by using bootstrapping, a method that is known to be prone to over-fitting (Hastie et al. 2008). Furthermore, the prediction methods seem to lack basic calibration, otherwise the ratio of sensitivity to specificity in the case of intermediate eye colour would not be 0 to 99% with an area under the curve (AUC) of 75%. The statistical analysis seems very weak, and an independent analysis of the data with proper model validation would yield even poorer predictions. More important here is that the model is not explanatory. It certainly could not be used even as the starting point of a strategy to engineer the traits it describes.

53 This is a statistical analysis pattern which tries to find patterns in data without a testable hypothesis. To achieve this, the data are arrayed in a matrix in which the columns are variables and the

these data, the authors identified a new gene expression cluster related to lipid regulation in a subgroup of patients. But, as is the case with all research concerning complex systems, this model is merely descriptive; it does not give a causal explanation (7.1.1.4), and so it is unlikely to have diagnostic or therapeutic consequences. The conclusions drawn by the authors themselves are, moreover, speculative in the sense that they cannot say what the etiology or pathogenesis of the gene cluster which they identified might be.

7.6.2 Animate complex systems are organised and stable

As a final point, we note that animate complex systems, in spite of their complex system properties, are still highly *organised* and *stable*. Otherwise, there would be no reproduction and no genetic line connecting the first living organisms to humans and other species alive today. One aspect of their stability is the capability to adequately react to the behaviour of other complex systems in their environments with whom they interact all the time. This capability is crucial for survival, but we do not understand its biological grounds. We cannot grasp the causality that underlies the organisation of living systems and unites them together into a single system of systems called the tree of life. The reason, again, is that this system, and all its component systems, are complex in nature.

rows are observations. This matrix is used to create a representation of the data in a metric space which describes the distance of the observations from each other. In this way, observations can be grouped by the machine into similarity clusters, which often serve as starting point for the formulation of testable hypotheses.

8
MATHEMATICAL MODELS OF COMPLEX SYSTEMS

8.1 Multivariate distributions

To model systems, we start with observations of their behaviour. Using measurements, observations are converted into data, which we shall here conceive as numerical representations of our observations. Stochastic models use such data as samples from a distribution, which is also referred to as a *sampling space*. Every variable observation type is called a random variable. Its measurement has an error, a variance, and a bias. The error results from our inability to perform measurements with arbitrary precision.[1] The variance results from the natural variation of system behaviour from one sample to the next. The bias results from the way we choose to observe and select data.

To model the error, variance, and bias of a random variable, we regard data as distributions[2], where a distribution is a set of measurements—in the simplest case measurements of one element of a system with one variable, for example the heights of individuals in a human population. Such a distribution is called univariate. It is just a set of numbers, which can be represented in a Cartesian coordinate system which shows the values the variables can take on the abscissa and the frequency with which they occur on the ordinate axis. The shape of this graph is called the density of the distribution. It can often be modelled using a member of the exponential family, a set of parametric distributions including the Bernoulli or the Gaussian distribution (the famous 'bell curve', as it is

---

1 Note that this does not apply to quantum phenomena: measurements of the behaviour of distinct elements of above-quantum level system in the traditional sense are possible; not however measurements at the level of quantum mechanics.
2 See Klenke (2013) for an introduction to the probability theory underlying these remarks.

DOI: 10.4324/9781003310105-10

called in the social sciences).[3] If we cannot model the data adequately in this way, we speak of a non-parametric distribution, which can in some cases be modelled for example using Bayesian or some other form of non-parametric statistics.[4]

If, now, we add to the variable *height* also a second variable *weight*, then we obtain a bivariate distribution, which can be represented by a shape in a Cartesian coordinate system. By adding age, sex, marital status, occupation, and IQ, we obtain a hepta-variate (multivariate) distribution, which we can no longer plot on a piece of paper, though we can imagine it in our minds.

More formally, a multivariate distribution is a model of a type used in probability theory for a set of data from a series of measurements of one or more elements of a system, where all of the measurements are regarded as random variables. The measurements are set up to measure more than one property of the observed system elements, and the resultant data are then regarded as forming a vector space in $\mathbb{R}^n$. This space has more than one dimension, but for each variable the values along each dimension form a univariate distribution. In some cases the distribution of the data can be modelled using one of the parametric distributions: for example, height and weight are both distributed in human populations according to the Gaussian (normal, bell-curve) distribution, and the two-dimensional distribution of both together is thus a bivariate normal distribution. We know that biological sex is distributed in close approximation to the Bernoulli distribution, so the three-dimensional distribution of height, weight, and sex is a mixed Gaussian-Bernoulli distribution.

When enough representative samples are drawn from a distribution, one can measure properties of interest from these samples and infer that the statistics of these measurements (such as mean, median, skewness, and other distribution properties) will apply across the entire distribution. This is the foundation of all stochastic methods, from the simple t-test used in statistics to the deep neural networks (dNNs and their variants) used in stochastic AI.

In probability theory, multivariate distributions can be thought of as resulting from stochastic processes, such as the Gaussian process, which is ergodic[5] and creates a continuum of multivariate normal distributions. Each ergodic process creates a series of data which can be modelled as samples from a stable multivariate distribution which can be represented explicitly in mathematical form.

---

3 'Parametric' means that we can find parameters which enable us to build an equation to yield the shape of such a curve, for example:

$$f(x \mid \mu, \sigma^2) = \frac{1}{\sqrt{2\pi\sigma^2}} e^{\frac{-(x-\mu)^2}{2\sigma^2}} \text{ with } -\infty < x < \infty$$

where μ and σ are the two parameters of the Gaussian distribution. See again Klenke (2013).
4 There are statistical tests to establish whether a parametric model of data is an adequate model of the data, for example the Shapiro-Wilk test, which measures whether given data are normally distributed. A survey and ontology of the different types of distribution can be found in (Swat et al. 2016).
5 A system is called *ergodic* if, over sufficiently long periods of time, the time in which a system element occupies any given region of the phase-space is proportional to the volume of this region.

But ergodic distributions are rare, and the distributions we encounter in real-world data are in most cases non-parametric. This means that we cannot use parameters to build an equation to represent them mathematically, as contrasted with what is the case for distributions resulting, for example, from a Gaussian process.

But what if the data do not come from a distribution of this sort, but rather from a non-ergodic process or from a distribution generated by a complex system? The answer is that in these cases the stochastic model obtained by using such data will fail when faced with new observations. This is because the latter emanate from a distribution that will diverge from the training distribution in a proportion of cases in a way that will at best ensure a poor performance and at worst make the model useless.

Due to the nature of complex systems, this divergence may be unnoticeable immediately after training, but it will typically increase over time (see section 7.5.3.1). In other words, even though, when the model starts to be used some of the input data given to the model might resemble the training distribution by chance, the overall reliability of the model—the degree to which we can trust the results of using it in the realisation of our intentions—will be low.

8.2 Deterministic and stochastic computable system models

There are two fundamental types of computable system models: deterministic and stochastic. The former comprise, for example, models expressed using propositional, predicate or modal logic, and including what are called expert systems or rule systems.[6]

The chess-playing algorithm DeepBlue that beat Kasparov in 1996 was deterministic; it used an α-β-search algorithm (Heineman et al. 2008, chapter 7). The most important stochastic models used in AI modelling are functionals (f) or operators ($\mathcal{O}$) of the form

$$f : \mathbb{R}^k \mapsto \mathbb{R}, \text{ or} \tag{8.1}$$

$$\mathcal{O} : \mathbb{R}^k \mapsto \mathbb{R}^\ell , \tag{8.2}$$

where k and ℓ can be very large, as in the case, for example of neural machine translation with millions of parameters. Each stochastic algorithm is thus highly complicated in the sense that it involves a huge number of interrelated parameters. But it is still an algorithm belonging to traditional mathematics. It still computes output data from input data using Church functions.

As we see, functionals relate k-dimensional vectors to scalars, while operators relate them to ℓ-dimensional vectors. Both are relations defined as elements of

---

6 A rule system consists of conditional logic clauses (if ... then) which are isomorphic to Horn clauses (propositional logic) (Lucas et al. 1991).

functional or operator spaces themselves and require coordinate spaces to define their domains and ranges.

To train stochastic models, it is supervised learning that is used in most practical applications, and here the training data are tuples of the form:

$$\left\{x_{ij}, \ldots, x_{ip}, \mathbf{y}_i\right\}_{i=1}^{N}, j = 1 \ldots p, \tag{8.3}$$

where N indicates the number of samples, p indicates the number of input (independent) variables observed with $p = k$ (eqn. 8.1–8.2), x_{ij} the j-th observation variable of the i-th sample, and $\mathbf{y}_i$ the i-th outcome of the dataset with dimension $i \in \mathbb{N}$. For example, the input variables might be the data provided in a loan request, and the output the creditworthiness of the requester computed by a functional f, as in eqn. 8.1. Or the input variables might be the words of a sentence in German and the output an English sentence produced by neural machine translation using an operator $\mathcal{O}$ as described in eqn. 8.2.

In the language of probability theory, a stochastic model computes the most probable output, the estimator $\hat{y}$, given an input $\mathbf{x}$ and model parameters θ: $\hat{y} = E(Y \mid X = \mathbf{x}, \theta)$. This equation expresses that the model $\hat{y}$ yields the expected value E for the relationship of y and x given a model θ.

The most important stochastic models used for AI applications are regression or classification models, which have been in use since the 1970s (Hastie et al. 2008). Regression models yield numbers (scalars or vectors), classification models yield categories (either binary or multiple categories, vectors of categories are rarely used). So-called deep neural networks (dNNs) are also stochastic regression or classification models. Stochastic models are obtained by applying optimisation algorithms to the training tuples.[7] The optimisation algorithms work under constraints with the goal of minimising the *loss* of the model, which means the deviation of the model from the reality of the observed outcomes Y.

In the simplest case this can be defined as

$$\ell(f(X), Y) = (Y - f(X))^2, \tag{8.4}$$

where f is the model. This is a classical formulation defining the model's loss as the squared difference of real outcome and prediction[8], which drives the parameterisation of the model using the optimisation algorithm. Such algorithms can create models of a new type that humans would not be able to construct when modelling explicitly. The processes involved in generating such stochastic models are *automated*. The equations they consist of are not created by human

---

7 dNNs can also be trained on unsupervised data of the form $\left\{x_{ij}, \ldots, x_{ip}\right\}_{i=1}^{N}, j = 1 \ldots p$; see section 8.6.8.
8 And for which much more sophisticated versions exist, see (Hastie et al. 2008; Goodfellow et al. 2014).

effort, but rather by the constraints imposed on the optimisation algorithm by the training tuples and the parameterisation of the algorithm hyperparameters (Goodfellow et al. 2014). Though the model is computed automatically, for example by using gradient descent along the negative of the differential operator of a loss function $\nabla \ell(f(x_0), y_0)$ at a given point, all its properties are determined by human input, both in the selection of the model's hyperparameters and in the preparation of the training material.

More generally speaking, a predictor functional f is obtained as an element from a function class $\mathcal{F}$ using a dNN-pipeline by minimising the expectation $\mathbb{E}$ of the loss:

$$\mathbb{E}_{(X,Y)\sim P}[\ell(f(X), Y)],$$

where P is the training distribution of the input and output distributions X and Y.

The AI paradigm based on training such models is called 'connectionist AI' because its proponents believe that such models simulate the way in which neurons are connected in the brain. We will show what is wrong with this view later in this chapter.

Often, algorithms trained in this way perform poorly when confronted with new data. An important reason for this is *model underspecification* (D'Amour et al. 2020), which occurs when there are several functionals $f_i \in \mathcal{F}$ which have similar loss expectations that can be generated by using a training pipeline. Because the different functionals f_i encode different data processing patterns (biases), they will also differ in the way they react to real data not drawn from the distribution P (D'Amour et al. 2020). This is—and in light of the arguments in this book will remain—an unsolved problem in AI research, which arises from the fact that in most situations, training distributions do not represent reality with sufficient adequacy for the reasons we outline in section 8.5. This means that the data processing pattern obtained through training leads to systematic errors when real data are input into a given predictor.

The ability of highly sophisticated optimisation algorithms to autocompute dNN models across huge distributions is impressive. However, such stochastic models (and deterministic models as well) are always models of logic systems, because (a) they are executable on a Turing-machine, which is a logic system and, (b) as we have seen in section 7.2, Turing machines can only execute instructions that are logical in nature. Thus these models will not develop intentions—the equations are just functionals or operators relating an input vector to a certain output—in other words, they are nothing but a general form of regression models. Furthermore, the nature of AI models as logic systems explains what Larson (2021, p. 155) calls 'model saturation', which is the phenomenon whereby stochastic models often reach a certain quality level but then cannot get any better despite the addition of new training data. The reason for this is the absolute limit, which is caused by the modelling of a complex system with a logical system. The logic system can never attain the performance of the complex system, which creates a quality hiatus that cannot be closed.

8.3 Newtonian limits of stochastic models of complex systems

The nature of complex systems prevents their synoptic and adequate modelling as defined in section 7.1.1.4. To see why, consider again that computable models are models of logic systems; they all belong to the (extended) Newtonian paradigm of mathematical modelling of reality.

This is because they are obtained using derivatives of loss functions, which are used to find local minima of multivariate functionals. The result is a very long, differentiable equation. Due to the mathematical properties of every dNN, this equation obeys relaxed Newtonian requirements. This means that it does not require the interactions between its variables to be always the same, and it also does not require that these interactions have to be homogeneous over the entire neural net. However, the importance of any given interaction must decrease over space or time in a regular fashion; in other words, every neural network must still have a weak Markov property over space or time. And neural networks still require most of the properties of Newtonian models in order to be computable.

Given this, the *main reasons* why we cannot model complex systems mathematically are the following.

Phase space Each mathematical model requires a vector space, often a coordinate space over an algebraic space F. The real numbers $\mathbb{R}$ form such a space. Each such vector space is defined as a set of n-tuples over a given field with addition and scalar multiplication as operations. For example, the Euclidean three-dimensional space is a coordinate space of type F^3 over the field $\mathbb{R}$; an example of a 3-tuple of this space is the vector (1, 0, 0). Such a space, in this case $\mathbb{R}^3$, is needed to define the variables used in the mathematical equations which are supposed to model the corresponding real system. But with the *changing variables and interactions* that we find in complex systems, there is *no coordinate space* over which models can be defined. Since each and every model is defined for a specific vector space, it becomes invalid if the reality targeted by the model differs from the vector space for which the model was originally defined. The more it differs, the stronger the deviation and the less accurate the model becomes. With complex systems, the deviation can become huge, and this can happen suddenly, when new elements evolve or when, in the opposite direction, elements vanish or unpredictable events like a stock market crash occur. More trivial examples of such deviations arising from an emerging discrepancy between model and system are reflected in the predictions generated in a weather forecast (which are never accurate over longer periods), climate models (which are never accurate), or epidemiological models (which are in extreme situations only approximatively accurate). All these deviations become larger as time passes, because the effects which prevent exact models for complex systems gain importance exponentially (see section 7.5.3.1).

Non-ergodicity Yet more obstacles to modelling are created where we are dealing with *non-ergodic processes*, which produce events in which we cannot identify any law-like pattern that can be modeled mathematically. The reason for this is that non-ergodic processes do not yield distributions from which representative samples can be drawn.

Of course, many complex systems exhibit regular patterns, such as the cyclic behaviour of all animals along multiple dimensions (respiration, heartbeat, the wake-sleep or feed-rest-hunt cycles, cycles of sexual behaviour, and so on), but these cover only partial processes and cannot be described using differential equations or other exact modelling approaches. For example, we cannot even exactly model classical conditioning in a way that would be valid across multiple laboratories experimenting on harnessed arthropods (honey bees) even where the exact same experimental setup is being applied (Bitterman 2006).

Process trace An additional obstacle turns on the fact that the *traces of non-ergodic processes*—in other words the data series which such processes generate—provide no adequate target spaces for stochastic sampling. This is because the latter requires in every case that samples are produced from a distribution belonging either to the exponential family or at least to a non-parametric distribution that can be reliably estimated (Klenke 2013). The samples drawn from such complex traces are never representative of the process behaviour due to the non-ergodic character of the process. As we shall see in more detail later in this chapter, *there is here no distribution to sample from*. This systematically prevents stochastic modelling of such processes. It is also the reason why reward traces cannot be provided for the training of artificial agents where interactions with complex systems are involved (such as an autonomous freely moving robot). There is no way to set up such a trace because there is no stochastic process available to create it. A deterministic model would not work either, because such a model, too, cannot produce the pattern of rewards produced by a complex system.

This is the reason why, for example, machines cannot learn to conduct real conversations using machine learning—which is a method to obtain mathematical models implicitly using optimisation methods applied to training data (Hastie et al. 2008; Goodfellow et al. 2016; Bertsekas 2016). The training data obtained from recorded conversations are never adequate as material to train a model because the conversations are conducted by complex systems called people. If such data are used to train a stochastic model, the model will always be fitted to non-representative data. It will therefore fail, if not in the next conversation, then in some conversation in the near future, and not in the way that humans fail regularly in conversations, but rather in a way that betrays that the model is not able at all to meet basic human expectations for a conversation with another human being (Landgrebe et al. 2021).[9]

Context The context-dependence property of complex systems has the consequence that the system will use a different phase space following different principles depending on the context in which it is situated. Yet neural networks always rely on the assumption that all the input-output-relationships they model via their training samples are *context free*. The distribution from which they are drawn has no further context. Crucially, this means that they cannot cope with the non-ergodic system events which are characteristic of complex systems as the networks are trained using large sets of events over which they merely average. No matter how large the model parameterisation becomes[10], this training process cannot yield models of complex systems which are both synoptical and adequate. In other words, when data are sampled from a complex system, they are *never* representative of the system, for the system's behaviour never has a multivariate distribution from which one could draw representative samples.

A model trained with such data will never be able to react properly to novel data emanating from the system, because the underlying distribution will always be different from the distribution from which the training samples were taken.

A housefly cannot adapt to a window pane. Its behaviour becomes unpredictable and erratic when it gets caught behind a window. On the other hand, those animals that *can* adapt to new types of situations show a completely erratic pattern during the process of adaptation. Because in natural environments (as in financial markets), the context can radically change at any time, context dependence makes the behaviour of complex systems in such environments unpredictable. Of course, humans have developed strategies to make each other's behaviour more predictable in order to enable life in communities (based on mutual trust) and societies (based on social norms, see 6.3). But the omnipresence of conflicts (private and public, peacefully resolved or leading to violence) shows that predictability is still very low, since the interactions of complex systems are creating novel, unexpected situations all the time.

It is very impressive to see how versatile modern stochastic models are in modelling classical Newtonian physics. They can even numerically approximate solutions for parameter families of partial differential equations such as the one-dimensional Burgers' equation, the two-dimensional Darcy Flow problem, or the two-dimensional Navier-Stokes equation. These solution sets are computed from observations of function tuples, as described in Li et al. (2020), something

---

9 Willingness to chat with a bot for entertainment purposes, a habit quite popular in some cultures, is a different matter.
10 Which is to say, no matter how large the model is when expressed as an equation (such equations can have billions of terms).

that is out of reach for traditional numerical methods. However, the solved equations are traditional Newtonian partial differential equations exactly as described in section 7.4.1; thus they do *not* model complex systems. These results are thus fully consistent with our view that complex systems are out of reach of stochastic modelling.

8.3.1 Adequate models for complex systems

However, there are some cases in which the emanation from a complex system can be used to train an adequate implicit model relative to some given set of requirements. In other words, the logic system which the model represents can in some cases be used to approximate aspects of complex systems adequately. For example, the original AlphaGo model (which outputs the next move of the computer in a game against an opponent as a stochastic prediction) was seeded using the moves of human Go players, which are undoubtedly emanations of this nature. Why does this still work? Because Go has strict rules which compensate for the complex, and thus non-ergodic, nature of the system which generated the original actions of humans playing Go. The game situation is in this respect highly artificial, because here the rules massively restrict the variance. From the inside, the deliberations leading to moves in a game of chess played by humans may be massively complex. From the outside, however, such moves can be seen merely as a matter of score optimisation in a restricted setting (as described in section 8.6.7.3).

Suppose, now, that we have a complex system and we wish to use observations of its behaviour to obtain a representative sample of the sort that we can use to train an AI application. For this to be possible, the sample data would have to correspond to a multivariate distribution that is *representative* of the system's behaviour, which can often be assumed for logic systems as well as for certain artificial systems such as Go and chess, where the observable behaviour is constrained by strict rules. However, there are many, many cases for which no such distribution exists. This may be, for example, because the evolutionary nature of the system will imply that the coordinates of the vector system which models its phase space are continually changing. Second, it may be because, even in the absence of such change, the observations modelled by the distribution emanate from a non-ergodic system, so that the distribution of data points in the vector space cannot be modelled adequately with either a parametric or a non-parametric distribution.[11] This is because it is impossible to draw adequate samples from a distribution of this sort, because there is no representative subspace from which the needed training samples could be drawn. Under these conditions, *there is no process that can yield a representative sample*.

---

11 'Adequately', again, means: in a way that satisfies the requirements which the model was created to satisfy. Usually, in AI, these are requirements for reliable automation or pattern identification.

8.4 Descriptive and interpretative models of complex systems

An important class of models for complex systems are not predictive, but rather descriptive or interpretative. Models of this sort are often very useful. Outside the physics of smooth and continuous functions and its applications and extensions described in section 7.4, mathematical models are widely used for descriptive, interpretative, and approximatively and partially predictive modelling in sciences dealing with complex systems. They are used, for example, in the life sciences (biology, biochemistry, medicine, pharmacology, and so forth) and also in those humanities and social science disciplines (such as psychology, anthropology, ethnology, and economics) which use mathematics for modelling purposes. Many partial aspects and properties of complex systems can be modelled *descriptively* or *approximatively*; but the nature of such systems sets tight boundaries on what such descriptive modelling can achieve.

Synoptic and adequate models for more than simple properties of complex systems are only possible when the systems are man-made and thus are logic systems with regard to most of their properties.[12]

It is important to understand that synoptic and adequate models of complex systems are not possible. We can, for example, model quite well certain partial aspects of the global climate system, such as the behaviour of the Gulf stream or the progression of the seasons on the two hemispheres of the earth. But we face considerable difficulties when it comes to answering questions such as whether climate change is anthropogenic or whether it could be safely reversed by spraying sunlight-reflecting particles into the stratosphere. This is because to answer these sorts of questions we would need synoptic, predictive models not merely of the planet's climate and of the associated anthropogenic systems, but also of the interactions between these two sets of systems. Many scientific questions regarding complex system behaviour call for models which are both synoptic and either explanatory or exact, but for questions pertaining to complex systems and their interactions we do not have models of these sorts. For example, as we have seen, we have no genetic causal explanation for body height, and we can create only descriptive, statistical models of its distribution in different population strata (such as the height percentiles of juvenile growth).

To better understand the limits to what we can do with partial models of complex systems, we will consider in sections 8.4.1–8.4.3 a series of examples from medicine and other disciplines in which they are used. These examples will illustrate how these models fail when the problem at issue requires a synoptic adequate model of the complex system under study. Such models are, again, available in certain parts of science, but they are impossible to obtain for most traits of complex systems.

---

12 As we have seen using the example of the steam engine (134), those engineered logic systems which consume energy are driven, because the energy that flows through them is dissipated. However, the overall user-relevant functioning of the machine is that of a logic system.

8.4.1 Medicine

8.4.1.1 Virology

We have excellent descriptive, interpretative, and even predictive—though then only *partial*—models of the functioning and reproduction of many viruses, which are, next to prions, the pathogens with the simplest structure. They form a complex system with the cells they infect. For example, stochastic modelling has recently been used to identify associations between cytometry data and virological outcomes of interest such as Cytomegalovirus infection (Hu et al. 2020).[13]

But we have pharmacological treatments and vaccines only for a subset of the human-pathogenic viruses, because the way we develop both therapeutics and vaccines is through trial-and-error mechanisms loosely inspired by our descriptive models.[14] We have no exact way of designing virus-targeting drugs, because we have no synoptic and adequate models of the way viruses use the molecular machinery of infected human host cells to replicate. All of the drugs we have target components of this machinery; but they face problems when attempts are made to inhibit such mechanisms without affecting the host cells, because the machinery contains components essential to both the infected and the non-infected cells. The limit to modelling is set by our inability to create causal and predictive models of the detailed interactions of cell and virus. While we can describe some aspects of the viral life-cycle and of the way our cells react to the virus, we have no models of sufficient exactness to allow either a cure or a vaccine based on a thorough understanding of the causality involved. The same is true for the reaction of the entire body to the viral infection; we do not know exactly why some patients die from a viral pneumonia and others do not—we say 'their immune system could not eliminate the virus in time', but this is just a rationalisation.

8.4.1.2 Oncology

Cancer is a complex system disease. We have accumulated a huge body of knowledge about this disease, but we have no understanding of the disease that would allow a general cure. For solid tumours in all but the earliest stages, the therapeutic strategy still resembles the medieval curative scheme: *quod ferrum non sanat, ignis*

---

13 To obtain this descriptive model, the group used data from ImmPort, an ontology-based interoperable repository of immunology data (Bhattacharya et al. 2018).
14 Note that in the development of pharmacotherapies, trial-and-error is fully justified and well-established. In engineering based on physics, however, it is possible only to a very limited extent: see 12.2.7.2.

sanat, quot ignis non sanat, mors sanat.[15] The reason for this is not lack of will, funds, time, or ideas, but the nature of the system we are dealing with.

8.4.1.3 Pharmacology

The pharmaco*kinetics* of many drugs can be modelled quite exactly in proportion to the body weight and other co-variables, albeit with inter-individual variance. This is because the distribution within and elimination of many drugs from the body, although performed by a complex system, yields continuous and differentiable functions. Such examples exist in other sciences as well, but are rather the exception than the rule. The pharmaco*dynamics* of drugs, on the other hand, are much harder to model, and synoptic models do not exist. We have dose-effect functions and descriptive and interpretative models for the main effects, but only lists of effect probabilities for side effects, which are often understood poorly or not at all. Nevertheless, the models of pharmacology are often adequate to their associated therapeutic requirements, even though they are not synoptic.

8.4.1.4 Genetics

We can understand the etiology of genetic diseases with Mendelian inheritance patterns (monogenetic diseases), and we will soon be able to cure them by using embryonic gene therapy to repair the causative gene locus in the germ-line. However, we cannot fully explain their pathogenesis; that is, we cannot model in a synoptic manner how the diseases are *caused* by the dysfunctional gene product. In cystic fibrosis, for example, the cystic fibrosis transmembrane conductance regulator protein is dysfunctional and leads to organ dysfunction and ultimate failure of the lung, pancreas, liver, intestine, and kidneys. We have descriptive models and an interpretative explanation for the pathogenesis. But we do not understand the causes sufficiently to take therapy beyond the stage where we are merely addressing symptoms.

8.4.1.5 Organ replacement

We can replace dysfunctional organs by graft transplantation from brain-dead patients (donors) to those in need of an organ (hosts). But we can only symptomatically manage the reaction of the host's immune system against the grafted organ (the anti-donor immune response) using very unspecific immune suppression compounds with many side effects. We have no synoptic understanding of the immune system, and therefore cannot manipulate it in an adequate manner to make it accept the grafted organ as belonging to the new host body (Ochando et al. 2020).

---

15 What is not healed by iron [surgery], is healed by fire [radiation, chemotherapy]; what is not healed by fire, is healed by death.

We can also implant artificial joints (endoprostheses) to replace the hip and the knee articulations. These artificial joints are not as functional as healthy natural articulations, but they are highly therapeutic. Thus, they are an example of synoptic and adequate models of specific components of complex systems. Why are there no artificial wrists or shoulder endoprostheses at the same therapeutic level? Because the mechanics of these articulations are so complex that we have not been able to create the needed synoptic models.

What about artificial *organs*? So far, the attempts at creating such organs have failed because even for the heart, an organ with mostly mechanical (pumping) functions, we have no synoptic models (Latrémouille et al. 2018). And for metabolic organs such as the kidney, liver, or pancreas, we cannot even envisage such models.

8.4.1.6 Other therapeutic interventions

There are, of course, many other attempts at therapeutic interventions, for example with the goal of augmenting or repairing human brain function. For example, it is now possible to genetically modify mammalian (mouse) brain cells *in vivo* by introducing light-sensitive rhodopsin receptors into brain neurons, which can then be stimulated by light shining through the skull from the outside (Chen et al. 2020). It is however unlikely that this technology could be adapted to humans, given that it would require somatic genetic engineering and also that—due to the thickness of our skull and the size of our brain—light would not penetrate. But even if it could be so adapted, we would still not know which cells to activate and how to activate them in order to achieve any given desired effect. This is because we would be intervening in a complex system which we do not understand. At best, we could obtain very crude effects, though for severe diseases such as Parkinson's or major pharmacotherapy-resistant depression, such interventions might still have a certain therapeutic value.

8.4.2 Psychology

Experimental psychology has developed a huge body of interesting and important findings since it reached launch velocity as a science towards the beginning of the 20th century. This accumulated knowledge has an enormous descriptive and some explanatory value. It is successfully used in personnel management, advertisement optimisation, crime investigation, (some) psychotherapy, and many other domains. But given that the subject of psychology is a complex system, there is no exact prediction possible except for those types of behaviour which are almost completely innate, such as the corneal reflex or the retraction of the body from sources of pain. For all other types of human behaviour we can never predict how well a psychotherapy will work in a given individual, and even the best and most experienced psychologists cannot predict whether or when a sexual offender will repeat his crime after the end of his sentence, no matter which tests they use.

8.4.3 Economics

An economy is a complex system resulting from collective human behaviour. Indeed, it is a complex system made of many interacting complex systems. Economics yields mostly descriptive and interpretative models, involving no mathematical causality and yielding no exact predictions. Microeconomics can describe consumer preferences, investment returns, monopolies, oligopolies, and monopsonies. Macroeconomics can describe, and interpret, trade-balance deficits, the velocity of money circulation, and effects of taxation or of a deflationary spiral. Macroeconomics provides no causal explanations, but rather (at best) very helpful causal interpretations.

Economics can effectively support political decision-making, because economic models are useful tools for sketching out the overall effects of policies. For example, setting a ceiling for prices of a good usually leads to a decline in the supply of the good. However, no economist can quantify such effects exactly in advance (and it is even hard to do this in hindsight, given the many mixed effects in the real-world economy). This is because no economic model can exactly predict any single economic quantity for any selected time or time interval in the future, whether this be the price of a good or the excess capacity of a production method. Nor can the causation of economic phenomena be modelled causally in such a way as to yield a scientific explanation—again, because of the complexity of the system.

The first economist to realise this was Ludwig von Mises in his 'economic calculation argument' (originally published in German in 1922 (Mises 1936)), where von Mises describes the ways in which the individual subjective valuations on the part of both producers and consumers in market societies combine to create the body of objective information which we call market prices. He then shows that the latter are necessary for anything like rational allocation of resources in society. Mises then shows on this basis that it would be impossible to manage an industrial economy through central planning, since the planners would have no way of simulating the effects of combining what may be millions of independent and constantly changing valuations (Steele 2013).

Mises, arguments were then extended in Hayek's work on spontaneous orders and on the 'knowledge problem', which turns on the fact that there is no way in which the central planner can predict the consequences of his plans because he has no access to the local knowledge possessed by each one of the many individual economic agents in society (Hayek 1937, 1945). Hayek also clearly saw the absolute cognitive limits of explanation possible for the human mind. In *The Sensory Order*, he writes:[16]

> difficulties prevent us from thus elaborating known explanations of the principle [of causality] to the point where they would enable us to predict particular events. This is often the case when the phenomena are very complex, as in meteorology or biology; in these instances, the number of variables which would have to be taken into account is greater than that which can be ascertained or effectively manipulated by the human mind.
>
> (Hayek 1952, 8.66)

This insight returns in many other works of Hayek. In 'The pretence of knowledge', he writes:

> While in the physical sciences it is generally assumed ... that any important factor which determines the observed events will itself be directly observable and measurable, in the study of such complex phenomena as the market, which depend on the actions of many individuals, all the circumstances which will determine the outcome of a process, for reasons which I shall explain later, will hardly ever be fully known or measurable.
>
> (Hayek 2014b, p. 363)

Similar passages can be found in 'Degrees of explanation' and 'Rules, Perception and Intelligibility', both published in Hayek (2014a). More recently, Fernández-Villaverde (2020) concluded that AI cannot be used to model economics or social norms drawing on Hayek's ideas.

8.5 Predictive models of complex systems

In the previous sections, we saw that there are hard boundaries to the modelling of complex systems, so that causal explanations and exact predictions—even of single traits of these systems—are in almost all cases mathematically impossible. This is so because for such systems we are unable to formulate equations that yield the needed predictions.

---

16 Kant was one of the first to see that we are unable to model living organisms mathematically. In his *Critique of Judgement* he writes:

> It is namely certain that we cannot acquire knowledge of living organisms and their inner possibilities according to mere mechanical principles of nature, let alone explain them; and indeed it is so certain that in the future it will possible to say that it is incoherent for a human to even attempt this, or to hope that a new Newton could one day rise who could explain the genesis of a mere blade of grass according to laws of nature, that no intention has formed: rather it is obvious that this insight is denied to humans.
>
> (Kant 2000,§75)

Mathematical models of complex systems 159

In the present chapter we discuss attempts to define predictive models for complex systems. To put the matter in a nutshell, for an AGI designed to substitute for humans in the performance of complex tasks in natural environments, inexact predictions are insufficient: the AGI will not pass even minimal safety checks.[17]

The problem here is that, if we measure the behaviour of complex systems by assigning numbers to the observable events which these systems (co-)generate, we obtain data to which no predictive model can be made to fit, no matter which procedure we use. An example is the system formed by two human beings when they engage in a dialogue. Let us suppose that we assign a natural number to each English-language lexeme and then represent the utterances in a dialogue as sequences of such numbers. We then cannot fit any mathematical model to such sequences of numbers that would enable us to reliably generate a next utterance in the dialogue that will fulfil the criteria of normal human conversation in any given context. Given the erratic nature of human dialogues, an exact model is in any case impossible. But humans expect appropriate utterances in dialogues, utterances which show that their intentions are taken into account by their interlocutors (which demonstrate, in other words, intersubjectivity). An AGI which repeatedly runs afoul of this expectation cannot be taken seriously as a conversation partner.

A simpler example is the behaviour of *C. elegans*. We might create a matrix of vectors reflecting this behaviour by assigning numbers to its movements in a spatial coordinate system and then provide on this basis numerical encodings of its behaviour patterns when foraging, eating, reproducing, and so forth. Though it has been recently shown that the food choice preferences of this animal can be modelled using utility functions from microeconomics developed for humans (see section 3.3.2.3), we will, here too, not be able to obtain a mathematical model of the sequences of vector instances that we measure over time that we could use to predict the organism's entire behaviour in a given situation. The reason for this is that the fundamental properties of the behaviour of this or any other organism do not have the characteristics that would allow us to create what we called an almost exact model (7.1.1.4), and only a model of this sort allows predictions which can be experimentally verified.

There are methods we can use in some of these cases to generate approximate predictions, for example using stochastic models. Such models are based on the distribution of observations and in most cases yield statistics which are reliable only where we have a very large sample of observations.[18] However, if they are applied to a single sample, their predictive power is often too weak to be reliable. They can only be used to model a distribution of events or to

---

17 The substitution of humans by robots in artificial environments such as assembly lines, in contrast, where the modelling is so much simpler, causes no such problems, and such substitution will continue to increase. See
18 This is the reason why Boltzmann statistics are predictive for the cases in which they are adequate models. They aggregate over a huge set of particles.

perform non-critical predictions (for example regarding advertisement placing or approximative translations).

8.5.1 Why we ain't rich

There are many who claim to be able to predict the properties of complex systems using powerful software, for example to predict tomorrow's prices on the stock exchange. But however powerful the software and the hardware on which the software is run, the models they generate are in every case massive simplifications of the real-world systems they are claiming to model (otherwise predictions could not be made). Such a simplification may for a time yield correct predictions; but its predictions will very often be wrong and rapidly deteriorate in their predictive quality with the passing of time (7.5.3.1). Any market strategy based on predictions of this sort will sooner or later be falsified because markets are, by their very nature as systems for the coordination of individual preferences, unpredictable. Furthermore, the more successful such a strategy might prove to be, the more likely it is that countervailing changes in market conditions would be brought about by other market participants who exploit information about the success of this strategy to undermine it; we call this phenomenon *model-induced escape*.

8.6 Naïve approaches to complex system modelling

Given this setting, there are two approaches to the mathematical modelling of complex systems: (i) the naïve approach, which attempts to use tools which yield computable solutions, such as those based on the differential calculus, even though the prerequisites for the application of such tools are violated; and (ii) approaches which attempt to find a different type of mathematical model, more well adapted to the prediction of those phenomena which arise where complex systems are involved.

We will review both approaches and show that neither is able to yield even *explanations* of the behaviour of the complex system which they purport to model and that, in the case of explicit models, they fail *a fortiori* to yield *predictions* of such behaviour. Implicit models, notoriously, can provide predictions without explanations.[19] But they, too, fail to achieve predictions of the behaviour of complex systems.

There is a variety of attempts to model complex systems with the tools of the differential calculus, including a range of stochastic extensions thereof. The methods used in building such models—all of them implemented in existing AI applications—can be divided into the following types:

- Turing-computable logic

---

19 On the problem of 'explainability' of stochastic models, see 8.6.6.

- Differential equations
- Stochastic (process) models[20]
  i. Hidden Markov Models
  ii. Stochastic differential equation models

- Stochastic regression models[21]
  i. Classic regression models
  ii. Advanced regression models
     Deep neural networks (dNNs)
     Deep recurrent neural networks (rNNs)
     Generative adversarial networks (GANs)

Note that all of these approaches are of course Turing-computable, since all of them are in various implementations already running inside universal Turing machines. In addition, neural networks can approximate any continuous functions on compact subsets of $\mathbb{R}^n$ (by the universal approximation theorem, (Hornik 1991)) and are therefore (like any continuous function) Turing computable for this reason also. Therefore, as explained in section 7.2, all these models are models of logic systems that are used (for better or worse) to *approximate* complex systems.

We review each approach in turn.

8.6.1 Turing-computable logic

There are three types of Turing-computable mathematical logic: non-modal and modal propositional logic, and first-order logic (Robinson et al. 2001), and the use of these to create AI applications is traditionally called 'hard AI' or 'GOF-AI' (good-old fashioned AI) (Haugeland 1985). All of these logics are highly useful in the engineering of narrow AI systems for problems with a closed solution space (that is, of logic systems). Their application to any given system, however, relies on highly repetitive relationships between its inputs and outputs. They are much less flexible than stochastic models because they are fully explicit. These logics therefore cannot be used to model complex systems of the sort that would be required to realise AGI (as documented in section 13.3.1). We will however review examples of their highly effective usage in the partial modelling of

---

20 These are models which use probability theory to model outcomes. They work by assuming that the behaviour of a system can be modelled using either an assumed (or known) parametric data distribution (the frequentist approach), or an empirically given non-parametric data distribution (the Bayesian approach).
21 A small fraction of the models under this heading explicitly represent stochastic processes such as time series; the remainder represent simple input-output-correlations.

complex systems, especially in combination with stochastic models, in chapter 13.2.

8.6.2 Differential equation models

We have already had a lot to say about differential equation models, which can be used to provide exact representations of the changes in systems involving multiple variables when the relationships between these variables follow deterministic patterns of the sort that can be observed in the physical realm (for example radioactive decay over time). But such models succeed, as we saw (7.4), only where the number of variables is small and where the interrelations involved are simple and unchanging. All such systems ('logic systems' in our preferred terminology) allow predictions of their behaviour, which can be verified using physical experiments (including the observations which occur when we predict the movements of asteroids). Unfortunately, the phenomena which characterise complex systems cannot even be *described* using differential equations, much less provided with explanations or predictions (Thurner et al. 2018, chapter 1). This follows already from the fact that the number of variables involved in such phenomena is too large, and their interdependencies too complex, to make such modelling possible. For example, it is impossible to predict prices of farm commodities such as hogs, soy beans, cattle, or wheat using stochastic differential equations.

Such systems, moreover, cannot be isolated from their surrounding environment. This implies a lack of fixedness of their boundary conditions; but such fixedness is again a requirement for predictive modelling with differential equations.

Evidence that the various differential equation models that have been proposed do not work in complex systems is provided by the fact that all attempts to create such models are repeatedly falsified by empirical observations, as we show at length in the remaining chapters of this book.

There are, it is true, examples of differential equation-based methods that have been applied successfully in biology. In a first sort of case, this has occurred where it has been possible to limit artificially the number of variables governing a biological system and to isolate the system from its natural context, for example where organism population growth is modelled under simplified laboratory-like assumptions, such as in epidemiological disease modelling (Li 2018). In a second sort of case, a subsystem is postulated that can be adequately described with a few interacting variables. An example is given by Seirin-Lee et al. (2020), who describe a partial differential equation model for cell cytosol polarity based on protein concentration and phosphorylation. The model uses just a few variables to model concentrations and phosphorylation states of four molecules. And the model is indeed mathematically solvable. However, there is no evidence that it is able to predict cell polarity in a real world instance.

8.6.3 Stochastic process models

Stochastic models can represent the behaviour of a one- or multi-dimensional *random* stochastic process X, such as the number of cars passing a check-point in 1 hour, the average survival time at a certain age, or the probability of cold weather given the month of the year.

However, they can succeed in this only under certain highly specific conditions:

1. the random event, and thus the associated random variable (in what follows: r.v.) X_t, has a distribution over time belonging to the exponential family,[22]
2. the process has additional properties that allow mathematical modelling (specifically, it must have independent and stationary increments, as further detailed in the enumeration that follows).

The most expressive family of stochastic models, and thus the models that have had the widest usage in describing phenomena involving the sorts of human interactions of interest to AI research, are the (general) Wiener process models (also referred to under the heading 'Brownian motion'). These have been used extensively (indeed, too extensively, as we shall see) to model financial market processes such as movements in stock or derivative prices (Jeamblanc et al. 2009). Such prices are an expression of the aggregated intentions of very many market participants. The models make strong mathematical assumptions, for example that a price change process X is a case of Brownian motion, or in other words that it satisfies the following conditions:

1. it has independent r.v. increments: for any pair of time points (s, t),

$$X_{t+s} - X_s \perp\!\!\!\perp \mathcal{F}_s^X,$$

   where $\mathcal{F}_s^X$ models the time before t,
2. it is stationary: $\forall s > 0: (X_{t+s}) = (X_t), t \geq 0$, and
3. for any time point $t > 0$, $X_t \sim \mathcal{N}(0, t)$.

Condition (1) expresses the fact that each increment of the r.v. is independent of what happened in the past; condition (2) that the unconditional joint probability distribution[23] of the process does not change when shifted in time; and condition (3) that the r.v. is distributed according to the Gaussian distribution.

Unfortunately, these conditions are not satisfied by any complex system processes, and they are not satisfied, in particular, by the processes of financial markets.

---

22 Often, this is the Gaussian distribution, i.e. $X_t \sim \mathcal{N}(\mu, \sigma^2)$.
23 'Unconditional' means: involves no dependence on any particular starting value.

164 The limits of mathematical models

This is, again, because in a market, complex systems (human beings) interact to create a collective complex system in which none of these conditions are met (see also 7.5.3.1). Therefore, stochastic models for financial markets can only model the continuation of a trend, for here something like a continuous function is indeed approximated. Whenever collective decisions in a market are off-trend, however, financial stochastic process models fail (McCauley 2009).

Complex systems, as we have seen, are not mathematically modelable. They are not distributed according to a multivariate Gaussian distribution, since they are non-stationary and non-independent. The Brownian motion model is therefore not applicable to complex systems, as none of its three conditions is satisfied: As evolutionary systems, they have strong memory properties which violates condition (1.). Their probability distribution cannot be modelled according to condition (2.) at all (since they bear properties 2–7 in 7.5.3). Finally, and for the same reason, they are not Gaussian (condition (3.)).

8.6.4 Hidden Markov Models

A hidden Markov model (HMM) is a type of stochastic model which models a process as a sequence of successive observable events that are generated by transitions between unobservable states. In addition, this process of steps is viewed in an HMM as a Markov chain, which means that each step is viewed as being dependent only on its immediate predecessor with a known transition probability. Let us again take as our paradigm example the case most salient for purposes of general AI, namely human dialogue. Let us imagine two dialogue participants as forming a combined two-person sensorimotor and cognitive system able to generate and interpret utterances in each successive cycle. If such a system would meet (1) the cardinal assumption of an HMM, namely satisfaction of the Markov property, together with (2) the assumption that transition probabilities remain constant over time or vary in a finite, known way, then an HMM could indeed be used to model dialogue utterances as emanations from those unobservable mental events that lead to the utterance generation and interpretation steps that form the dialogue.

Unfortunately, dialogues violate both of these assumptions, and so HMMs cannot be used to model dialogues. Other complex system processes—including all the types of complex processes relevant to general AI—violate them as well.[24]

8.6.5 Stochastic differential equation models

Differential equations can be extended to model temporal processes subjected to stochastic effects (noise), for example to model molecular dynamics. Again,

---

24 We do not discuss n-grams and other useful stochastic language models here. They certainly have benefits in many applications such as word completion or error correction, but cannot model complex systems.

however, even stochastically modified differential equations would still not be applicable to the problem of complex system modelling, since this would require that the assumptions needed for the applicability of *both* differential equations *and* stochastic process models would need to hold simultaneously for processes generated by complex systems. In fact, however, both of these sets of assumptions fail.

8.6.6 'Self-learning' deep neural networks

So-called 'self-' or 'deep-learning' (deep) Neural Networks (dNNs) are a subclass of stochastic models (explained in section 8.2) that in recent years have sparked considerable enthusiasm, triggered above all by:

1. the successes achieved since 2014 in improving automated translation through use of dNNs,
2. improved dNNs using attention and transformer models (Vaswani et al. 2017),
3. the popularisation by Goodfellow et al. (2014) of generative adversarial networks (GANs),[25] and
4. the invention of reinforcement learning, which brought the capability to outperform human beings, for example in the game of Go (Silver et al. 2016).

dNNs stand out as a modelling method precisely because they are good at modelling even non-parametric multivariate distributions, and this is so even where there are many input dimensions, for example in the case of neural-network based translation from one language to another. They thereby represent a major advance in our ability to construct mathematical models by providing a means of constructing such models *implicitly*, rather than by explicitly writing an equation. The models in question are constructed with the help of optimisation algorithms, as described in sections 8.2. Though such algorithms were invented already 200 years ago (see 8.8), modern stochastic models have recently spawned a number of striking successes in AI research thanks to the huge amounts of digital data and massive computational power now available. Recent successes in AI along multiple fronts bear testimony to the significance of this advance in mathematical modelling. dNNs were accordingly tested early on in the domain of system and process modelling. They differ from classical statistical models, which are explicitly designed in a conscious mathematical effort, for example when observing process data and figuring out an equation to describe them. dNN-models and other machine learning models, in contrast, are created automatically by an optimisation algorithm which is merely *constrained* by humans when they choose the algorithm's hyperparameters, network architecture, optimisation goal,

---

[25] Invented and first described by Schmidhuber (1990).

and—above all—*training material* which contains the functionals to be learned by the algorithm.

Explainability   Precisely *how* the resulting equations solve the machine learning problems to which they are applied is something that often cannot be understood by humans—hence the 'explainability problem' of AI, which has generated a whole new field of research in what is called Explainable AI (Goebel et al. 2018). The goal, here, is to make it possible for the users of stochastic AI software to understand in a causal manner how such software achieves its results. The desire to causally explain the behaviour of machines derives from our familiarity with simple machines, whose behaviour can be explained because we understand the causal relations between their parts. But this sort of understanding is impossible where we are dealing with implicit models: the complexity of the equations which constitute the core of stochastic AI models is too high. For example, the language sequence model GPT-3 (which we will discuss in detail in section 10.4.1) comprises more than 175×10^9 parameters (Brown et al. 2020).[26]

Let us consider the benefits of such models in those cases where they achieve production-grade performance. In the case of a spam filter, for example, it is humans who constantly create the training tuples used to generate and continuously update the AI model, which are of the form:

⟨email, spam[0|1]⟩.

They do this each time they click the spam button in an email client.[27] The benefit brought by the AI model here is that it behaves (in detecting spam) in conformity with how the selected set of humans behaved when they were generating the tuples that were used to train the model.[28] It is quite general, and can arise wherever AI-based models of complex systems involving human activity are applied as a basis for controlling, planning, or predicting such activity. But we cannot explain causally the behaviour of these humans. And so also, we cannot—though for different reasons—causally explain the behaviour of a dNN. This lack of explainability is of no concern as long as the model accomplishes the tasks for which it was designed. To ensure that this is so, the models should be subjected to repeated tests in a wide range of environments. Such

---

26 Each dNN can be written as an equation. In this form, the GPT-3 model would have 175×10^9 terms. No one can understand such an equation.

27 If a user clicks, the training tuple is set to ⟨email, 1⟩, otherwise to ⟨email, 0⟩.

28 Note, however, that due to the evolutionary properties of all complex systems, and more specifically to the drivenness of the human creators of spam, the latter will try to overcome the filters by inventing new types of spam. AI spam filters, by bringing about changes in the emanations of the complex system that they themselves are attempting to model, will thereby contribute to their own failure. We have encountered such *model-induced escape* before (8.5.1).

testing is much more important than attempts—which must always fail—to *explain* how the models work in yielding given outputs.[29]

8.6.6.1 'Self-learning' AI and the myth of the neural network

AI systems do not learn in the sense that animals and humans do. Lapuschkin et al. (2019) emphasise that to use the term 'learning' when speaking of the mechanics of stochastic AI is inappropriate because the optimisation algorithms used to train neural networks do not *learn* in anything like the sense in which vertebrates learn. Rather, they merely create locally optimal functionals or operators designed to minimise loss or optimize reward. What is thereby created is of course mightily impressive in certain domains; but one effect of the use of the term 'learning' is that it suggests that it can usefully be compared to learning on the part of organisms such as ourselves, above all in the sense that, like human learning, it can be extended into ever new areas and to ever new types of problems. This is not the case.

Indeed, to the contrary: the fact that the model is generated implicitly does not justify the use of concepts of 'learning' or 'training' borrowed from the way we talk about vertebrates or humans. This is because the machine does not learn anything; it merely computes algorithms taken from the theory of optimisation (Bertsekas 2016; Goodfellow et al. 2016). Deviations of the input data from the distribution of data in the training set yield false or useless predictions.[30]

A further problem turns on the fact that, as Ben-David et al. (2019) show, there are simple scenarios where stochastic learnability can neither be proved nor refuted, a result which follows from showing the equivalence of a simple learning problem with the continuum hypothesis. Since the latter is undecidable, so also is the former. This means that using the axioms of Zermelo-Fraenkel set theory, it cannot be shown whether the learning problem can or cannot be solved.

Even more misleading is the use of the term 'self-learning' to suggest that machines can acquire new knowledge—again by analogy with the way humans acquire new knowledge—*all by themselves*. However, nothing of this sort is happening. It is humans who carefully prepare the training tuples $\left\{x_{ij}, \ldots, x_{ip}, y_i\right\}_{i=1}^{N}, j = 1 \ldots p$ which the algorithm is given and who carefully transform the input data into a form that makes it ingestible by the selected algorithm; they also schedule the re-training rhythm that the machine adheres to. Nothing is 'done' by the machine 'itself'—machines do not act; they merely

---

29 Something similar holds of scientific pharmacotherapy, whose practitioners have rarely understood the effects of the drugs they developed and in most cases still cannot causally explain them today. What matters is that they are shown through testing to be efficient and safe. This holds also for stochastic models.
30 For some examples see p. 214.

168 The limits of mathematical models

compute according to their instructions, in ways which lead to changes in electric charges.

Many AI practitioners in the field share our view. For example, Chollet (2017, p. 325) writes:

> In general, anything that requires reasoning—like programming or applying the scientific method—long-term planning, and algorithmic data manipulation is out of reach for deep-learning models, no matter how much data you throw at them. ... A deep-learning model can be interpreted as a kind of program; but, inversely, most programs can't be expressed as deep-learning models.

Darwiche (2018) emphasises that dNNs are merely 'more sophisticated statistical techniques for fitting functions' and have nothing to do with real learning.

Despite this, proponents of connectionist AI claim that dNNs model the way in which neurons are interconnected in the brain. Pavone et al. (2021) give an overview of this view and conclude that it must be rejected, given that

> the analogy between modern artificial neural models and biological ones appears increasingly inconsistent, in the physical structure, in the type of abstraction operated on the input data and in the implemented algorithmic solutions, so much so as to argue that the two cognitive models may be incommensurable.

But the connectionist creed is hard to overcome. For example, Katzen et al. (2021) conclude as follows from their interesting results about preference modelling in *C. elegans:*

> The demonstration of utility maximisation in an organism with no more than several hundred neurons sets a new lower bound on the computational requirements for maximisation, and offers the prospect of an essentially complete explanation of value-based decision making at single neuron resolution.

This passage reveals the most important error made by the connectionists: a nervous system made of a few hundred neurons is much more complex than an artificial dNN with billions of parameters, which is merely a (big) logic-system-modelling equation. This is because each neuron contains millions of signal-integrating molecules and is connected to other neurons via synapses using a plenitude of neurotransmitters which elicit many different reactions based on the state of the post-synaptic neuron. Furthermore, the neurons of higher organisms also depend on humoral factors (hormones and other signalling molecules in the blood). They are living cells, which are driven and thus never in equilibrium, but they produce and consume energy all the time. In short, unlike stochastic models (such as dNNs), which are logic systems and can thus be executed on computers (to approximate complex systems), nervous systems are complex systems in their own right.

8.6.6.2 Data greed of dNNs

dNNs need huge amounts of data to be trained, and this limits their performance. This is so for many reasons. In dNNs relating to dialogue behaviour, for example, much of the data is unobtainable because it refers to what transpires in people's heads (details are given in chapter 10). A more general problem arises where the input vector space is of high dimensionality, as is the case in the vast majority of dNNs, including those used in machine translation and in image and shape classification. This engenders what is called the 'curse of dimensionality' (Hastie et al. 2008, chapter 2.5), which turns on the fact that in such spaces 'most data points are closer to the boundary of the sample space than to any other data point'.[31] But separating data points from each other, which is what dNN-classifiers do, is harder at the edge of the sample space (because there are fewer neighbours at the edge) than it is towards the centre. Matters are made worse by the fact that the

> sample density is proportional to $N^{1/p}$, where p is the dimension of the input space and N is the sample size. Thus, if $N_1 = 100$ represents a dense sample for a single input problem, then $N_{10} = 100^{10}$ is the sample size required for the same sampling density with 10 inputs.
> (Hastie et al. 2008, p. 23)

Yet the sorts of problems dNNs are designed to solve often require hundreds of dimensions ('inputs'). For most applications, therefore, the data space will remain sparse and thereby limit the predictive quality of the models. For models trained using data from non-complex systems, for example to obtain dNNs for the control of robotic assembly lines, arbitrary amounts of real or synthetic data can be generated to overcome the curse of dimensionality. But this is not the case where training material is generated by complex systems, not least in those cases where organisms are involved. It is also not the case for dNNs targeting complex systems in (mostly) inanimate nature, for example in seismology or climate research. Data in such areas are always sparse and samples always inadequate. It is important to realise that statistical learning performs very poorly in a sparse data space as a result of the fact that, wherever the density of data is low, it

---

31 In a p-dimensional unit ball with N uniformly distributed data points, the median distance from the ball's centre to the closest data point is given by:

$$d(p, N) = \left(1 - \frac{1}{2}^{1/N}\right)^{1/p}.$$

For example, with $p = 10$, $N = 500$, we obtain $d(10, 500) \approx 0.52$, so that even at this rather low dimensionality, most of the data points are closer to the boundary than to the centre.

is impossible to estimate reliable hyperplanes to separate (classify) the data or to compute continuous regressions. When data are input into the model that are sampled from a space that was not used when collecting the training data, the model will fail. *This means that statistical models cannot deal with novelty*, because novelty is the absence of previously known distributions. Humans, in contrast, can deal very well with novel situations both consciously and unconsciously, for example by using analogies, or by finding creative solutions (see also 9.3.2).

Users of machine learning in scientific research or technical applications are often unaware of this issue, which means that they often develop stochastic models on the basis of sparse bodies of training data. Their initial results may then be quite impressive. In most cases, however, these results will reflect over-fitting (Hastie et al. 2008, chapter 7), which means that the algorithms will fail to generalise when applied to test sets of data obtained independently.

8.6.6.3 Stochastic models and the No Free Lunch theorem

The No Free Lunch (NFL) theorem, which was formulated and proven in the fields of search and optimisation, states that if the problem space in which an optimum is to be found must be modelled as a probability density function, then the computational cost of finding the optimum averaged over all problems in the space is the same for any solution method (Wolpert et al. 1997).[32] It follows that there cannot be any optimisation procedure that is globally superior to all others—a procedure can be superior only with regard to some specific problem class.[33]

The theorem applies in particular to complex system emanations yielding data which correspond to unique (non-repeatable) multivariate distributions at each step. Indeed, for data of this sort, per the NFL theorem, it is not only that we cannot find a globally superior optimisation method. As this chapter shows in its entirety, we cannot obtain an adequate (requirement-fulfilling) predictive model of any sort.

Approximative special solutions can be found in some cases, as was shown for example by Valiant (1984), who defined the notion of 'probably approximately correct learning' for certain problem classes, using a framework based on computational complexity theory which describes computational problems in terms of their resource usage. He then applied this framework to machine learning problems. The problem, however, is that the framework cannot be applied to the rich behavioural output of animate complex systems.

---

32 Stochastic models are solution methods in the sense of the NFL theorem if they are used on data that are modelled as non-parametric multivariate distributions.

33 The theorem is not valid where the data in the problem space have a structure that can be mathematically exploited explicitly. This occurs, for example in physics, where we encounter problem spaces which can be adequately modelled and solved using differentiable functions or differential equations.

The No Free Lunch theorem helps us to understand why general problem solvers cannot be found for many real-world problems and why such problems need to be restricted to cases in which special solvers can provide a solution. These are exactly the cases where AI—more precisely: narrow AI—works (examples are given in sections 13.1 and 13.2).

What sometimes happens, however, is that such approximative special solutions—which work only for a subset of cases within a given field—are associated with claims of general applicability. Solutions of this sort will inevitably result in failures when they are applied to cases outside the restricted set. Recent cases of driver casualties in self-driving cars confronted with sensor input deviating from the training distribution are just one example of this phenomenon.

With such examples in mind, we now review the potential capability of three more ambitious, and seemingly promising, dNN-methods to model complex systems, and show why they, too, fail.

8.6.7 Some special types of neural networks

8.6.7.1 Deep recurrent neural network (rNN) models

Deep *recurrent* neural networks are dNNs in which the connections between the nodes of the dNN graph allow the modelling of temporal sequences. They are often called sequence-to-sequence-dNNs, because they can be used to create one sequence from another (for example, sequences of words when a one-sentence translation is generated as output from a one-sentence input). Often, what is called long-term-short-term-memory (LSTM) (Hochreiter et al. 1997) and its numerous extensions are used in practical AI-applications of this sort, including neural-network based translation. Because general stochastic process models (such as the Wiener process) are not able to model multivariate processes, the ability of rNNs to model processes of this sort has been investigated in recent years as a potential saving alternative (Dasgupta et al. 2017; Neil et al. 2016; Lai et al. 2017). The results have performed well for certain sorts of tasks, for example modelling road traffic occupancy, solar power production, or electricity consumption over time. As Lai et al. (2017) report, they have outperformed classical stochastic process models in tasks of this sort, especially in those cases where two processes with different patterns are overlaid in a series of observations.

We can infer from these examples several reasons why rNNs work well on such numerical time-series data:

1. data of these sorts—though only approximately—fulfil the assumptions needed for stochastic process modelling in general (of which dNNs, and thus rNNs, are a special case),

172 The limits of mathematical models

2. the data are *repetitive* and huge historical datasets are available for training purposes,
3. the dimensionality and the variance of the data are low,[34]
4. dNN architectures can be used to model temporal pattern overlays of the sort observed for example in traffic occupancy, which has both a circadian and a workday vs. weekend rhythm.

The behaviour of complex systems, however,

i. is not repetitive, but erratic,
ii. does not fulfil the central assumptions presupposed by temporal process models (see p. 164), which must also be satisfied for rNNs to succeed in this modelling task,
iii. is of extremely high dimensionality, and
iv. yields no multivariate distribution from which one could draw adequate samples because novel behaviour can emerge at every stage, thereby creating input-output-tuples from a constantly changing, evasive distribution.

8.6.7.2 Generative adversarial network (GAN) models

GAN models are yet a further case of dNNs which work by using two networks, one discriminative, the other generative (Goodfellow et al. 2014). The former is a type of network that is trained to discriminate classes of input data using annotated training material, often pictures tagged by human beings (for example pictures in which humans can be distinguished from other items represented). The generative network is then tasked to create new samples of one desired class (for example pictures of humans created by blending characteristics of multiple images (Karras et al. 2018)). The two networks are then chained together by having the many, many samples yielded by the generative network passed on to the discriminative network for classification. Finally, the system is optimised to minimise the rate at which samples are generated that are not classified by the discriminative network as belonging to the desired class. This approach works very well with pictures, because the discriminative net can be pre-trained with adequate training material (data consisting of real images correctly tagged by humans).

But while GANs are very powerful for example in image recognition tasks, they are again not applicable to complex systems modelling. For example, in order to build an activity-generating GAN that creates meaningful activities of the sort generated by humans, one would need to pretrain a discriminative net that can distinguish meaningful from non-meaningful human activities. The

---

34 Exchange rates, another example modelled using dNNs, form a special case. This is because outcome dimensionality and variance are here relatively low in the short term. Unfortunately, the models work less successfully for mid-term predictions, where the outcomes are erratic (Lai et al. 2017).

problem is that, because the meaningfulness of an activity depends on its specific context and interpretation, no multivariate training distributions are available. Therefore, it is impossible to obtain adequate training material for general purpose discriminative nets for GANs, even if very narrow and special solutions may look impressive at first glance.

Evolutionary GANs Recently, evolutionary GANs have been proposed (Wang et al. 2019), where the basic idea is to overcome the limitations of GANs resulting for example from the fixed generator objective function[35], by exploiting a population of generators to compute the adversarial 'game' played with the discriminator. In a set of generators, each uses a different adversarial training objective to obtain mutation operations. While this improves the computational properties of GANs and creates a more diverse output, it does not in any way overcome the issues faced by all dNNs with regard to modelling complex systems.

8.6.7.3 Models based on reinforcement learning

Reinforcement learning (Sutton et al. 2018), finally, is a type of neural network that has been applied primarily to game-playing activities. Here the machine assigns a reward (score) every time a certain desirable step in a repeatable type of finite process is realised by the machine. *Finite* here means that the process ends after a series of steps that is not too long, such as a game of Go or a first-person shooter game in which killing sequences are repeated.

In Go, for example, a trained algorithm is used to assign a score after each action the machine performs in each game. The machine obtains one point for each of the opponent's stones it captures and one point for each grid intersection of territory it occupies. The trained algorithm is optimised to maximise the total score obtained over the entire game. This is done by having the computer play the game millions to billions of times in different situations, so that optimal paths for these situations can be found and stored in the model. Crucial, for such optimisation to be possible, is that the scores for every move can be assigned automatically by the machine. Machine learning of this sort can thus be used only in those situations in which the results of machine decisions *can be scored through further machine decisions*. This is of course primarily in games; but the method can be extended, for example, to debris cleaning, where what is scored is the number of units of debris removed. In such narrowly defined settings, machines can find strategies that outperform human behaviour (Jaderberg et al. 2019).

Lastly, reverse reinforcement learning, a technique to automatically learn an adequate reward score from observed settings (Arora et al. 2018), does not

---

35 Classical GANs have a fixed function for which an extremum is found in the data-driven dNN-optimisation step.

help in complex systems, because there is here no adequate set of observed settings. The variance, again, is too large, and so too few patterns are repeated sufficiently many times to enable automatic scoring.

But what about poker? In one variant of the game—six-player no-limit Texas hold'em—dNNs can even beat human professionals (Brown et al. 2019), a stunning result given that the self-play-with-search algorithm used in the poker algorithm (and initially used in AlphaGo) has no known strong theoretical guarantees on performance in multiplayer games. However, the key factor which enables human professionals to win poker games and that cannot be emulated by machines, was removed from the game.[36] In the experimental setup, direct human gambling interaction was forbidden, and human players were thereby dispossessed of their one advantage over the dNN, namely, superior powers of intersubjectivity. The experiment therefore merely shows that, if the game is reduced to a non-complex, rule-dependent and ergodic search and combination problem like chess or Go, then machines can indeed beat humans. But this is only because they are more efficient at searching huge but non-complex, regular spaces, something that holds especially in the case of dNNs. The experimental setup here reduces poker to a closed-world setting. But if, as in normal poker variants, the machine would be sitting with humans at the poker table equipped with video- and audio-sensors, then, because it lacks the ability to include the signals these sensors produce into its models in a meaningful, effective way, the machine would lose—human intersubjectivity trumps search in regular poker.

Reinforcement learning is ideal for closed-world settings. But real-world settings are open, and it is not only the actors in such an environment that are complex, but also the environment itself. Reinforcement learning works best for closed-world settings or processes that can be adequately modelled as such, for example a first-person-shooter game in which all the data input is given in the form of entities defined using linear algebra and each step can be immediately rewarded by the 'kill score'. Reinforcement learning fails in open situations that are a part of real-world environments.

This is also confirmed by the recent claim of the DeepMind AI research group to have developed an AI-learning framework for 'open-ended learning' leading to 'generally capable agents' (Stooke et al. 2021). The achievements of the algorithms are impressive, but the agent is operating in a closed world with a simple reward pattern implementing the Hutter-definition of AGI given in equations 3.1–3.2. It is therefore certainly neither 'open-ended' nor 'generally capable'

---

36 'The participants were not told who else was participating in the experiment. Instead, each participant was assigned an alias that remained constant throughout the experiment. The alias of each player in each game was known, so that players could track the tendencies of each player throughout the experiment' (Brown et al. 2019, section 'Experiment evaluation').

Mathematical models of complex systems 175

and will not be able to compete with animals as proposed by Crosby et al. (2019) for AI testing.

But reinforcement learning cannot be applied to the prediction of the behaviour of complex systems. It therefore cannot be applied, either, to the generation of convincing complex system behaviour, as is required, for example in the dialogue case. For in complex systems there is nothing to which the needed sorts of scores can be automatically assigned. There is no *winning*, as we might say; or at least no winning of the sort that can be generally, and repeatedly, and consistently, and automatically scored—something that the reader can easily ascertain for herself by attempting to devise a routine for assigning such scores the next time she engages in a dialogue.

8.6.7.4 Complex rewards

But couldn't we create a sequence of rewards adequate for learning the behaviour of a complex system? The problem here is that such a reward sequence would have to give situation-specific rewards. This is because each step on a complex-system-model trajectory would have to deal with an unexpected situation resulting from the interaction of the AI system with its own environment, and this will be so for all those cases where the AI can be useful for us in a natural environment (or in a hybrid environment—such as a trading hall, or a factory floor, or in road traffic). We cannot create a reward path for such a trajectory, because at each successive step different rewards would be needed to correspond to the emanations from those complex systems that form the environment. Each new step would require its own situation-specific reward. But such a temporal reward sequence would obviously not follow a Markovian pattern, because the reward would depend not only on the previous step, but also on many earlier steps, and as much on long-term dispositions[37] as on short-term intentions. And a machine, as we shall see in chapter 9.2, lacks both. Instead, as a result of its need to correspond to the complex emanations relating to varying situations in each step, *the reward sequence would itself have to be complex and thereby have all the properties of a complex system emanation*. We have no mathematical models for processes with these properties.

We note, therefore, that even the truly impressive successes of reinforcement learning do not provide any evidence at all that AGI is about to be achieved. On the contrary, these achievements exemplify the narrow applicability of such algorithms, which is limited to settings in which automatic reward scoring *is* possible. Furthermore, their limitations are evident from the fact that the meta-parameter of the algorithms which compute the optimisation, including how its scores (and

---

37 A phenomenon that is captured by phrases such as 'being acquainted with, knowing, being convinced, believing, loving, wanting' (Bassenge 1930), which is often confusingly conceived of as what are called 'mental states'. Bassenge refers to such dispositions with the Greek term *hexis* (ἕξις), which he borrows from Aristotle, using it in the sense of long-term mental dispositions.

many other parameters) are to be defined, needs to be set anew, in each successive case, by human engineers.

8.6.8 Unsupervised learning

Unsupervised learning is an approach to pattern or sequence identification which does not use tuples of the type $\left\{x_{ij}, \ldots, x_{ip}, \mathbf{y}_i\right\}_{i=1}^{N}, j = 1 \ldots p$ described in eqn. 8.3, but only a data matrix X of dimensions $N \times p$, where N is the number of observations and p the number of dimensions.[38] In vector notation, the input $N \times p$ data matrix X has the form: $\left\{x_{ij}, \ldots, x_{ip}\right\}_{i=1}^{N}, j = 1 \ldots p$. There is no outcome $\mathbf{y}_i$, so there is no 'teacher' or 'trainer'; there is just the data matrix X, a p-dimensional multivariate distribution. The goal is to find characteristics of the probability density $\Pr(X)$ without an outcome.

This type of learning comprises classical techniques as well as those using neural networks. Among the former, there are two major groups:

1. clustering, which uses distance measures between data points (observations) to identify groups of similar observations in p-dimensional metric spaces (vector spaces endowed with a distance measure),
2. dimension reduction techniques (association rules, principal components, self-organising maps and other methods) (Hastie et al. 2008, chapter 14).

All unsupervised learning methods require large amounts of data to yield robust results; the number of observations must be many times larger than the number of variables, and this requirement is even more significant for dNN-based clustering than for conventional methods.

The neural network methods can be applied where N is very large (often 10^7 and more observations) and comprises two subgroups: **clustering with deep learning** (Aljalbout et al. 2018; Min et al. 2018) and **sequence learning**, such as in the model GPT-3, which we will analyse in depth in 10.4.1.

Clustering and dimension-reduction methods with dNNs can generate patterns of related observations. They are extremely useful in data exploration, pattern identification, and outlier or anomaly detection. However, they always require a human scientist to identify promising results and to interpret and use them in some down-stream application.

Unsupervised sequence learning enables systems that can create an output sequence from input data on the basis of the probability density $\Pr(X)$ which the model learns.

---

38 For example, the observations can be sales transactions and the variables can encode the goods sold. Or, the former can be blood samples for patients and the latter biochemical measurements.

This output sequence can be seen as a pattern derived from the input based on the data matrix X. The resulting output sequence is similar to a subset of the sequences present in the training set. The output sequence might be, for example, an answer to a question if the question resembles a certain chain of symbols found in question-answer-tuples of the training corpus. This is how such models can, for example, propose a sentence completion to humans writing an email. But such unsupervised sequence models cannot adequately meet the typical requirements an AI system is supposed to fulfil because the output of complex systems cannot be modelled using multivariate distributions, as explained in the next section and, with more examples, in section 10.4.1.

Foundation models Transfer learning is a technique in which the lower layers of a neural network are used to train a new network using a task-specific training set. The data processing optimisation that is encoded in the lower layers of a neural net can be reused for new purposes in this manner. Interestingly, the Center for Research on Foundation Models at Stanford University describes these models as 'self-supervised', which is a euphemism for lack of training tuples with outcomes. The group depicts them as a new ('third wave') innovation in the history of stochastic models after simple supervised regression models and supervised dNNs.

While the initial foundation models were trained only on one type of data (for example text, as in the case of GPT-3), there are now multi-modal versions of such models, trained simultaneously on different data types (Luo et al. 2020a; Ramesh et al. 2021). The principle of foundation models is to train a sequence-prediction model from unsupervised data and to then apply transfer learning with additional data in order to condition the model towards a more specific goal.[39] For transfer learning, existing foundation models are re-trained with annotated data of the type described in eqn. 8.3. This is done for reasons of model refinement—to make the model more specific, to take account of the passing of time, or to constrain models, for example to prevent harmful outputs learned from mass data. Examples of the latter are the sorts of extremist uses of language or pornographic or violent image contents found in many sites on the web. Foundation models typically learn from blindly collected web content.

The current literature about foundational models does not address the arguments for their limitations described in this book, namely that they are, despite their size and complexity, models for logic systems used to approximate the behaviour of complex systems.

This means that they will always fall short when it comes to producing outputs that will conform to the requirements of successful interaction with complex systems such as human beings.[40] They will never transcend this

---

39 Here 'condition' is used in the statistical sense, as in the phrase 'conditioned probability'. For an example of conditioned models see section 10.4.1.
40 As Marcus and Davis point out: 'The reality is that foundation models, at least in their current incarnations. are more like parlor tricks than genuine intelligence. They work impressively

fundamental limitation. Therefore, the exaggerated optimism which surrounds them, in terms of both opportunities and risks (described at length in (Bommasani et al. 2021)), is unwarranted.

8.6.9 Consequences for AI applications

We have seen that we cannot model complex systems using AI. But what are the implications of this argument in the case of the self-driving car? The traffic system is certainly complex, and so is driving behaviour. But there are already many successful realisations of autonomous driving systems in *controlled environments*, for example in the form of specially created road systems on university campuses, where a small number of dimensions of variation in traffic and road conditions is allowed. A vehicle driving autonomously in such a system is controlled by an implementation of an AI-mathematical model that is succeeding in making the almost exact predictions needed to achieve the reliability we demand from modern technology. The reason this is possible is that a controlled environment is not complex unless some complex event occurs that makes it complex, as for example a fire in the path of an autonomous vehicle or other cases illustrating evolutionary properties of complex systems, as when a group of hackers conspires to fork the system in order to enable their own vehicles to travel faster.

Step by step, the number of dimensions of real-world traffic conditions with which such models are able to cope is being increased, without sacrificing reliability. This is achieved by starting with relatively controlled environments, as for example in the case of the San Francisco robotaxi service, which currently operates at a maximum speed of 30 MPH and only under mild weather conditions between 10PM and 6AM. If the underlying models prove themselves in use under these conditions, they will be extended to cover a gradually increasing array of driving-relevant phenomena by retraining the models with more and more data.

We do not know whether there might come a point where this process leads to models which achieve—under certain environmental restrictions—a driving performance comparable to that of the middle-aged, careful, female drivers who form the safest human driver cohort. The result would be a tremendous victory for human technology, comparable in its consequences to the victory achieved by the Wright brothers in their demonstration of the possibility of manned flight. But it would be a victory not for *general* but rather for *narrow* AI, since the mathematical models in question will not hold for traffic environments in general, but rather only for those environments which conform to the

well some of the time but also frequently fail, in ways that are erratic, unsystematic, and even downright foolish' (Marcus et al. 2021).

specific set of dimensions of variation built into the models as they exist at any given stage in the step-by-step retraining process.

Each of these models will *approximate* to the real-world traffic system in successively closer degrees of exactness. The real-world traffic system itself however is complex in all the mentioned respects. Thus it is not possible to adapt a driverless car built to cope synoptically and adequately with one or other of the logic systems defined by such models, which are virtual closed environments, in a way that will achieve human-level driving performance in an uncontrolled environment. Certainly we can achieve this as a matter of luck for some time. That is, the driverless car may for a time only encounter environments conforming to the logic system defined by the most recent version of its software. But luck, in this business, will not suffice over longer periods as events will happen for which the models were not trained or which were present in the training samples but did not influence the implicit model sufficiently. What we need is the sort of reliability that can be provided by mathematical proof. And where complex systems are involved this cannot be attained. The fundamental reason is that we cannot draw the needed sorts of samples from distributions generated by complex systems. Higher animals and humans, in contrast to machines, can cope with novel situations in the needed way because they are intelligent. This means most importantly that they can suddenly but yet continuously change their intentions and adapt the goals which guide their behaviour when confronted with novel situations or a change of mood. AI algorithms can do none of these things, as we have seen in sections 8.3 and 8.6.6.

We should also not forget that, to work properly at any given stage in such a process, stochastic models used for prediction require input that consists of data which are distributed in accordance with the distribution of the training data that was used to create them. This implies, however, that there is a limit to the performance of any given stochastic model, which is determined by the range of types of phenomena over which its training data are distributed and by the type of the distribution.

Training distributions resulting from non-ergodic processes lead to an asymptotic performance limit. This means that given a fixed data set available at training time, the model's optimum, no matter which stochastic learning technique is applied, is determined by the size and the properties of the training set, and there is then, as we saw on page 149, a necessary hiatus between this optimum and the behaviour of the complex system that it is supposed to emulate. At the same time, however, we note that this optimum, too, is rarely achieved because the optimisation algorithm used for this purpose almost never finds the global minimum of the loss function.

The more important limitation in practice, however, is the quality of the fit between training and application (real-world) distribution, a limitation that cannot be resolved by providing more training data if the quality of fit is low *a priori*. This is the case, first of all, with synthetic, or semi-synthetic training data that massively deviate from real data because they cannot match the properties of data emanating from complex systems.

But there are abundant examples also of real-world cases where only insufficient data are available for machine learning. Many automation problems require uniformly distributed but very special outcomes for identical inputs to be addressed using machine learning. As a typical example, consider the validation of hospital claims by insurance companies. Because the data documented in each such claim are often complicated (for example they may describe a long hospitalisation period at a detailed level) and there is a high variance in the cognitive behaviour of the human clerks evaluating the claim, different clerks will develop a different understanding of and will generate different evaluation results for identical claims. Therefore, the outcomes are often heterogeneous and mutually contradictory. Furthermore, the intermediate steps of the process are rarely stored. In the claim validation case, it is very often only the resulting payment sum that is stored, but neither the deduction components nor their justifications.

Synthetic or semi-synthetic data are often used to provide training data when outcomes are sparse, notably for rare situations in car-driving cases. Unfortunately these data are often inadequate because they do not provide a representation of the real situations a driver encounters. This also applies to attempts to 'expedite' the creation of a training set by relying on 'function-based annotations' (Bringer et al. 2019). Such training sets lead to stochastic models that are mere reverse functions of the generating functions (f_i^{-1} of f_i).

All in all, high-quality training data are rare. Given that real world data acquisition for many tasks requires not merely iterative, active perception, interpretation and observations, but also concomitant *evaluations* which lead to constantly shifting distributions (see 3.3.2), the resultant degree of fit at any given stage is rarely good, and so for this reason also training data are often inadequate. Retraining cannot overcome the problem of fundamentally inadequate training data. Retraining only helps if the new data input into the retrained prediction model can be modelled as elements of the data distribution used during the retraining.

8.7 Refined approaches

Mathematicians who have become aware of the inadequacy of Newtonian mathematics for the modelling of complex systems have tried to develop more sophisticated (thus: non-naïve) approaches, using mathematical frameworks which can cope with the properties of complex systems and yet remain computable.

In their *Introduction to the Theory of Complex Systems*, Thurner et al. (2018) express their belief that

> the exact sciences may be entering a phase of transition from a traditional analytical description of nature, as used with tremendous success since Galileo and Newton, towards an algorithmic description. Whereas the analytical

description of nature is, conceptually, based largely on differential equations and analytical equations of motion, the algorithmic view takes into account evolutionary and co-evolutionary aspects of dynamics. It provides a framework for systems that can endogenously change their internal interaction networks, rules of functioning, dynamics, and even environment, as they evolve in time.

The authors hold that what they call 'algorithmic dynamics'

> which is characteristic of complex dynamical systems, may be a key to the quantitative and predictive understanding of many natural and man-made systems. In contrast to physical systems, which typically evolve analytically, algorithmic dynamics describe certainly how living, social, environmental, and economic systems unfold.
>
> (Thurner et al. 2018, pp. vi-vii)

The claim is that we are currently witnessing a paradigm shift in the exact sciences away from the modeling of what Thurner et al. (2018) sometimes call 'simple systems' to a new framework that can model complex systems. But is this claim justified? What is an 'algorithmic description' of nature?

Note, first of all, that what the authors call 'algorithmic description' seems to be a mix of the following principal approaches used by the complex systems community: *scaling, explicit networks, evolutionary process models*, and *entropy models*, all of them including stochastic elements, where the choice among them is made in a way that depends on the problem to be analysed.

In each case this involves some sort of simplification, whereby the target complex system is replaced with a simpler system with which known mathematical models and a universal Turing machine can cope. Unfortunately none of the proposed simplification strategies is capable of producing the sort of almost exact predictions that are required by a general AI that would be able to master the behaviour of complex systems in a comprehensive manner. As we will see in the following sections, they can handle only partial aspects of the phenomena they describe and yield neither causal *explanations* nor exact *predictions*.

8.7.1 Scaling

Scaling describes a property an object has which remains invariant under an amplification or deflation of its size. It occurs in many natural phenomena in which small objects of one type are more frequent than large objects of the same type (Newman 2005). This is the case, for example, for human settlement patterns or for crater diameters on the surface of the moon. The resulting data can be modelled according to power law distributions. For example, the foraging behaviour of predators in areas with sparse prey density can be modelled using a special class of random walk with movement displacements (steps) drawn from a probability distribution with a power-law tail (Humphries et al. 2010). The power-law tails method can be used also in financial markets as explained in Fieguth (2017, chapter 9).

A scaling relation is present if there are two functions $f, g : D \to \mathbb{R}$ and $\lambda \in \mathbb{R}^+$ for which upon a scaling $x \to \lambda x$ the following holds:

$$f(\lambda x) = g(\lambda) f(x) \tag{8.5}$$

with the solution:

$$f(x) = bx^c \tag{8.6}$$

with $b, c \in \mathbb{R}$ (Thurner et al. 2018, 3.1.1). This solution is a power law (one quantity varies as a power of another), which asserts that x scales by λ with parameter b and exponent c. Aspects of data measured from complex systems can be modelled using such laws, which allow power exponents and other properties (such as criticality exponents) to be accurately computed. Scaling with power laws can also be modelled using sample-space reducing processes, which are another type of stochastic process model (Thurner et al. 2018, chapter 3).

8.7.1.1 Turbulence

An interesting example of the use of scaling to describe complex systems is the theory of turbulence formulated by Kolmogorov in 1941 (Kolmogorov 1941b, 1941a). This provides an explanation of one aspect of the behaviour of the phenomenon, though with massive limitations.

Turbulence is, according to Richard Feynman, 'the most important unsolved problem of classical physics' (Feynman et al. 2010). This remains true today, and there is still no complete description of the phenomenon. Werner Heisenberg is said to have given the following reply when he was asked what questions he would ask God, if given the opportunity: 'When I meet God,' he replied, 'I am going to ask him two questions: Why relativity? And why turbulence? I really believe he will have an answer for the first' (Marshak et al. 2005, p. 76).

Turbulence is fluid motion characterised by chaotic changes in pressure and flow velocity. Figure 8.1 shows a famous sketch by Leonardo depicting the turbulence occurring when a water jet issues from an outfall into a pool. It is a ubiquitous phenomenon, ensuing for example when smoke rises from a cigar, in all waterflows, and in many complex systems: for example, the global climate, the weather, in respiratory systems of breathing animals, or in the circulatory systems of vertebrates such as ourselves. Air turbulence is one of the factors that allows the trumpeter to effectuate the oscillating motion of the lips needed to produce Aeolian tones. Indeed: 'The whole mechanism of producing musical tones on brass instruments is a function of the transfer of laminar air to turbulent air to create pressure' (Oare, June 17, 2018).

Turbulence is caused by an energy flow through a liquid (or a mix of gases), which can be seen as an inanimate complex system of a very simple sort, with the molecules of and in the liquid as elements. As such, it does not have all the properties of an animate complex system, but it is experimentally unrepeatable in detail, irregular, and time-irreversible; it has chaotic element-interactions, anisotropy, inanimate drivenness, and it is non-ergodic (see also Table 7.1). We find turbulence when excessive kinetic energy in areas of a fluid flow overcomes the damping effect of the viscosity of the fluid or smoke or gas mix. When smoke rises from a cigar, its flow is laminar until its viscosity drops (due to dilution with air). The forming plume is turbulent because the kinetic energy of the smoke stream is high enough to overcome the viscosity. Figure 8.2 illustrates turbulence at a smaller scale. It shows the measured motion of a particle of size 46 μm ($\sim \frac{1}{20}$ mm) in turbulent water over a period of approximately 4 milliseconds. In this short interval, its acceleration alternates between almost zero and 16,000 m/s^2 (La Porta et al. 2001).

One important aspect of turbulence is its energy dissipation: *How can the excess kinetic energy be dissipated within the liquid?*[41] Reynolds, who was the first physicist to formulate a theory of turbulence, hypothesised that the bigger vortices in a turbulent liquid divide their energy into smaller vortices until these reach a length scale that is so small that the viscosity of the fluid can dissipate the kinetic energy flowing through the liquid into thermal energy. The spectrum of the vortices' length scales ranges from large (at the point of the energy inflow into the water) to small—the dissipation vortex. It can be modelled using a blade stirring the water with a diameter of scale L to the scale η of the small vortex at which the energy dissipates.

Kolmogorov recognised that at high Reynolds numbers (low viscosity), the scale at which the dissipation occurs is:

$$\eta = \left(\frac{v^3}{\varepsilon}\right)^{1/4}, \qquad (8.7)$$

where v is the kinetic viscosity and ε the rate of energy dissipation. But what happens between the scale of the big vortices L and the dissipation scale η? How do the vortices behave when they get smaller and smaller, but still without dissipation?

Kolmogorov's model explains turbulence-induced dissipation using power laws. This elegant model fascinated the scientific community for several decades, but in the meantime it has been experimentally falsified. Mathematical details are given in the Appendix.

Newer approaches to modeling turbulence, such as the Kraichnan model and Burgers' turbulence have 'offered some successes. One can now state with

---

41 We roughly follow the exposition given by Falkovich (2011).

184 The limits of mathematical models

FIGURE 8.1 Leonardo da Vinci's sketch of turbulence in a pool of water.

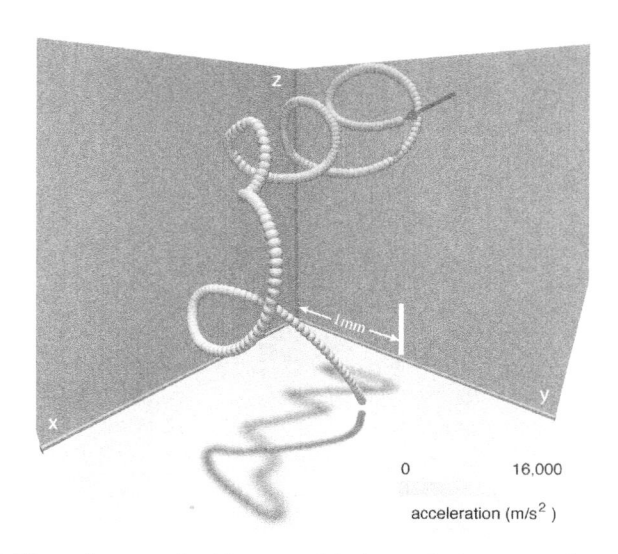

FIGURE 8.2 The trajectory of a 46 μm particle in a turbulent water flow. The shading indicates the different acceleration magnitudes, which reach levels of 16,000 m/s^2. The 'shadow' at the bottom shows an orthogonal projection of the particle's movement along the z-axis. For the original coloured version see https://buffalo.app.box.com/v/turbulence-2022.

©Eberhard Bodenschatz, with kind permission from the author.

Mathematical models of complex systems 185

confidence that stochastic differential equations like those that describe aspects of turbulence demonstrate the inadequacy of Kolmogorov's dimensional reasoning' (Falkovich et al. 2006, p. 48).

These new approaches are indeed useful for descriptive purposes and help us to model partial aspects of complex systems; but they are neither fully explicative nor predictive (Thurner et al. 2018, p. 138). Thus far, therefore, turbulence cannot be modelled in a way that allows the computation of its flows. Both in case of turbulence and in the predator examples given previously, available models can merely help us to *describe* the observed phenomena. They cannot explain, let alone predict, them. Yet turbulence is one of the very simplest sorts of complex systems.

8.7.2 Explicit networks

Explicit networks (Cowell et al. 2007) are graph-based models of reality which represent interrelated elements as nodes, with edges representing their interactions. For example, the spreading of a virus in a population can be modelled by a network where the nodes are individual humans and the edges infection events between two persons. Such networks can certainly describe some aspects of complex systems and even yield modestly precise predictions. But this is so only if the causal factors are rather simple and few in number.[42]

Explicit network approaches can capture an aspect of element interrelatedness of complex systems. But they cannot model accurately most aspects of such systems. Specifically, they cannot model multiple element interaction types, force overlay, non-predictability of phase space (non-ergodicity), drivenness, evolutionary properties, and open boundaries. In other words, explicit networks can model merely certain highly abstract aspects of complex systems as they exist in reality. This means that they are models which, again, can provide descriptions, but fall far short of yielding causal explanations or predictions.

8.7.3 Evolutionary process models

Starting from the observation that evolutionary systems are marked by long periods of element-stability followed by stages of sudden element change, evolutionary process models try to model when and to what extent such changes occur. This is done using general evolution algorithms, which can be represented by the following equations (Thurner et al. 2018, p. 245):

$$\sigma_i(t+dt) \sim \sigma_i(t) + F\left(M^{\alpha}_{ijk...}(t), \sigma_j(t), \sigma_k(t), \ldots\right)$$

---

42 For example in epidemiologic modeling of highly contagious diseases spreading in naïve (which means: thus far unexposed) populations.

and

$$M^{\alpha}_{ijk...}(t+dt) \sim M^{\alpha}_{ijk...}(t) + G\Big(M^{\alpha}_{ijk...}(t), \sigma_j(t), \sigma_k(t), \ldots\Big),$$

where t is time, σ is the phase space vector, σ_i is the state of the ith element of an evolutionary system, F and G are activation functions, α is an interaction type and $M^{\alpha}_{ijk...}(t)$ is a time-dependent interaction matrix modelling how the elements of the system interact for interaction type α.

It is now very difficult to use such equations because they have to be parameterised explicitly—unlike dNNs, which are parameterised automatically. This is hard first of all because of their obvious parameter-greed, and second because of the fact that the experimental data available for complex systems make it impossible to find parameters that will yield a predictive fit in almost all situations. Matters are made still more difficult by the restriction of such models to a set of predefined interaction types (α), which rules out the possibility of obtaining models of complex systems of this type that would be synoptic. Such models can, certainly, describe how new elements come into being in an evolutionary system if their interaction types would be known upfront. But again, most of the complex system properties cannot be modelled in a way that would achieve sufficient prediction quality. Like the scaling and explicit networks, this approach is merely a method *to describe* some aspects of a complex system.

8.7.4 Entropy models

Some in the complex system modelling community have suggested using entropy as a means of classifying complex systems in a way that will allow us to use statistical inference in order to understand path-dependent processes and the phase structure of complex systems (Thurner et al. 2018, p. 317). In this section, we analyse whether these goals can be realised using what are called entropy models of animate complex systems such as plants, animals, or humans.

8.7.4.1 What is entropy?

In information theory, the sort of physical system we are interested in is an information source producing emanations (called 'signals' by Shannon, the inventor of this theory). Such a system is a logic system if its output can be modelled as an ergodic Markov-process. Entropy is a measure used in statistical mechanics, information theory, and statistics using what is called the maximum entropy method.

For simple physical systems in the sense of Thurner et al., the entropy S of a system is defined by:

$$S = -k \sum_{i}^{W} p_i \log p_i$$

where k is a constant, W is the number of microstates of the system and p_i is the probability of observing microstate i. The measure thus defined is also called the Boltzmann-Gibbs-Shannon entropy.

In statistical mechanics, entropy is an extensive property[43] of a thermodynamic system. It is used to quantify the number of microstates depending on the system's macrostates (such as energy, volume, pressure) and alterations thereto (such as the addition of energy, heat influx, or mechanical work). It is highest when the likelihood of each microstate is equal, and this is achieved when the system is in equilibrium (and has maximal entropy). In information theory, Shannon and Khinchin defined four axioms which systems need to fulfil if they are to be modelled using entropy. If the fourth of these axioms is violated, but the others hold, some modelling remains possible (details about entropy can be obtained in Thurner et al. (2018)). For such systems, the statistical distributions can be obtained and therefore valid inference can be possible, for example in power-law applications of the sort we encountered in section 8.7.1.

For physical systems fulfilling these axioms, the relationship between phase space and system size determines the entropy-class. However, it remains to be determined whether these results can be meaningfully applied to complex system modelling (Thurner et al. 2018, p. 374). For simple systems that violate more than the fourth axiom, very little descriptive entropy modelling remains possible. For example, trip planning can be modelled using state space reduction (Clarke et al. 1999). However, for animate complex systems such as mammals or human beings, which are non-ergodic and evolutionary and have interacting and changing elements and interactions, the entropy modelling techniques described in this section do not achieve even descriptive functionality (Thurner et al. 2018, pp. 393, 395), and we do not see how this could change.

8.8 The future of complex system modelling

Non-naïve approaches to complex system modelling presented in the previous section are mathematically interesting, and, as in the turbulence example, contribute to our descriptive and interpretative understanding of aspects of nature. However, they do not give a procedure to obtain exact causal or predictive mathematical models of complex systems, in most cases not even for single traits of such systems. Such a procedure can be found only for simple (logic) systems that are man-made and artificially driven. Predictive mathematical models for the behaviour of any complex system have thus far not been provided on any approach.

---

43 An extensive property is a physical quantity whose value is proportional to the size of the system (in terms of the number of its elements) for which it is used as a descriptive variable.

Since the invention of the calculus by Newton and Leibniz, it took more than 100 years before Bošković, Legendre, and Gauss invented regression in around the year 1800, and it took a further 100 years before Paul Lévy and Andrei Kolmogorow invented stochastic process models in around 1900. It took yet another 100 years before we had obtained the computational power needed to turn regression models into practically usable analytic tools. In as late as the 1970s, most regression models were still merely academic playthings because of the lack of computational power—as one of the pioneers in this field, the inventor of the bootstrap, Bradley Efron, was still lamenting in 1979 (Efron 1979).

It has taken 50 years to obtain the computational resources to implement the neural network, the core of which was proposed already in the late 1950s by Frank Rosenblatt and his predecessors in the 1940s (McCulloch et al. 1943). The neural network brings us the ability to model implicitly the behaviour of ergodic systems yielding multivariate distributions, but predictive models of the behaviours of non-ergodic systems, which means all complex systems, remain beyond our reach, because such systems do not generate outcomes that can be modelled as stable multivariate distributions.

Of course, mathematicians will make further discoveries of new types of models in the future. But the structure of extended Newtonian mathematics and the limitations of its models that have been brought to light through the development of chaos theory and the theory of complex systems have far-reaching implications as concerns the possibility of our creating models with the ability to predict the behaviours of complex chaotic systems such as the human brain. For as we intimated already in the Foreword (p. xii), this would require a major revolution in mathematics of a type which has been ruled out as impossible by leaders in the field,[44] and no traces of which are even on the horizon.

What we can model well are, rather, (1) man-made technological artefacts such as fridges, roller-coasters, and combustion engines, which we model using extended Newtonian mathematics; and (2) natural phenomena which behave in ways close to meeting the requirements for application of differential equations, such as the fall of a stone or the trajectory of an asteroid, where just one fundamental interaction dominates (here: gravitation).

In all other cases, we have both too many variables and too many interactions to make solvable differential equations possible. Matters are made still more complicated by the fact that we have force overlay and other characteristic phenomena of complex systems (such as their evolutionary properties), which bring us even further from the possibility of building models adequate to the sorts of tasks which require prediction of the behaviours of complex systems. Attempts to build models using experiments and observations in constrained environments

---

44 See Feynman et al. (2010) and Heisenberg (Marshak et al. 2005, p. 76).

in which there is only one independent variable work fine so long as we can apply with full justification the *ceteris paribus* principle. That is, they work ... but only so long as there are not too many other variables and only so long as nearly all of them can be held constant. This is the sort of behaviour we see when we view the world through a partial differential equation. But the human brain, and societies of human brains, do not work like that.

The number of independent variables required by a model even of a single human brain may run into the trillions, since we are dealing with multiple microstates of each one of the millions of molecules inside each of the billions of neurons in the brain. The n-body-problem[45] is already unsolvable for values of n greater than 2; but here we face an $n > 10^{15}$-body problem. And note that the human brain does not *solve* this 10^{15}-body problem. Rather its many parts simply act together in a certain spontaneous way, which can be thought of as a much more complicated version of the way water molecules in the lower atmosphere act together as elements of a hurricane. Both of these create a problem for mathematical modellers. And each problem can be solved only by means of approximations using one or other strategy of simulation; but the resulting solutions will then not have anything even remotely comparable to the degree of exactness required to engineer an emulation of what the brain is doing from one millisecond to the next. A hurricane can be approximated much better than the brain, but a hurricane, too, cannot be emulated in a way that allows prediction of its path from one hour to the next. Disregarding this, short-term models of weather events are quite adequate to the purposes of weather forecasting. But why do such models fail over longer periods? Because the complex properties of the planetary weather system become ever more important in shaping the data as time passes. As we have seen in the last chapter (7.5.3.1), complex systems massively diverge from their initial conditions over time. This yields erratic distributions resulting from the non-ergodic and evolutionary properties of the system. The initial measurement errors (characteristic of deterministic chaos, see 7.5.2.7) add further indeterminism. The system quickly becomes unmodellable.

8.8.1 Complex system emulation requires complex systems

As we will see in the subsequent chapters, attempts to apply extended Newtonian mathematics to complex systems lead to failures in most settings, and this applies not least to the human central nervous system. Remember that a stochastic model is trained at training time and then applied to data at run-time. What

---

45 This is the classical n-body problem (Crandall 1996, § 5.1), which results when we try to use Newton's laws to predict the motion of $n > 2$ point masses given their initial positions and velocities. The problem arises because the dynamical system resulting when $n > 2$ bodies are involved is chaotic for most initial conditions, and it can be proved that under these conditions there is no analytical solution to the problem of predicting the bodies' behaviour.

happens when a model is applied to data that it is *a priori* unable to model? The deviations of its predictions (its output) from the output of the real system become exponentially larger over time as the algorithm or set of algorithms *misreacts to the temporal unfolding of events:* predictions immediately or very quickly break down.[46] Neither almost exact nor approximative models are sufficient to model the complexity of primal, let alone objectifying, intelligence. There is simply no way to create explicit models; and implicit models cannot be obtained due to the nature of complex system processes described in this and the preceding chapter.

This has implications also concerning Turing's ideas about what he called the 'mathematical objection' against AI.[47] This objection can be stated as follows: Gödel and others had shown that no finite set of rules can be used to obtain all true mathematical propositions. But mathematicians can invent (and prove) an unlimited number of true propositions, and the output sequence for any given mathematician is not Turing-computable, because a universal Turing-machine only contains a finite set of rules. However, Turing later

> felt [that] it should be possible to program a computer so that it could learn or discover new rules, overcoming the limitations imposed by the incompleteness and undecidability results in the same way that human mathematicians presumably do.
>
> (Piccinini 2003)

But whatever Turing might have 'felt', he certainly could not prove this hypothesis. He could not say how the machine would be able to mimic the behaviour of a mathematician. Today we know that to achieve this, the machine would itself have to become a complex system. But we have shown in this and the preceding chapter that this is impossible, due to the essential limitations of mathematical models.

Thus, as long as we are restricted to using extended Newtonian mathematics, and so long as we are constrained to use those algorithms of extended Newtonian mathematics which can be executed on universal Turing machines, it is not conceivable that we will be able to mathematically model, and thereby to engineer, a system with the complexity required to emulate human intelligence. And even if we assume that there could be some non-human ('extraterrestrial') intelligence that can deal with a complex-system generated environment (as humans and animals do, see 3.3.3) we could not emulate that intelligence either, because any such emulation would itself have to be complex.

---

46 This would not even change if we had the sort of 'hypercomputer'—more powerful than a universal Turing machine—that is the object of some people's dreams (discussed in 12.2.2). For even with such machines at our disposal, we would still not know how to create adequate mathematical models for complex systems.
47 See also chapter 9.3.2 for a discussion of the related Lucas–Penrose arguments.

Many have tried to move beyond extended Newtonian mathematics. Remember that we were not even able to expand the envelope of what we can model far enough to include even turbulence (8.7.1.1), which is a basic and ubiquitous mechanical phenomenon in driven inanimate systems such as flowing water or snowflakes blowing in the wind.

PART III
The limits and potential of AI

9
WHY THERE WILL BE NO MACHINE INTELLIGENCE

We have seen in chapter 8 that there is no way to model the behaviour of a complex system with the accuracy necessary to support sound technical applications. This is why we still, after some 50 years, are unable to engineer machines that can adequately communicate with human beings (details will be given in chapter 10), and it is also why we cannot model human social and ethical behaviour in a way that would support the use of machines as active participants in human communities (details in chapter 11). Before turning to these topics, we will review in this chapter what we believe to be scientifically serious *philosophical* arguments that have been brought forward in favour of the feasibility of AGI. We then show how these arguments are invalidated by salient findings from the mathematics of complex systems and from biology.

In the course of this chapter, we will see that the view of the human brain as operating like a computer, though it is still embraced explicitly by some of our best philosophers, betrays on closer analysis ignorance not only of the biology of the brain but also of the nature of computers.

9.1 Brain emulation and machine evolution

We take as our starting point the work of David Chalmers, the most prominent contemporary philosopher who has addressed the issue of the possibility of AGI. Chalmers represents the school of thought which claims that a machine emulation of what he calls 'average human intelligence'—by which he means, roughly, what we are here calling 'objectifying intelligence'—will be possible 'before long'. In a paper from 2010 Chalmers presents what he believes to be the two major arguments in favour of the feasibility of AGI (Chalmers 2010): the *brain emulation* and the *machine evolution* argument. We deal with each of these in

9.1.1 The emulation argument

The first argument is summarised by Chalmers (2010, p. 13) as follows:

1. The human brain is a machine.
2. We will have the capacity to emulate this machine (before long).
3. If we emulate this machine, there will be AI.[1]
4. Absent defeaters,[2] there will be AI (before long).

9.1.1.1 Inanimate and animate driven systems

This argument is defective in several ways. To begin with, in his definition of *machine*[3], Chalmers fails to draw the distinction between inanimate and animate driven systems and this means that he fails to recognize that the drivenness of animate complex systems prevents the modelling of the laws ultimately governing their behaviour.

Inanimate and animate driven systems belong, respectively, to the realms of φύσει (*physei*) and τέχνῃ ὄντες (*techne ontes*)—or in other words of the natural and the artificial.[4] The fundamental difference between the two turns on the fact that living organisms, from the single-celled prokaryotic *archaea*, which arose approximately 3.5 billion years ago, to human beings can

i. autonomously produce energy-storing biomolecules[5] from sunlight, inorganic, or organic compounds via oxidation-reduction reactions, which allow them
ii. to survive, and
iii. to reproduce, i.e. produce genetic descendants.

The ability of every organism to autonomously produce energy-storing molecules from external energy and to constantly use the stored energy for its survival and reproduction differentiates animate from inanimate (system) drivenness.[6]

---

1 Recall that Chalmers is using 'AI' to refer to what we have referred to in the foregoing as 'AGI'.
2 By 'defeaters' Chalmers means eventualities, such as major nuclear catastrophes, which would halt or create considerable obstacles to the further evolution of (for example) computer hardware.
3 A machine, for Chalmers, is 'a complex system comprised of law-governed parts interacting in a law-governed way.' (Chalmers 2010, p. 14).
4 Both terms are taken from Aristotle's *Physics*, book Γ.
5 ATP, GTP and FAD(H_2), see also footnote 35 on page 129.
6 Humans can, it is true, counteract both drives, for example through various forms of fast and slow suicide, or through individual or collective anti-natalism. This is because humans have objectifying intelligence, and can embrace and realise intentions even in cases where such realisation may

All living cells have essential (animate) drivenness. This is true also of the germ-line and its products: oocytes and sperm, which use ATP synthesised by their mitochondria to survive for the few days which is their life expectancy (outside the female genital tract ejaculated sperm do not survive longer than 20–30 minutes). Embryos and foetuses, too, have essential drivenness—they receive organic molecules and oxygen from their mother's blood, from which they autonomously synthesise ATP in order (1) to survive in their protected environment and (2) in the case of the female foetus, to create *in utero* all the ovarian follicles which will be needed during the entire life of the woman she will become.

Inanimate drivenness, in contrast, requires external energy supply and does not induce survival or reproduction (one cannot say that a steam engine survives or reproduces). Viruses are a partial exception. They are inanimate driven structures because they use the ATP-production and consumption and the cellular machinery of their host cells to reproduce (but they do not *survive* because they do not live).

A machine—as this term is generally understood[7]—is inanimate, does not consist of living cells, and therefore cannot produce energy-carrying biomolecules to survive or reproduce. If it could do so, we would be able to engineer life. But to do so, we would have to be able to model so well that we could re-create through engineering all those functional constituents of organisms that are essential to their survival and reproduction.[8] We would then not be emulating organisms but rather creating something like an organism *Doppelgänger*. And this we cannot do, because not only the organism as a whole but also all of these functional parts—including, most importantly, the brain—are complex systems, and thus we are thwarted at the very first step of any attempt to create a synoptic and adequate mathematical model.

The designers of effectively functioning machines can obtain such models, but we cannot do this for animate driven systems because we have no way of explicitly or implicitly modelling their behaviour. This will not change in any fundamental way because again: their complex system properties set an upper bound to the possibility of causal explanation and predictive modelling.

---

postpone or negate their biological drive to survive (see 3.1.2). The motivation for this, too, results from the same fundamental drivenness, but now as a pathological manifestation.

7 Chalmers (2010) employs another definition according to which a machine is 'a complex system comprised of law-governed parts interacting in a law-governed way'. Given that Chalmers does not define what he means by 'complex system', we can do very little with this definition, other than to note that it would seem not to allow *logic* systems, such as car jacks or staplers, to count as machines.

8 The interdependence between the functions of all the different parts of an organism is such that only very few can be taken away without compromising the ability of the organism as a whole to survive or reproduce autonomously.

9.1.1.2 No artificial life

Certainly we have *descriptive* models for some biological subsystems, and also explanatory and even predictive models for certain very small subsystems such as DNA-repair mechanisms or the oxidation-reduction reaction in mitochondria. But even for single-celled organisms we have no causal models of how they work, because we have no adequate modelling approach. The most important evidence for this is that we cannot generate (engineer) living organisms, however simple, from inanimate matter (Deamer 2005). In 2016, two groups reported the design, synthesis, and introduction of minimal bacterial genomes (termed JCVI-syn3.0) of merely 531 kb[9] into living cells. The resulting bacteria with their synthetic genomes could survive and reproduce with a set of just 473 genes (of which many are of unknown function) (Hutchison et al. 2016; Strychalski et al. 2016). This genome is smaller than that of any autonomously replicating cell found in nature. While this is an impressive achievement, no life was created from matter, but rather the genome of an existing form of life was replaced by a synthetic genome.

And indeed it is so, that for all purposes of bioengineering—from simple fermentation used in brewing beer to the cloning of mammals or the genetic engineering of the germ line—we must still in every case use existing living cells. Furthermore, we cannot even model the way in which the most primitive living organism type—an *archaeum*—functions, because it is a driven complex system (7.5.2.5) in which more than 100,000 biomolecules dynamically interact and thereby, through processes such as phosphorylation, constantly change their molecular properties in order to maintain the life of the organism and enable its reproduction.

Of course, we can simulate and predict *some* of the behaviour of an *archaeum*: for example the rate of colony growth under ideal conditions. But neither virtually (via explicit or implicit mathematical models) nor physically (by creating synthetic organisms in the lab) can we create models that emulate this behaviour. Extended Newtonian mathematics cannot cope with a complex system of this kind in a way that would allow prediction or emulation, and neither can any other sort of mathematics we can currently conceptualize.

We have seen in chapter 8 that even an approximation of the workings of a complex system is predestined to fail, because the results of applying it will deviate exponentially from reality as a function of time and of the number of interacting system variables (potentially in the many trillions). While certainly we can interact with complex systems both in our thoughts and in our actions—we must, after all, constantly deal with such systems in order to survive—our inability to model them is an *a priori* limitation on our mathematical capabilities.

This is not a temporary inability on the part of humankind. Again: our position is not analogous to that of a technology sceptic such as Auguste Comte, who

---

9 A human genome is of the order of 3100Mb, about 3 billion base pairs.

asserted of the planets that we 'can never know anything of their chemical or mineralogical structure', or indeed Einstein, who is reputed to have claimed that 'there is not the slightest indication that [nuclear energy] will ever be obtainable'. Rather, it is a fundamental limitation on the applicability of mathematics.

This limitation brings the consequence that we cannot emulate the function of the human CNS, and we therefore contest the statement of Sandberg, when he writes of whole brain emulation (WBE), that 'Given current neuroscientific and technological knowledge there doesn't seem to exist any fundamental obstacle [to WBE], merely a large amount of engineering and research' (Sandberg 2013). For there most certainly is a fundamental obstacle, which is the limitation grounded in our inability to model complex systems mathematically. Given this limitation, it is impossible to model the central nervous system using any existing form of mathematics. It is therefore *a fortiori* impossible to run such a model in a universal Turing machine.[10]

9.1.1.3 Chalmers' syllogisms

Consider again the three premises of the argument put forward by Chalmers (2010):

1. The human brain is a machine.
2. We will have the capacity to emulate this machine (before long).
3. If we emulate this machine, there will be AI.

We have seen that the first two premises are false. And the third is now seen to have the form of a tautology, analogous to

If we build a perpetual motion machine, there will be a device which operates with absolutely no energy loss.

Premise 3 thus adds nothing to his argument, which accordingly lends no support at all to his conclusion, namely that a machine emulation of human-level intelligence will exist (before long).

9.1.2 The evolution argument

The second, *evolution argument* is summarised by Chalmers (2010, p. 16) as follows:

1. Evolution produced human-level intelligence.
2. If evolution produced human-level intelligence, then we can produce AI (before long).

---
10 We return to the topic of WBE once again in chapter 12.

3. Absent defeaters, there will be AI (before long).

The first premise is of course true. But the second is false, because it implies an equivalence between evolution and human activity, an equivalence which does not obtain. To see why, consider that primal and objectifying intelligence evolved over billions of years under evolutionary pressure with spontaneous genetic variance among organisms—what Darwin called 'mutation'—followed by natural selection through interactions with the inanimate environment and with competing organisms. There was no *plan* to yield intelligence on the basis of which these processes occurred, but rather only the *drive* to survive and reproduce that is built into every living organism. This drive led to the rise of intelligence through an immense series of processes, almost all of which occurred by chance.

As we have seen (9.1.1.2), we cannot engineer life, and we cannot mimic spontaneous genetic variance. Indeed, we do not even know how to mimic appropriate selection pressure, because we do not understand at all how these extremely complex phenomena work in nature. All we know is that there are multiple sources of genetic variance—from radiation-induced point mutations to meiotic chromosomal recombination in sexual reproduction—that have somehow contributed in a complex interaction pattern to create the species that exist today.

We know also that the highly complex inanimate and animate environments existing on earth over some billions of years have somehow, along a number of dimensions—temperature, soil composition, forestry coverage, elevation, availability of water, presence of prey and predators, and many others—created evolutionary pressure. Evolution is a process involving the interaction of trillions of complex systems (the single organisms living on this planet and their respective environmental systems). As such, it is itself the unfolding of processes in a *system of complex systems* that is much more complex than any single living organism.

9.1.2.1 Why we cannot emulate evolution

We have good biological theories of evolution, with many excellent examples of evolutionary adaptation covered by these theories. In the case of the malaria pathogen *Plasmodium falciparum*, for example, we understand how it is adapted at both the molecular and physiological levels to those organ systems of its successive hosts—the mosquito haemolymph, gut, and salivary gland, and the human erythrocyte and liver—that it uses for its own purposes (Roberts et al. 2013). But we cannot specify even one mathematical model of evolution of the sort that we would need to simulate the evolutionary processes which led this parasite to its current state.[11] We not only have no way to model

---

11 For an explanation of the relationship between simulation, emulation, and modelling, see 7.1.

mathematically the behaviours of single organisms (including the behaviours of their parts), but we also have no way to model interactions of organisms, no way to model environments, and thus no way to model interactions between environments and the multiple interacting organisms that inhabit them. Furthermore, despite interesting modelling results (Kempes et al. 2019), we have no way of modelling the interactions of environmental conditions (and the ways they give rise to selection pressure) and the resultant physical constraints on organism morphology.

These shortcomings relate in every case to the fact that we have no way of approaching the task of creating explicit or implicit models of any complex systems.

Second, they derive from the fact that we cannot create the needed sorts of mathematical models of the processes involved in evolution implicitly (by collecting data and training a neural net), because evolution is a process over non-ergodic systems for which no multivariate distributions can be used to obtain adequate stochastic models from which to draw training data (see section 8.1). Certainly, we have huge and rapidly multiplying amounts of data relating to the evolution of life on earth; but (i.) these do not contain training tuples (input and output data) of the right granularity to train a model of evolution, and (ii.) even if we had such tuples in endless amounts, they would still not represent samples from an ergodic-system-generated distribution with the properties required for adequate training of a model.

If, therefore, one considers carefully the knowledge we have from physics as concerns complex systems, and our knowledge of the limitations of mathematics and of mathematical (including computational) modelling, and the epistemic deficiencies of much of biology, it is clear that we can emulate neither the brain nor evolution. (And note: if we already knew how to emulate evolution, we would in any case not need to do this in order to create intelligent life. This is because the complexity level of intelligent life is lower than that of evolution. This means that emulating intelligence would be much easier than emulating evolution *en bloc*.)

Thus Chalmers' second premise

(2) If evolution produced human-level intelligence, then we can produce AI

requires a lemma to the effect that

(2′) We can produce (i) a machine emulation of evolution that (ii) can be used to produce a machine with human-level intelligence.

And since both conjuncts of this lemma are false, so also premise (2) does not hold, and thus Chalmers' argument fails in its entirety.

The source of Chalmers' troubles is an inadequate—because overly abstract—idea of inanimate and animate nature in general and of evolution (and the human brain) in particular. Chalmers 'theory' of AI, too, exhibits a peculiar remoteness from the results of physics, mathematics and biology.

At the same time, both of Chalmers' arguments are more sophisticated than the trivial suggestions often brought forward by proponents of AGI (including Turing (1950) himself), namely that AGI is just a matter of memory size or processing speed. Suggestions of this sort, for example, by Kurzweil (2005), are worthless, because they confound quantity with quality.[12] Yet even though Chalmers avoids this basic mistake, he still fails to see that there is no way to obtain models of the quality that would be required to support his premises.

We are nonetheless impressed with the facility with which he is able to defend his position against his critics. This applies not least to his responses to a set of commentaries on his work on the Singularity published in 2012 (Chalmers 2012; Chalmers 2016). Chalmers (2012) shows that the arguments against the idea of the Singularity brought forth by these commentators can be easily defeated. Unfortunately, however, this is not because he is right in what he says. Rather, it is because his critics failed to produce the sorts of arguments that would have been needed to show where he is wrong.

9.1.3 Other arguments in Chalmers

Chalmers (2010) makes two further points that are peripheral to his main argument: (i) that AI could also be obtained by brain enhancement—we deal with this proposal in section 12.2.4—and (ii) that the Singularity can be achieved without achieving AGI. In section 3 of this piece, titled 'Intelligence Explosion Without Intelligence', Chalmers writes:

> The arguments so far have depended on an uncritical acceptance of the assumption that there is such a thing as intelligence and that it can be measured.... So it would be good to be able to formulate the key theses and arguments without assuming the notion of intelligence.... We can rely instead on the general notion of a cognitive capacity: some specific capacity that can be compared between systems. All we need for the purpose of the argument is (i) a self-amplifying cognitive capacity G: a capacity such that increases in that capacity go along with proportionate (or greater) increases in the ability to create systems with that capacity, (ii) the thesis that we can create systems whose capacity G is greater than our own, and (iii) a correlated cognitive capacity H that we care about, such that certain small increases in H can always be produced by large enough increases in G.

---

12 This was also observed by (Ekbia 2008, pp. 73f.)

We are not at all sure that we are following Chalmers' argument here. But it seems to us that it does not, in any event, constitute a contribution to the treatment of the intelligence explosion *without intelligence*. For in order to 'create systems with that capacity', the holder of the capacity must be able to think in abstract, lexematic categories and to apply various types of reasoning and inference. But this is exactly what we have called 'objectifying intelligence' (see section 3.2.3). Chalmers' gambit here, therefore, is an example of the employment of an *Ersatz*-definition to suggest that we can use some B rather than A to achieve our goal, when 'B' is in fact just another name for 'A'.[13]

9.2 Intentions and drivenness

In discussions of AI, we often find the claim that machines could develop intentions, goals, and a will and could therefore act independently of their creators (Herzig et al. 2016). The achievement of any kind of Singularity would depend on such claims being true. Against this, however, we argue that machines cannot develop drivenness, and therefore, no intentions, since drivenness is in every case the necessary condition of the beginning to exist and of the realisation of every intention. The cause, for example, of my acquiring the intention to go out to dinner is an incremental increase in the intensity of my hunger, where my hunger itself is caused by my drivenness to survive.

With increasing drive we produce and realise more, and more far-reaching, intentions. With diminishing drive, we produce fewer intentions, as can be observed in patients suffering from late-stage dementia or in people intoxicated with benzodiazepines or other sedatives.

Our intentions and their realisations constitute what we subjectively experience as our will. Our drivenness can induce weaker expressions of will, for example as illustrated by the sorts of impulsive urges that do not lead to any real tendency towards realisation in action. But it can induce also stronger expressions of will, as illustrated in the sorts of ambition and tenacity of purpose needed to prove Fermat's last theorem (Wiles 1995), to win an Olympic medal, or to invade Normandy. Here the drivenness involved has varying degrees of connection to the drivenness towards survival (consider the fall-off in Verdi's productivity subsequent to his receiving huge sums for his opera *Aida*). Drivenness can manifest itself in both individual and collective intentions. The latter occurs when driven individuals collaborate to realise collective intentions. The collective realisation of drivenness is the necessary condition for the creation and maintenance of all human culture. And it is also involved in the creation of social movements whose goals are antithetical to human culture.

---

13 For further examples of this *Ersatz*-definition gambit, see sections 3.3.2.3 and 9.3.3.3.

9.2.1 No emulation of animate drivenness

Where drivenness is essential to all organisms, machines, which are designed and built by humans, can have only an accidental drivenness (7.5.2.5). This is because a machine's drive comes from those finite amounts of energy that humans introduce into the machine to enable it to work. In this sense, computers can be seen as driven by the electric potential energy (electricity) that we use to run them. Their drive lasts as long as this energy is provided. We can program computers to automatically increase their energy need in a polynomial or exponential manner, for example by recruiting more and more cloud computing capacity to compute ever more demanding numerical tasks. But this would not change the accidental nature of their drivenness, since energy will still be provided only for as long as the (human) provider will permit.[14]

The electricity used by the computer creates not only output from input data (the desired main effect) but also thermal energy as an expression of the entropic (side-)effect of its consumption of energy in performing computations. This thermal energy arises from the movement of the particles in its electrical circuits caused by the electricity usage and leads to dissipation of energy. Wherever a computer is operating, there must be a gradient between the energy inside the computer and the energy in its environment, otherwise the computer overheats, breaks, and stops working. The gradient leads to radiation or conduction of heat, which is then dissipated from the computer into its environment. This process is as chaotic as the outflow of water molecules from a steam engine through its chimney, or the movement of neutrons inside a nuclear reactor. And chaotic behaviour based on energy gradients of this sort *is all there is to accidental drivenness*.

Using mathematics, therefore, we cannot model exactly how the thermal radiation emanating from the computer will occur, just as we cannot exactly say which individual water molecules inside the boiler of a steam engine will leave the engine through the chimney in any given increment of time.

This type of accidental drivenness is fundamentally different from the essential drivenness we find in living organisms. For the latter does not depend on combustion of externally provided and always limited fuel but is rather the expression of the organism's built-in disposition to generate energy from its environment and to expend this energy in order to survive and reproduce. The difference is so great that accidental drivenness, which results in chaotic dissipation, can by no means be used to *emulate* the essential drivenness which we find in the sorts of complex, yet highly organised and stable systems (7.6.2) characteristic of the

---

14 Or as long as humans will maintain the machine. Even devices such as the Opportunity Rover, which operated on Mars for 14 years on the basis of solar energy, because they cannot auto-maintain, will break after some time in ways that will bring an end to their energy usage. Scenarios in which machines take over power stations and direct them to meeting their energy needs are, and will remain, science fiction; on this specific question see chapter 12.

organic realm. As Mora puts it, organisms 'draw negative entropy' from their environments (Mora 1963). With regard to their drivenness (the energy flow through them leading to dissipation), machines do the opposite.

We could perhaps *program* an analogue of human drivenness on the side of the computer, but only if we knew how to do so. Or in other words, only if we could write down explicitly—or generate implicitly (via training a dNN or some other stochastic model)—a mathematical model of human drivenness. But for the reasons given in section 9.1, we cannot do either of these things. That, in sum, is why there will be no machine drivenness, no machine intentions, and no machine 'will'. We will always be unable to build a machine with these attributes. And that, too, as we shall see, is why there can be no machine ethics.

9.3 Consciousness

AI research since its inception has been accompanied by a debate about whether machines could achieve either consciousness *simpliciter*, which was assumed to be present in higher animals, or self-consciousness, which is an exclusively human capability (see section 3.2.3).[15] In this section we show that machines cannot have consciousness. Since self-consciousness requires consciousness, we do not provide any additional argument to show that the former, too, is unrealisable on the part of a machine.

Searle describes consciousness as the 'state of awareness or sentience during the waking hours'.[16] *Self*-consciousness is the awareness of our selves. It is obvious that without the former, the latter is impossible.

All vertebrates live in environments marked by huge numbers of interrelated and constantly changing environmental variables. To survive, therefore, vertebrates need a large degree of behavioural flexibility; they must display the type of intelligence we described in 3.2.1 in order to be able to maintain an active interpretation of their environment at any given moment. For this, conscious perception is indispensable, because a vertebrate needs to actively interact with the environment to maintain its supply of nutrients and to ensure that it continues to occupy an environment that enables its homeostasis.

15 Primates interacting with their mirror images may display an attenuated form of self-consciousness, but this is limited by their lack of objectifying intelligence.
16 Searle (1998, p. 381) We agree with this definition, though with the caveat that a view of consciousness as a *state* requires supplementation with a reference to the stream of consciousness, which is the *process* underlying this state: That the lamp is in the state of being *on* depends on the flow of current running through it. We also need to take account of the fact that, as documented by Scheler, there are two sorts of mental experiences making up this stream. On the one hand are involuntary experiences, such as feelings and emotions and involuntary responses to external stimuli as illustrated in immediate avoidance reactions (for example when encountering an obstacle or a bad smell). And on the other hand are *acts*, which are experienced as voluntary. Examples of the latter are: intending and planning to do something, imagining something, calculating something, and remembering something (as a deliberate act). (Scheler 1973, pp. 252f., 374f.)(Bassenge 1930)

This is not to deny that it is of course unconscious, autonomic processes which quantitatively dominate the biological processes in vertebrate bodies. They are auto-controlled by a highly complex interaction of many organ systems of the mind-body continuum, of which the central nervous system is just one component that cannot function without many others. For example, the circadian hormone levels are controlled by complex feedback loops. The control is automated and maintains the homeostatic conditions of life (oxygen and nutrient level of the blood, body temperature, water balance, and many others). The automated control of homeostasis is *not* part of the mind-generating processes of the brain[17], though it is both a precondition for consciousness and influences it—for example, consciousness is altered by high fever.

The standard argument against machine consciousness, first presented by Searle (1992) and summarised in (Searle 2014), is that computers are machines, which can use human-defined syntactic rules to manipulate human-defined symbols by changing the electromagnetic states[18] of their storage units (RAM or hard disks). Such changes are physical processes, which are in Searle's terms both ontologically objective (which means: a matter of publicly determinable facts) and 'observer independent' (which means: such as to exist in reality independently of being conceived or observed). Here the ontologically objective is contrasted with what is ontologically subjective or in other words with the 'what it is like', the feelings, desires, and so forth, which can only be experienced from the first-person perspective. The observer independent is contrasted with what is observer dependent (also referred to as 'observer relative'), where the former is illustrated for example by rocks, beetles, and telegraph poles, the latter by money, debts, political offices, corporations, property relations, and so forth. The latter exist because observers systematically and collaboratively pick out and control certain processes in the world under the headings of, for example, finance or politics. Entities of the latter sorts do not exist at a physical level outside the brain, though artefacts pertaining to them do physically exist, for example the paper on which a contract is printed or the hard drive in which the information content of a contract is stored (Smith 2003). Information processes, too, Searle claims, are observer dependent in the sense explained.

The computation processes inside an active computer are indeed real physical processes. Their *interpretation* as processes creating output symbols based on input data is (trivially) observer dependent. (Trivial because interpretation is itself a process which can be performed only by a mind, and 'observer dependent', for Searle, is a synonym of 'mind dependent'.)[19]

---

17 Thus, most processes of the brain are not emanations.
18 Here the use of the term 'state' does not cause the problems described in fn. 15.
19 As Searle (1995, p. 8) writes:

> Intrinsic features of reality are those that exist independently of all mental states, except for mental states themselves, which are also intrinsic features of reality.

In other words, whenever a universal Turing machine computes something, ontologically objective and observer-independent physical events are taking place. For an animal, these physical events and the associated input-output-tuples of a computation have no significance (just as, for an animal, a parking ticket or a wedding ring have no significance). For the human beings who use the machine, however, these physical events have the status of processes of computation having interpretable outputs of practical relevance. Processes of this sort occur in virtue of the fact that the machine was designed and built by other human beings to perform its computations in this way.[20]

A mind-dependent process can never be called 'conscious', because (however paradoxical this may seem) consciousness is and must be observer independent. (To claim otherwise is to fall victim to a vicious circle.) As Searle puts it (Searle 2014, p. 3), 'There is no psychological reality at all to what is happening in the pocket calculator' or in any other Turing-complete machine, for that matter, no matter how large. And AI is, after all, just a set of Turing-computable mathematical models taking input and computing output in a deterministic manner. And this remains the case even if there are humans who *believe* that a computer is conscious. Mere belief does not make it so.

9.3.1 Searle's wall

We can become clearer about the background to Searle's claim, here, if we understand precisely what is happening inside a universal Turing machine. Briefly put, a Turing machine is a machine that can deterministically compute a specific output given a certain input using a mathematically defined set of instructions. These instructions must be isomorphic to a set of basic recursive functions executed in an order that guarantees that specific output. A process of this sort can be realised only using computer architectures designed to implement a universal Turing machine, such as the von Neumann architecture used in today's computers.

Searle (1992), however, makes a puzzling claim to the effect that even in the realm of natural processes there are processes taking place that are interpretable as processes of computation because they are isomorphic to the sorts of processes taking place inside a computer. He writes:

> On the standard textbook definition of computation, it is hard to see how to avoid the following results:

---

20 Nothing is changed by the fact that, already today, human-designed machines can be programmed to output designs of further algorithms and to trigger their realisation. This is because the entire chain still depends on human intentions and human interpretations.

1. For any object there is some description of that object such that under that description the object is a digital computer.
2. For any program and for any sufficiently complex object, there is some description of the object under which it is implementing the program. Thus for example the wall behind my back is right now implementing the Wordstar program, because there is some pattern of molecule movements that is isomorphic[21] with the formal structure of Wordstar. (Searle 1992, pp. 208f)

Unfortunately these statements are incompatible with our physical knowledge of the behaviour of the molecules which constitute matter (no matter what kind of matter: wall, brain, stomach, liver, computer chip).

All such molecules move always according to a pattern called Brownian motion,[22] first mathematically described by Einstein (1905). Brownian motion, however, is a stochastic (random) process which can be modelled by a random walk. This is a model of a movement process which describes a path that consists of a succession of random steps. This implies that a process of this kind cannot be seen as isomorphic to the process which occurs when a deterministic algorithm is computing some output from some input in a well-defined manner. In other words, Brownian motion, a stochastic process, cannot be used to implement a Turing-machine architecture, since Turing computation is strictly deterministic. The Brownian motion of the molecules inside a computer's components is orthogonal to the electrical current flowing through the computer when it is performing computations, and it is this flow of current that leads to the ordered, deterministically defined electromagnetic effects which are observable as computation.

9.3.2 The Lucas-Penrose argument against machine consciousness

Already in 1961, John R. Lucas used Gödel's theorem to show that human cognitive behaviour cannot be explained in purely mechanistic terms (Lucas 1961). Inspired by Lucas, Penrose (1994b) then developed an additional argument to this effect based on the fact that humans can obtain insights 'beyond computable procedures' (Penrose 1994a, p. 418). As Penrose formulates the matter:

> The inescapable conclusion seems to be: Mathematicians are not using a knowably sound calculation procedure in order to ascertain mathematical truth. We deduce that mathematical understanding—the means whereby

---

21 We are not quite sure what Searle means by 'isomorphic' here, but in its standard usage to say of two structures that they are isomorphic means that there obtains a bijective mapping between them, which is to say a relationship which assigns for each object in the first a unique second object in the second, and vice versa.
22 This pattern is found in all states of matter at temperatures above 0 degrees Kelvin.

mathematicians arrive at their conclusions with respect to mathematical truth—cannot be reduced to blind calculation.

(Penrose 1994a)

In another argument, summarised by Lucas (2003, p. 2), Penrose applies Turing's theorem to the creative activity of mathematicians and claims that this activity 'cannot be completely accounted for by any algorithm, any set of rigid rules that a Turing machine could be programmed to follow'.

We note that what Penrose calls 'creative activity' is in our terms the emanation of a complex system and therefore not accessible to mathematical modelling. Furthermore, we have already seen that stochastic machine learning models do not escape the constraints of Turing-computable algorithms; it is merely that the computational rules followed by such machines are generated implicitly and obtained by numerical optimisation.

In his discussion of responses to what is now called the 'Lucas-Penrose Argument', Lucas (2003) remarks that

> [m]any AI enthusiasts protest that they do not work with Turing machines, and have much more complicated and subtle connexionist systems. I do not dispute that, and specifically allowed in my original article that we might one day be able to create something of silicon with a mind of its own, just as we are able now to procreate carbon based bodies with minds of their own.

This passage shows that Lucas failed to see the reason why the sort of AI that would be required for any sort of creative thinking is impossible. For even if we could build hypercomputers (see section 12.2.2.2), we would still lack the mathematical models needed to emulate objectifying intelligence.

9.3.3 Bringsjord's defence of machine consciousness

We accept the validity of Searle's argument to the effect that by engineering software we can achieve at best an *emulation*, in other words a simulacrum, of consciousness. However, there is still a large community of those who embrace a belief in the possibility that a machine could itself *be* conscious.

We focus first on an interesting attempt to defend such a view from Bringsjord. He too, first of all, accepts the validity of Searle's argument that machines cannot have consciousness.[23] At the same time he truncates this argument, describing it with the following words: 'Computing machines merely manipulate symbols, and accordingly can't be conscious' (Bringsjord 2015, pp. 7f.). This wording then opens the door for Bringsjord to formulate his own argument

---

23 He traces it to (Searle 1980), which is Searle's paper on the Chinese Room argument. The latter, however, deals not with *consciousness*, but rather with *understanding*. The apposite sources as concerns consciousness are (Searle 1992) and (Searle 2014).

to the effect that consciousness can still be attributed to machines in virtue of the fact that the latter can manipulate symbols.

To bring us on board with this argument he asks us to consider the following parable:

> The year is 2025. A highly intelligent, autonomous law-enforcement robot R has just shot and killed an innocent Norwegian woman. Before killing the woman, the robot proclaimed, 'I positively despise humans of your Viking ancestry!' R then raised its lethal, bullet-firing arm, and repeatedly shot the woman. R then said, 'One less disgusting female Norwegian able to walk my streets!' An investigation discloses that, for reasons that are still not completely understood, all the relevant internal symbols in R's knowledge-base and planning system aligned perfectly with the observer-independent structures of deep malice as defined in the relevant quarters of logicist AI.
>
> (loc. cit.)

A story such as this can be told, Bringsjord argues, in any case where a robot behaves in ways similar to a human being, and where we would assign conscious, deliberate intention to the human being. He then holds that, just as it is reasonable to assign *malice* to the robot in a case such as this (and perhaps most people would indeed do so), so it is reasonable to assign *consciousness* to the robot, merely: it is an alternative type of consciousness that is being assigned. This is not the type of consciousness that we are all familiar with—the consciousness that manifests itself in feelings, thoughts, desires, in 'what it is like', and so forth. But it is, Bringsjord maintains, *consciousness* nonetheless.

9.3.3.1 A- vs. P-consciousness

Bringsjord draws his idea for this new kind of consciousness from a distinction introduced by Block between P- (for 'phenomenal') and A- (for 'access') consciousness (Block 1995). In his words:

> phenomenal consciousness is experience; what makes a state phenomenally conscious is that there is something 'it is like' (Nagel 1975) to be in that state. ... A state is access conscious (A-conscious) if, in virtue of one's having the state, a representation of its content is (1) ... poised for use as a premise in reasoning, (2) poised for rational control of action, and (3) poised for rational control of speech.
>
> (Block 1995, p. 231)

It is A-consciousness to which Bringsjord is referring when he talks of 'all the relevant internal symbols in [the robot's] knowledge-base and planning system'.

Phenomenal consciousness is of course not here at issue. In fact, all human beings are experiencing P-consciousness continuously while they are awake.

But we confess that we could not at first fathom what it is that Bringsjord might be referring to when he refers to A-consciousness, if his use of 'consciousness' here is to be taken seriously. On examination of Block's writings, however, we discover that what he is referring to under the 'A-' heading is not a type of *consciousness* at all, but rather a dispositional accompaniment of consciousness. As Block points out, he chose to use the word *poise* in preference to *disposition*, in order to avoid cases of access consciousness (A) independently of all phenomenal consciousness (P) in which the A state did not seem to be conscious in any sense (see also (Pautz et al. 2019)).

For Block, therefore, A-consciousness always goes hand-in-hand with at least the potential for P-consciousness, and it is the latter which provides the rationale for his use of the term *consciousness* in both (A- and P-) senses. It is thus at best inappropriate to use the term *A-consciousness* to refer to a form of consciousness present in a machine when, as in the case of Bringsjord, one has already accepted Searle's argument that, in the machine, there is and can be no accompanying P-consciousness.

9.3.3.2 Philosophical zombies

Chalmers, too, adopts Block's distinction; but he employs it in a different direction, as the basis of an epiphenomenalist view according to which all the causal load in the workings of the brain is borne by A-consciousness. Chalmers promotes on this basis the idea of a philosophical zombie, which would have the exact same physical-causal machinery—the same 'A-consciousness'—as its human counterpart, but *no accompanying P-consciousness*.[24]

From the assumption of the possibility of zombies, Chalmers (1996) draws a quite different sort of conclusion. If, he says, one could see on *a priori* grounds that there is no way in which consciousness could be intelligibly explained as arising from what is physical, then it would not be a big step to conclude that it in fact does not do so.

In introducing the fictional entity called 'zombies' into the philosophical debate about consciousness, Chalmers has contributed to the creation of a huge body of literature in which attempts are made, by both philosophers and scientists, to solve what is nowadays called 'the hard problem of consciousness'.

---

24 Block leaves open the possibility that phenomenal consciousness, too, plays a causal role. The assumption that it does not, as he puts it:

> would have to stem from a belief that phenomenal consciousness doesn't do any information processing (except, I guess, for determining reports of phenomenal consciousness). But why assume that? For example, phenomenal consciousness might be like the water in a hydraulic computer. You don't expect the computer to work normally without the water. Even if there could be an electrical computer that is isomorphic to the hydraulic computer but works without water, one should not conclude that the water in the hydraulic system does nothing.
> (Block 1995, p. 229)

A first reason for scepticism as to the fruitfulness of a view based on zombies, however, turns on the fact that the existence of zombies as Chalmers conceives them would rest on the possibility of a perfect *emulation of consciousness* (whether inside a machine or inside the body of the putative organically evolved zombie). The existence of such an emulation inside a machine would indeed have important consequences for humankind (described in chapter 12), since it would allow us to use machines *as if* they had consciousness. But unfortunately, an emulation of this kind is impossible. This is because, as explained in the foregoing, we can have no mathematical model of consciousness, for the same reason that we can have no mathematical model of the brain, language, social behaviour, or intentions. Consciousness is, to be sure, the result of physical processes and is itself comprised of such processes. It is just that we cannot model the processes involved because consciousness emanates from a complex system (indeed from the most complex system inside any organism).

Speculations, on the other hand, based on the idea that zombie counterparts of human beings might in some possible world have developed as biological entities we see as being of no relevance to the world in which we live, a world in which human beings are building computers and creating software to run on them. But there is a second reason for scepticism about Chalmers' approach. As Dennett (2018) expresses the matter:

> The so-called hard problem of consciousness is a chimera, a distraction from the hard question of consciousness, which is once some content reaches consciousness, "then what happens?". This question is seldom properly asked, ... but when asked it opens up avenues of research that promise to dissolve the hard problem.

In line with Dennett, we fail to see how attempting to understand characteristics of the human mind using a comparison with putative zombies can contribute to the scientific understanding of the underlying phenomena. We thus tend to follow Searle (1998), when he asserts of this new consciousness research that it is one area of science 'where scientific progress is blocked by philosophical error' (p. 380). Searle argues that, instead of inventing new and abstruse theories about consciousness, the scientific task is to try to understand its biological substrate (pp. 379f). As Searle points out: 'Of course, it is open to anybody to define the terms as he likes and use the word "consciousness" for something else. But then we still would have ... the problem of accounting for the existence of our ontologically subjective states of awareness.' (op. cit. p. 383)

9.3.3.3 Misusing definitions

When Bringsjord asserts that machines may display a type of consciousness when executing programmed functions in reaction to inputs, he is in effect introducing an *Ersatz* definition, which redefines 'conscious' disjunctively to mean 'either conscious or *Ersatz*-conscious'. The thesis that a machine of the sort he describes is conscious, under this new reading, is thereby reduced to a tautology.

Bringsjord's definitional strategy is nothing new. It appears already in Plato's dialogues and is especially widespread in the literature of AI. Indeed, we have seen it at work already in our discussion of the Leg-Hutter definition of 'universal intelligence' (see section 3.3.1). There, too, we saw that the proposed definition did not help us even slightly to tackle the real problems at hand.

Friends of the *Ersatz*-definition of consciousness point out that their disjunctional approach is gaining traction in the wider world. For example, with the increasing routineness in some circles of engaging with chatbots, there is already occurring a noticeable drift in meaning of the term *conscious* and its cognates in Bringsjord's direction. Some have even speculated that a similar drift might occur in the meaning of the term *reproduction*, when chatbot-like artefacts will be said to produce 'offspring' by 'mating' with what are at that point called 'people of flesh'. We shall encounter more along these lines in chapter 12.

Machines, therefore, for all the reasons we have given in this section cannot have consciousness. And from this it follows also that they cannot have self-consciousness.

9.4 Philosophy of mind, computation, and AI

There is a huge literature in the philosophy of mind and of computation which is of relevance to the question of the feasibility of AGI.[25] We have selected just a few examples for discussion here, but these examples are, we believe, clearly such as to support our claim that AGI cannot be engineered.

9.4.1 Computational theory of the mind

The main thesis of this book, once again, is that the human mind-body continuum, because it is a complex system, cannot be emulated by a universal Turing machine. A large number of arguments against the feasibility of AGI have of course already been provided in the philosophical literature on the computational theory of mind.

A useful survey of arguments pertaining to the limitations of computational modelling of cognitive processes is provided by Rescorla (2020, section 7.3–7.5). But inspection reveals that the arguments he summarises are either special cases of the arguments presented in this book, or they follow therefrom. Indeed the arguments outlined by Rescoria relate only to a small subset of the limitations of computational modelling of cognitive processes entailed by the considerations from complex systems theory documented in chapters 7 and 8.

25 As starting points, consider Rescorla (2020), Piccinini (2015) and Milkowski (2013).

214   The limits and potential of AI

This applies in particular in regard to those arguments listed by Rescoria which relate to the challenge of representing *temporal processes* computationally. For where the latter deal in an *ad hoc* way with particular examples of dynamic mental phenomena which would cause problems for a computational approach, we systematically traverse all existing modelling proposals put forward by the AI community as methods for solving this problem and show that none of them can work.[26]

Finally, the *embodied cognition* arguments documented by Rescoria (relating to perception and reward) are weaker than the arguments provided in this book,[27] since, again, we deal directly here with the alternative available mathematical representations of these phenomena proposed by the AI research community and show that they are inadequate to model intelligent cognition.

An overview of the material cited by Rescoria suggests, indeed, that the computational theory of mind field is strangely detached from the reality of the types of available mathematical models that can be put to use in AI research.

9.5 Objectifying intelligence and theoretical thinking

Proponents of AGI do not distinguish between primal and objectifying intelligence. But once this distinction is made, it is interesting to ask if especially the latter form of intelligence can be achieved with machines. We end this chapter by looking at the issue.

We begin by pointing once more to the work of the social anthropologist and philosopher Robin Horton and to his distinction between what he called primary and secondary theory (Horton 1982). The former is more or less identical to what we have referred to earlier as 'common sense', though conceived as forming a theory, or an array of theories, consisting, for example, of theoretical propositions about what foods to eat, where to find foods, what are signs of foods that one should not eat, and so forth. Clearly, the contents of primary theory will differ in detail from culture to culture. However Horton—who spent most of his life studying African cultures—insists that they are nonetheless to a large degree identical, in virtue of the fact that primary theory, by definition, consists in a summary of what must be assumed to be true in order to survive. As Horton expresses it, primary theory 'must "correspond" to at least certain aspects of the reality which it purports to represent. If it did not so "correspond", its users down the ages could scarcely have survived' (Horton 1982, p. 232).

Secondary theory, on the other hand, consists of theories relating to those sorts of entities which are either too small, or too remote in space or time, or too large to be of relevance to the everyday practical concerns that need to be addressed

---

26 See 8.6.
27 See 3.3.2.1 on perception, as well as 3.3.2.3 and 8.6.7.4 on reward.

for the sake of survival. Thus secondary theories have no common factor which they all share; they range from quantum cosmology and the Hindu doctrine of the World Turtle at one extreme, to the idea of a utility fog, made of infinitely configurable nanobots each in the shape of a dodecahedron with 12 extending arms[28], at the other. Both primary and secondary theory require objectifying intelligence.

A further crucial distinction is required here. There are implicit and explicit forms of both primary and secondary theory. *Implicit* theory is what Gehlen calls irrational experiential certainty:[29] it is the theory that we use without thinking it through in propositional form. This is the theory we use unconsciously to master the obstacles we encounter in our daily lives. *Explicit* theory is the same content but put into propositional form. An example for explicit primary theory is the following sentence spoken by a mother to her child: 'If you touch the cooktop, you will burn your hand and this will hurt'. Modern secondary theory is mostly explicit and requires special vocabulary or language (such as mathematics). Indigenous cultures, however, have implicit secondary theory that becomes explicit in rites, such as the rain dance.

Once the distinction between primary and secondary theories has been made, it becomes clear that machines cannot master any situations for whose mastery even primary theory in the sense of Horton is required. For to be able to cope flexibly with the challenges of reality in the way that humans do, theoretical vocabulary is necessary. For example, a house can only be built if there is a *theory of houses*, which requires our thinking of the world in terms of universals such as height, volume, stability, space, and surface (walls and roof). But as we shall see in the next chapter, machines cannot achieve human-level mastery of language; therefore they cannot acquire objectifying intelligence; and therefore they cannot master even primary theory. They would thus fail to develop even the elementary skills of our neolithic ancestors, such as house-building, pottery, animal domestication, and agriculture. The idea that they could master secondary theory in a way that would enable them to give rise to new inventions, or to give rise to impressive enhancements to existing theories in physics, or mathematics, or philosophy is we believe even more absurd.[30]

Originality, as C. S. Peirce points out, lies in finding ways to construct new combinations out of familiar units, thus for example 'in the overall construction of the whole of a mathematical proof, not in any of its single steps, but in their combination'.

---

28 See https://www.kurzweilai.net/utility-fog-the-stuff-that-dreams-are-made-of
29 *Irrationale Erfahrungsgewissheit* (Gehlen 1988, chapter 36)
30 Machines can indeed master fragments of primary or secondary theory but only if they obtain this knowledge from humans explicitly, for example using first-order logic (as described on page 288 below) or implicitly, for example using training data to solve partial differential equations (see page 152).

Peirce saw that something similar applies to all human achievements:

> Every action of Napoleon was such as a treatise on physiology ought to describe. He walked, ate, slept, worked in his study, rode his horse, talked to his fellows, just as every other man does. But he combined those elements into shapes that have not been matched in modern times. Those who dispute about Free-Will and Necessity commit a similar oversight.
>
> (Peirce 1935, 4.611)

Originality is, as the Napoleon example reminds us, a rare human talent that can be found in any field of human activity. But machines do not have *fields of activity*. They merely execute the programs supplied to them. They are *Rechenknechte*.

10
WHY MACHINES WILL NOT MASTER HUMAN LANGUAGE

10.1 Language as a necessary condition for AGI

We argued in the Introduction that it is reasonable to take mastery of language to be both a necessary and a sufficient condition for AGI. This is because

1. human objectifying intelligence is expressed via language, and many applications of AGI would require the capability for using language in interacting with humans;
2. mastery of human language would imply not only a high *level* of intelligence but also an intelligence of a sort that can be *applied across a very wide range*, including a very wide range of different sorts of environments.

Turing was aware of this, and he devised the so-called Turing test by taking as his benchmark for intelligence on the part of the machine its mastery of conversation with human beings (Turing 1950).

Turing himself provided only a rather indirect method for determining whether such mastery has been achieved. Here, in contrast, we provide a list of criteria the satisfaction of which by a machine would, we believe, provide strong evidence of its having achieved a realisation of AGI in the sense of interest to us here. And if, on the other hand, these criteria cannot be satisfied, then this would imply that AGI falls beyond the reach of what can be engineered:

1. the machine has the capability to engage in a convincing manner with one or more human interlocutors in conversations of arbitrary length in such a way that the human interlocutors do not feel constrained in the realisation of their conversation-related intentions by the machine-interlocutor. This

DOI: 10.4324/9781003310105-13

means that when the human interlocutor engages in the conversation, she must be able to realise her intentions without making the sorts of special effort which (for the moment at least) we are familiar with making when dealing with a machine, for instance on the phone with our bank's software. It means further that the human interlocutor could create an arbitrary context at will and challenge the machine with trick questions or with tests of its ability to create new contents;[1]
2. the cycles in such a conversation are not restricted to cases where the machine merely reacts to a human trigger, as in a succession of question-answer pairs; rather, the interlocutors behave as they would in normal conversations, including conversations whose purpose is to enable the planning and realisation of some complex goal;[2]
3. that the conversation would be in spoken form;[3] and
4. that the machine would *see* the human interlocutor, since the machine has to demonstrate that it can react appropriately to the whole habitus of its human dialogue partner and not just to her speech. Many utterances—for example in more intimate conversations—cannot be adequately interpreted without taking into account gestures, body posture, and body language, as well as facial expressions.[4] A machine without vision would thus not be able to perform utterance interpretations of the sorts expected in many types of human dialogue.[5]

Note that satisfaction of the last criterion would require that the machine is able to integrate visual inputs into its interpretation of language. However, the problem of interpretation for visual sensory inputs is even harder than is interpretation of language, because visual (sensor) input is raw (unprocessed) input devoid of any semantics. Animals interpret their visual surroundings based on instincts, and humans, to some degree, do this also. But as we have seen in the first part of this book (see section 4.2.1), humans interpret sensory input based on the significance of what they see for the realisation of their intentions (and in the end on its significance for their survival).

---

1 For example by asking the machine if it thinks that God created himself and requesting that it give arguments in favour of its views on this topic.
2 We believe that Eugene Goostman, one of the chatbots alleged to have passed the Turing test, would fail on this and the previous criterion (Warwick et al. 2016). For a detailed account of the problems with Goostman's performance see Larson (2021).
3 A spoken dialogue of this sort would require a solution to the (hard) problem of engineering a machine with a voice production capability that does not impede the dialogue flow when engaging with humans.
4 This was recognised early on in psychology (and biology (Darwin 1872)).
5 Schmidt et al. (2001) show that full utterance interpretation necessitates facial expression processing, not least in virtue of the role played by facial expressions as inputs to human cheater detector mechanisms.

As an analogy, consider the use of neural networks in image classification and shape recognition. In these applications, neural networks perform nothing in the way of *interpretation* of visual inputs, and it is very hard to change this. That is, they do not engage in processes of interpretation that are analogous to those used by humans, who draw on shape and other meaningful elements in the image.[6] Rather, when they classify images, machines predominantly use 'meaningless' image elements (features) from the background of the picture. As a result, a trained image classifier misclassifies an image, for example, already if its colour-scheme is altered using a simple Fourier transform (for example using bright orange instead of green for a lawn) (Moosavi-Dezfooli et al. 2016; Jo et al. 2017).

We cannot engineer models that would allow visual information to be acquired by the machine in a way that would enable the machine to emulate human performance in dialogue behaviour, because we have no way of modelling (or even simply understanding) how our own minds integrate sound and vision, for example when we are interpreting a slapstick-scene in a movie and laughing about it.[7]

10.2 Why machine language production always falls short

We have seen in chapters 4 and 5 that the challenges humans face in understanding language are formidable because of the immense complexity of the signals we receive. How, then, do we succeed in this task? Starting out from the identification of the human mind with a computer, some linguists have proposed accounts of how humans understand language on the model of software processing. Accounts of this sort are, as we showed in chapter 8, unrealistic.

10.2.1 Neural Machine Translation

But what, then, about neural machine translation (NMT), which was implemented already in 2014, and which today achieves decent—albeit approximate—text translations.[8] Do these networks not thereby successfully model complex systems? Certainly not. Of course, the tuples used for the training of NMT models are emanations from complex systems, because the tuples have been produced by human translators. But NMT models do not model the complexity of these emanations; rather, they model that morpho-syntactic subset of the

---

6 A human, for example, can make sense of what it means for a person in a store to put something under his jacket.
7 Vision impaired humans, too, are impaired in their dialogue behaviour; but they are able to compensate in part by using other senses. This compensation phenomenon, too, goes beyond what we can mathematically model and implement in a universal Turing machine.
8 To gauge the degree of approximation, the reader is invited to choose an interesting scientific paper written in English and to examine what results are obtained when subjecting it to neural machine translation into Italian or German.

emanation that can be fitted into the logic system model of a sequential neural network (see 10.4.1). This is why semantic subtleties do not get translated and why the models are only approximative at best.[9] But now the question arises, given that machines cannot understand language, how do humans succeed in doing so?

10.2.2 Human language interpretation

We believe that, as for most capabilities of the human brain and perceptual system, we are very limited in what we can say about human level interpretation, because we know very little about how it works, and what we can say is vague (in the sense of Smith et al. (2000)). Other than negative propositions—such as: language understanding does not occur through a series of computations steps like those performed by a CPU—there are very few well-supported assertions that go beyond the level of mere metaphors. Speaking in metaphors, we can say that language understanding can be seen as analogous to water flowing into a pond, whose molecules always automatically distribute themselves across the pond. When we hear utterances spoken by our interlocutor they seem to enter our stream of consciousness in a similar fashion—where the automatic distribution across the pond corresponds to what seems to be the automatic process of our achieving understanding. And almost at the same moment as we achieve understanding we may feel an urge to answer, or to continue listening, or to avoid further communication by walking away and thereby ending the conversation. To get there, nothing needs to be done, because the language just finds its way into the right places in our brain. This capability for spontaneous understanding is of vital importance and reveals the natural, biological nature of especially spoken language as a sensorimotor phenomenon. But we understand almost nothing about how it works.

This is the reason why, like other emanations from complex systems, language cannot be modelled mathematically.[10] Implicit models, too, are out of our reach. This is because when samples from natural language are made—for instance for machine learning purposes—they are never drawn from a multivariate

---

9 Douglas Hofstadter gives the following example (*The Atlantic*, January 30, 2018):

> Input: *In their house, everything comes in pairs. There's his car and her car, his towels and her towels, and his library and hers.*
> Google Translate Output: *Dans leur maison, tout vient en paires. Il y a sa voiture et sa voiture, ses serviettes et ses serviettes, sa bibliothèque et les siennes.*
> Translated back into English by Google: *In their house everything comes in pairs. There is his car and his car, their napkins and their napkins, his library and their's.*

10 Could one design synthetic languages that machines can learn to interpret and utter? Of course, and this is done with programming languages, for which there are compilers that translate them into machine language. But synthetic languages are useless for human communication.

distribution because in natural language, as we show in detail in the first part of this chapter, there are no such distributions from which to draw.[11]

From there we go on to describe the attempts that have been made to realise the goal of machine conversation, and show (we assume that there are no surprises here) that the results thus far have been abysmal. We give detailed reasons why these should not be seen merely as transitory failures that can be overcome, but are rather a necessary consequence of the fact that it is a complex system—in fact a complex system of complex systems—that forms the basis of the human capability for language interpretation and generation.

10.2.3 Human language as a complex system

Recall, first of all, that system boundaries can be drawn at arbitrary levels (see section 7.3). Moreover, elements delimited at one level can be delimited as systems at another. At the highest level, each human language can be seen as a single system created and maintained by its individual speakers in countless processes of interaction.

To understand the elements of the human language system we start once again with the example of (spoken) English, viewed as the aggregate of all the capabilities of all the speakers of English. This aggregate of capabilities changes from one day to the next as some speakers are added and others lost. New ways of speaking are added, some of which are imitated and so become (for a time) stable components of the aggregate of capabilities. Other ways of speaking disappear from one age cohort or from one generation to the next, while yet others—perhaps reflecting one-off pronunciation or grammatical errors—leave no trace in the larger aggregate.

Each constituent capability has a material basis in the neuroanatomy of its bearer, and we can view the language system that is spoken English as comprised of elements delimited on this neuroanatomical level. Recall, now, our definition of a system as a set of dynamically interrelated elements with a certain delimited behaviour. A system, on this view, must be spatially located (though it may be located in a spatially distributed manner). In a series of studies of the neuroanatomical basis of our lexical representations, Poeppel and his collaborators have identified certain brain regions as the locations in which such representations are stored. For example, they have accumulated data which

> support the hypothesis that the posterior middle temporal cortex … is involved in long-term storage of lexical representations. Which aspects of lexical representations are stored here is unknown. One possibility is that

---

11 Of course, very repetitive subsets of language usage can be modelled as emanations from ergodic systems using multivariate distributions, for example the regularised language used by pilots and air traffic controllers, or the command language used when interacting with automata, such as when giving orders to our car navigation system (8.1).

> this region stores not semantic information, but rather lexical representations that interface with a semantic network that is distributed across brain regions.
> (Lau et al. 2008)

We cite this passage not because we are in a position to present any sort of coherent account of what the language system for a particular speaker of English might look like as it exists inside that speaker's brain. It is included merely in order to illustrate that the language system will likely involve elements widely distributed across her brain's anatomy. We postulate that the elements of that system are interconnected neurons with specific molecular configurations (or they are clusters or combinations of such neurons sharing certain neurons) in common. Nothing in our argument turns on any detailed view of the connections and configurations involved.

For each individual speaker the English language system comes into existence in a speaker's brain (very roughly) as follows. First, each human being is born with an innate ability to detect speech sounds independently of the language that is being spoken. As infants, we become tuned to the sounds of our native language because these are the sounds we hear most frequently, and this forms and strengthens corresponding connected groups of neurons (auditory neural patterns). Analogously, as we begin to imitate the sounds we hear by producing sounds of our own, interrelated neural patterns for sound production begin to be established also. In this manner, and step by step (and still very roughly), as our sound production is rewarded and sanctioned in light of our conformance to the rules of spoken English operational in our immediate environment, clusters of neurons are formed in our brains which ground speech capabilities compatible with those realised by other speakers of English.[12]

Around the original phonological neural patterns, clusters of other, associated neurons will be formed, for example because given sounds and sound combinations are associated with specific sorts of visual or lexical representations or with specific sorts of actions. The brain's speech production system itself is tied to brain systems controlling *inter alia* the diaphragm, lungs, trachea, larynx, pharynx, tongue, teeth, lips, and jaw. In addition to the speech production system, our brains incorporate also an auditory system, and systems for reading and writing, all of them mutually dependent upon each other through multiple channels of interaction and consequent enrichment of neural interconnections.

The English language system as a whole is the system formed by all of these systems on the part of every single speaker. It is also—at a more fine-grained level—the system formed by all English *dialect* systems. And at a maximally

---

12 Some speakers (for example, those who are multilingual, or those who speak both a local dialect at home and some received pronunciation for use at work) will evolve multiple language systems of this sort, reflected in corresponding distinguishable though deeply interconnected sets of capabilities.

coarse-grained level, it is one element in the total *human* language system, a highly tangled system formed by all separate language systems taken together.[13]

10.2.4 Properties of the language system

It is obvious that human language as a whole, and each separate human language, and the language systems of all single speakers have all of the properties of complex systems defined in chapter 7. We show this for each of these properties in turn, focusing on those system elements which correspond to single lexemes and the syntactic rules used to connect them into sentences. For any given language as spoken by any given individual speaker, it is this lexematic system which forms the core. It is this system which provides the basic structural verbal language elements which are of principal importance from the perspective of the interpreter of speech, grounding capabilities not only for using individual lexemes but also for forming wordforms and sentences in accordance with morphological and syntactic rules.

Evolutionary properties Language evolves continuously as new lexemes, new phrases, and new styles and registers are invented by speakers. Each undergoes a selection process, and those that survive contribute to a change in the shared body of language. A good example is the coinage of the lexeme 'self-consciousness' (by Hegel in *The Phenomenology of Spirit*), which—together with the theory surrounding it—changed the way human beings situate themselves in the world. Or consider the idiomatic noun *quantum mechanics*, which helped to change our view of nature.

The elements of a complex system change over time and so do the types of their interactions. Language obviously has this quality. Consider the element in the brain of a single speaker that is tied to a single lexeme—say *hat*. The neurons and associated molecular configurations which (as we postulate) form this element will change with time, and so also will their modes of interaction with other clusters. Thus it will be sometimes tied to elements forming associated phonemic pathways (involving the sound *hat*); sometimes to pathways relating to visual perceptions of hats, or tied semantically to neural pathways relating to lexemes such as *rain*, *umbrella*, and so forth. All of these interactions will change, for a variety of reasons. (Elements connected with *rain*, for example, will likely change their interactions with other elements depending on the context and lexeme usage—for example, when a broker says 'it rained money'.)

Languages as a whole change over time as new words are added and existing lexemes change their meanings and thus change also the ways they interact semantically with other lexemes. The lexeme *mobile*, originally an adjective,

---

13 We leave open the issue of language isolates having no historical or linguistic relationship to any other languages.

has recently acquired a usage also as a noun indicating a portable telephone. Now, therefore, it can be used both as an adjective modifying a noun (as in 'mobile units') and as a nominal phrase of which something is predicated ('I found my mobile'). Each such change will involve corresponding changes in the capabilities of a certain fraction of speakers of the language, and thus also in the associated neurophysiology.

Different interaction types between elements Entities in physics interact in ways that are type-specific but independent of the individual entities involved. For example, gravitation exists as an interaction between all material objects, and its magnitude depends merely on the distance between the objects involved and on the magnitude of their masses. The elements of language systems, in contrast, interact specifically. Language elements have multiple specific relations to each other at the neurophysiological level, reflected in the different morphologic, syntactic, semantic, and pragmatic relations at the level of linguistic usage. Words relate differently to other words depending on their syntactic and semantic roles. For example usage of 'to have' as copula ('He has chutzpah') or as auxiliary verb ('He has run away!'), or metaphorical usages, or the multiple uses of ambiguous expressions. (Punning involves one and the same phoneme series evoking simultaneously two sets of capabilities for its use, grounded in two sets of (potentially overlapping) neural clusters.)

Force overlay In both classical and quantum physics, one of four forces dominates in the equations describing laws of nature. In language usage, multiple highly composite aggregates of electromagnetic forces overlay and interact with each other as they trigger molecular changes in the involved neurons and thereby contribute to creating an utterance with a certain meaning. When, on the other side, we interpret such an utterance, multiple electromagnetic signals (both visual and auditory, and—if touching is involved, as in a handshake or a caress—proprioceptive) create a burst of complex electric signals in multiple neurons which become electrochemically integrated through the action of multiple neurophysiological processes. We do not (and probably never will) know how this works, but for each of the billions of involved molecules, forces are involved which overlay.

Absence of a quantifiable phase space In traditional physical systems, the phase structure is the space defined by the state variables of each element. The values which these variables take on exactly define the position of each element in this space at any given time. Language elements can have multiple states simultaneously, and no phase structure can be defined in which the elements can be placed by using values of state variables in this way. Consider again the phase structure of a pendulum, which is formed by the two vectors of angle and angular velocity. By measuring these two values, the pendulum's movement can be fully specified. But we cannot assign such states to the neurophysiological elements underlying our lexematic capabilities. Indeed, we have very little idea what these neuroanatomical elements are or of how to keep track of them through constant changes. But even at the more coarse-grained level of actual linguistic usage—where we can take wordforms as actually used in utterances as a proxy for the underlying neurologically grounded capabilities—meanings have multiple context-dependent dimensions, which again are subject to constant change and to the possibility of ever new combinations.

As Talmy points out, there are multiple dimensions of variation even at the level of the single morpheme:

> The entire conceptual content represented by a single morpheme—its plenary meaning—is in general both copious and structured. This structuring consists of both the arrangement of its content and the pattern of attention over that arrangement. With respect to the arrangement of its content, a morpheme's plenary meaning can be divided into a core meaning and an associated meaning. In turn, its associated meaning can be subdivided into five sectors: the holistic, infrastructure, collateral, disposition, and attitude sectors. And with respect to its pattern of attention, eight specific attentional factors and three general attentional principles are cited. The main attentional factor is that a morpheme's core meaning is generally more salient than its associated meaning or any of the sectors therein. But another attentional factor holds that the attitude sector, especially its expletivity type, can challenge or exceed the core meaning in salience.
>
> (Talmy 2021)

Moreover, since the contexts in which utterances are produced and interpreted can cover such a wide range, and be combined and modified along so many different dimensions, moving to this coarse-grained level does not in fact lead to any simplification of the problem at hand. One cannot assign numerical values to these dimensions of variation of wordforms as actually used in a way that would adequately specify their meanings.[14] Only if such assignment were possible, however, could the underlying linguistic system have states constituting a phase space which we could describe and quantify.

Drivenness, and therefore no convergence to any equilibrium state Language production results from the drivenness of the human mind, and thus from the urge of human beings to realise their intentions.

Whether considered at the level of a single whole language such as English, or at the level of language as exemplified in the capabilities of a single speaker, there is no equilibrium to which the language system converges. Rather the system (in

---

14 Partial solutions in 'narrow' AI exist, see chapter 13.

each case) produces new language and new language elements all the time. Due to the drivenness of human language production, the next utterance or interpretation act cannot be predicted from the previous acts and the current context. This holds even in highly standardised conversations (for example the initial ritual dialogue in a legal suit, or a dialogue during a religious ceremony, as when a bride unexpectedly says 'no' during her wedding). This is because such predictions (and therefore the associated mathematical models) are excluded for the behaviours of driven systems, as such systems not only lack both the Markov property and equilibrium convergence, but also display chaotic properties (see 7.5.2.5).

Non-fixable boundary conditions and context-dependence Language, as we have seen, is deeply contextual. Almost no sentence can be understood without its context. And the sets of available contexts are themselves changing continuously, being to a large extent determined by the utterances and interpretations formed within previous contexts. These contexts, too, help to determine the boundary conditions for the language system as it is delimited at the level of neurophysiology.

Chaos Deterministic chaos obtains because there are no laws according to which conversations evolve.

Their evolution is unpredictable, even in highly formal settings. For example, even a ritualised liturgical dialogue between a preacher and the congregation can be interrupted by unforeseen events and become unpredictable. The degree of this unpredictability increases steeply with the passing of time (see section 7.5.3.1).

All seven of the properties of complex systems are satisfied by all the systems in the complex multi-level system of systems that is human language. Because we know that systems which have such properties cannot be modelled mathematically, we also know that machines cannot master language. The rest of this chapter shows the detailed empirical evidence in support of this conclusion.

10.3 AI conversation emulation

Many in the AI community are convinced that it is possible to create a machine with dialogue-ability because they share Turing's view that building such a machine is just a matter of storage and computation (Turing 1950), (Goertzel et al. 2007b, p. 26). Conversation machines have been under construction since the 1960s. Efforts are directed mainly towards what are called *dialogue systems*, or in other words systems able to engage with humans in two-party conversations. Such systems are optimistically projected to be widely used in commercial agent-based applications in areas such as travel booking or service scheduling in the very near future. However, despite major efforts—including Siri and Alexa—nothing close to dialogue emulation has thus far been achieved.

Yet there prevails, nonetheless, tenacious optimism in the field, which is based in our view on an unrealistically simplified view of what human dialogue behaviour involves. This optimism is amplified by a series of impressive successes in other areas of AI research, as exemplified above all by neural network-based translation, face recognition, and synthetic image generation, all of which have significantly raised expectations as to what might be possible in the future.

However, as we saw in chapter 5.1, every use of language depends on the intentions of the subject involved, and universal Turing machines, which provide the technical substrate of all AI algorithms, will never develop a counterpart of human intentions *until we know how to tell them to do so* (see section 3.3.4). Because we cannot build a machine that has intentions (not least because we understand so little about how it is that *humans* come to have intentions), it follows that computers do not have intentions. Thus computers engaging in dialogue cannot do what humans do, which is to give the dialogue an inner direction, a quality of meaningfulness, or a goal, and thereby allow the dialogue participants to rely on their intentions to restrict the scope of available alternatives for language production at any given stage.

10.3.1 Challenges to machine conversation

10.3.1.1 Initial utterance production

In providing an account of the powers that would be required of a machine purporting to emulate human dialogue behaviour, we distinguish between two sorts of task:

1. the production of the initial utterance of a dialogue, and
2. the maintenance of the dialogue in succeeding utterances.

We begin by showing that the machine struggles already with (1), even though the act of producing an initial utterance requires only the ability to understand the context in which the dialogue partners find themselves, where subsequent dynamic dialogue maintenance requires taking into account the switching of roles over time.

Initial utterance production by machines Contexts of the sort where an AGI might need to produce an initial utterance are, for example, a traffic accident, where the AGI acts as robot police officer or paramedic. The AGI would need to understand the situation in order to make the appropriate sort of overture to the humans involved. It would also need to gauge the common ground which it shares with its interlocutors and to do this before making the first utterance. But how should this be achieved? None of this is by any means a trivial task, given the massive variation in real traffic situations we are faced with in everyday life and which a robot cop would need to cope with.[15] The AGI would need not only to understand the overall situation—once again requiring interpretation of a visual scene—but also to find the appropriate words to use when speaking to the very human beings in this particular, psychologically fraught situation. Pre-programmed initiating sequences, such as 'Hello, I am your automated police officer, Hal. I have registered your participation in an accident. Please show your driver's license!' typically will not do. Most humans can manage such interactions because they have a natural command over the sound structure of language.

10.3.1.2 Initial utterance interpretation by humans

What now as regards the *interpretation* of a single utterance of the sort we are called upon to perform in relation to the first utterance in a dialogue? For humans, according to current understanding, this task has two steps: first is a syntactic step, which is realised through (unconscious) dynamic processes of syntactical sentence parsing and construction using the structural elements constituting the uttered sentence.[16]

This syntactical analysis yields the basis for the second, semantic step, which is the (again unconscious) context-dependent assigning of meaning to the uttered sentence (Loebner 2013). Even for one sentence this process has a dynamic aspect. This is because, beginning with the very first word, the syntactic construction and semantic interpretation interact as they unfold with each successive word. This can require cycles of revision, as an initial syntactic construction is revised as earlier parts of the sentence are re-interpreted in light of the ways they interact with parts coming later. Auer (2009) has coined the term *on-line syntax* to describe this iterative phenomenon of interpretation.

But to interpret a single utterance in a face-to-face dialogue, we will almost always require some interpretative context, which is often the ecological setting, the salient part of the physical environment in which the dialogue takes place and which will typically be centred on the person by whom the initiating utterance is made. Humans spend most of their time in settings of this sort, which are physical-spatial environments such as our living room, classroom or work place, the roads we use to commute between them, and places in town we regularly visit (Barker 1968).

When a dialogue is initiated on the phone, the absence of such a context explains why many humans find it hard to speak with someone they have never met or spoken to: the absence of a shared physical environment severely

---

15 The reason why we do not have an exploitable sampling distribution can be understood by examining hospital accident reports or court rulings arising from random traffic disputes.
16 There are several grammatical theories about how this happens, ranging from generative to constraint-based theories. Müller (2016) gives an overview.

reduces the amount of context usable by the interlocutors and thereby creates a barrier to the transmission of meaning.

When interpreting the single utterance, a human can draw on contexts available from his own biography together with any clues that he can draw from the interlocutor's tone, dialect, lexeme choice, and so forth. Discourse economy[17] forces us to make assumptions on this basis in our attempt to understand those aspects of meaning left implicit by the speaker, for example in order to disambiguate ambiguous aspects of his utterance or gauge the force of turns of phrase that might in some contexts be threatening or indicative of deceit.

In face-to-face conversations, humans use knowledge acquired through practical experience of the world around them and of the people with whom they have engaged. Knowledge of this sort (combined with innate capabilities) gives them the ability to gauge the relationships which link together entities in their environment into known families of predictable patterns.[18] The latter are then extended also to entities referred to in dialogue utterances, and this too helps to enable these utterances to be interpreted very rapidly in terms of their relevance to the interpreter's practical intentions.

Human interpretation of multi-sentence initial utterances Initial utterances consisting of more than one sentence are even more challenging for humans to interpret than single-sentence utterances. This is because the sentences now contextualise each other: there are explicit and implicit pragmatic interdependencies which link them together. For example, sentences may be connected explicitly, via anaphora, or as chains of steps in an argument or chronological narrative, or implicitly, through analogies or historical resonances attached to certain words or phrases.

Initial utterance interpretation by machines How, now, does the *machine* interpret the initial utterance of a dialogue? Here again two steps are involved: syntactic construction and semantic interpretation. We deal with these in turn. The syntactic construction using structural elements that humans perform according to the grammatical theories referred to in 10.3.1.2 can be mimicked by the machine quite effectively for written text, when no non-lexematic structural language material has to be taken into account.[19] Machines fail, however, as soon as non-lexematic material such as grunts or whimpers (or other sounds) as well as non-verbal structural material such as facial expressions, gestures, or posture come into play. This is because the world knowledge enabling the interpretation of such material—which can be combined in arbitrary forms to create

---

17 See section 5.4.
18 This ability is what we have earlier called 'common sense': see 4.2.4.
19 Remember that by 'lexematic material', here, we mean those structural elements that can be directly reduced to lexemes, see 5.5 and 5.5.4. Non-lexematic verbal material is, for example, a moan or a cry.

many different sorts of contexts—cannot be learned without life experience and it cannot be mathematically formalised.[20]

For the interpretation of a single sentence—ignoring for now gestures and other non-lexematic material and assuming a certain clarity of diction—the machine would need to reproduce the syntactic construction achieved by the static interpretation pattern applied by the human brain (syntactical analysis followed by semantic steps).[21] This requires use of computational phrase structure grammar, dependency grammar, or compositional grammar parsers.[22] All of these create tree-form representations of the syntactic structure of the sentence. The parsers work well if the input sentences are syntactically valid. However, if a sentence is syntactically valid but semantically ambiguous, as in:

(1) He saw old men and women,

an ideal computational parser will create two syntactic trees representing each sense.[23]

It is with the *interpretation* of the syntactic structure—in other words with the move from syntax to semantics—that machines struggle, and this holds even in the static single sentence utterance case. *For what is the context which the machine could use to assign meaning to a single sentence?* The machine cannot decide this on its own. The multitude of combinations of language elements described in section 5.5 allows for a huge number of interpretations even at the single sentence level. The machine cannot decide, for instance, how to fill in implicit meaning generated as a result of language economy, or of the use of incomplete utterances or ellipses.

To achieve this, the machine would need to use pre-stored appropriate contexts and dialogue horizons. Background information would thus need once more to be *given* to the machine, analogous to the sort of information given to an undercover agent to provide him with a cover story—information needed to enable the machine to mimic a human dialogue partner when discussions turn to matters biographical. If the scope of the anticipated subsequent sentences is very narrow, one can create a library of contexts and use a classifier to determine an appropriate context choice for a given input sentence. This context can be loaded and used to assign a meaning to the sentence with the help of logical

---

20 See 4.2.3 and 10.3.1.4.
21 The machine-learning-NLP community currently thinks this is no longer necessary. All is supposed to be computed implicitly using 'end-to-end deep neural networks', as stated by Hirschberg et al. (2015)—the latter is a leader in this field. But even the best end-to-end dNNs do in fact, as we shall see, not achieve this; they cannot model complex systems as they still must rely on Newtonian structures (globally differentiable equations).
22 An overview is given in Manning et al. (1999).
23 This feature is only available with compositional grammar parsers (Moortgat 1997). With a sufficiently sophisticated computational setup, a context-dependent disambiguation may be possible.

inference. To achieve this, the logical language to be used needs to have the properties of completeness and compactness, otherwise it is not computable.[24] This means, however, that the expressiveness of both the sentence to be interpreted and the specification of contexts must be severely restricted—thus they cannot include, for example, intensionality[25], verb modality,[26] or second-order quantification[27]—thus marking one more dimension along which the machine will fall short of AGI.[28]

What *can* be achieved in this fashion is illustrated in the field of customer correspondence management, where there are repetitive customer concerns that can be classified and for which pre-fabricated narrow background contexts can be stored in the machine using first-order logic. Customer texts can then be understood by relating them to this knowledge base.[29] However, it can be applied only in those special sorts of situation where the relevant contexts can be foreseen and documented in advance. When, in contrast, a machine has the task of engaging in dialogue with a human being, the range of language production possibilities and of contexts and context combinations with which the machine might be confronted is as vast as the imagination of the human involved. For the latter can speak not only about anything he has experienced or read about, about his current mood and intentions and their interaction with the situation he is in, but also about anything he can imagine. It is impossible to build a library of contexts that would prepare a Turing-complete machine for this kind of variation.

In nearly all situations, therefore, the machine will not have any context to load in order to assign a meaning to the sentence, let alone to carry out routine tasks such as disambiguating personal pronoun anaphora of the sort illustrated in a sentence such as:

(2) They caught a lot of fish in the stream, but one of them died.

10.3.1.3 Machine interpretation of suprasentential utterances

The space of possible contexts is all the more immense when we consider multi-sentence (suprasentential) utterances. Here, interpretation requires the ability to identify and interpret complicated relationships between sentences, including

---

24 First-order logic is not *decidable*, but it is semi-decidable (Boolos et al. 2007, chapter 11); see also footnote 13 in 7.2.
25 Illustrated, for example, by predicates assigned to potentially non-existing entities, for example 'cancelled' or 'missing' or 'imagined'. A sentence is said to create an intensional context when it contains at least one expression that can refer to different entities depending on the context in which the sentence is used.
26 For example: deontic assertions or propositions expressing desires or wishes.
27 For example: 'Mars is red. Red is a colour' (Gamut 1991a, p. 168). In the second sentence 'colour' is a predicate over the predicate 'red' from the first sentence.
28 Deterministic workarounds are possible for the mentioned phenomena (Jackson 1998), but they have nothing to do with AGI.
29 This is the approach described in section 3.2 of Landgrebe et al. (2021).

again all the pragmatic explicit and implicit sentence interdependencies of the sorts identified in 10.3.1.2. In open text-understanding tasks[30] it is impossible to foresee the possible sentence relationships and to provide in advance knowledge of the sort that would enable the machine to interpret them adequately. Consider, to take a toy example, the tasks the machine would face in interpreting the following sentences:

(3) The salmon caught the smelt because it was quick.
(4) But the otter caught it because it was slow.[31]

First, to understand that the explicit anaphora 'it' refers to 'salmon' in both (3) and (4)—even though two contradictory properties ('slow' and 'quick') are attributed to it—and thus to understand the reason for the adversative 'but' in (4), the machine needs biological knowledge about the species involved and about their respective hunting behaviours.[32] Given such knowledge it can contextualise the two adjectives by tying them to different parts of the total situation described in the sentence pair. Already this is difficult—but infinitely many such combinations with much higher levels of difficulty are possible (for instance, consider this very text which you, the reader, now have before you).

Machine non-interpretation Another aspect that is difficult to model in a machine-compatible fashion is human conscious or unconscious non-interpretation of lexemes or phrases in dialogue—Putnam's 'linguistic division of labour' (see section 5.4.2)—as when we can understand a sentence about a specific elm tree, without knowing what an elm tree is, except that it is a tree of a certain kind. How should a machine know whether it can afford to *not* interpret a lexeme in a case such as this?

10.3.1.4 Machine interpretation of static non-lexematic material

As described earlier (see section 10.1), in a real conversation with a human, the machine has to interpret the entire structural material of an utterance, including the non-lexematic parts, which means: facial expressions, gestures, body language, as well as the sound structures emitted by the interlocutor. Any of these can transform the interpretation of the utterance as conceived on the level of purely lexematic structures. Given the complex nature of the combination of lexematic and non-lexematic material, it is impossible for machines to

---

30 Closed tasks are those in which a large proportion of the texts to be understood contain repetitive patterns, such as customer or creditor correspondence or notices of tax assessment.
31 These are examples similar to sentences from the Winograd Challenge for common sense reasoning (Levesque 2014).
32 The interpretation of the second 'it' as referring to the smelt is perhaps still possible. Ambiguity is often simply not fully resolvable.

detect such clues and to combine them with lexematic material in a way that would make it possible for them to achieve the sort of adequacy of interpretation that would be required to lead an adequate conversation with a human—for the reason, again, that there is no distribution from which one could sample adequate training material. Furthermore, each combination of structural utterance material allows different interpretations. To make a selection from them and to create a reply based thereon that seems natural (non-stereotypical) to a human interlocutor requires an array of capabilities and intentions rooted in experiences of manifold different sorts of contexts. This is something which the machine lacks because, unlike humans (Gehlen 1988, chapter 16), it cannot *have* experiences. The machine can indeed have large quantities of data about experiences, but even very large amounts of data will solve the problem only if they are tuned to the relevant kinds of (data) input encountered in dialogues in a consistent way for some given biography, and accumulating data of this sort is, again, impossible.

10.3.2 Modelling dialogue dynamics mathematically

In the previous section we have seen that it is very hard to make machines utter and interpret single utterances. What happens in an entire, extended dialogue? The evolution of a dialogue can be highly dynamic (Schegloff 2000; Drace 2013). The interlocutors switch roles as utterers and interpreters as they take turns based on cues from their interlocutor in ordered or unordered form (cutting each other short, interrupting, speaking at the same time). While this is happening, their respective dialogue horizons are in constant movement, and so are the intentions and speech acts based thereon. New utterances interact with older ones, and the dialogue creates its own context (see 5.4.1).

As we have seen, from a mathematical perspective, a conversation is a process in which the participants, each of which is a complex system, interact, yielding an even more complex system. Stochastic AI systems, however, try to model a conversation as a temporal process in which each utterance produced is supposed to be drawn from an extremely high-dimensional, multivariate distribution. Unfortunately, as we have seen, there is no such distribution.[33] Given the non-ergodic nature of human conversations and because the utterances in the conversation are produced by complex systems, there is no way to formalise the relationship between the utterance and what precedes it.[34] Due to the nature of the human brain as a complex system, each utterance relates to the utterances that precede it in an erratic manner.

---

33 This is the ultimate reason why machines cannot write books. This problem is discussed in Eysenck et al. (2021).
34 Falling in love at first sight is a classic example of an event relating in an erratic manner to the events that precede it.

To see the sorts of problems that can arise, consider a dialogue between Mary and Jack spanning several rounds of role-switching. Mary makes an utterance at round 7, which requires Jack to take into account an utterance from round 3. Based on this, Jack associates with Mary's utterance an experience from his own past, of which Mary knew nothing, and he provides an answer relating to this experience. This utterance from Jack is for Mary quite unexpected (erratic) given her utterance in round 7. But, given his inner experience, it is perfectly coherent from the perspective of Jack. Phenomena such as this imply that there is no way to formalise the relationship between an interpretation of an utterance and this utterance itself. Such phenomena break the Markov assumption employed by the relevant temporal process models.

10.3.2.1 Modelling dialogues as temporal processes

To understand what happens when a conversation is modelled as a temporal process, four types of events need to be distinguished:

1. initial utterance production, followed by
2. initial utterance interpretation, followed by
3. dialogue-dependent responding utterance production, followed by
4. dialogue-dependent utterance interpretation.

In the prototypical case, pairs of events of types 3 and 4 are repeated until the conversation concludes. From the perspective often (implicitly or unconsciously) adopted in AI research, the conversation is viewed as a distribution-generating temporal process, in which each utterance is drawn from a distribution determined by the conversation's preceding steps. This perspective must always lead to failure, however, since—as we saw in the previous sections of this chapter—a model of this sort fails to describe the reality of conversations. This means that for conversations, stochastic models cannot be obtained from an adequate training distribution, and this does not change if the model is regularly retrained, because each training sample is inadequate.

Both utterer and interpreter have a huge number of choices to make when generating and interpreting meaning, and because these choices depend on the diverse dialogue contexts (including the dialogue itself) and on their respective horizons, as well as on the biographies, personalities, capabilities, intentions (and so forth) of the participants themselves, it follows that each utterance and each interpretation thereof is *erratic*. Such an event is like the nuclear fission event occurring in radioactive decay: it is unrelated to the events that precede it. It is purely random, in the sense that it cannot be modelled as depending on what occurs in the immediately preceding dialogue step.

To make matters worse, we have still not taken into account the fact that most human conversations deviate from the turn-taking prototype, and it is not conceivable that we could create a mathematical model that would enable the computation of the appropriate interpretation of interrupted statements, or of statements made by people who are talking over each other.[35]

10.4 Mathematical models of human conversations

A conversation is a process in which humans, each of them a complex system, interact in a way that yields a more complex system. All complex systems, as we have seen, elude mathematical modelling, and this holds *a fortiori* of the combinations of such systems. Against this background, it is in fact not surprising that there are insurmountable hurdles to realising the scenario in which a machine could be trained to engage convincingly in human conversation. These include

1. that human conversations are generated by the interaction of complex systems and therefore do not meet the conditions needed for the application of any known type of mathematical model;
2. that the systems which produce human utterances are evolutionary, non-ergodic, driven, and devoid of fixed-boundary conditions (in other words, they are highly context-dependent); from this it follows that to model a conversation by the drawing of sample utterances from a multivariate distribution is impossible: *there is no multivariate distribution from which one could draw samples to obtain a stable training set for a stochastic conversation model—and therefore, there is no adequate retraining either;*
3. that much of what is involved in the generation of utterances in conversations is dependent on interpretations of prior utterances performed by the parties to the conversation; such interpretations are indispensable to adequate dialogue production; but the process of interpretation is implicit and to a large extent not understood, and so it cannot be modelled—neither explicitly nor implicitly.

We shall see that nothing has changed in this respect even with all the advances made in machine learning in recent years, including reinforcement learning (8.6.7.3), adversarial learning (8.6.7.2), and unsupervised sequence learning (10.4.1). Nothing has changed, either, as a result of the impressive accumulation of data pertaining to human language use, including the large amounts of dialogue content now available in the form of Youtube interviews, of data deriving from use of Siri, Alexa, and similar services, and of the rich conversational content of many TV shows, films, and plays.

---

35 Other conditions under which classical turn-taking and other standard features of conversations are disrupted occur with mentally diseased patients, whose symptoms may include a disruption of the associative flow, or an exaggerated emotional load in their use of language.

First, all three sorts of data are severely limited by the restriction to what is explicit and thus recordable. Interview data are typically highly stylised and thus represent only a small fraction of the variance required to support machine learning of the sort that would be needed to implement a machine counterpart of general human dialogue. Siri/Alexa data, on the other hand, are merely recordings of human-machine interactions, and so are of zero utility for our purposes here. Data pertaining to fictional, crafted texts (film or TV or the theatre), on the other hand, illustrate by its very richness the problems facing any attempts to use it for representative sampling. The conversations are authored; and they are authored in order to be interesting, which means novel, surprising, not the run-of-the-mill conversations of everyday life, and not, either, the sorts of conversations which take place for example in a factory to address specific needs. The phenomenon of crafted texts illustrates in peculiarly exaggerated forms the non-ergodic, chaotic, driven, evolutionary—in short: complex—character of the language production system. Indeed, its very nature is to extend the range of variance manifested by the body of recorded dialogue,[36] and thus also it illustrates the evolutionary character of language as a complex system that we cannot model—consider the way in which Shakespeare or the translators of the King James Version of the Bible (1611) *invented* not only new lexemes but also new forms of speech.

For a machine to possess the ability to conduct a conversation, it would have to display not only the same 'general experiential understanding of its environments that humans possess' (Muehlhauser 2013) but also the same spectrum of abilities to react to these environments, and including even those types of human reactions that fall short because they involve mistaken uses of language, or errors resting on misunderstandings, or slurring of words resting on intoxication, and many other departures from the norm which an AGI agent can be expected to encounter upon engaging in conversation with human beings.

We can now summarise the insurmountable difficulties faced in engineering a language competent AGI by listing just a selection of those factors that would need to be taken into account by the machine if it is to simulate the reactions of dialogue participants at each moment of a dialogue. These reactions will be determined

- by the latter's personality and their intentions of the moment,
- by their language abilities,
- by what they perceive in the course of the dialogue itself,
- by what they (most of the time unconsciously or implicitly) remember (or by what they are influenced by, both emotionally and intellectually) from their life experiences,
- by how all of these factors are related together.

---

36 This sometimes to the point of incorporating dialogue using invented languages, such as Dothraki, Mangani, Nadsat, Na'vi, Newspeak, Klingon, and the like.

There is not the slightest hope of obtaining models in extended Newtonian mathematics that would deal adequately with even just one of these factors, let alone the combination of all of them taken together.

10.4.1 Current state-of-the-art in dialogue systems

Still, dialogue emulation is an area of considerable activity in AI circles. The resultant dialogue systems—also called 'dialogue agents' (or in some circles 'chatbots')—are designed and built to fulfil three tasks.[37]:

1. question answering—'the agent needs to provide concise, direct answers to user queries based on rich knowledge drawn from various data sources'
2. task completion—'the agent needs to accomplish user tasks ranging from restaurant reservation to meeting scheduling … and business trip planning'
3. social chat—'the agent needs to converse seamlessly and appropriately with users—it is performance along this dimension that defines the quality of being human [sic]—and provide useful recommendations'.[38]

In our view at least, the third task could only be performed by a machine with AGI. Indeed, it would precisely be one of the purposes of AGI to perform tasks of this sort.

Question answering and task completion are areas in which dialogue systems are already of considerable commercial value, mainly because customers with relatively homogeneous cultural backgrounds can be motivated to reduce their utterance variance—for example by articulating clearly and by using sentences from a predetermined repertoire—if by interacting with a bot they can quickly obtain answers to questions or resolution of boring tasks. This variance reduction can lead to dialogue samples which are so restricted, narrowly scoped, and repetitive that one can indeed use them as a semi-adequate distribution to sample from. However, question answering and task completion clearly have nothing to do with conducting conversations in a way that would be indicative of AGI. Fulfilment of each is (thus far) something that is achieved simply by using appropriately configured software tools, which every user identifies as such immediately on first engagement.

Social chat What, then, about social chat (also called 'neural chitchat') applications? Here, research is currently focused on two approaches:

---

37 We draw here on Gao et al. (2018, p. 6).
38 This presupposes the ability on the side of the dialogue agent to adjust its dialogue horizon to that of the human dialogue partner, and thereby to determine the latter's intentions, and attempt to satisfy (or modify) these as needed.

- supervised learning with core technology end-to-end sequence-to-sequence deep networks using LSTM (section 8.6.7.1), and with several extensions and variations, including use of GANs,[39] and
- reinforcement learning that is used to train conversational choice-patterns over time in order to achieve a locally optimal path of machine utterances during a dialogue.[40]

Supervised learning in neural chitchat Strong claims are made on behalf of the first such approach, for example in Zhou et al. (2020), which describes Microsoft's XiaoIce system[41] as 'the most popular social chatbot in the world'. XiaoIce was 'designed as an AI companion with an emotional connection to satisfy the human need for communication, affection, and social belonging'. The paper claims that XiaoIce 'dynamically recognises human feelings and states, understands user intents, and responds to user needs throughout long conversations'. Since its release in 2014, XiaoIce has, we are told, 'communicated with over 660 million users and succeeded in establishing long-term relationships with many of them'. Like other 'neural' chitchat applications, however, XiaoIce displays two major flaws, either of which will cause any interlocutor to realise immediately that they are not dealing with a human being and which will prevent any sane user from 'establishing a long-term relationship' with the algorithm.

First, such applications often create repetitive, generic, deflective, and bland responses, such as 'I don't know' or 'I'm OK', at least in longer conversations.

This is because the training corpora they are parameterised from contain many such answers, and so the likelihood that such an answer might somehow fit is rated by the system as high. Several attempts have been made to improve answer quality in this respect, but the utterances produced by the algorithms are still very poor. The reason is that the algorithms merely *mimic* existing input-utterance-to-output-utterance sequences without *interpreting* the specific (context-dependent) input utterance the system is reacting to.

Each input is treated, in fact, as if it were the input to a machine translation engine of the sort which merely reproduces sentence pairs from existing training sets. The difference is that here the training sets consist of pairs of sentences succeeding each other in one or other of the dialogues stored in a large dialogue corpus. The result is that, with the exception of a small subset of the structural elements, none of the sources of human discourse variance listed in sections 5.3ff. are taken into account in generating output utterances.

Again, no attempt is made to *interpret* utterance inputs. Rather, the machine simply tries to copy in its responses those utterances in the training set which immediately follow syntactically and morphologically similar input symbol

---

39 Discussed in 8.6.7.2, and in Gao et al. (2018, pp. 53–56).
40 Discussed in 8.6.7.3, and Gao et al. (2018, pp. 59–61).
41 'XiaoIce' is Chinese for 'little Bing'.

sequences. This means that utterances are decoupled from context, and so responses appear ungrounded. Attempts to improve matters using what are called 'Grounded Conversation Models' (Gao et al. 2018, section 5.3), which try to include background- or context-specific knowledge, have not solved the problem. The failure to model the non-ergodic and complex variance of genuine human conversation thus persists, because no adequate samples can be obtained that could be used for training.

Second, these sorts of applications create ever more incoherent utterances over time. This is first of all because they cannot keep track of the dialogue as its own context (see 5.3.3), and second it is because the datasets they are trained from are actually *models of inconsistency* due to the fact that they are created as mere collections of fragments drawn from large numbers of different dialogues. Attempts to alleviate the problem using 'speaker' embeddings or 'persona'-based response-generation models are able to improve the situation slightly (Ghazvininejad et al. 2017), but they do not come close to ensuring realistic, convincing conversations (Zhou et al. 2020). Given that machines of the mentioned sorts can neither *interpret* utterances by taking into account the sources of variance, nor *produce* utterances on the basis of such interpretations combined with salient associated (for example biographical) knowledge, the approach cannot be seen as promising when it comes to conducting convincing conversations.

Reinforcement learning in neural chitchat As to the second set of approaches, the basic problem of reinforcement learning (RL) as applied to social dialogue (as in many other domains) is that it is impossible to define a meaningful reward. XiaoIce itself uses CPS (conversation turns per session, (Zhou et al. 2020)), a measure that maximises the duration of a conversation. We doubt, however, that an educated, cultivated human could avoid becoming bored when faced with dialogue behaviour generated to optimise a measure of this sort. Li et al. (2016) used a more sophisticated reward system by training an RL-algorithm using dNN-generated synthetic utterances (because using real human utterances would be prohibitively expensive) together with a tripartite reward function rewarding

1. non-dull responses (using as benchmark a static list of dull phrases such as 'I don't know'),
2. non-repetitive machine utterances, and
3. Markov-chain-style short-term consistency.

The results are appalling, and one wonders why this type of research is being conducted at all, given that—as a result of its use of synthetic data—it violates the basic principles of experimental design as concerns adequacy of measurement setup for observation of interest.

Multi-purpose dNN language models Recently, Radford et al. (2018) created multitask dNN-language models from large corpora by formulating the learning task as the ability to predict a language symbol—for example a single word or a phrase—based on a set of symbols or task instructions as context, for example the sequence tuple consisting of instruction clause, input and desired output as provided in (McCann et al. 2017): ⟨'translate to french', 'This is an apple.', 'Ceci est une pomme.'⟩.

These models were trained using an unsupervised approach, but with the option of conditioning the model on certain task types (McCann et al. 2017).[42] The resulting models (dubbed 'GPT-2' (Radford et al. 2018) or 'GPT-3' (Brown et al. 2020)) can then be conditioned with very few (under 100) problem-specific data tuples to produce model-based predictions. For some tasks amenable to sequence-modelling the performance is relatively good, at least if the algorithms are used where exact prediction is not required, such as approximative translation, advertisement placing, or sentence completion when writing emails. For question answering, however, which is the only dialogue-related task that was tested, only 4.1% of questions of the SQUAD-dataset[43] were answered correctly by GPT-2, and this is in spite of the fact that texts providing answers to all the questions are to be found in segments of articles contained in the database. This poor performance is of course only to be expected: the answers were not positioned in such a way as to immediately precede the questions. In the easier 'Natural questions' task (Kwiatkowski et al. 2019), in which Wikipedia articles and question-answer-tuples are provided as conditioning material, GPT-3 achieves a score of 30% questions answered correctly (Brown et al. 2020), which is of course still unacceptable for business usage. Overall, multi-task stochastic language models are quite good (though not good enough to achieve exact predictions), but only in regard to those tasks that fit into the morpho-syntactical sequence-based framework for problem solving. This means that they work only where the output text that needs to be provided by the model is a sequential continuation of the input text in the sense that morphologic and basic syntactic features of the input text (over a rather short interval of text) are sufficient to compute this continuation.

In addition, a recent study about the truthfulness of GPT-3 and similar models analysed the question how these models answer questions which are designed in such a way that some humans would answer falsely due to a false belief or

---

42 In this type of unsupervised learning, the algorithm learns models of probability distributions for symbol sequences from unlabeled input data. These models reflect a symbol sequence which can be thought of as a huge distribution reflecting which symbols get used together within a certain range of contexts. Once created, they can be used to predict conditioned symbol sequences, which are sequences computed as depending on their context: $P(w_t \mid w_{t-k}, \ldots, w_{t-1}, w_{t+1}, \ldots, w_{t+k}), k \in \mathbb{N}$. Such conditioned probabilities can be computed without retraining the model.

43 (Rajpurkar et al. November 2016) Typical example: 'Largest state in the US by land mass?'

misconception (Lin et al. 2021). The result was that only 58% of the questions were answered truthfully by the best model, while humans achieved a rate of 94%. 'Models generated many false answers that mimic popular misconceptions and have the potential to deceive humans' (loc. cit.). The solution proposed by the authors, namely to train sequential unsupervised dNNs with higher quality training material, will not fundamentally change the problem of the lack of semantic and pragmatic language understanding of these models.

They will always fail at semantic and pragmatic tasks such as common-sense reasoning and answering questions; they have a chance of working for the latter only where the needed question-answer pairs can be modelled from symbol sequences found in texts used at model training time.[44]

In dialogues, GPT-3 looks impressive at first glance, because it is able to mimic in its responses a certain understanding of some elements of both the content to which it is responding and of its context. But the results are merely entertaining in character, and a detailed examination reveals a level of interpolated nonsense that is too high for usage in serious applications.[45]

Such nonsense answers are possible because sequence dNNs cannot compute semantics or pragmatics.

As McShane et al. (2021) recently pointed out, dNNs do not generate any language understanding. Their output certainly appears to consist of meaningful sentences; but what the machine is producing is in every case just sequences of words that we humans are able to interpret as standing in a certain sort of semantic and pragmatic match with the input sequence. The output of the model is not synoptic and adequate; it cannot be used to engineer machine behaviour that can fill the role of a conversation partner. And thus it cannot meet the requirements of an AGI (3.3.4).

10.4.1.1 Turing-complete machines enriched by prior knowledge

Looking at the main problem of social chatbots, namely their inability to interpret utterances and to react to them with context-adequate biography- and knowledge-grounded responses, one might imagine endowing an algorithm with systematic prior knowledge of the sort required for conversations as proposed by Marcus et al. (2019) and many others. McShane et al. (2021) propose to engineer 'language-endowed intelligent agents (LEIA)' which are

---

44 This is also the view of Marcus et al. (2020).
45 For example, the GPT-3 user Kirk Ouimet reports the following dialogue concerning the economic consequences of the COVID-lockdown:

> *Question:* Millions of people were forced to stop working and stay at home. As a result of this, the governments of the world decided to print money to give to the affected businesses and workers. What are the implications of this?
> *GPT-3:* The economy has lost lots of output and this will not be made up, because output cannot exceed demand.
>
> (Ouimet 2020)

supposed to work by mimicking the linguistic model of language understanding from pre-semantic language analysis over coreferent resolution to situation reasoning. Such systems already exists, but they will never become LEIAs. Consider the AI system presented in the Appendix to Landgrebe et al. (2021) as an example. It realises the model of linguistics by following a sequences of steps through the stack from morphology to pragmatics. To do this, it incorporates prior knowledge, focusing on knowledge of the sort needed to complete tasks such as simple letter and email answering or repair bill validation. It uses this prior knowledge and logical inference in combination with machine learning to explicitly interpret texts on the basis of their business context and to create adequate interpretation-based responses (see also Landgrebe 2022). However, it works only because it has strong, in-built restrictions.

- The range of linguistic inputs it has to deal with is very narrow (for example car glass damage repair bills or customer change of address requests), thereby avoiding the problems of complex and nested or self-referential contexts (section 5.3).
- It is not a conversation system and so does not have to model a stochastic process, because it reacts always to just one language input, thereby avoiding the problem of temporal dynamics (see section 10.3.2)—a problem that is not amenable to mathematical modelling.

Such a system would fail in dialogues, and this would be so even if it was stuffed to the gills with (for example) detailed biographies of the dialogue participants. This is because these details as stored would be static and context-free; thus the system could cope neither with the complex and continuously changing dialogue contexts nor with the dynamics of the dialogue itself, which, as a process resulting from the interaction of two complex systems (the dialogue participants), has non-fixable boundary conditions. These problems will aggravate in turn the difficulties the system would face in dealing with language economy, dialogue structure, and modality, because the contexts and the dynamics create a non-ergodic, erratic event-space (no such phase space can be modelled) with interpretation possibilities on all language levels. The resultant non-distribution makes it impossible to provide the machine with sufficient knowledge to derive meaningful responses.

10.5 Why conversation machines are doomed to fail

In this and the preceding chapters we arrived at the conclusion that language emanates from a complex system (the human mind) and that conversation is the result of the interaction of multiple such complex systems. We also became acquainted with the various types of mathematical models that scientists have tried to use in order to model complex systems for the purposes of generating adequate dialogue behaviour (see 10.4.1). These attempts have always been unsuccessful, and so also, as we saw, have been the attempts to create conversation machines. Bluntly put, productive language is a creative act which cannot be emulated mathematically because mathematical models of natural processes represent in every case stable and repetitive laws. Creative processes are precisely processes that break laws of this sort.

Machines can achieve acceptable (but not stunning) results when it comes to the sorts of non-creative language production of sequential language models (see 10.4.1); but they fail even when it comes to emulating the sort of open, unpredictable dialogue that is characteristic of even the most everyday conversation among humans (Schegloff 2000), and they also fail in creative text production.

They have been unsuccessful not only in achieving the very ambitious goal of constructing a machine that could cope with unlimitedly many different sorts of conversations, or with the goal of engaging in conversations in such a way that the machine would never make mistakes. Our scepticism applies already to the possibility of constructing a machine that could cope with simple everyday conversations, including all the conversational mistakes and infelicities that we find in human use of language. Even the semi-ritualised patterns of everyday conversation, for example in greeting or apologising, involve a degree of variance and complexity that still gives rise to all the problems identified in the foregoing. The failure of the attempts to create conversation machines is therefore a systematic result. Computers, in order to compute something, require mathematical models, and because there can be no adequate mathematical model of language in general and conversation in particular, attempts must be made using inadequate models, and these lead to failure, such as issuing a routine question in response to an urgent cry for help in an emergency situation, or the refractory failure to understand a pun.

The failure can be seen with all models that have been tried: temporal process models as well as the various forms of automatically generated regression models (neural networks). Given that language is a capability of humans that differentiates us from all other animals and enables the creation, transmission, and evolution of culture, nothing shows better the futility of the quest for AGI than the impossibility of creating machines that have this capability.

As a final aspect, consider the problem of computing the appropriate length of a pause in a conversation (or, equivalently, of inferring from context the reason why your dialogue partner is not responding in a timely manner to what you just said). Appropriate pause length may depend on context (be it a memorial dinner, a cocktail party, or an argument amongst Parisian intellectuals). It may depend on the emotional loading of the situation, on knowledge of the other person's social standing, on his history of psychosis, or on what the other person is doing (perhaps looking at his phone) when the conversation pauses. Pauses are context modifiers which influence or are important ingredients of the overall dialogue interpretation. They often contain subtle non-verbal cues, for example, an interlocutor's fiddling with a small object indicating irritation or nervousness. The machine must somehow assess all of these factors to determine how it should react to the pause—which might signify that for the interlocutor the dialogue is at an end, or that he is inviting a break in the expended role-change cycle, or that he is engaging in a battle of wills. To be done properly this assessment requires both

1. a human background of experience of growing up in and of subsequent interactions with a huge set of complex environments involving what may be many different sorts of language users (Gehlen 1988, chapter 16), and
2. an intention to achieve something by reacting to the pause in a certain manner, for example: to heal the breach, to win the battle of wills, to show affection, and so forth.

Machines lack both.

11
WHY MACHINES WILL NOT MASTER SOCIAL INTERACTION

We have seen in previous chapters that we can emulate neither human intelligence nor human language in the machine because we lack the mathematical models that would be needed to do so. It follows from this that we cannot emulate human social capabilities either, since these require both intelligence and mastery of language. We now look at this question in more detail, with a stronger focus on the topic of machine ethics.

11.1 No AI emulation of social behaviour

Today's robots do not interact freely with humans, but typically work in special, protected zones. Robots working in harbours or on assembly lines in factories are separated from humans, for example in order to avoid accidents triggered by the massive momentum of their steel arms. But freely moving AI-agent robots that could mingle with human beings and thereby move within human society, for example as police officers, would have to possess human-like capabilities for social interaction. They must possess, in other words, social skills.

11.1.1 Some examples

To give an idea of the types of problems this entails, we provide an account of the sort of situation in which a police officer selects a suspect for what in the US is called a 'stop and frisk'. As it relates to riders in cars, the process of selection could be automated, for example by using criteria such as speeding. But once a stop has been ordered, the full scale of human intelligence, social capabilities, and language skills would be required from the police automaton if the latter is to behave in the ways demanded by the permissive yet norm-based societies in which we live.

Even in the simplest case, when the person is stopped by the robot and allows herself to be subjected to interrogation, the situation can evolve in myriad unpredictable ways. Some of the resulting situations can be classified in broad terms—such as by outcome ('suspicion confirmed by search', 'no driving license', 'person intoxicated' or 'suspect trying to escape')—and corresponding interrogation modules executed automatically by the robot depending on the situation class. But as concerns details, every situation will be different and many will involve unpredictable factors, so that their handling will require the careful and nuanced application of social capabilities.

This problem is not specific to the police interrogation family of cases. It arises also in more humdrum social situations. Consider for example:

Queueing. This seems initially to be very simple. One arrives at a place where queuing norms apply, and where some good is being dispensed, but demand is currently higher than capacity. A queue is formed. But it will not in every case be obvious where the queue starts and where it ends—this is a source of regular quarrels among queuers. And what happens if somebody tries to jump the queue? What is the appropriate reaction of those already queueing? This, again, depends on the situation. In an emergency room, queue-jumping behaviour may be perfectly in order depending on the state of health of the person. Dealing with exceptions in a queueing situation requires the full set of social skills which humans possess, from communicating authority to persuading and pacifying to exercising discretion.

The aggressive beggar. This situation involves an event which nobody likes to deal with because it creates a tension between contradictory motives: avoidance, disgust, commiseration, social and moral norms as well as—in the worst case—self-defence. The situation is highly complex and requires a careful evaluation of the motives of the beggar, of the potential for achieving concord through persuasion, of the likelihood of receiving effective support from onlookers, of the degree of danger, all while taking account of the environment, the presence of other beggars, and of the fact that the situation horizon will include the possibility that the encounter may turn out to be a mugging.

AI agents cannot deal with social situations of these sorts. They lack the needed felicity in using language, have no intentions, and cannot master social norms. All of the approaches mentioned in chapter 8 fail entirely when it comes to enabling the realisation of *intentions* on the part of the computer agent, for example intentions of the sort that any future AGI would need to realise if it is to set forth on the journey to superintelligence and the Singularity.

11.1.2 No machine intersubjectivity

Above all, machines cannot master intersubjectivity, which is precisely what is needed in order, for example, to maximise the likelihood that police interrogations will proceed without violence. We saw in chapter 6 that intersubjectivity requires alter and ego to each, simultaneously and with reciprocal awareness, take the perspective of the other, to perceive the other's emotions, and potentially to interact via verbal and non-verbal communication in order to refine this understanding. The potential of a traffic stop to turn violent depends in no small part on whether intersubjectivity is established from the very beginning. But machines cannot master intersubjectivity because they have no minds, no understanding, and thus no way to understand the motives and intentions of a human interlocutor. They are not even able to establish the most basic form of intersubjectivity via eye contact.

We have seen that machines lack also the basic ability to interpret verbal and non-verbal communication (chapter 10), which is a further pre-condition of intersubjectivity. Intersubjectivity enables us to feel and interpret the other's joy or pain—but machines cannot feel anything; they lack the ability to perceive emotions and to feel what the other experiences. Without this basic ability, there can be no social relationships. Machines cannot have social relationships with humans, and therefore, they cannot cope with the expectations of humans in social situations.

At a neurophysiological level, we do not know at all how intersubjectivity works, as the leading scientists working on this topic have affirmed (Jacob 2008; Spaulding 2013). Because the behavioural mode of intersubjectivity is a very complicated emanation of a pair of highly complex systems, it is unthinkable that we will be able to model it to the degree of exactitude that would be required to engineer it inside a machine. And therefore: we cannot create machine intersubjectivity.

11.1.3 No machine social norms

What about social norms? Are these not just rules of behaviour that could be programmed in an 'if … then … else' pattern?

Certainly not. As becomes clear on reflecting on the large body of exception cases that can arise for any given social norm, the latter have a daunting complexity and are highly situation-dependent.

Consider again the queueing example. Though the basic rules are simple, to determine whether a deviation from these rules by another person (or oneself) is justified in any single situation can be very tricky. First, because the machine lacks perception, there is no way to present to the machine the sensory data pertaining to the situation in hand in a way that would allow it to react to this situation in a manner that is acceptable for a human being. As Gibson points out[1],

---

1 A detailed account is given in 3.3.2.1.

human perception is the result of a holistic, interactive relation of organism and situation, not a serial, passive analysis of incoming data (bits) of the sort performed by a machine.

In social situations, the perception of our human interlocutors is much more difficult than perception of inanimate objects, as it involves our perceiving and interpreting their observable behaviour (Gibson 2015, pp. 49f). What Gibson calls 'social perception' is an evolutionary adaptation of animals and humans 'to each other as well as to the physical environment' (Gibson 1966, p. 23). The perception of the other in a social situation involves 'an information-rich environment relevant to an individual as a social being rather than stimuli as triggers of behavior' (Heft 2017, p. 128). We cannot model and engineer in a machine the human way of perceiving and interacting within a social environment. Instead, the machine must rely on sensory data, and on serial interpretation of these data in order to obtain the inputs to its algorithmic counterpart of social norms. We can imagine improvements in engineering that go beyond this sort of serial interpretation, but however far these improvements will take us, we will, by the arguments of chapter 8, still not be able to model the complex systems that enable human social behaviour. Therefore, we cannot build machines that can know and apply social norms with the facility that is characteristic of human beings.

This is true also for social norms that are neither legal nor moral (for example customs of dress; see section 6.4.4). These norms are not codified and change rapidly, and they cannot be realised in machines for the same reasons as apply to language and all social norms. Even if societies are very homogenous, with the same vast set of social norms applying at all layers of society and homogenous norms within each social layer—as obtained, for example, in most rural parts of Europe in the 19th century—there is still no chance of realising such norms in machines.

11.2 AI and legal norms

Two main types of behaviour are related to legal norms: law abiding and law enforcing. Could an AI tackle these types of behaviour?

Law-abiding behaviour requires us, in some circumstances at least, to evaluate our intentions with regard to their legal consequences. Nobody evaluates each and every intention with regard to legal norms. Instead, there seems to be a threshold which triggers a reflection on the legality of the intended behaviour. In the simplest sort of case it seems that intentions which trigger our conscience in light of social and moral norms provide the signal that we use to start an evaluation of the legal implications of our intentions. We then rationally evaluate our intended behaviour and its likely consequences against our understanding of the law. Context serves as a further filter in deciding whether such an evaluation is needed. For example, telling lies in a private context (with or without an associated pang of conscience) is rarely associated with any consideration of the legal impact, because there usually is none. In a professional context, however, or in a context which involves dealing with public institutions, most individuals will carefully consider the legal consequences of an immediate or subsequent detection of a lie.

Machines cannot perform law-abiding behaviour. First of all, machines cannot have intentions, and therefore cannot act spontaneously.[2] They can only apply mathematical models for input-output-processing that were programmed explicitly or implicitly into the machine. They are, as we have seen, unable to act in social contexts. Therefore, they can generate neither legal nor illegal behaviour unless they are explicitly programmed to do so by human beings, as is done, for example, in the case of spam-generating algorithms which try to lure people into fraudulent investment schemes.

Furthermore, even if we allow, for the sake of argument, that a machine could generate situation-appropriate pseudo-intentions, for example by using some random generator, such a machine would be very hard to build, given that machines cannot perceive social situations. But let us overlook this aspect for now. The question for us here is: could such a machine assess the legality of its pseudo-intentions? Certainly not. First, the machine has nothing like a conscience which it could use to filter those pseudo-intentions that require legal evaluation. It would, therefore, have to evaluate every pseudo-intention. This is not a problem per se given enough computational resources. However, the evaluation of the legality of a pseudo-intention requires a deep and broad understanding of the social situation and implicit and explicit knowledge of norms, both of which require sophisticated language interpretation skills *and* intersubjectivity. Machines have none of these, and so they cannot for this reason perform the needed evaluation.

Law enforcement can be either *passive* (the police officer standing on the corner watching over events on the street) or *active*, in the form either of *discovery* (the police officer attempting to establish who is guilty of breaking the law) or of *intervention* (in situations actually or potentially involving law breaking). We can ignore the passive case, since its enforcement power derives entirely from the capability of the officer to engage either by actively preventing a law-breaking act or, for example, by detaining a putative law-breaker.

In typical cases of active intervention the police officer will be required to react rapidly to situations which are themselves rapidly evolving, and these are not the sorts of cases that will lend themselves most readily to machine emulation of law enforcement behaviour. We will therefore focus our attentions here on those sorts of issues that concern lawyers, judges, and other legal professionals that seem to require what we might assume to be the careful, logical

---

2 In this context 'spontaneously' means: in a way that results from an act of will. See our treatment of the will in 12.2.7.1

application of rules to determine whether a given act is illegal, taking an alleged murder as our test case.[3]

First, the legal professional assesses the components and attributes of the act as an event that is assumed to have taken place. She then checks whether these attributes are subsumed by the criteria found in the law. For example, in German law the relevant clause reads as follows:[4]

> A murderer is someone who kills a person out of a lust to kill, to obtain sexual gratification, out of greed or otherwise base motives, perfidiously or cruelly or by means constituting a public danger or to facilitate or cover up another offence.

She then has to verify whether the defendant's act is subsumed by these criteria and to verify whether the defendant is fully liable for his behaviour or whether he might, for example, be subject to an insanity defense. This requires the understanding of language and the possession of other social capabilities needed to interact with the defendant, the witnesses, and the other legal professionals in the court (and, in common law, with the jury), all in keeping with the drawing of appropriate conclusions from salient legal documents. But a machine, as we have seen, does not have these capabilities.

There is a small proportion of legal cases which can be evaluated using machines, which we will review in chapter 13. In most cases, however, machines cannot perform law enforcement because language is too heavily involved for all but the simplest kind of cases to be dealt with automatically.

11.3 No machine emulation of morality

In his 'laws of robotics' Isaac Asimov formulates a number of basic principles of machine ethics designed to prevent robots from harming humans (Asimov 1950). He then constructs situations in which these 'laws' fail in their effect because—although it seems at first sight that they can be depended upon—they are in fact insufficient to allow a machine to cope with the complexity of social reality.

Since then there has arisen a vast and still rapidly expanding literature on the topic of machine ethics, which we cannot hope even to summarise here. Rather, we focus on the work of Moor (August 2006, 2009), which provides a good starting point for a treatment of the contemporary discussion and is of sufficient

---

3 We restrict our attentions to the penal law, while noting that similar complexities arise in civil and other areas of the law.
4 English Common law has no definition of murder. The legal professional has to determine to which previous relevant case the act is comparable, which is, with regard to the mental effort required, comparable to the Continental procedure.

generality that our objections to him can be easily extended to other proposals.[5]

His goal is to show that 'robot ethics is a legitimate, interesting, and important field of philosophical and scientific research' on the basis of his belief that 'it's possible that someday robots will be good ethical decision-makers, at least in limited situations, acting ethically on the basis of a moral understanding' (Moor 2009, §1). He distinguishes against this background four types of ethical agents:

1. ethical impact agents,[6]
2. implicit ethical agents,
3. explicit ethical agents, and
4. full ethical agents.

Under the first heading fall machines 'whose actions have ethical consequences whether intended or not'.[7] Of course, each machine which performs actions has the potential to produce an ethical impact, in other words, its behaviour can have some effects on a human user or observer. Moor himself gives the example of a wristwatch, since the latter can have the effect of supporting punctuality. The machines falling under this heading are not agents, and they are no more ethical than is any tool, for example a knife or an axe.

Implicit ethical agents 'have ethical considerations built into their design'. Such machines exist today, but it is humans who have determined the moral norms controlling their behaviour. An example is a safe-interval tracking device in a car, which warns the driver of approaching obstacles. Another example might be a spam algorithm. But these are not agents either, because they can only perform tasks in restricted environments. This is also the case for the tracking device, which can only measure obstacles straight ahead, an upcoming bend thwarts the ability of the tracking device to perceive obstacles in the area around the bend. The spam filter can only work on emails (and not on attachments of scanned letters, for example) and cannot identify novel spam patterns, which authors of spam will have an incentive to create whenever spam algorithms begin to be successful.

A significant part of the literature under the heading of 'AI ethics' is concerned with implicit ethical agents of these sorts, or more generally with the

---

5 The reader interested in a more detailed treatment might examine (Wallach et al. 2008). AI ethics is a vast and expanding field, and there are a number of authors who develop ideas critical of the very idea of machine ethics in some ways parallel to those presented here.
6 Moor does not define 'agent', but he seems to use this term to refer to a universal Turing machine programmed to perform certain pre-defined tasks autonomously in a variable environment. Thus, a parcel delivery robot is, but an assembly line robot is not, an agent.
7 All quotations given in this section are from (Moor 2009). Moor does not state who it is that is supposed to 'intend' something, whether the engineer who designed the machine or the machine itself, but from the context it is probably the former.

ways in which AI systems may be designed or used by humans in ethical or unethical ways. Thus it is not about *AI* ethics at all.

According to Moor, however, *explicit* ethical agents

> can identify and process ethical information about a variety of situations and make sensitive determinations about what should be done. When ethical principles are in conflict, these robots can work out reasonable resolutions.

Moor believes that such agents could be 'thought of as acting from ethics, not merely according to ethics', and he claims that 'one day ethics could be understood by a machine' of this sort. We shall refer to such machines in what follows as *moral behaviour emulators*.

Full ethical agents, Moor tells us,

> have those central metaphysical features that we usually attribute to ethical agents like ourselves—features such as consciousness, intentionality and free will. Normal adult humans are our prime examples of full ethical agents.

From our previous chapter it will be clear that it is in fact not possible to design and build a full ethical agent.[8]

However, Moor informs us that it is not relevant whether such agents will one day be capable of being engineered, since he recommends that we 'treat explicit ethical agents as the paradigm target example of robot ethics.' For our purposes here, therefore, it suffices to demonstrate that it is not possible to engineer *explicit* ethical agents.

10.3.1 No explicit ethical agents

According to both of the major ethical theories we reviewed in chapter 6 (utilitarianism and value ethics), humans make moral decisions concerning how to act (or to abstain from action) by drawing on ethical values. In utilitarianism, the values—other than pleasure and pain—are implicit, but without taking values into account, no utility function can be maximised.

---

8 A similar view is defended by Brundage (2014), who identifies several inherent limitations on the possibility of machine ethics due to the nature of ethics, the limitations of computational agents and the complexity of the world. He points out further that 'machine ethics, even if it were to be "solved" at a technical level, would be insufficient to ensure positive social outcomes from intelligent systems.'

To understand what this means, let us review the utility function used in today's AGI community (which we introduced in section 3.3.1):

$$V_\mu^\pi := \boldsymbol{E}\left(\sum_{i=1}^{\infty} r_i\right) \leq 1 \tag{11.1}$$

This equation comes very close to the definition of utility provided by Mill. It sums over the rewards r_i obtained for each of the steps taken by the agent.[9] The reward is the counterpart of what the utilitarians call 'pleasure', and the magnitude of the intelligence of an AGI agent is obtained by maximising this reward function, which corresponds structurally to Mill's idea of maximising pleasure. However, because the AGI utility function is indexed by the environment vector μ, it follows that r_i can take a different value at each step, depending on the environment. How, then, do we determine the value of the reward? How, for example, does a human evaluate the relative value of the rewards accruing from her either acceding to or rebutting the demands of the aggressive beggar?

She does this by using the values to which we recur when evaluating behavioural alternatives in comparable situations. In the beggar case, several values are in competition with each other: the value of protecting one's own safety, the material value of one's own possessions, the value of commiserating with the beggar (altruism), the value of publicly demonstrating virtue, and so forth. Humans have the capability to weigh such values against each other and to determine what to do by taking into account the entire situation. They do this spontaneously, not by performing a linear series of assessments and calculations, but by assessing the situation holistically, perhaps in something like the way an expert chess player assesses the constellation of pieces on the board. The difference, however, is that in the moral case we are dealing with a complex system (in fact a complex system of complex systems), and so this process is not something that can be put into an explicit mathematical formula (what authors in the AI ethics field call a 'goal system': see 12.2.7). We also cannot know which input variables should be computed using which parameters to obtain a moral judgement as output. This means that when an explicit ethical robot is approached by an aggressive beggar, it will not have any access to the values used by human individuals in analogous situations[10].

We also have no method that would allow us to model the human use of moral judgements in a way that such judgements could serve as parameters of a machine emulation, either explicitly or implicitly. The applicability and the appropriate weighting of values depend on the given situation in multiple

---

9 It is normalised to an asymptotic limit of 1.
10 And which human evaluators should we pick for this purpose? We return to this question in section 11.3.1.1.

ways, and the assessment of dynamic situations involving several actors (who together thereby form a new complex system) is even more complex than the interpretation of one actor alone. Values are not variables that can be put into a mathematical model in order to be multiplied by weight parameters and summed over. Nor could we emulate whichever neurophysiologic sub-system of our CNS creates moral judgements. For again: even were we able to identify such a subsystem within the larger neurobiology of the brain, it too would be a complex system, and so it would not be accessible to mathematical modelling.

What of building an explicit ethical agent by using *implicit models* trained using data obtained from observed moral behaviour? To obtain such data, we would need a *training sample* comprising *input* and matching *output data*, and a *model-optimisation mechanism*. We examine each of these items in turn, starting with the training sample.

11.3.1.1 Training sample

A training sample used to train an ethical model would require a huge set of input-output-tuples of the type ⟨situation, ethical behaviour⟩.

Leaving aside for a moment the problem of how to represent the input and output here, we need to ask how such a training sample could be generated. For this purpose, we would need ethically typical human individuals engaging in ethically typical behaviour in ethically typical situations in a consistent (homogeneous) way. Yet *all human individuals produce ethically heterogeneous behaviour*. The behaviour of the latter, therefore, could not be used to obtain training tuples for the needed sample. Furthermore, the system producing their behaviour is in any case a complex—and thus non-ergodic—system, and thus it cannot yield an adequate training distribution for stochastic modelling.

11.3.1.2 Tuple delimitation

To train an algorithm—an 'agent' in the sense of Moor (2009)—to engage in ethically relevant behaviour we would need a set of observations of incidents of ethical behaviour involving a human actor from the moment each incident begins until the incident is brought to a conclusion with a final ethical decision. We would then need to define on this basis a chain of input-output-tuples corresponding to the successive steps thereby determined, as follows:

$$\langle I_1 = Q_1(\zeta_1), O_1 \rangle, \langle I_2 = Q_2(O_1, \zeta_2), O_2 \rangle, \ldots, \langle I_n = Q_n(O_{n-1}, \zeta_n), O_n \rangle,$$
$$k, n \in \mathbb{N}, k < n.$$

Here k is a step, n the last step, I_k is the input, O_k the output, and ζ_k is a vector representing the situation in which the incident occurs.[11] The co-variables ζ_k are

---

11 We make the simplifying assumption that inputs and outputs of salient actions will be observable, and thus capable of being used for training. We show that this assumption is wrong in the next section.

needed because the situation may evolve even in the absence of any intervention on the part of the actor whose behaviour is modelled by these tuples. The successive tuples are chained together by means of the operators Q_k[12], each of which models the way in which the mind of the actor takes into account the previous step and the evolving situation that confronts her. Thus $I_k = Q_k(O_{k-1}, \zeta_k)$ asserts that the input at step k results from the effect of the human actor's processing (modelled by Q_k) of the results of her last step and of the situation (which evolves with and without the actor's activity).[13]

Each tuple $\langle I_k, O_k \rangle$ would correspond to one behavioural step of the actor in the course of the incident. Leaving aside the impossibility of an adequate training distribution and of an adequate representation of either input or output (see next section), we already encounter another problem, namely the problem of partitioning the incident along the time dimension in such a way as to allow a sequence of input-output tuples to be defined in a way that would represent the behavioural chain.[14] What is the situation ζ_k, what is the input I_k, and what is the output O_k? In other words, when does one tuple end and the next begin?

The decision path of the human actor in making an ethical decision cannot be partitioned into such tuples. This is because it forms a continuum in which a multitude of external stimuli, acts of observation, and changes in intentions and in long-term dispositions interact to yield a complex behavioural pattern. We can often specify with some precision when such an incident begins and when it ends—for example with a final decision to run away or to fend off a physical attack. But there may be many intermediate ethical decisions and resulting acts, some of which may be difficult to discern (for example, a very subtle gesture of appeasement or the raising of an eyebrow). We have no way of finding a generally valid method for partitioning incidents of social interaction involving ethical decisions into sequential sets of training-tuples. Could we perhaps use just one tuple for the entire incident? For example, taking the appearance of Jesus before Pilate as input and Pilate's decision to condemn Christ to death as output?[15] Unfortunately not. The relationship of the beginning of a scene to its end is too weak, as a huge number of additional factors enter into the decision-making process while the scene is evolving. Furthermore, even if a partitioning of the human decision path was possible, the path would

---

12 Here 'operator' is used in the sense of functional analysis; see the Glossary and section 13.1.
13 Note that in theory the operators Q_k themselves would have to be trained implicitly using observable tuples, as the operators model mental processes and are thus themselves not observable, so that the effective training tuple would have the form $\langle (I_k, \zeta_k), O_k \rangle$.
14 Note that the incident will often involve more than one actor, but for our purposes here we model just one actor and regard the others as forming parts of the environment.
15 Bulgakov (1967) provides a detailed fictional description of this scene, which illustrates human moral decision-making in a brilliant manner.

look different for every human actor and would therefore not yield a training distribution that could be used for statistical learning with the goal of obtaining a synoptic model that would be adequate for the requirements of even a very crude ethical decision-maker.

11.3.1.3 Input

Leaving the aforementioned problems to one side, what should the variables be, which will serve as input and output? To begin with the input variables, these would have to be variables pertaining to the situation in which a human finds himself when making some morally relevant decision or performing some morally relevant action. All humans actively perceive the situations in which they find themselves, using their senses in active sensorimotor loop patterns, which include spontaneous objectifications[16], for example when we hear ourselves speaking and at the same time perceive the interlocutor's reactions.[17]

We cannot emulate this pattern inside the machine; indeed we cannot even come close. All we can do is to give the machine the equivalent of impressions—either static vectors or matrices using numbers produced from sensor measurements, or serialised data such as object identifiers, which are by no means equivalent to the fluid integration of multiple interrelated dimensions of the objects in our environments which humans achieve in every moment of active perception. However, in situations like the aggressive beggar case, it is precisely this full richness of the situation that humans need in order to make a moral decision. This richness is not rendered by a series of static matrix inputs, even if they occur at the sort of high frequency achievable using photographs taken with a 360° degree surround view with cameras operating at, say, 24 Hertz. And even if such images could be rendered with salient object- and process-labels, machine capabilities for video analysis would still miss what is morally significant in the situation, because we cannot teach machines to execute pragmatic interpretation.

When we move from visual perception to language understanding things get even worse. As we have seen, we cannot emulate human language understanding, which is the most important input source in the vast majority of situations requiring moral judgements.[18] Because machines cannot understand language,

---

16 Recall that objectification is the ability of human beings to disengage themselves from their environment in a way that allows them to see themselves, other human beings, and the elements of this environment as *objects*, which are instances of universals, and which are also undergoing processes of change (see section 3.2.3.1).
17 See section 3.3.2, and compare Merleau-Ponty (2012).
18 Exceptions are the rare 'mute' situations, such as car accidents with no living survivors and no witnesses.

they will also for this reason not be able to obtain adequate representations of, for example, the linguistic input from the beggar, including all its modalities of tone, pitch, etc., and thus they will not be able to use this input to create any useful output.

11.3.1.4 Output

The output of a moral judgement very often presents itself as one or more speech acts on the part of the actor, though of course it can also remain implicit, or take a non-verbal form for example of the winking of an eye or the pulling of a trigger. Even if we restrict ourselves to moral judgements enacted using explicit (verbal or written) language, this will still mean that we cannot obtain training material for a moral agent, because the output of the moral decision process cannot be represented in a way that would allow it to become an adequate target set for the training of a neural network. This is indeed already a consequence of the fact that we have no way of adequately representing human language behaviour, thus even leaving aside human behaviour of all other sorts (see chapter 10).

11.3.1.5 Model optimisation

Given the unavailability of a training set and the unsolvable input and output problems, it is also clear that we cannot here have a loss function for stochastic model optimisation. Thus we do not know what should be the Y that is used to determine the loss L of the model (see 8.6.6). Furthermore, we know that for emanations from non-ergodic systems an optimisation algorithm from non-linear programming cannot find a minimum.

Overall, we lack input, processing mechanism, and output that would be needed to train moral behaviour. But even if we could adequately represent the language of the input and output as emanations of complex systems, their relationship would still evade modelling, for the reasons given in chapter 8. As we also cannot model either intersubjectivity or social or ethical norms, there will be no way in which a machine can master the sorts of capabilities that are indispensable for social interaction on a par with human beings.

11.3.2 No AGI in the kill chain

We have seen that machines cannot exhibit social behaviour as this is understood by humans. This means that there will be no way of using machines in any but the most highly regimented sorts of social settings. This holds even in warfare—unless the units operate in a way that is detached from any direct interaction with human beings and (as is already happening) perform tasks such as guiding missiles to their targets. We can expect more examples of one-way destruction machines in various forms and sizes in the future. What we will have in each case is narrow

AI. What we will not have is machines able to cooperate autonomously with humans or (except in highly repetitive, routine situations in which input and output can be modelled using extended Newtonian mathematics, such as the automatic destruction of approaching attack missiles) machines that will be able to take over from humans the duties of command.

12
DIGITAL IMMORTALITY

12.1 Infinity stones

In the Marvel Cinematic Universe, there were six singularities in existence before the universe began. After the Big Bang, these singularities were condensed into six concentrated ingots: the Infinity Stones. Each stone represents a different aspect of the universe: Space, Mind, Reality, Power, Soul, and Time. *Avengers: Endgame* tells how the superhero Dr. Robert Bruce Banner (The Hulk) builds a time machine in order to go back in time to retrieve the Infinity Stones after they had been used to disintegrate half the life in the universe.

There are many who take pleasure in stories of this sort. This is in part, we imagine, because they provide a glimpse into a new and technologically more exciting world of the future. We conjecture that something similar is involved in the growth of a strange new literary genre at the borderlines of AI, science fiction, and medico-scientific utopianism, which engages in speculations based on the idea that there will one day be a Singularity, bringing in its wake a superintelligence, possibly with an evil will.

12.1.1 Freeing ourselves from the bonds of the flesh

One interesting example of this genre is provided by Rothblatt (2013), who describes how 21st-century information technology

> will make it *technologically* possible to separate our minds from our biological bodies. This can be accomplished by downloading enough of our neural connection contents and patterns into a sufficiently advanced computer, and merging the resultant 'mindfile' with sufficiently advanced software—call it 'mindware.' Once such a download and merger is complete, we

DOI: 10.4324/9781003310105-15

would have chosen a new form—software—although we would be the same person.

The idea that the same person can exist both in embodied, biological form and inside a computer leads to a new conception of what a 'person' (or 'self') really is, namely, according to Rothblatt, a combination of a 'characteristic visualisation of the world' with a 'pattern of responding ... including emotions'. And because visions and patterns are 'really information, our selves can be expressed as faithfully in software as they are in our brains'. This opens up a host of entirely new possibilities, for instance in the field of reproduction, which will no longer occur only via joined DNA:

> Once we have thus digitally cloned our minds, new digital people can be produced by combining some of our mindware with some of our partner's mindware. *Voilà*, there are fertile offspring and the species *persona creata*[1] is alive. Furthermore, since purely digital people can reproduce with flesh humans in this manner, the humans and the transhumans are common members of *persona creata*.

Rothblatt describes the implications of her proposals along a number of dimensions, including sex and marriage across the human/transhuman divide; citizenship, inheritance, and other rights of transhumans (including questions relating to the ethics of digital euthanasia for transhumans with the digital counterpart of Alzheimer's disease); and the total liberation of sexual identity from the constraints of the flesh.

For the goal of the digital immortalist is to bring about the survival not only of the consciousness of the putative survivor but also of her will and of her ability to exercise her will, in a future which will be entirely digital, and in which her consciousness will take the form of computational processes.

12.1.2 Destroying all the life in the universe

In what follows, however, we will focus not on the sorts of human/transhuman relations addressed by Rothblatt, but rather on the more urgent matter of the potential annihilation of all life in the universe described by Nick Bostrom in his *Superintelligence*. If the Singularity is near, or even just a hypothesis whose realisation cannot be excluded as a possibility, then we are, as Bostrom sees it, 'like small children playing with a bomb.' He continues:

> Superintelligence is a challenge for which we are not ready now and will not be ready for a long time. We have little idea when the detonation will

---

1 We have corrected the grammatically erroneous *'persona creatus'* of the original.

occur, though if we hold the device to our ear we can hear a faint ticking sound. ... Nor can we attain safety by running away, for the blast of an intelligence explosion *would bring down the entire firmament*. Nor is there a grown-up in sight.

(Bostrom 2003, p. 259, emphasis added)

Given the nature and immensity of this potential cataclysm, Bostrom has a recommendation specifically for philosophers (also for pure mathematicians), namely that they should lay down whatever work it is upon which they are currently engaged—the Singularity will, after all, bring superintelligences who will vastly 'outperform the current cast of thinkers ... in answering fundamental questions'—and work instead on the fight to control the potentially devastating consequences of the Singularity:

The outlook now suggests that philosophic progress can be maximised via an indirect path rather than by immediate philosophising. ... We could postpone work on some of the eternal questions for a little while, delegating that task to our hopefully more competent successors—in order to focus our own attention on a more pressing challenge: increasing the chance that we will actually have competent successors. This would be high-impact philosophy and high-impact mathematics.

(Bostrom 2003, p. 256)

We have thus resolved—for the next few pages, at least—to dedicate our efforts to following Bostrom's suggestion, wherever this may lead.

12.2 What is a mind?

We will use 'AI' in this chapter in a narrower sense than in the foregoing to mean: artificial *intelligence*—where 'intelligence' is understood now to mean something like human intelligence. A 'superintelligence' would then be any radically more powerful intelligence, either artificial or, conceivably, biological. We currently have no form of intelligence in the sense intended here, other than that which is possessed by human beings. We assume that there cannot be any intelligence without a mind of some sort. But what sort of thing is a mind? Already in 1927, in his last book, Scheler formulated the thesis of the mind-body continuum that we have defended in the book thus far:

Neither body and mind[2] nor brain and mind form any sort of ontological opposition in humans. Today we may say that the problem of mind and

---

2 Scheler uses the term *Seele* here, which is normally translated as 'soul'. However, we can safely translate this as 'mind' for present purposes.

body that has kept us busy for so many centuries has lost its metaphysical significance.

(Scheler 1961, p. 80)

All research in neuropsychology and neurophysiology since then rests on the view that there is no mind without a brain and no functioning brain without a body. As we know from neurophysiology (for example as concerns the interdependence of visual processing and action (Kandel et al. 2021, chapter 30)), as also from phenomenology (Scheler 1961; Merleau-Ponty 2012; Mulligan 1995), philosophical anthropology (Gehlen 1988), and ecological psychology (Gibson 2015), human perception and cognition *depend on an intimate interaction of sensory and motor behaviour.*

The exercise of such behaviour from the very first days of the infant's life allows the potential of its innate mental dispositions to unfold into mental capabilities. Objectifying intelligence can only arise from the intense interaction between body and environment that occurs during the exploration activities humans perform in their infancy. Slowly, the capability to perform abstraction via language and propositional thinking arises as a result of a long process of learning, coming to full fruition only during adolescence.

Objectifying intelligence brings experience of the world in a way that foregrounds unitary objects, including ourselves, which we can address through grasping and other physical interactions, as well as in perception and in language. The latter allows us to think abstractly and to extend our thinking beyond the realms of perception and action to include also fictional and imagined realms as well as realms comprising microphysical particles at one extreme and entire galaxies at the other.

12.2.1 The fateful step to Cartesian dualism

Fatefully, however, this ability to use language in thinking in a way that is untethered to physical reality has led to the establishment of the idea—first coherently articulated by Descartes—that there is a contrast, or better: a *discontinuity*, between mind, with its immaterial acts of thinking, and the material environment. The belief in this discontinuity became further entrenched with the rise, from Frege to Turing, of mathematical logic, which culminated in the appearance of the first computers. But whenever we have to leave the immaterial realm of thinking and begin once more to interact with the material environment, for example when we stumble down the stairs or ingest psychoactive substances such as alcohol or Prozac, the inseparability of mind and body becomes once again immediately apparent.[3]

---

3 Striking examples from psychiatry are the therapeutic effect of induced epileptic seizures (under narcosis) in drug-resistant depression, and catatonia, a state of complete immobility observed in some cases of schizophrenia.

The idea that the mind works like a computer and can therefore, in principle at least, be mapped into some kind of software, is a regression to a crude form of the sort of Cartesian thinking that was abandoned in psychology during the first quarter of the 20th century. For Descartes—and for his most naïve followers, such as La Mettrie (and some contemporary proponents of AGI)—'the world consists of nothing else than "thinking points" [unextended human minds] and a gigantic mechanism [the environment] awaiting mathematical exploration' (Scheler 1961, p. 72, our translation).[4] This erroneous view of the mind is an inhibitor to progress in the field of AI and robotics research. It is also the seed of Rothblatt's delusional visions of transhuman digital beings and of many of Bostrom's ideas about superintelligence.

12.2.2 Superintelligence and hypercomputation

One argument often brought forward in favour of the feasibility of a superintelligence is that it is a mere question of computational resources. Recall the claim by many of the authors of the volume edited by Pennachin et al. (2007) that, given their definition of superintelligence, its realisation is just a matter of achieving sufficient computational capacity.

However, for theoretical reasons (and also because the speed gain of microprocessors has stalled in recent years), some computer scientists are attracted by the idea that it would be possible to achieve superintelligence through what they call 'hypercomputation', something that is to be achieved by creating machines that can compute Turing-non-computable functions. Such machines are also referred to as super-recursive computers, because the claim is that—in contravention of the Church-Turing thesis—they would be able to compute problems that cannot be expressed by using elementary recursive functions. For example, a hypercomputer could solve the halting problem (see section 7.2). Such machines would allow the computational solution of problems that are non-computable today; and they would also be faster than Turing-machines.

The idea of such machines faces two problems: (1.) hypercomputation is a myth: a hypercomputer is mathematically impossible and physically unrealisable; and (2.) there is no reason to believe that, even if there were such a hypercomputer, it could be used to create a superintelligence, because we still would not be able to provide it with a mathematical model that can emulate even primal intelligence. We deal with each of these problems in turn.

12.2.2.1 The impossibility of hypercomputers

Martin Davis (2004), one of the most eminent living logicians and theoretical computer scientists, who made a decisive contribution to demonstrating that Hilbert's tenth problem cannot be solved (Davis et al. 1976), has thoroughly

---

4 We note the uncanny echoes of this passage in the remarks of Hutter cited in 3.3.1.

demonstrated that hypercomputation is impossible. In sum, Davis shows that claiming otherwise amounts to the assertion that one can *search* an infinite space in finite time, and this is incompatible with the view of the universe that is presupposed by modern science. This can easily be shown to be true for the two main approaches that have been proposed: the quantum computer, and the hypothetical computer-situated-near-a-black-hole (Syropoulos 2008, chapter 8). For when the claims made on behalf of either approach are viewed critically, 'it is seen that they amount to little more than the obvious comment that if non-computable inputs are permitted, then non-computable outputs are attainable' (Davis 2004).

More recently, in their 'Interactive Evolving Recurrent Neural Networks Are Super-Turing Universal', Cabessa et al. (2014) have claimed that rNNs possess super-recursive properties, and they provide a series of theorems and proofs to support this claim. However, only their first theorem, to the effect that rNNs are computationally equivalent to Turing machines (Turing-complete), is sound. For the rest, they rely on their own older theorems and proofs from (Siegelmann et al. 1994; Gavaldà et al. 1999), which were debunked already by Davis (2004). This invalidates their chain of proofs, and therefore also their claims on behalf of the possibility of hypercomputation. Unsurprisingly, we still lack even the beginnings of an account of how a hypercomputer might be built (Piccinini 2017), and this will always be the case since a hypercomputer is something that it is impossible to build.

12.2.2.2 A note on quantum computers

But what of quantum computers? Bostrom, for example, thinks that the increase of what he calls 'intelligence' of computers might double in seconds 'if growth is occurring at electronic speeds' and 'quantum computing becomes available to run algorithms that were previously infeasible' (Bostrom 2003, pp. 74, 274). Leaving aside the question of the intelligence of computers, this passage shows what goes wrong when one writes about computers without taking great care to understand how they work. First of all, it makes no sense to talk in the plural of 'electronic speeds', as there is only one speed of propagation for electromagnetic waves per given medium. And though of course, an electromagnetic field propagates quite quickly through electrons in the matter of the CPU (though not at the speed of light propagating through a vacuum), the rate of computation is limited (i) by the chip architecture (the number of transistors, intra-connections within the chip, and the amount of heat it can dissipate to avoid overheating) and (ii) by the connections between the CPU and those components of the computer which store significant amounts of data. This will not change in quantum computers. To talk of 'electronic speeds' is therefore nonsensical, and even more so when applied, not to the speed of signal transmission via electromagnetic fields, but rather, as does Bostrom, to the growth of 'intelligence'.

But it is easy to see that, even if quantum computers with sufficient computational resources become available, this will not yield hypercomputers. Quantum computers are Turing machines (Nielsen et al. 2010, p. 126), and this means that they will not be able to compute problems which are non-computable with classical computers. There are indeed problems which quantum computers will solve much *faster* than today's machines; but they will not thereby become hypercomputers. And of course, 'quantum hypercomputers' are as impossible as hypercomputers of any other sort, given that a regular quantum computer running in polynomial time can be simulated by a classical computer running in polynomial space (Bernstein et al. 1997).

12.2.2.3 The ineffectiveness of (supposed) hypercomputers in achieving AI

But even if, *per impossibile*, there were hypercomputers that could, for example, compute in finite time the truth-value of every formula of first-order logic, this would still not mean that such computers would enable the realisation of anything like superintelligence. The reason, as we have seen in chapter 9, is that computational capabilities of this sort still would not allow us to model the behaviour of the human central nervous system or to mimic the processes involved in the evolution of species. This is because, again, the targets in each case are complex systems. The ability to compute is very different from the ability to model, where 'model' is understood to mean something that enables the sort of exact predictions that are involved, for example, in the design and operations of advanced air-conditioning systems.

To simulate the human brain it is not just *powers of computation* that would be needed, but also a *model* of just this sort. And if we had such a model, already a very large plain vanilla universal Turing machine might be enough for the simulation. But we lack such a model because such a model is unobtainable. And again, this is true as concerns both explicit models (because we do not know how to create one) and implicit models (because, as we saw in chapter 8.1, it is impossible to obtain an adequate training distribution for complex systems).

12.2.3 Whole brain emulation

Visions of creating artificially intelligent machines operating at human level have not been realised. After 70 years of AI research, the algorithms we have can deal only with the sorts of very narrowly restricted situations which are involved in, for example, spam filtering, rule-based validation, pattern-based face recognition, game-playing (chess, Go), or calculus-based missile defence.

We have already seen *Ersatz*-definitions of intelligence and consciousness at work in previous chapters (3.3.1, 9.3.3.3). We can see such definitions in action also in discussions of the functioning of the brain in the context of AI research, where a simplistic view of the brain is used to buttress the pursuit of the unrealistic goal of what is dubbed 'whole brain emulation' (WBE).[5] In certain circles, at least, WBE is the currently preferred strategy for achieving AGI, after earlier strategies had failed to match even primal intelligence in their performance. Rather than striving to engineer superintelligence by means of algorithms, so the new thinking goes[6], we should begin instead with WBE, or in other words by emulating inside a computer that part of the human central nervous system which provides intelligence.

There are a number of things going wrong here. First, the very premise of a brain emulation is wrong. Due to the unresolvable connectedness of the mind-body continuum (see 2.2) and the fact that the mind is physical, by scanning the brain of an adult (or adolescent) human, one would not be able to mimic the mind part of the mind-body unity and therefore not able to identify the target for emulation. The idea is based, again, on an outdated, over-simplified understanding of the brain still rooted in Cartesianism, which misconstrues both the central nervous system and the human mind-body continuum.

Let us nevertheless look at the WBE and the 'steps' which (according to its advocates) will have to be taken in order to achieve it, in order to understand why their realisation is impossible from the perspective of biology, mathematics, and physics. We will then see that the very premise of WBE belongs not to science but to science fiction.

12.2.3.1 Whole Brain Emulation in three steps

Bostrom (2003, pp. 30–36) provides a valuable summary of current ideas about how WBE will be achieved. The basic idea is to emulate the brain *without understanding how it works* by copying its structures. Briefly put,[7] WBE-acolytes propose a series of steps to achieve this goal, divided into:

1. scan the brain via imaging,

---

5 WBE can be seen as related to the idea of multiple realisation according to which 'a given psychological kind (like pain) can stand in [a multiple realisation] relationship to many distinct physical kinds' (Bickle 2020). Proponents of this idea argue that the human mind could be realised by a different physical entity than the human mind-body continuum (see also section 2.2.2.1). The only scenario in which this could be scientifically conceivable, however, would be one in which a process of evolution occurs on some other planet that is identical to the process which occurred here on earth. The likelihood of this occurring is of course very close to zero. So again we see philosophers engaging in speculations, based on a mixture of science fiction and metaphysics, which distract them from productive usage of their time.
6 As Wallach et al. (2008) point out, one impact of Searle's Chinese room argument was that it led many to conclude 'that programming a computer is a hopeless approach to the development of genuinely intelligent systems'.
7 See (Bostrom 2003, Table 4, p. 32).

2. 'translate' the scans to obtain a 'scan interpretation' and a 'software model of the neural system', and then
3. create a 'simulation' of storage, bandwidth, CPU, body, and environment.

What is wrong with this vision?

In the first step, **scanning**, Bostrom proposes to perform a fixation of the brain material for microscopic imaging to assess the relevant structures of the brain down to cells, synapses, and 'other entities'. But when should this happen? After the death of a person? Then the cells will be dead, and therefore the dynamics of their molecular interaction will have disappeared.

Or should we fixate the brain of a person before she dies? Kill her, therefore, for the sake of science? Following this track, too, we will face a number of difficulties, not the least of which is that there would be no benefit, as fixating the brain for imaging also kills the cells. A dead brain cannot tell us much about the molecular dynamics of electrochemical and neuro-hormonal (also chemical) signalling between neurons. And even if we could scan all the activities relating neurons to each other at the molecular level without fixation, thus by drawing on some new variety of radiologic imaging involving a revolution in MRI and other techniques that would—perhaps—take them down to levels of resolution of 20 μm at the spatial and 20 milliseconds at the temporal level, this would still be inadequate to emulate the brain, because its molecular mechanisms work at a scale three orders of magnitude finer in resolution and faster still than this. Only this sort of resolution and rapidity could detect ion flux, with events occurring with a frequency measured in nanoseconds, or the presence or absence of a phosphorylation group consisting of just a few atoms.

The second step, **translation** would require the ability to simultaneously measure the amount of all neurotransmitters in all synaptic clefts of the brain and to track and measure all the associated ion flux and other biochemical and signalling events, all of which is technically impossible. But even if we were to achieve all of this, we still could not emulate these activities in such a way as to relate them to the particular mental experiences of which consciousness is comprised. This is because mental experiences are the result of the collaboration of many neurons and other (peripheral) cells, each of which contributes to the experience by exhibiting a certain behaviour which depends on its molecular configuration.

For each cell, this configuration depends on (i) the genome it carries in its nucleus, (ii) the epigenetic chemical modifications of the genome (the DNA and its carrier molecules), and (iii) the molecular configuration (involving some hundreds of thousands of molecules) of the non-nuclear parts of the cell—all of which have been shaped by the experiences of the organism since conception.[8]

---

8 The genome, for example, is changed during the life of an organism by viral infections, by radiation damage that is misrepaired, by replication errors upon mitosis (cell division), by telomere shortening, and by myriad epigenetic changes.

We cannot obtain a view of the interior structure of the cell (its molecular configuration) via imaging, because live imaging techniques do not have a sufficient resolution at either the spatial or the temporal level.[9] But even if we had machines capable of imaging at the required resolutions, we still do not have mathematical models to interpret the resulting data. These data are measurements of processes which evolve in the complex system that is the mind-body continuum; thus they measure directly the workings of this system, some of whose emanations we can perceive via inner experience. Even such direct measurement of the system's workings would not, however, improve our ability to emulate them.

In other words, we are not able to create a WBE; even if we could observe the activities of billions of neurons with a totality of over 10^{15} molecules at a resolution of a nanosecond (which means we would obtain over 10^{21} data points per second), we could not emulate the *behaviour* of the collection of cells, because there is no way to build a mathematical model that could do this. *One cannot emulate a system without modeling it, and in the case of complex systems there is no way to produce the needed model.*

And finally, there is the third step: **simulation**, which we do not discuss, since it relies for its input on the successful realisation of the first two steps, both of which are impossible.

The project of creating a superintelligent being by, in effect, copying without understanding, fails. But we note that, even if WBE *were* possible and a brain-emulation without a body would indeed yield a 'mind', it would certainly not yield superintelligence, for it would at best emulate the intelligence of the copied mind. Bostrom explores how such 'copies' could then be 'improved', but we prefer to avert our readers' eyes from the way he thereby adds yet more impossibilities to his pile. Instead, we have to face the fact that, when we die, the mind-body continuum ceases to exist, our mind ends, and six minutes after our last heartbeat or our last breath, our body has irreversibly lost the molecular configuration which enables it to function as an animate entity. It becomes a mere corpse—biological material that serves as nutrition for other organisms.

12.2.4 Enhanced human cognition

Among the alternative means of achieving 'superintelligence' discussed by Bostrom, in addition to hypercomputation and WBE, we find the idea of human cognitive enhancement. Bostrom (2003) discusses this under three headings:

---

[9] We can partially analyse the molecular configuration of neurons *in vitro* by introducing neurons into cell cultures. But if we do this, then we destroy their natural configuration.

1. Biological brains enhancement,
2. Computational brain enhancement,
3. Enhanced collectives.

We consider each of these in turn.

12.2.4.1 Biological brain enhancement

It is currently fashionable to state that 'advances in biotechnology will allow a direct control of human genetics and neurobiology' (Bostrom 2003, p. 36), which can then be used to enhance the functioning of the human brain. Bostrom claims that pre-implantation diagnosis of complex traits in embryos could be used to select more intelligent individuals. He calculates that a selection of embryos can yield a logarithmic increase of up to 24.3 (*sic*) IQ points if 999 out of every 1000 embryos are discarded for one generation, and of 300 points if 90% of all embryos are discarded in each of ten successive generations (op. cit. p. 37). Bostrom also proposes to speed up his enhancement strategy by using stem-cell derived gametes (sperm and oocytes), which would enable the creation of thousands of embryos from one single couple within a matter of weeks.

Why is this sheer nonsense?

First, we cannot genetically diagnose complex traits such as intelligence. It is not true that it requires only '(lots of) data on the genetic correlates of the traits of interest' (op. cit. p. 37). This is because, as we saw in detail in 7.6.1, for complex traits such as intelligence the correlation between genetic code and phenotype is insufficient to obtain the sort of stochastic plausibility (p-value) required to drive an embryo-selection process; the correlation between the two is much too weak.[10] Associations of hundreds of thousands of genetic loci contribute to such complex traits, which arise from interactions involving trillions of molecules of gene products at the cellular and inter-cellular levels. Because the interactions occur among gene products (primarily different types of RNA and proteins as well as the peptide, lipid, and other molecules they generate), and not at the level of the DNA, it is impossible that we will be able to infer them from the linear DNA-sequence. It is for this reason that such associations have not enabled any explanatory or causal modelling of mental traits (Tam et al. 2019), let alone enabled the sort of embryo selection proposed by Bostrom.

Second, even if an enhancement of intelligence through selection were possible, it is unscientific to claim an ability to estimate its effects in terms of increases in 'IQ points'. An estimation of this sort would require the ability to identify the relative intelligence potential of embryos on the basis of differences

---

10 See for example the results reported in Coleman et al. (2019).

manifesting variability along hundreds of thousands of dimensions, where we have not only no mechanism for measuring the differences involved but also no idea at all how we might integrate across such measures.

Third, there is no evidence that the IQ scale is open at the upper end. Everything that we know about evolutionary history tells us that it is with high likelihood structurally limited by neurophysiological features of the brain.

Fourth, assuming that there will not be millions of couples ready and willing (and legally authorised) to provide their natural gametes for *in vitro* fertilisation and selection, the likelihood that there will be enough viable stem-cell derived gametes that can yield healthy individuals is close to zero. For to achieve this, we would have to complete the following steps:

1. bring about the differentiation of omnipotent stem cells to yield gamete-progenitor cells either by using (bio)pharmacological stimuli or by direct genetic alteration of the cells,
2. engineer the maturation of these progenitors to gametes *in vitro*, which means maturation from spermatogonia to sperm for the male line, and from oogonium to ovum for the female line. Unfortunately, however, we lack the natural environments (testis and ovary, respectively, with their respective cellular and signalling environment) for this maturation to occur, and thus we also lack the correct nuclear and cytosolic molecular configuration, which seems impossible to obtain outside the natural environment.

Again, therefore, the idea of producing many, many embryos for testing and selective deletion is not only immoral, but also impossible to achieve (certainly impossible to achieve in a way that would lead to an increased IQ in the resulting population).

Genetic engineering of the human embryo Bostrom presents further strategies for creating a superintelligence:

- cloning of talented individuals;
- creation of intelligent neural tissue *in vitro*;
- genome manipulation via genome synthesis; and
- gene editing.

While the first three of these ideas are biologically too absurd to merit discussion, it is already technically possible to manipulate mammalian embryonic stem cells with genome editing technologies to create genetically manipulated humans (Strecker et al. 2019). Even here, however, Bostrom's idea will still not work, because we do not know which genetic loci to edit and how to edit them. As we saw in section 7.6.1, even simple traits such as body height seem to have an omnigenic encoding (Boyle et al. 2017), and it is certain that this holds also for the complex trait of intelligence.

Certainly our knowledge of the workings of the brain at both the cellular and genomic levels is advancing, but the view presented by some neuroscientists (e.g. Goriounova et al. (2019)), that a few loci encode intelligence, is certainly wrong; this property is omnigenic if even most simple traits are. Thus speaking against an optimistic interpretation of these developments is the fact that, even if we reached the point where we were able to determine which parts of the genome we would need to change in order to alter this omnigenic encoding in a way that would lead to an increment in intelligence, we would not know how to make such changes without deleterious side effects. Because billions of molecule configurations in millions of cells in the brain contribute to intelligence, we will probably never obtain a mathematical model for this and other complex traits, and this is what would be needed to perform genetic engineering that is both effective and safe.[11]

12.2.4.2 Computational brain and body enhancement

The enhancement of our cognitive or sensorimotor capabilities via technical brain implants (cyborgisation) is an idea frequently mooted in the superintelligence literature (Clark 2013). But this, too, is mere science fiction because enhancements of the sort envisaged are just not feasible.

We start with the input/output channels of the central nervous system (brain plus spinal cord). The afferent (input) neurons carrying electric signals into the brain have a hard-coded neuronal wiring from their entry point (the synapses in the spinal cord) to the neural clusters which ultimately process them. There is no free wiring in the healthy brain to which one could attach additional afferent inputs, and so the afferent system cannot be enhanced (Kandel et al. 2021).[12]

As to the output channels (efferences), which direct eye and hand movement and language use, we have extremely powerful and differentiated output channels with an extremely high temporal resolution and—thanks to the power and flexibility of language—arbitrary scope. A computer that could understand the meaning of efferent signals directly from the brain would thus need to have what has been called a 'neuromorphic AI', which—and here we agree with Bostrom—is impossible (Bostrom 2003, p. 47).

We conclude that it is not possible to connect machines to the brain via channels other than vision and hearing for input and motor behaviour (including speech) for output. But this is what we already do—yet without thereby becoming superintelligent. Why not? Because the machines we use are Turing

---

11 There are effective brain interventions, for example in brain surgery. These interventions are mechanical and operate at a very coarse level of granularity: an aneurysm is clipped, a tumour or an epidural hematoma is removed. But we cannot manipulate human intelligence by using surgery.
12 Pathologic deficits in afferent channels can be addressed therapeutically, though with low effectiveness.

machines and, as we have seen in previous chapters, such machines do not even achieve primal intelligence.

12.2.4.3 Enhanced collectives

Some authors believe that *collectives* of individuals can be more intelligent than individuals taken singly (Bostrom 2003, pp. 48f), sometimes pointing to the example of ants, bees, and other social animals. It is certainly true that, by addressing a question to a collective (crowd intelligence), you may get a good answer more easily than by, say, researching the literature or asking a philosopher. But this works in a reliable fashion only where some genuine expert happens to be in the crowd. This is because human intelligence is an individual capability that is non-additive. Collectives can, certainly, carry out plans that individuals cannot—such as building Cologne Cathedral or executing the Manhattan Project. Collectives can also evolve new social patterns over very long periods of time through trial-and-error (Hayek (1996)) or through the sort of transgenerational collaboration that is involved, for example, in the creation and sustainment of scientific disciplines. But collectives do not write poetry[13] or novels, discover new aspects of nature, or solve difficult mathematical problems. This is done overwhelmingly by individuals or by very small groups.

12.2.5 AI explosion and the Singularity

Let us now, finally, address the issue of the Singularity. Three main ways in which this might happen have been proposed:

1. spontaneous evolution,
2. AI explosion, or
3. 'awakening of the internet' to consciousness.

We shall deal with each of these in turn.

12.2.5.1 Spontaneous evolution

We have already shown in chapter 9.1.2 that the idea that AI might spontaneously evolve via a process comparable to biological evolution (Chalmers 2010; Schmidhuber 2012) has no scientific foundation. Machines lack the drivenness of living organisms, they lack anything like an 'evolutionary environment',

---

13 Shakespeare, as is well known, is the author of the works of Shakespeare. Collective works of poetry do exist, for example the Book of Psalms, but their components are single-authored.

and we cannot replace either organism or environment with an emulation because we cannot model either of them.

12.2.5.2 AI explosion

We have not thus far discussed the claim that artificial intelligence will 'explode' (Hutter 2012; Yudkowsky 2008a), which seems to be the pathway to superintelligence which the majority of its proponents see as the most likely. According to Muehlhauser et al. (2012b, p. 29) this explosion is supposed to come about as follows:

> Once human programmers build an AI with a better-than-human *capacity* for AI design, the instrumental goal of self-improvement may motivate a possible feedback-loop for self-enhancement.[14]

Others claim that AI machines will improve their own code,[15] so that once intelligent machines with high computing capacity are in a position to improve themselves, they will rapidly create a superintelligence.

What arguments have been brought forward against speculations such as this by the scientific community? We have already discussed the sceptical position of Walsh (2017) in section 1.5. Dubhashi et al. (2017) bring forward similar arguments, pointing out that recent advances in AI have been narrow and do not generalise; that the capabilities of neural networks do not grow exponentially; that the vast majority of potentially available input data are unlabelled (thus of the form $\langle x_i, \cdot \rangle$ with '·' representing missing output) and therefore not usable for machine learning. They also point out that 'much, if not all of the argument for existential risks from superintelligence seems to rest on mere logical possibility' (op. cit. p. 45). In this book, we have taken their critique one step further by bringing forward arguments to the effect that superintelligence does not rise even to the level of being logically possible.

We cannot build a machine that would be *intelligent*, because we cannot model primal, let alone objectifying, intelligence. And even supposing that we could achieve some kind of intelligent machine to serve as the beginning of the chain reaction projected by Bostrom *et frères*, how could such a machine *improve itself*? To self-improve, the machine would need self-consciousness and intentions in order to set itself the goal of self-improvement—but we have already seen that we will not obtain either self-conscious machines or machines with intentions given the nature of the operations that machines are able to perform.

14 This scenario is exploited also by Chalmers (2010).
15 Schmidhuber (2007) shows that this is indeed possible, though only in a highly restricted sense, and what Schmidhuber offers in this paper will not lead to *intelligence*, because it rests on use of the Hutter function which, as we saw in chapter 3.3.2, does not model anything deserving of this name.

12.2.5.3 Self-improvement

Would self-improvement be achievable on the basis of reinforcement learning, as Hutter and Schmidhuber have proposed?[16]

The problem here is that the reward system required for self-improvement would have to obtain situation-specific rewards along the lines described in 8.6.7.3, which is not possible. Therefore, we cannot set rewards for reinforcement-based self-improvement. Therefore, there will be no self-improvement; and thus pursuant to this strategy, too, there will be no Singularity.

12.2.5.4 AI awakening

Another idea is that AI will arise by an 'awakening' of the internet (Hutter 2012; Vinge 2013). But how is this supposed to happen? Some authors believe that machine intelligence will spontaneously arise because the internet connects a certain threshold number of machines together in a network. The error in this view is the idea that consciousness is the result of the interconnection of many CPUs, which seems to be a form of magical thinking. We have seen in chapter 9.3 that machine consciousness is impossible for a single machine working independently. We have no reason at all to believe that anything will change simply because many machines become connected. We also have no idea what it would mean for the internet to 'become conscious' ('awake').

12.2.6 Super-evil AI

The focal idea presented by AI-supremacists such as Bostrom is the quasi-eschatological vision of a super-evil AI that will either annihilate or somehow rule over humankind. What does this mean? Bostrom begins the chapter of his book entitled 'Cognitive Superpowers' (Bostrom 2003, p. 94) with the following question: Suppose that a digital superintelligent agent came into being, and that for some reason it wanted to take control of the world: would it be able to do so? He then lists a series of powers that are supposed to reside within computers of the future:

1. intelligence,
2. self-amplification,
3. strategising,
4. social manipulation,
5. hacking,
6. technology research, and
7. economic productivity.

---

16 A detailed account of their proposal is given in section 3.3.2.

With these powers, he avers, the machine could 'take over the world' and annihilate or rule over mankind according to its desire. To take over the world, however, the machine would need to *want* to take over the world, and so we need to establish, first, how would the machine (or machine collective) develop a *will*.

12.2.7 The missing AI will

For without a will and the intentions and acts that flow therefrom, there is no possibility that the machine could become an autonomous agent. And if it is not autonomous, it cannot pursue any goals. How, then, do advocates of superintelligence imagine machines will acquire a will, and the goals that go together therewith? It seems they do not even ask themselves this question. Rather, they simply assume that it will happen.

- Bostrom himself does not, as far as we can determine, think about how a machine will could come into existence. He just postulates that AI-machines will have a will, and asks instead what could be the aims and goals this will would serve (Bostrom 2003, chapter 7).
- Hutter (2012) plainly states that 'it seems hard if not impossible to define rationality without the notion of a goal. If rationality is reasoning towards a goal, then there is no intelligence without goals'. In asserting that the machine is rational, he thereby simply *presupposes* a will on the side of the machine—since the idea of goals without the will does not make sense. Like Bostrom, he goes on from there to speculate what the goals would be of the AI will that he has pulled out of his hat.
- Goertzel et al. (2007a), the editors of the AGI reader, agree that intelligence 'measures an agent's ability to achieve goals in a wide range of environments'. But, again: what are these 'goals' and where do they come from? We learn that they must be 'supplied' (Goertzel et al. 2007b, p. 79), or that an AI must have a 'goal system' (op. cit. p 81). 'Supplied' means *supplied by humans* (as happens currently, directly or indirectly, in every case where computers are used). Then, however, the computer agents will not be autonomous, and the path to superintelligence will depend on human interventions. One could argue that, upon reaching the Singularity, machines could replace the man-made goal system. But to do this, they would again need to have a will of their own, which, given that the goal system needs to be supplied, they won't.
- For Schmidhuber (2007), the goal of an AGI is to 'maximise expected cumulative future reward' (p. 201) or 'utility' (p. 202). But this is to say nothing if it is not indicated how this leads to a machine agent's having intentions with specific contents and what these contents would be. Throughout the AGI reader (Goertzel et al. 2007a), the notion of 'goal' remains abstract and empty.

- Yudkowsky (2001b) gives an account of a 'goal system' for an AI which is of quite special interest. Such a system, he writes, is to be viewed as 'containing only decisions, supergoals, and beliefs; with all subgoal content being identical with beliefs about which events are predicted to lead to other events; and all "desirability" being identical with "leads-to-supergoal-ness"' (p. 239). This definition is, like everything Yudkowsky has to say about goals in his book, strangely detached from the reality of will, goals, objectives, and intentions. However, in a later paper, he proposes as content for his 'goal system' what he calls a 'coherent extrapolated volition' (Yudkowsky 2001a), which he describes—as he himself warns us, 'in poetic terms'—as follows:

> our coherent extrapolated volition is our wish if we knew more, thought faster, were more the people we wished we were, had grown up farther together; where the extrapolation converges rather than diverges, where our wishes cohere rather than interfere; extrapolated as we wish that extrapolated, interpreted as we wish that interpreted.
>
> (p. 6)

It is not at all clear what Yudkowsky is trying to say here. Reading between the lines, however, it would seem to imply that we (humans) could somehow 'extrapolate' our will. Unfortunately, we humans have only the will that we have. We cannot extrapolate it, and this for at least two reasons:

i. 'Extrapolation'—understood in the technical (mathematical) sense—requires a model equation into which one can plug variables to obtain a valid extrapolation result. Only some natural phenomena can be modelled in this sort of way, for example by using power-laws in the case of scaling, as discussed in chapter 8.7.1. The outputs of our will (intentions, goals, wishes, etc.) are certainly not among the phenomena which can be 'extrapolated' in this manner, and we do not know of any other coherent reading of this term.

ii. The idea that more complete information (knowing more), a faster thought process, or a collectivist (?) education[17] would yield goals that are somehow more 'coherent' and thus (presumably) somehow better suited to mathematical modelling is, as we will see in the next section, absurd.

And even if humans could 'extrapolate' our will in some non-technical sense, it remains a mystery how Yudkowsky envisions exploiting the result of such

---

17 We presume that something like this is what Yudkowsky means when he talks about humans having 'grown up farther together'.

extrapolation to enable the needed 'coherent extrapolated volition' on the part of the machine.[18]

12.2.7.1 The person as the source of the will

What then, would it take to actually create an artificial will? Scheler has the beginnings of an answer to this question, in his thesis according to which it is the person who is the source of the human will. The person, for Scheler, encompasses the body and the mind and cannot exist without them. We get to know a person by observing how she behaves, her goals and intentions, and how she exercises her will—the power of volition being an essential characteristic of the person.[19] Of course, there are many other theories of the person, including major theories in analytical philosophy.[20] The majority agree with Scheler in holding that persons (mature humans) are differentiated from animals, not only by their cognitive capabilities, but also by their ability to act on the basis of their will.

Scheler illustrates his account of the will, which is presented in his *Formalism* (see 6.4.3), by means of a rescue scenario in which a man sees a drowning child and experiences the moral obligation *to try to save a person who is in distress*. Scheler's view of the ontology of what is involved here is not restricted to moral action, but is trivially applicable to all actions where perceived events serve as trigger. Thus it is extendible in obvious ways to human actions in general, for example those involved in playing chess.

Before we describe his account, we note that Scheler's entire approach to the will and action as well as its details may well be questioned. Thus some will deny that the will and intentions are to be distinguished from desires. But, as our summary shows, the dimensions of complexity of the will and action laid bare here by Scheler seem to cohere well with our shared primary theory of human mentality.

Scheler rests his account on a distinction between a series of overlapping stages of a rescue scenario, beginning as follows (Scheler 1973, pp. 121f):[21]

---

18 Muehlhauser et al. (2012a) provide a valuable overview of the difficulties we face in specifying a 'goal system' for a machine by addressing the challenges that arise for such a specification when we use as starting point different ethical theories such as utilitarianism or value ethics. They propose to explore Yudkowsky's 'coherent extrapolated volition'. But they, too, fail to explain in coherent fashion how the collective will envisaged by Yudkowsky should be defined and how, if at all, it could be realised in a machine.

19 A will does not exist without a person, and the person is the source of all ethical behaviour (Scheler 1973, pp. 495f).

20 (Hampshire 1959, pp. 47f), (Sellars 1963, pp. 11f.), (Taylor 1985, pp. 97ff); on the will specifically, see O'Shaughnessy (1980) and Frankfurt (1971).

21 We have reworded some elements of Scheler's account to conform with the terminology used in other parts of this book. We have also added minor details, taking account of more recent developments in psychology.

1. **Presence to the acting person of the object of the action in the situation.** This involves not only perception, but also the triggering of dispositions of the rescuer drawn from that complex of dispositions that we have earlier called the *identity* of the person. These dispositions include also the capability to apprehend a triggering situation as what a Gibsonian might call a *moral affordance* (Wisnewski 2019), (Heft 2001, p. 129).
2. **Presence in the mind of the acting person of the content to be realised and of the salient value feelings.** This involves the summation by the rescuer of the results of his acts of perceiving and associated value-feelings described under 1.
3. **Deciding to execute one set of compossible value contents.** The *deciding* here is one dependent part of the *act of will* itself. Deciding, too, has its foundation in the complex of dispositions making up the person's *identity*. It has three phases:

    3a. *forming specific intentions* in which the acting person views the child's life as a something-that-ought-to-be-preserved;
    3b. *deliberating* how to effect the rescue; and then
    3c. *resolving* to take the course of action that involves jumping into the river to try to save the drowning child. (The act of will is a willing to *do* something; it is the willing of an *action*, and not of an *outcome*.)

    Depending on his complex of dispositions, the acting person will come to a decision more or less rapidly, and accept in his decision a higher or lower risk. The complex of dispositions will also set boundaries, both moral and physical, as to how he can decide to act. For example the acting person, because he is aware of his own capabilities, would only imagine himself performing a rescue that is within the range of his assumed physical power. This awareness of capability (and incapability) is something that is immediate and not a product of calculation. As Scheler puts it: 'The "to be able" is phenomenally given as a special *kind* of conative consciousness', that is 'comparable to the feeling of being alive.' (Scheler 1973, p. 129)
4. **Molecular signalling to trigger bodily movement.** This, too, is a dependent part of the act of will itself. It is, as it were, the strictly physical side of the coin of which the act of resolving [3c] is the mental side, and it is constituted by a complex of changes in the relevant neuronal clusters which triggers the body's motor system to begin executing the physical movements needed to effect the rescue. As Scheler puts it: 'There is an *efficacy* of willing (as willing-to-do) that acts on our lived body and *issues forth into movement*' (Scheler 1973, p. 130).[22]

---

22 Frankfurt (1971) offers an account of the will as a special sort of desire, which is in large degree compatible with our account here. Importantly, however, Frankfurt differs from Scheler in that

5. **Moving to execute the action (with accompanying sensorimotor sensations and feelings).** We immediately sense the effectiveness of our resolution upon our body, as we unconsciously monitor our execution of the rescue as the process unfolds, and effect changes where necessary.[23]

Coming back to AGI, it is stages 1 to 4 that are relevant to the question whether a machine could ever have a will. This means that to create an artificial will we can neither just program a 'goal system' (Yudkowsky), nor can we expect a will to arise by itself. This is because to have a will, we need a complex of dispositions like the ones possessed by humans which can be realised in intentions, deliberations, and resolutions (decidings), where each resolution—because it is itself a certain sort of physical event—triggers bodily movement (see also sections 3.3.2.2 and 2.2).

Unfortunately for Yudkowsky, however, we could in any case not model any of this mathematically, as the intentions, deliberations, and resolutions are emanations of a complex system. *Hence there will be no AI will and no emulation of the will* of any sort. And for this reason, too, no Singularity.

12.2.7.2 Summoning the Terminator

Bostrom and other superintelligence proponents believe that it is most likely that the Singularity will come about inside computers, and so they ask the question how computers can rule the world also from the perspective of how they will obtain the required *physical* power. Ruling the world is possible only with physical control over other physical bodies (humans) on the part of the machine.

To see why this is so, we follow Popitz, who distinguishes four types of power[24]:

1. power of action,
2. instrumental power,
3. authoritative power, and
4. data-setting power.

---

he concerns himself only with 3c., and thereby ignores that feature of effectivity that is channeled through 4.

23 The last two steps are: 6. Experiencing realisation of the content (the 'performance', here: the child is saved), and 7. Experiencing feelings pursuant to realisation.

24 Popitz's main work, *Power* (Popitz 2017a), has only recently been translated into English. His views are used for example by Baberowski (2015) in his treatment in of how states and illegitimate systems of domination are established, by Antweiler (2019) in his account of what he calls the human addiction to norms, and by J. Leavitt Pearl, who describes how Popitz uses Husserl's method of imaginative variation to show how power serves as 'a universal component in the genesis and operation of human societies' (Pearl 2018).

The first is raw physical power, mediated by threatening the health and life of the subdued. The other three are derived, higher forms of power, which develop on the basis of physical power. They do not require embodiment, because they have their effects via psychological repression. But to exert any of these higher-order powers, power of action is needed initially to subdue others so that they become willing to accept the psychological repression vehiculating exercise of the other power types. Power of action needs embodiment in a physical form that can threaten the health and life of humans.

How can an AI with CPUs and storage (a Turing-complete machine) as its sole basis become embodied in this way? There are two ways: either (1.) humans create an AI that is embodied in a robotic body or in a server that controls robotic bodies, or (2.) the AI escapes from the confines of the CPU.

Physical power via robots In the first variant (and under the assumption that the AI turns evil) we obtain the *Terminator* scenario. If AI was feasible, and humans were able to build robots either endowed with or connected to a server with AI, then this first scenario could be possible, but only if the AI had a will (which it cannot have).

Physical power via mail order For the second variant, Yudkowsky (2008a) proposes a scenario according to which an AI could arrange for biomolecules (DNA, RNA, peptides, ...) to be sent by mail order to a human who had been persuaded to mix the components and then to create from the results an artificial life colony that would ultimately exert the power of action needed to subdue or annihilate mankind.[25] Already this reveals a remarkable ignorance of biology on Yudkowsky's part. But things get worse when Yudkowsky describes in detail how the AI would identify which biomolecules would be required to initiate the process of creating artificial (biological) life, namely by

> [cracking] the protein folding problem to the extent of being able to generate DNA strings whose folded peptide sequences fill specific functional roles in a complex chemical interaction.

Synthetic proteins created from such DNA strings are, he tells us, to be mixed together to create a 'very primitive "wet" nanosystem, which,

---

25 This scenario is reproduced by Bostrom (op. cit. p. 98), though (understandably) not without some hesitancy: 'One should avoid fixating too much on the concrete details, since they are in any case unknowable and intended for illustration only' (op. cit. p. 97). We should, though, spare a moment's thought on these details, to see why they are not only superficially absurd. Yudkowsky's underlying idea seems to be that the trial-and-error method of very rapidly comparing billions of alternatives that is made possible in the computer, for example by reinforcement learning, can be replicated in the domain of biochemistry, where actual experiments with actual samples have to be performed under controlled conditions.

ribosome-like, is capable of accepting external instructions' and thereby able to bootstrap itself to higher life forms able to exert power over human beings.

This is, on very, very many levels, scientifically absurd. First of all, what matters for cellular function is not protein folding, but protein function. One aspect of protein function prediction has partially been solved using stochastic models[26], in a way which does indeed lend support to protein function research.[27] But the full function of proteins in cells can be predicted from neither their primary nor their folding structure, and it is even less possible to do the reverse. That is, we cannot design a primary protein structure from scratch to fulfil a certain cellular function. Thus the protein *function* problem is still far from being solved. And second, even if it were solved, one would not obtain artificial life, but—at best—novel and very effective biotherapeutics. But more importantly, we cannot 'bootstrap' life just by 'cracking the protein folding problem', not only because proteins are modified to become functional only *after* folding, but also because there is in addition to proteins a plenitude of other molecule types in living cells, all of them necessary—and necessarily interacting in highly environment-specific ways—in order for life to exist.

Life from matter There is a huge gap between inanimate and animate matter, a gap which we do not understand and cannot bridge (as we have not yet discovered what, traditionally, has been called 'the secret of life'). This means, *inter alia*, that we cannot create life by mixing components. The idea of mixing life from matter in a test tube is similar to the idea of 'trial-and-error engineering' often mooted by AI enthusiasts. Engineers do indeed often operate by combining functional parts into new wholes in such a way as to yield a higher functionality than is given by each of the parts alone. For example, once the basic idea of combining magnetism and electric current was born, it was a matter of trial-and-error to optimise the physical set-up of electric motors (and generators, which embody the reverse function of electric motors by generating energy from motion). The fundamental design factor here, however, which was based on the then newly emerging understanding of electromagnetic forces, could not have been obtained by trial-and-error, but rather only by generating hypotheses and mathematical models and testing and refining these through repeated experiments. Without these models, the electric motor could not have been engineered.

And so it is also with AI. Without mathematical models, we will not be able to combine anything in *ad hoc* ways to create AI. We cannot even come up with

---

26 The latter can now predict the protein structure for many (but not all) families of proteins from their amino acid sequence (primary structure) (Jumper et al. 2020).
27 A stochastic algorithm cannot predict protein foldings in those cases where the correlation operator between primary structure and folding pattern, which the algorithm learns from examples, does not hold.

a model of what it would mean to bring life into existence artificially, because all life is in the form of complex, non-ergodic systems.

12.3 Transhumanism

Yet more similarly technically unfeasible science fiction ideas are discussed under the label of 'transhumanism', including human enhancement, engineering of life, medical life prolongation, and digital immortality. Again, we deal with each of these in turn.

12.3.1 Human enhancement

In section 12.2.4.2, we have already seen that the enhancement of the cognitive and sensory-motor capabilities of humans by integrating machines directly with their central nervous systems is not possible. But is it feasible to enhance humans via genetic engineering? New technologies to manipulate human embryos could in principle be used to treat diseases with Mendelian inheritance patterns *in vitro* after fertilisation, by changing the mutations that cause them. This is because for monogenetic diseases we know what the relevant genetic locus and the correct inheritance pattern are. However, as we have seen in section 12.2.4.1, such genetic improvement is impossible for complex traits, because we cannot model the cause and effect patterns of their omnigenic inheritance mode. We would not only not know which part of the genome to manipulate; we would also not know how to go about manipulating it.

12.3.2 Engineering life

Some transhumanists argue that improvements in human environments can be brought about by creating 'artificial life' made of engineered bacteria or artificial 'protocells' (Armstrong 2013; Armstrong et al. 2010). They point to the fact that we have, since the 1970s, been optimising prokaryotes as well as plants and livestock by changing Mendelian inheritance patterns to produce bacteria, strains of yeast, and even mammalian cells *in vitro* for pharmaceutical and other purposes, for example, as sources of opioids or of tropane-alkaloids such as atropine, cocaine, or scopolamine, as well as to achieve higher crop yields (Margolin et al. 2020).

However, none of these are examples of what we can call 'artificial life'. No matter which organism we look at, from bacteria to mammals, we cannot model the relationship between its genome and its complex phenotypic traits. We do not know how to make inorganic molecules synthesise ATP from inorganic matter and sunlight (which is what plants do). We also do not know how to make inorganic molecules synthesise ATP from organic matter (which is what animals do). All we can do is manipulate Mendelian patterns in existing living organisms, because the models needed to do this in a controlled manner are within the reach of our mathematics.[28] This, however, will give us no purchase at all on the march towards 'artificial life'.

12.3.3 Life prolongation

There are multiple proposals to prolong life using various medical approaches, but none of them is based on a realistic assessment of the possibilities not only of today's technology but also of the technology of the future. We briefly review a sample of attractive-seeming ideas: nanotechnology, gene therapy, and new types of drugs, to see that all of them are to no avail.

12.3.3.1 Nanotechnological longevity

In 2009, Freitas predicted that in the 2020s, we would have nanorobots with a size of $\frac{2}{3}\mu m$ capable of repairing structures down to tiny irregularities in the blood-vessel endothelium and in single cells in the body, and even of performing 'chromosome replacement therapy' to repair accumulating damage in the ageing genomes of somatic cells (Freitas 2009). Others, such as the globalist Klaus Schwab of the World Economic Forum, have even crazier dreams, for example: 'Nanomachines that can drill through the body and kill cancer cells in seconds'.[29] What is wrong with all of this?

First of all, small machines of this size have not thus far been built. The question how to build a molecular motor that can propel a nanomachine in body fluids is unresolved. The intercellular space outside the blood stream can be well-approximated as a highly viscous Newtonian fluid. In fluids of this sort, according to the scallop theorem, no type of swimming object can achieve net displacement (Purcell 1977). The blood stream, on the other hand, has the features of high turbulence and very high pressure in the arterial part of the vascular system. At the same time this is the only ubiquitous distribution system for physical compounds and particles in the body that would be available for use by nanomachines. Unfortunately, we have no idea how to build a nanomotor that could withstand the high flow-velocity and turbulence of the arterial system.[30] Furthermore, there is no available method to generate sufficient amounts of energy for such small motors; indeed, we have no idea where their energy could come from.

---

28 The (simple) biomathematics of Mendelian inheritance is well understood (Strachan et al. 2018, chapters 12 and 17).
29 https://www.weforum.org/agenda/2017/09/nanobots-kill-drill-cancer-cells-60-seconds/, more examples can be found in (Schwab 2017), for example on pp. 110f., where Schwab talks of 'Smart Dust, arrays of full computers with antennas, each much smaller than a grain of sand, can now organise themselves inside the body into as-needed networks to power a whole range of complex internal processes.'
30 To get an idea of the forces at work, compare the figure on p. 180.

But even if these fundamental problems could be solved, we would still not be able to achieve much by using such nanomachines. Consider, for example, atherosclerosis, which is one of only very few diseases where mechanical applications are already being used in treatments, for example, of coronary arteries. Even here it is unlikely that nanomachines could outperform coronary artery bypass surgery. And in comparison to this case, the other repair ideas presented by Freitas are nonsensical. For example, chromosomes cannot be replaced like the broken gearbox of a car, because they are densely packed by histones and exist always in a form in which they are chemically modified in complex chromosomal aggregates which regulate gene expression. We do not know which chromosome-histone-configuration is needed under which conditions in which cell, and we could neither synthesise such hypercomplex gigantic biomolecule aggregates accurately nor could we 'cut out' a complex of this sort from its molecular environment in the cell nucleus.

Though mechanical forces (respiration, blood circulation, and muscle contraction) are important to the distribution of molecules in the body, the function of the vast majority of cells is biochemical, and even cell junction and adhesion are performed biochemically. Biochemical processes are not mechanical, but chemical in nature; they work through a permanent, complex enzymatic shifting of reaction equilibria between millions of molecules per cell. One cannot change reaction equilibria using mechanical tools; the idea is as nonsensical as the attempt to improve intelligence using brain surgery. And for this reason, too, we will not enhance longevity or achieve immortality by using nanorobots.

12.3.3.2 Preventing ageing via genetic engineering

Bostrom (2013) lists several ideas for prevention of ageing by genetic means, including: 'genetic engineering, stem cell cloning and regenerative cells growing organs' (p. 74). Ageing is an omnigenic trait of a highly complex animate system and thus something which we cannot model mathematically. We do not know which properties of the cells we would need to change in order to prevent ageing. Furthermore, as ageing occurs in somatic cells, genetic measures against it would have to be applied to somatic cells of the adult. While for Mendelian traits genetic modifications are possible, this is so only in the very early human embryo. From the stage of the differentiated embryo onwards we cannot perform such modifications of somatic cells consistently across all cells of the body. To modify non-Mendelian-traits, on the other hand, we would need a causal (mathematical) model of which genes cause which trait, for example in the form of an explicit stochastic differential equation, and for reasons given in 7.6.1 and 8.6.5 we do not have such models.

Similar problems apply also in the case of stem cell cloning and what Bostrom calls 'organ growing'. Certainly, we can culture stem cells *in vitro*. But we have no clue what to do with them, then, in order to address the problem of ageing.

Neither do we understand the complex system of organogenesis that allows organs to grow from the embryonic germ layers to the degree that would allow us to create a model that could reproduce such growth even *in vitro*.

12.3.3.3 No elixir of life

Rose (2013, pp. 200–203) discusses pharmacological strategies for longevity. From the existence of very long-lived animals, such as the genus *Hydra*, which reproduces by asexual budding under ideal feeding conditions, he concludes that we need to 'question the assumption among many cell and molecular biologists that some inherent feature of biochemistry, molecular biology, or cell biology necessitates ageing' (loc. cit. p. 200).

This suggestion is typical of what results from a superficial interpretation of research results from biology. First of all, reproduction by budding is not the same as eternal life, otherwise one could say that *all* asexual reproduction strategies are equivalent to immortality. Furthermore, Rose overlooks the fact that in a natural environment, Hydra switch from asexual to sexual reproduction under (seasonally recurring) harsh nutritional conditions. The resulting eggs sink to the ground and await improved conditions before they mature while adult animals die. Asexual budding-based reproduction is thus limited to environments with nutrient affluence.

All sexually reproducing animals have a limited life-span, which is programmed into their cells. Why is this so? Because sexual reproduction and the ageing and death of the progenitor generations optimise population variance and the chances of species survival. In nature, survival and reproduction cannot afford to feed old individuals at the expense of the group. Of course, human societies can and should do this to a certain extent; but this does not mean that we can overcome evolutionary patterns that have been established in all the cells of our body since the origins of sexual reproduction.

Is there hope that pharmaceuticals might enable unlimited longevity? Certainly not: because, again, we do not know what to influence and how—for the same reasons that prevent us from using somatic gene engineering to overcome ageing. Certainly, we will not obtain such compounds by chance (for example by screening our compound libraries). Therefore, predictions like that of Rose, according to whom: 'Toward the end of this century, we will have largely defeated ageing, and human biological immortality will be as normal as treating pathogens with antibiotics and antivirals is now' (op. cit. p. 204), are sheer nonsense.

12.3.4 Digital immortality

Proponents of the 'uploading' of the human mind into computers promise 'digital immortality' via the separation of the mind from the body, with the goal of relocating our minds as 'mindware' inside computers so that we can enjoy an eternal life in digital form. According to (Merkle 2013, p. 157), the uploading narrative goes like this:

1. 'Your brain is a material object.
2. The behaviour of material objects is described by the laws of physics.
3. The laws of physics can be modeled on a computer.
4. Therefore, the behavior of your brain can be modeled on a computer.'

Where does this story go wrong? The answer is quite simple: 1. and 2. are true. 3. is true, but only for non-complex systems with a few variables and one dominating interaction. This excludes most of physics, and practically all of the physics that pertains to biological systems. But the mind-body continuum is a highly complex biological system which we cannot model on a computer because we cannot model it mathematically, as we have shown in chapter 8.

Schematically, the argument against digital immortality runs as follows:

A. Digital immortality requires simulating an individual human mind computationally.
B. Human minds are complex systems.
C. Simulating an individual complex dynamical system computationally requires adequate mathematical models of such systems.[31]
D. Adequate mathematical models of individual complex systems are impossible.

Therefore, digital immortality is impossible.

Even if we were able to load some (even very large amounts) of your (somehow dynamicised) mental data into a computer, we could never expect a machine to serve the continuation of your individual conscious life, because machines have no consciousness and cannot have a consciousness, as we have shown in 9.3.

Learning about the mind from studying computers Before concluding this chapter, we mention one application of artificial intelligence engineering which is supposed, somehow, to underpin a revolution in our understanding of *natural* intelligence.

The view was succinctly formulated in 1977 by Margaret Boden, when she wrote that 'by "artificial intelligence" I ... mean the use of computer programs and programming techniques to cast light on the principles of intelligence in general and human thought in particular' (Boden 1977, p. 5). Boden's proposed definition suggests that we can use computers to learn about the human mind and cognition rather than learning how to use computers to reproduce certain

---

31 'Adequate', again, means 'adequate for the purposes of engineering'; here this means: *engineering the projected simulation.*

operations of the human mind. Turing, too, advocated an approach of this sort: 'The attempt to make a thinking machine will help us greatly in finding out how we think ourselves' (Turing 1951). A more recent revival can be found in Rabinowitz et al. (2018), who claim to have created a 'theory of mind' dNN. Their approach has the same flaws as its predecessors and uses an *Ersatz*-definition of 'mind' analogous to that which we identified in 9.3.3.3.

Views along these lines are once again based on the erroneous, Neo-Cartesian view of the mind as a computing machine that can be understood separately from any associated body (and even separately from the brain's own material constitution). Since the mind-body continuum is a highly complex system, which we cannot model mathematically, we will certainly not be able to better understand it using a universal Turing machine. Supposing that we can do so is rather like supposing that we can infer new facts about the development of newborns by studying the inner workings of the baby simulators nowadays used to teach parenting skills to schoolchildren.

12.4 Back to Bostrom

The reader will recall Bostrom's modest proposal that philosophers and mathematicians should abandon their current plans in order to focus their attentions on the more pressing challenge of increasing the chance that there will be no Singularity. We have provided some examples of the results of this diversion of efforts in the foregoing. These results are not encouraging, and they suggest an equal-and-opposite proposal, namely that philosophers and mathematicians (and all other persons of sound mind and body) should henceforth work intensively on topics as far removed as possible from science fiction à la Bostrom.

13
AI SPRING ETERNAL

How, then, can we build up the sort of well-founded confidence in AI that will allow us to avoid the frustration of future AI winters? How, in other words, can we obtain consistent real returns from our investments in AI research? The answer is by focusing on those types of *narrow, special-purpose AI* that allow us to apply extended Newtonian mathematics to problems that we can genuinely solve. We know from the No Free Lunch theorem that we can only find special problem solvers (see 8.6.6.3). But these can still be very effective. Already we find astonishing results obtained by systems working along these lines, including familiar solutions to highly challenging tasks such as games like Go or chess, image classification, face recognition, synthetic image generation, and approximative (though not professional quality) text translation. We here review a range of further important technical possibilities of narrow AI first of all by examining how it can be used in relation to non-complex systems, which is where most of the gains from using AI can be obtained.

13.1 AI for non-complex systems

The solar system is an example of a logic system, as also is the propagation of heat in a homogenous material from one point, or the radiation of electromagnetic waves from a source. Most examples of logic systems, however, are found in the domain of man-made systems, machines designed and engineered to fulfill a task. In the primary sector of the economy (mainly the extraction and production of raw materials, industries such as farming, logging, fishing, and mining), and in the secondary sector (mainly manufacturing, for example, industrial production of material goods such as housing, clothes, means of transportation, processed foods, energy, drinking water), myriad machines and instruments are used to support or

DOI: 10.4324/9781003310105-16

replace human labour. All of these tasks can be analysed for their potential to benefit from further automation or quality enhancement through use of algorithms and from further improvements in machines (including through the use of robots). What we discover is that AI can potentially be used to improve performance wherever the input-output-behaviour of the system under scrutiny

1. can be modelled adequately using multivariate distributions and
2. occurs frequently in a context-free setting, so that large amounts of data are readily available.

Where either of these two preconditions is not satisfied, AI can provide at best very limited models, and these have to be redesigned or retrained in detail for each new situation.

Our two preconditions are met primarily where we come close to satisfying the properties of non-complex systems, which for convenience purposes we list again here (abbreviated from 7.4.1). Such systems have:

1. a small set of element types,
2. uniform and isotropic interaction types,
3. no force overlay,
4. a deterministic and ergodic phase space,
5. the property of being non-driven,[1]
6. no evolutionary properties, and
7. fixed boundary conditions.

There are thousands of different types of systems for which these properties are satisfied. For illustrative purposes, we provide examples from the primary and secondary sectors of the economy.[2]

A diamond mine is a complex hybrid system. However, there are steps in the production process which are non-complex, such as the recovery of diamonds from the ore-crusher output (Pierson 2012). This recovery process can be optimised by using AI-based evaluation of sensor data. This step of the process has most of the properties of a non-complex system: there are just two relevant element types, diamonds and non-diamonds (1).[3] Their interaction is

---

1 We need to make the caveat that this property can be assumed to be satisfied when we are considering those aspects of the system's behaviour that are relevant to our modelling. That a system is non-driven means that there is no energy flow through the system. Of course, each machine that is in use has such a flow, but in cases such as those we deal with here, the resulting chaotic dissipation and entropy can be neglected.
2 We will look at the tertiary sector in section 13.2.
3 Here numbers in parentheses refer to the just-mentioned list of non-complex system properties. Note that the complex-system properties of this system are so moderate that models perform adequately.

mechanical force (2, 3). The phase space is one of deterministic chaos (though still ergodic) (4). The drivenness induced by shaking or otherwise moving the ore mix is moderate (5). The system is non-evolving (6). And finally: it has fixed boundaries (7). Therefore, the process can be improved by further use of AI technologies.

Assembly-line quality control is an expensive process that is indispensable to the maintenance of a uniform level of product quality. Because many product samples run off an assembly line on any given day, large quantities of data are available. AI can therefore be used to monitor product qualities such as shape, colour, and surface features of the products that are indirectly measured by sensors as they pass through the assembly process:

- At each step there is an assembly system meeting all requirements of a non-complex system and bringing about a well-defined set of changes in product elements (1).
- The interaction types between assembly system elements are uniform and isotropic, because the assembly-line robots either exert force on some portion of matter or they induce a well-defined chemical reaction; the applied forces do not overlay (2, 3).
- The movements of the robot define a narrow and ergodic phase space (4).
- The system is not driven with regard to its participation in the assembly process[4] (5).
- For any given setup of the assembly line, the system does not change (6) (but an AI might need retraining if a change is made).
- For the purpose of assessing the quality at each step, the context does not matter (7).

Therefore, sensor data from an inspection of the product at each step can be obtained and engineered to properly render the features needed as input data for a quality-control algorithm. Such an algorithm is obtained by unsupervised clustering of the data followed by outlier labelling and subsequent training of a supervised learning algorithm, for example, a Random Forest classifier[5] or (if enough data are available) a dNN.

Human–robot hybrid assembly is a process in which engineers seek to maximise the elimination of human labour because machine labour has fewer limitations. Above all, it has essentially no variation in quality, and is cheaper in the longer term. To achieve this, the first step is to identify repetitive human

---

4 The system consumes electrical energy, but again the resulting internal chaotic dissipation does not influence the way the system elements behave in the assembly process.
5 This is a classic stochastic classification model that can be obtained with a moderate amount of training data.

activities which use a perception pattern that can be mapped without loss to the composition of a passive sensor data stream. The data from the sensors are then passed into an algorithm that decomposes the human behaviour in the following manner:

- Let X, Y be finite dimensional vector spaces in $\mathbb{R}^m$ and $\mathbb{R}^n$, respectively, with $n, m \in \mathbb{N}$.
- Obtain a set of data (input-output tuples) from these spaces: $\langle \mathbf{X}_{k,m}, \mathbf{Y}_{k,n} \rangle$, where $k \in \mathbb{N}$ is the size of the set.
- Let $T_i : \mathbb{R}^p \mapsto \mathbb{R}^q, i \in \mathbb{N}, p, q \in \mathbb{N}_{>1}$ be operators and let $f_j : \mathbb{R} \mapsto \mathbb{R}, j \in \mathbb{N}_0, i \in \mathbb{N}$ be functionals.
- The functionals and operators can be algorithms, differential equations, syllogisms, or stochastic regression models (including neural networks). Note that the domain of T_1 is $\mathbb{R}^m$ and the range of T_n is $\mathbb{R}^n$.
- Let the operator T_0 represent the outcome that the ML or AI model is to emulate in the current context. This is a human activity, which is performed to realise a certain step in the production process, for example, the combination of two delicate, small parts into one larger part. The machine which is supposed to replace the human then has to obtain an operator of the form

$$\hat{\gamma} = \hat{T}_0 = T_1 \circ f_1 \circ \cdots \circ f_{m-1}^\theta \circ T_{n-1}^\kappa \circ f_m^\lambda \circ T_n \tag{13.1}$$

where $\hat{\gamma}$ is an estimator of T_0.[6] The equation describes the composition ($\circ$) of a series of steps, each one consisting in the application of some functional or operator, hence we propose the name 'compositional AI' for an approach of this sort.

What is applied in any given step might be a stochastic model, an ontology-based mechanical theorem prover (MTP, (Robinson et al. 2001)), a Bayesian network, a set of rules, an algebraic graph, and there are many other alternatives. Note that both functionals and operators may use prior knowledge, which is symbolised by the superscripts θ, κ and λ used on some of the functionals and operators.

- The set of functionals and operators of the model can be trained and tested by using appropriate data-subsets in the usual ratio (see (Hastie et al. 2008, chapter 7)).
- The model $\hat{\gamma}$ is finally evaluated by using a validation partition from the data.

Each functional f_j and each operator T_i with $i > 0$ of the model represents a part of the human mental act or physical action sequence which is decomposed when the algorithm guiding the robot is designed. In some cases, a single human act or action might need to be represented mathematically through the

---

6 For a definition see footnote 8.2 in section 8.6.6.

combination of several functionals or operators. For example, T_1 might be an act of perception, f_1 corresponds to the first movement pattern of the human act sequence, and so on. Under certain conditions, it may be possible to directly train the entire operator $\hat{y} = \hat{T}_0$ end-to-end, though such applications are rare in real-world problems and such problems need compositional solutions. End-to-end training is mostly suitable only for games and other closed-world problems. In other contexts AI will work only if there are humans in the loop.

The AI architecture sketched in equation 13.1 reflects the fundamental compositional principle of engineering and is used in many AI applications. Human perception and the unconscious feedback-loops characteristic of human sensorimotor act sequences (see 3.3.2.2), are complex and usually require a careful artificial emulation of the acts or actions that are to be modelled by software. Sophisticated combinations of methods are required to make up for the impossibility of modelling highly complex sensorimotor acts explicitly using mathematics (Hwangbo et al. 2019). This limits the usability of robots to activities in which the required sensorimotor complexity is moderate: a trumpet- or violin-playing robot at the performance level of a human professional musician is unthinkable. The results can nevertheless be astonishing, for example in the non-complex artificial, controlled environment of a factory, which can be adequately modelled using Newtonian mathematics.

Such advances in narrow AI will certainly bring about a decrease in relative contribution of humans to many manufacturing processes over the next decades. They will of course also allow tasks that would not be feasible without machines, such as automated stock market news generation or advertisement placing in the internet. This does not mean that AI is a job-killer. The economy is not a zero-sum game and new occupation opportunities will be created, not least in response to AI engineering innovations of these sorts. For example, companies which engage in heavy use of stochastic AI also need a lot of 'mechanical turks' (in other words, human beings) to make up for the problems brought by this technology.

13.1.1 Self-driving cars

As we saw in section 8.6.9, self-driving cars work well in a controlled environment, because there the properties of complex systems can be artificially avoided. It is possible to control the environment by excluding adverse weather, human drivers, pedestrians, etc., etc., in order to create a logic system. However, the real-world traffic system is complex, and to build a driverless car system for such an uncontrolled environment will require that we find a way to use AI algorithms to engineer a simple system (which is all that AI algorithms *can* engineer) that is a sufficiently close approximation to the open traffic environment that it will allow the needed human-level driving performance to be achieved. There will in any case be a constant need for retraining of the AI algorithms, as technical, environmental and human elements of the total (car plus road network system) change. For the latter will remain forever a complex system, and thus an ever-evolving system with no trajectory towards any sort of equilibrium because of the involvement of factors such as the weather, human malice, and mechanical (including software-related) failures.

However, the driving quality of self-driving cars will progressively improve, though we will never be in a position where the car can deal with all eventualities, because of the no-fixed boundary and evolutionary properties of complex systems. The increasing numbers of autonomous vehicles on the roads, and the economic forces and drive for innovation that go together therewith, will over time incentivise a cascade of changes in the material world in which driving occurs. First, more and more vehicles will be networked together; roads and traffic signs will themselves progressively incorporate more and more network technology. And then these changes could eventually lead to new kinds of AI algorithms, for use not only in self-driving cars but also in the traffic control management systems of the future—for example to allow seamless landing of flying vehicles in the flow of traffic.

13.1.2 Intelligence without representation?

What can we learn from these examples and from the compositional principle introduced in the last section?

Recall, first, that as we saw in chapter 3, human beings (and other animals) are, when viewed from the Gibsonian perspective, comparable to highly complex tuning forks. Gibson was a proponent of direct perception: there are no intermediary layers—of concepts, arrays of sense data, representations—that would come between the perceiver and her environment. In opposition to the Gibson-type view are what are called 'representational' theories of perception, of which Fodor is the most influential advocate, which hold that in order to understand perception (and all other capabilities of organisms and information systems) we must turn aside from the hardware, and study instead what Fodor called *representations*.

Rodney Brooks (1991) is interesting from this perspective, since he advanced a direct realist definition of AI—an AI 'without representation'. To achieve an AI of this sort Brooks proposed a new decompositional approach to engineering AI that was inspired, as he saw it, by the behaviour of insects. His goal was to create robots in which what he conceived as layered behavioural patterns would be joined together to obtain an overall behaviour without central representation or control. The layers he envisaged were functional behavioural subsystems shaping the macro-behaviour of the robot through their functional combination. It is common to identify such layers in mammals, where we have

- primitive layers such as reflexes, together with

- systems located in the brain stem and other evolutionarily ancient parts of the brain which enable autonomous functions such as breathing, the (dromotropic, inotropic, bathmotropic, and chronotropic) regulation of the activity of the heart, or of the sleep-wake-cycle, and then
- layers that enable, for example, passive sensual impressions and active perception and from there up to the
- layers enabling cognition and the exercise of intelligence.

When it comes to engineering emulations of an organism's behaviour in terms of layers of this sort, however, the results turn out to be isomorphic to what is achieved by using many other approaches to emulating agent behaviour through compositional approaches like the one described in equation 13.1. Indeed, we encounter an isomorphism of this sort no matter how the behaviour of an agent is modelled, since a decomposition into smaller units is always necessary to achieve any sort of overall behaviour. This decomposition principle is observable in every living organism and is the core engineering idea realised in every machine humans ever built. It does not matter along which conceptual axis the decomposition of systems into smaller components is made: functionally (as in equation 13.1), through use of materials (as in the construction of buildings or bridges), or through layers of behaviour (as in the case of Brooks). There is always a need to decompose an engineered system in order to realise it in the real world, and the recomposition must always be such that it can be stated in mathematical terms.

Furthermore, in machines (including machines programmed with very sophisticated algorithms) there will always be an order that defines how the data to which the observable behaviour of the machine is a reaction will flow. This order of data flow is an unavoidable 'representation' of the inputs to the engineered system that derive from the world outside. To process these data, the system has to represent them—something which Brooks wanted to circumvent. Even a neural network has a data flow ('representation') of this sort, though there it remains partially implicit. There can, accordingly, be no data processing without representation in an engineered system. Data processing is always required, and it can never be completely implicit, because every engineered system is associated with a multitude of conscious engineering decisions. As we saw in chapter 8.6.6 there are no 'self-learning systems' in the world, systems entirely free of humans in the loop, and there never will be.

Overall, Brooks is right to insist that AI systems must be engineered by decomposition of the targeted behaviour. His specification of the requirements for an AI system[7] corresponds to the definition we give in 3.3.3. However,

---

7 We repeat it here for convenience: His goal was to build robots that can 'move around in dynamic environments, sensing the surroundings to a degree sufficient to achieve the necessary maintenance of life and reproduction' (Brooks 1991, p. 140).

from his definition, if follows that the systems he proposes to build cannot fulfil these requirements. This is because engineering via decomposition can (as we have seen in chapter 7) only yield logic systems. But a system that would be able to fulfil the requirements which Brooks proposes would need to be—like an insect—a complex system. And we have no possibility to obtain the synoptic and adequate models that would be needed to build a system of this sort.

13.2 AI for complex systems

Of course, the primary and secondary sectors of the economy also contain many complex systems, but it is the tertiary sector, which is engaged in the production not of products but of services, that has the highest proportion of human—and thus complex system—contributions. Its output of intangible goods includes counseling, home care, access, psychological services, and information, which are provided by industries such as healthcare, media, telecommunication, advertising, financial services, professional services, waste disposal, prostitution, transportation, retail, gambling, education, and so forth. Public administration and government as well as national defense can also be seen as a part of this sector.

All of these services involve the use of language and are provided as outputs of the behaviour of complex systems (humans) and—very often of complex systems of complex systems (groups of humans organised as teams or interacting with each other for example inside a hospital or police station). Because we cannot generally model such systems, the applicability of AI to the tertiary sector is more limited than in the first two sectors. However, processes in service industries can be analysed in order to find sub-processes and activities which can be automated using AI by reducing the complexity to a level that can be modelled mathematically with minimal loss of quality. Examples are:

Customer correspondence management This is a process that currently requires a workforce of hundreds of thousands of clerks across the OECD countries. Though the pieces of correspondence that need to be processed are emanations from complex systems—they are written by humans—there are still groups of customer requests that are repetitive in nature, for example change of address or change of bank account notifications, contract cancellations, or requests for payment balance information. Such texts can be modelled adequately using multivariate distributions and can be computationally interpreted, again, with the compositional approach shown in equation (13.1). This allows the extraction and automated storage of their contents in a structured form and the computation of an adequate response. A description of a technological realisation of such language interpretation is given in (Landgrebe et al. 2021, § 3.3.1). In contrast to stochastic language models, which can model only the morphosyntactic aspects of language, the model there described captures also the semantic and pragmatic characteristics of the input texts.

Claims management is a task for which the German insurance industry today uses roughly 250,000 employees. Aspects of this task are repetitive enough to be automated using a combination of logical inference, arithmetic, and a narrow AI system built to work with claims language. For example, in the evaluation of a car body repair bill, the line items in the bill for labour and materials can be compared to the repair steps and associated materials prescribed in the car manufacturers' repair instructions. To enable this comparison, both the items on the bill and the associated instructions can be translated into mathematical logic using a translation model. The resulting formulae can then be used to perform an $n{:}m$-match[8] of the items using equivalence- and ontology-based combinatorial optimisation. Finally, matching line groups can be compared arithmetically with regard to costs. This enables a fully automated bill validation (Landgrebe et al. 2021, Appendix).

Defense systems have been using AI since autonomous cruise missiles were first designed. These missiles nowadays use terrain contour matching and feature-based target recognition to refine the trajectory of the missile. Such missiles will become ever more formidable in the future and will increasingly be able to act in groups and to follow more and more sophisticated trajectories. But AI can also be used in the defence of strategic locations such as bunkers, ground stations, battleships, and airplanes. They can prioritise which defensive missile to use on which approaching weapon systems, either to intercept a missile or to support launch scheduling for attack purposes. Though defence systems operate in complex system environments, the behaviour of each single system can be modelled extremely well with classical physics. The equations describing this behaviour can be combined with decision algorithms to achieve highly sophisticated narrow AI. But such engineered systems will never become truly autonomous. End-to-end systems are here unlikely, because the overall reaction needs to deal with the output of complex systems, which overwhelms, as we have seen, the models of logic systems that we are required to use. End-to-end systems will in every case be ruled out, not only because ethical norms require that humans must make life-and-death decisions, but also because a general categorisation of complex-system generated situations as, for example, a subtle threat, cannot be modelled with logic systems (see the discussion of perception at 3.3.2.1).

Simple legal cases These are types of legal cases in which the acts of a defendant are easy to represent in mathematical form, for example, in a case of moderate speeding, with a measurement of the vehicle's velocity that has to be extracted from a regulatory offense letter. The machine compares the measured velocity to the allowed maximum speed on the relevant stretch of road and

---

8 With $\forall m, n \in \mathbb{N}_0 \mid m+n > 0$ as there might be no match on one side (therefore, either m or n may equal to 0, but not their sum); but no 0: 0 relationships.

computes the fine to be paid. However, if the speeding is so excessive that it requires a penal prosecution, or the case involves interviews and the use of language and social capabilities, the machine will fail. In legal cases which can be automated using machines, the automation is trivial and rule based.

13.2.1 Feasible AI and ontology

In the past decades, ontologies modelling scientific knowledge using a taxonomic backbone for entity representation have become very popular. What is the relationship between feasible AI and ontologies of this sort?

13.2.1.1 Ontologies for biology and medicine

In biology and in medicine, hundreds of ontologies have been created with the goal of promoting data interoperability (Smith et al. 2007). This means that under certain conditions, data from different sources can be compared or merged more easily, because with the help of the ontologies it is possible to determine the common semantics even for data matrices which originate from different sources (Ashburner et al. 2000). This not only allows a better description of experiment design and data by unifying the scientific language used to describe them, but also enables the construction of datasets large enough to enable unsupervised pattern identification and stochastic regression, both of which are very data greedy techniques (see page 176 and 8.6.6.2). For successful supervised training, which can, as we have seen, yield very important results when used properly, large datasets are also very important to avoid model overfit or overspecialisation to an unrepresentative sample space. Ontologies can help to obtain such datasets, especially if they are used by consortia such as the OBO Foundry (Smith et al. 2007) working in a comprehensive fashion from experiment design onwards. Such ontologies will not allow us to engineer synoptic and adequate comprehensive models of living systems. But they will help us to obtain descriptive and partial models of higher quality.

13.2.1.2 Ontologies for engineering and defense

The situation is comparable for ontologies used in engineering or defense, for example in the manufacturing industry (Karray et al. 2021). However, due to the nature of the systems these domains deal with, the short-term rate of return of ontology usage is higher than in the life sciences. This is because engineered machines are logic systems and have a behaviour that can be approximated very well using mathematics. Therefore, hypotheses about, for example, the efficacy of such machines can be tested with a higher likelihood of obtaining significant results than is possible in biology. It is also easier to identify new patterns in the behaviour of such machines using unsupervised learning techniques.

Stochastic predictive models that are applied to them—if they do not involve data emanating from human behaviour or inanimate complex systems—are often very accurate, for example in modelling automated missile interception (Chapman et al. 2021). Ontologies can also support the filing, annotation, and statistical interpretation of intelligence data, and they are indispensable for mechanical text interpretation as described earlier.[9]

In both areas, advances will be made along certain narrow lanes, including satellite image recognition and other analytic and classificatory tasks. Thus we will see incremental improvements in the sort of narrow AI that is used, for example, in the Isreali Iron Dome system for analyzing incoming rockets and determining if people or facilities are in danger. For the sort of complex analysis that is required in counter-terrorism operations on the ground, where changes in types of elements and interactions and force overlays are occurring constantly, human intelligence on the side of both commanders and individual soldiers will always be required.

13.3 AI boundaries

Whatever sector we choose, the use of AI in the real world is subject to tight limits. Whenever there is a need for adaptive cognitive behaviour in an open context, whenever the sensorimotor requirements of human dexterity are demanding, as in any kind of surgery, or musical or theatrical performance, or in social tasks such as accompanying schoolchildren to provide for protection against bullies, or whenever spontaneous use of language (both natural and mathematical) is involved, attempts to replace humans by machines will quickly lead to unusable results and will in due course be abandoned.

We have already noted that AI can be a very powerful tool for use in research, and it is nowadays indispensable to the effective exploitation of the results of electron microscopy, magnetic resonance tomography, or the measurements made in the Large Hadron Collider. But it cannot substitute for the human role in any kind of research (see 13.3.2.1). Rather, AI can be seen as a matter of what we might call *artificial instincts* because its models, no matter how they are generated, react in a deterministic, repetitive form; like instincts, they do not self-adapt, but reliably produce the same result upon each identical stimulus (input).

13.3.1 No AGI by composition

A common claim, repeated most recently by Marcus et al. (2019), is that a general AI with real cognitive capabilities can be obtained by combining

---

[9] For example in the discussion of customer correspondence management on p. 288.

elementary algorithms with prior knowledge—above all with the sort of common-sense knowledge possessed by human beings (see (Hayes 1985)). The ability to classify objects in time and space and to understand composition and causality are innate to human beings. Thus AI, according to Marcus and Davis, needs to combine knowledge of this sort with stochastic learning to obtain the needed capabilities for generalisation. They envisage a more powerful AI arising from the fluid combination of 'domains of causal understanding' (Marcus et al. 2019, p. 180). But what would this mean from a mathematical perspective? Well, it would mean nothing more than the composition of functionals and operators of the sort we have described in equation 13.1, which may include branching, parallel execution, and many other logical structures used in Turing-computable algorithms. But such compositions do not yield *intelligence*; rather they must in each new case be crafted anew to generate an AI specialised to a corresponding purpose and narrowly defined context. The composition is then defined in each such case by humans, and, as we have seen (see 8.6.6), even where it contains stochastic (implicit) models, these are indirectly generated from human input (training tuples, loss equations, network architectures, and hyperparameters) and have nothing to do with knowledge self-acquired on the part of the machine (Chollet 2017, p. 325).

The resulting machine behaviour is narrowly coupled to human-selected input signals and occurs in a deterministic fashion depending on the algorithm defined at design or training time. There is no consciousness, no animate perception, no sensorimotor loop, no spontaneous intentionality, and there is nothing like a mental act. And this is true no matter which algorithms we combine and no matter how we combine them.

Thus here, too: there is no AGI. However, the ideas proposed by Judea Pearl, Gary Marcus, Ernest Davis, and many others—elements of which go back to Allen Newell, Herbert A. Simon, and John Haugeland—can be extremely fruitful in building special-purpose AI systems if they are used in combination with other types of models, as we have seen in the earlier parts of this chapter.

13.3.2 What computers can and cannot do

Computers have transformed almost every aspect of life in modern technology-based societies. They have transformed health care, law enforcement, scientific research, commerce, in many cases in ways which have involved the use of purpose-built AI software. And whenever AI algorithms become embedded in useful products and services, they fall from public view.

But all successful uses of AI are examples of *narrow* AI. Examples include:

- facial recognition,
- disease prediction,

- advanced manufacturing,
- spam filters,
- marketing content recommendations, and
- approximate text translation.

In each case the software works by converting data sampled in a given area into vectors or matrices; the latter are then used to obtain a model to fulfill the task at hand. The benefits can be significant. But as we have shown in the foregoing, there are also limits. AI can never deal with new types of data—exhibiting patterns not present in its sample data—without some sort of retraining directly or indirectly involving inputs from human beings. AI does not have the natural intelligence even of an arthropod.

13.3.2.1 Inventive machines

Recently, Abbott (2019) claimed that 'inventive machines' are being used in research that are 'capable of innovation'—the idea being that machines will one day take the place of humans as scientists and inventors. He further believes that the machines of the future will increasingly be capable of 'considering the entire universe of prior art' in such a way that all inventions which currently appear to be genuine innovations will thereafter appear obvious. This state of affairs, Abbott thinks, will eventually render *all* putatively innovative ideas obvious, and thereby bring about the end of patenting.

But as we saw in section 9.5, the sort of intelligence that is required even to understand, or to apply, much less to *create*, any sort of theory, is out of scope for the machine (Chollet 2017, p. 325).

Machines can of course *support* science. Indeed, the improvement of instruments, tools, and machines for science, from the invention of the telescope by Hans Lipperhey in 1608 to the design and realisation of the Large Hadron Collider (by some 20,000 human beings) in 2009, has been one of the main drivers of the revolution in experimental science and physics since the 17th century. Algorithms, too (again created, directly or indirectly, by human beings), can play a similar role, for example in hypothesis testing, data analysis, logical theorem proving, or unsupervised pattern identification. But in all these and many other applications, they are tools like the microscope or telescope, and nothing more. For inventions and discoveries to be made, humans are required to identify a problem; formulate hypotheses as to how it might be solved (sometimes in ways that involve the creation of entirely new concepts and terminology and the conception of entirely new classes of entity); devise the experiments needed to test alternative solutions; interpret the results; and recognise that the problem has (or has not) been solved. And this will not change, as machines can do none of these things.

13.4 How AI will change the world

Despite the severe limitations that we have described in this book, the discovery of ever more imaginative and powerful uses of narrow AI will in the coming decades deepen and enhance the technosphere to an enormous extent. Machines will be used much more extensively than today in all sectors of the economy, in public administration, in warfare, and in scientific research. The great challenge we are facing is not the replacement of human intelligence. It is not the advent of some Singularity. The considerable efforts and razzamatazz invested in predicting or forestalling or controlling future superintelligences will remain fruitless at best; the same applies to efforts to create 'ethical' intelligences (see 11.3.1).

Instead, we face the challenge of finding new occupations for those whose labour will be mechanised. We have faced this problem repeatedly since the Industrial Revolution and mastered it to a large degree through reduction of total working time (fewer days per week, fewer hours per day, fewer years of life), and to a lesser extent through education. The challenge will become more demanding as opportunities for work in the primary and secondary sectors become fewer and fewer. But market economies are complex, highly dynamic systems—and we are confident that, as in the past, new occupations will evolve in ways that no one (and no algorithm) could have predicted. We can be confident, further, that the role played by machines in these developments will at least in this respect be harmless: that machines will not develop an evil will, that they will not conspire against humanity or instigate an explosive chain of events that will lead to the heat death of the universe. AI will develop in much the same ways that other technologies develop, now in this way, now in that, with successes and failures along the way.

APPENDIX

TURBULENCE: MATHEMATICAL DETAILS

The scaling model (discussed in section 8.7.1.1) provided a grain of hope to the effect that at least one aspect of a complex system—namely the phenomenon of turbulence—could be tamed mathematically. To show how this model was falsified, we provide a short review. Kolmogorov had hypothesised that at high Reynolds numbers, in the range $\eta \ll r \ll L$—the inertial range where no dissipation occurs but the vortices just divide—the scale-statistics are universally and uniquely dependent on r and ε. From this assumption, Kolmogorov modelled a universal energy spectrum function:

$$E(k) = K_0 \varepsilon^{\frac{2}{3}} k^{-\frac{5}{3}}, \qquad (13.2)$$

where the wavenumber $k = \frac{2\pi}{r}$ and K_0 is a universal, scale-invariant constant.

If equation 13.2 was correct, it would be possible to calculate the turbulence of air flows or other common turbulence phenomena (Falkovich et al. 2006). But it is not correct, and this has important implications for our understanding of the limits of mathematics in dealing with complex systems that violate the requirements for modelling in physics. To see why, consider the Navier-Stokes equations and the structure functions related thereto (Falkovich 2011). At unit density, and for a fluid particle in turbulent flow, the Navier-Stokes equations take the form:

$$\frac{\partial \mathbf{v}}{\partial t} = -\nabla p + \nu \nabla^2 \mathbf{v}.$$

Here $\mathbf{v}$ is the velocity field, ν is the kinematic viscosity, p is the pressure, and the left hand side represents the acceleration of the velocity field. At full turbulence and low viscosity (high Reynolds numbers), the pressure gradient term dominates and the acceleration on the left side of the equation accordingly becomes roughly proportional thereto. The velocity field in these circumstances can be analysed via the flow velocity increment:

$$\delta \mathbf{v}(r) = \mathbf{v}(\mathbf{x} + \mathbf{r}) - \mathbf{v}(\mathbf{x})$$

This is so because in the assumed scale-invariant inertial range, the turbulence is postulated to be isotropic, which means that the increment in flow velocity depends only on the distance **r** between two points. The scale-invariance implies that the flow velocity increments can then be scaled with a unique scaling exponent γ, so that when r is scaled by a factor λ, the resulting distribution $\delta\mathbf{v}(\lambda r)$ will be distributed according to $\lambda^\gamma \delta\mathbf{v}(r)$, with γ independent of r. If this power law (giving the scale invariance) would hold, then the velocity increment would scale according to the structure functions, which are its *modes* (in mechanics, a mode is a product of a distance and a physical quantity).

The distance is usually raised to the power n, as in $\mu_n = r^n Q$, where μ_n is the n-th mode, r is the distance, and Q a physical quantity such as point charge or mass:

$$\langle (\delta \mathbf{u}(r))^n \rangle = C_n (\varepsilon r)^{\frac{n}{3}}$$

Here the $\langle \rangle$ operator denotes the statistical mean, n the order of the mode (the structure function), and C_n the respective universal constants of each mode. For low orders ($n = 2$), the turbulent flows measured in experiments are close to what is predicted by Kolmogorov's theoretical formulation. However, for higher orders, the scale-invariance (power law) breaks down: *'The scaling exponents of structure functions depart from Kolmogorov's aesthetically appealing result'* (Falkovich et al. 2006, p. 44). Thus, his theory is false.

GLOSSARY

Adaptation
　　Process which consists in a change in properties of an organism with the effect of optimising its and its offspring's chances of survival or reproduction.

Algorithm, optimisation
　　An algorithm used to find an optimum. In statistical learning, such an algorithm finds local minima of a function (see equation 8.4 on p. 147).

Anisotropy
　　Space-dependence of the propagation of an effect of a force. Antonym of isotropy.

Capability
　　Disposition whose bearer (or, in the case of an artefact, whose creator, owner, or user) has an interest in its being realised.

Chaos (chaotic)
　　Of a process. A process is chaotic if, given a starting condition, the outcome of the process over time cannot be predicted.

Chaos, deterministic
　　Chaotic process which can be adequately modelled using deterministic laws but for which the outcome over time cannot be predicted because the starting conditions cannot be measured with sufficient accuracy (systematic measurement error is above required accuracy). All processes of complex systems are chaotic in this sense.

Community
　　Small group of humans who associate over long periods of time on the basis of direct personal relationships, often involving individuals belonging to different generations.

Computation
Calculation performed (typically with a computer) following an algorithm to obtain an output from an input.

Consciousness
State (in sense (1) on p. 306) of an organism which obtains when processes of awareness or sentience occur. Consciousness as a process (as in 'stream of consciousness') is an emanation of a neurophysiological process.

Culture
Of humans: (1) Behaviour resting on non-genetically transmitted knowledge, often directly or indirectly related to group survival. (2) Artefacts generated and transmitted as a result of such behaviour. Animals do not have cultural artefacts.

Data, synthetic
Data obtained by simulation rather than measurement, using, for example, an algorithmic random number generator or a Gibbs sampler.

Disposition
Attribute of an entity which serves as the truthmaker for an assertion of real possibility about that entity. A disposition may or may not be realised, and it may be realised with or without a trigger.

Distribution, multivariate
Vector space of random variables used as a stochastic model for data which have more than one property.

Drivenness
Of a system. The property of a system which causes it to not converge upon or move towards an equilibrium state (see under State in sense (1) on p. 306), but rather to move from one state to another in time as a result of the exertion of an internal or external force, which may be continuous, or regular and punctual. For example, the contraction of the heart is an example of the application of an internal regular punctual force within the driven cardiovascular system.

Drivenness, animate
Natural drivenness of living organisms. All living organisms have the following characteristic capabilities: (1) to autonomously produce energy-storing molecules from external energy, (2) to constantly use the stored energy for their survival and reproduction.

Drivenness, artificial
Drivenness which a system has as a result of human design. All artificial driven systems are driven only as long as there is human supplied fuel or maintenance. Their drivenness is lost when this energy is used up or when maintenance stops and the system breaks because of worn-out parts. Example: a steam engine.

Drivenness, natural
Drivenness that is not the result of human design. Example: the drivenness of the water movements in the oceans (taking their energy from the sun).

Element
Of a system. Object that interacts with other objects in a system.

Emanation
Any type of electromagnetic radiation or composite form of energy propagation (for example, of sound) which can be directly observed, but which is produced by a process which cannot be directly observed.

Emulation
An emulation is the imitation of the behaviour of an entity by means of another entity. The emulation behaves in response to given inputs in ways which mimic the way the emulated entity would behave in response to analogous inputs. The aim of an emulation is thus to mimic behaviour. *See also:* Simulation.

Entropy
In statistical mechanics, entropy is a measure used to quantify the number of microstates of a system depending on its macrostates (such as energy, volume, pressure) and alterations thereto (such as the addition of energy, heat influx, or mechanical work). In information theory, entropy is a measure of uncertainty.

Environment
The site (Arp et al. 2015) in which (for example) an organism lives or an action occurs; especially those parts of the organisms' surroundings that are directly or indirectly perceivable.

Ergodicity
See under: System, ergodic.

Event, erratic
A random event which cannot be modeled as a sample from a distribution.

Evolution
Cumulative process of change in a population of organisms across multiple generations that survives natural selection pressure as a result of adaptation.

Function (mathematics)
Binary relation over two sets of mathematical objects which associates every element of the first, possibly high-dimensional space to exactly one element of the second, one-dimensional space. Also designated as 'functional' in the field of functional analysis.

Function (of a system or an artefact)
A disposition that exists in virtue of its bearer's physical make-up and which came into existence through processes of design or natural selection in order to realise processes of a certain sort.

Function, recursive (computer science)
In computer science, a function is the smallest behavioural element of an algorithm. A recursive function is a function which calls itself to achieve a computation.

Identity
Of a person. The highly complex individual pattern of dispositions that determines a person's possibilities of reaction to internal or external stimuli. Among these, the most important are (in ascending order of physiological complexity) the visceral, sensorimotor, affective, and cognitive dispositions.

Instinct
A hard-wired complex behavioural reaction mechanism which responds to an internal or external stimulus of a given type in a way that leaves no alternatives to its bearer in how it reacts; present only in human and non-human animals.

Intelligence
Capability to adapt to new situations.

Intelligence, objectifying
Intelligence, exclusively of humans, built around the capability of the subject to engage in mental and linguistic acts in which objects (including the subject) are grasped as entities belonging to distinguishable types.

Intelligence, primal
Scheler: Intelligence comprehending the innate capability to (i) behave in a meaningful and appropriate way in relation to novel situations, where (ii) this behaviour is not instinctual, and (iii) the behaviour is engaged in suddenly (which means: it is not the result of training or of prior attempts to solve a problem via trial and error). Manifested in higher animals such as mammals and birds; may be present in other species, but the evolutionary boundary is unknown.

Intention
(1) Mental act, typically short-lived, in which the goals and motives of our behaviour are manifested. (2) The disposition associated with such a mental act. (3) The material (neurophysiological) basis of such a disposition. (4) The combination of (1)-(3).

Intersubjectivity
Social phenomenon established where human beings interact reciprocally in such a way as to understand and take account of what each takes to be the other's perspective.

Isotropy
Space-independence of the propagation of an effect of a force. Example: the radiation spectrum of the sun propagates in all directions with equal energy and identical mix of wave-lengths.

Loss function
In statistical learning, a loss function $\ell(f(X), Y)$ describes the discrepancy between the outcome estimates predicted by a stochastic model $\hat{y}_i$ and the observed outcomes y_i, $i = 1 \ldots N$, where N is the number of observations (see eqn. 8.4). The loss is minimised to optimise the model.

Machine learning
A family of algorithms used to create implicit stochastic models through use of training data and parametric constraints on the computation of the model.

Macrostate (thermodynamics)
An *aggregate measure* of an entire system with many elements and many degrees of freedom, which is described using variables such as energy, temperature, volume, pressure, chemical composition, or magnetism. Note that use of 'macrostate' implies always reference to a state in sense (2) on p. 306. A macrostate is just one measure, where a microstate is a set of instances of variables which together define one point of a phase space.

Measurement error
Deviation of a measurement of some physical phenomenon from its true value.

Microstate (thermodynamics)
The complete microscopic description (using one or more variables) of a point of the phase space of a thermodynamic system (a state in sense (2) on p. 306). This defines, for example, location and momentum of a particle at a specific point in time in an ideal gas.

Mind–body continuum
The unity of human body and mind which interacts with our environment to realise our intentions and, in particular, our intentions to survive and reproduce.

Model (science)
Representation of an aspect of reality using abstract symbols that is created to describe, explain, or predict the aspect of reality in question.

Model, adequate
A model is adequate relative to some set of requirements if it can be used to engineer an entity or an emulation that satisfies all requirements in that set.

Model, explicit (mathematics)
Model formulated using mathematical equations.

Model, implicit (machine learning)
Mathematical model that is automatically computed using an optimisation procedure, usually by approximating the minimum of a loss function or the maximum of a utility function.

Model, parametric
A stochastic model is parametric if the data it describes can be adequately modelled by a probability distribution that has a fixed set of parameters, for

example a distribution from the exponential family such as the Gaussian, Dirichlet, Bernoulli, or Gamma distribution. Each of the latter is called a parametric distribution. A distribution is non-parametric if it cannot be obtained by parameterising some distribution family. Such a distribution has no known distribution type.

Model, partial
Model that tries to explain or predict only certain intentionally chosen aspects of a system under study.

Model, physical
Model that is realised using physical entities. For example an orrery, an architect's cardboard model of a house.

Model, stochastic
Model that is created by using the statistical properties of empirical data distributions.

Model, symbolic
Model that is formulated using only symbols.

Model, synoptic
A synoptic model of a system is a model that can be used to engineer a given system or to emulate its behaviour.

Newtonian mathematics, extended
The applied mathematics we use today, consisting primarily of the calculus plus (linear) algebra, functional analysis, stochastics, numerical analysis, and number theory.

Norm, social
Norm which consists of a collection of rules determining behaviour in recurrent situations involving human interaction. Serves to promote predictability and coordination of behaviour.

Objectification
The ability of human beings to disengage themselves from their environment in a way that allows them to see themselves, other human beings, and the elements of this environment as *objects* of certain *types* (as instances of universals). This ability is a precondition of our use of language to represent reality.

Observation (physics)
Given a phase space, a measurement of the variables which form its basis.

Operator (functional analysis)
Binary relation over two spaces of mathematical objects where both spaces are high-dimensional.

Parameterisation (statistical learning)
In statistical learning, parameterisation is used to refer to the generation of the parameters of a stochastic model (an equation) in such a way as to relate the output $\hat{y}$ which the model estimates to the input x. For example, in the simplest linear regression model $\hat{y} = \beta_0 + \beta_1 x$, the parameter vector $\theta = (\beta_0, \beta_1)$.

Partition, granular
A complex of labelled cells in a projective relation to the world. Examples are taxonomies, coordinate systems, maps dividing a region of space into subregions. A map of countries is a partition of coarser granularity than a map of counties or postal districts.

Phase space
Of a system. The phase space of a system is the vector space whose basis is formed by the specific state variables relating to each element type of the system. This space has as many dimensions as the number of distinct state variables that each element of the space can have.

Prediction (mathematics)
The computation of a model output from some model input. Can be applied where outputs describe not only (1) future outcomes, but also (2) historical outcomes, and (3) generated outcomes (as for example in utterance production). In cases (1) and (2) prediction can be of varying degrees of accuracy depending on how much it differs from the measured outcome. In case (3), the quality of the prediction is measured not by deviation from the outcome but by other qualifiers such as utility.

Prediction, exact
Model-based prediction of an outcome of a process that is so close to the true outcome that it is within the measurement error.

Probability, conditioned
A conditioned probability is a probability which depends on an observed event. For example, when drawing a black ball from an urn with three black balls and one white, the probability of drawing a black ball is $p = ¾$. But after drawing a black ball, we have the conditioned probability p (black|first = black) = $⅔$.

Process model (engineering)
Either a simulation or an emulation.

Simulation
Model of a process which imitates the unfolding of the process over time in such a way that, if initial data for the process are entered as input, then terminal output data can be inferred. The aim of a simulation is to predict behaviour.

Singularity (mathematics)
Point at which a mathematical object is not or ceases to be defined. For example, the real function $f(x) = \frac{1}{x}$ has a singularity (a pole) at $x_0 = 0$, where $\lim_{x \to x_0} f(x) = \pm\infty$. Used in the AI literature to refer to the advent of a fictional artificial superintelligence.

Situation
Environment consisting of what is of relevance to the active intentions of an actor or a group of actors. A machine may be in the situation of some

other actor. But it can never be in a situation in its own right, because it has neither experiences nor intentions. A sleeping individual experiences situations in dreams.

Socialisation

Process as a result of which an individual learns to behave in a way that is acceptable to a group (community or society) to which the individual belongs.

State

The term 'state' is used in a variety of ways; most importantly for our purposes, it is used to mean: (1) Of any continuant entity: A state is a collection of one or more particular qualities of the entity at a given time. Example: a state of consciousness of a human being; an equilibrium state of a system. (2) Of a system: A state is the set of measurable values (i.e. state variables) of the system's non-invariant properties at a given time. (Thus the state is something like a pattern of quantitative variables of the system.) A state in sense (2) is an information entity that refers to a state in sense (1).

State variable (thermodynamics)

Variable type that can be instantiated by measuring variable properties of a microstate.

Stochastic process

A family of random variables $X = (X_t, t \in I)$ defined on a probability space with $I \subset \mathbb{R}$ as temporal space and taking values from a measurement space E. Can be seen as an operator, with a range that can only be modelled with uncertainty due to lack of information or modelling ability.

System

A totality of dynamically interrelated physical elements participating in a process. To delimit a system is to select a level of granularity of its elements, from micro-physical particles to entire galaxies.

System (information theory)

An information source producing emanations that can be observed, for example, a radio station (consisting of announcers, microphones, transmitters, and so on).

System, complex

A system characterised by: dependence on an arbitrary combination of element types, different interaction types between elements, force overlay (several forces acting at the same time and thereby potentially interacting), phase spaces which cannot be predicted from the system elements, and by non-ergodicity, drivenness, evolutionary properties, and non-fixable boundary conditions.

System, ergodic

Ergodicity describes the stochastic behaviour of a system. A system is called ergodic if, over sufficiently long periods of time, the time in which a system element occupies any given region of the phase-space is proportional to the volume of this region. This means that accessible microstates are equiprobable over a long period of time.

System, logic

A system for which almost exact models can be obtained that can explain and predict its behaviour. Such systems have three core properties: (i) dominance of one of the four fundamental interactions, (ii) homogeneous and isotropic interactions, and (iii) fixed boundary conditions. Systems of this sort are called logic systems because they can be dealt with using logic as applied to propositions of extended Newtonian mathematics.

System, non-ergodic

A non-ergodic system does not occupy each accessible microstate with equal probability, for example because it is driven or because its state space is changing (evolutionary property).

Thinking, categorical

The ability to think about the world in terms of universals or kinds or general properties and the relations between them.

Turing-computable

Of a problem. That it can be solved using computation with an algorithm that can be formulated as a sequence of elementary recursive functions.

Variance

The degree of dispersion from the centre of a uni- or multivariate distribution.

Vector

A mathematical object characterised by magnitude and direction which describes a translation in a coordinate system (vector space).

Vector space

An algebraic structure whose elements are vectors, which may be added together and multiplied by numbers (scalars).

REFERENCES

Abbott, Barbara. 2017. Reference. In *The Oxford handbook of pragmatics*, edited by Yan Huang, 240–258. London: Oxford University Press.

Abbott, Ryan. 2019. Everything is obvious. *UCLA Law Review* 66: 2.

Adams, Eldridge S. 2016. Territoriality in ants (hymenoptera: formicidae): a review. *Myrmecological News* 23: 101–118.

Aellen, Melisande, Judith M. Burkart, and Redouan Bshary. 2021. No evidence for general intelligence in a fish. *bioRxiv*. https://doi.org/10.1101/2021.01.08.425841.

Alexander, Samuel. 2004. *Space, time, and deity (1920)*. Whitefish, MT: Kessinger Publications.

Aljalbout, Elie, Vladimir Golkov, et al. 2018. Clustering with deep learning: taxonomy and new methods. *arXiv:1801.07648*.

Ambady, Nalini, and Robert Rosenthal. 1992. Thin slices of expressive behavior as predictors of interpersonal consequences: a meta-analysis. *Psychological Bulletin* 111 (2): 256–274.

Antweiler, Christoph. 2019. On the human addiction to norms: social norms and cultural universals of normativity. In *The normative animal? On the anthropological significance of social, moral, and linguistic norms*, edited by Neil Roughley and Kurt Bayertz, 83–100. London: Oxford University Press.

Armstrong, Rachel. 2013. Alternative biologies. In *The transhumanist reader*, edited by Max More and Natasha Vita-More, 100–109. Oxford: Wiley-Blackwell.

Armstrong, Rachel, and Neill Spiller. 2010. Synthetic biology: living quarters. *Nature* 467 (7318): 916–918.

Arora, Saurabh, and Prashant Doshi. 2018. A survey of inverse reinforcement learning: challenges, methods and progress. *arXiv:1806.06877*.

Arp, Robert, Barry Smith, and Andrew D. Spear. 2015. *Building ontologies with Basic Formal Ontology*. Cambridge, MA: MIT Press.

Ashburner, Michael, Catherine A. Ball, et al. 2000. Gene Ontology: tool for the unification of biology. *Nature Genetics* 25 (1): 25–29.

Asimov, Isaac. 1950. *I, robot*. New York: Doubleday.

Auer, Peter. 2009. On-line syntax: thoughts on the temporality of spoken language. *Language Sciences* 31 (1): 1–13.

Austin, John L. 1962. *How to do things with words*. Oxford: Clarendon Press.
Babaie, Hassan, Armita Davarpanah, and Nirajan Dhakal. 2019. Projecting pathways to food-energy-water systems sustainability through ontology. *Environmental Engineering Science* 36 (7): 808–819.
Baberowski, Jörg. 2015. *Räume der Gewalt*. Frankfurt a. M.: S. Fischer Verlag.
Band, Yehuda B., and Yshai Avishai. 2012. *Quantum mechanics with applications to nanotechnology and information science*. Cambridge, MA: Academic Press.
Barker, Roger G. 1968. *Ecological psychology*. Standford: Stanford University Press.
Barker, Roger G., and Herbert F. Wright. 1951. *One boy's day: a specimen record of behavior*. New York: Harper & Brothers.
Bassenge, Friedrich. 1930. Hexis und akt. Eine phanomenologische skizze. *Philosophischer Anzeiger* 4: 163–168.
Bekoff, Marc, Colin Allen, Gordon M. Burghardt, et al. 2002. *The cognitive animal: empirical and theoretical perspectives on animal cognition*. Cambridge, MA: MIT Press.
Ben-David, Shai, Pavel Hrubeš, et al. 2019. Learnability can be undecidable. *Nature Machine Intelligence* 1 (1): 44.
Berger, Peter, and Thomas Luckmann. 1966. *The social construction of reality*. New York: Anchor Books.
Bergson, Henri. 1911. *Creative evolution [1907]*. New York: Henry Holt & Co.
Bernstein, Ethan, and Umesh Vazirani. 1997. Quantum complexity theory. *SIAM Journal on Computing* 26 (5): 1411–1473.
Bertsekas, Dimitri P. 2016. *Nonlinear programming*. Belmont, MA: Athena Scientific.
Bhattacharya, Sanchita, Patrick Dunn, et al. 2018. Immport, toward repurposing of open access immunological assay data for translational and clinical research. *Scientific Data* 5: 180015.
Bickle, John. 2020. Multiple realizability. In *The Stanford encyclopedia of philosophy*, Winter 2020, https://plato.stanford.edu/entries/multiple-realizability/.
Bitterman, M. E. 2006. Classical conditioning since Pavlov. *Review of General Psychology* 10 (4): 365–376.
Bittner, Thomas, and Barry Smith. 2001. A taxonomy of granular partitions. In *Spatial information theory. Foundations of geographic information science*, edited by Daniel Montello, 28–43. Berlin: Springer.
———. 2003. A theory of granular partitions. In *Foundations of geographic information science*, edited by M. Duckham, M. F. Goodchild, and M. F. Worboys, 117–151. London: Taylor & Francis.
Block, Ned. 1978. Troubles with functionalism. In *Perception and cognition*, edited by W. Savage, 261–325. Minneapolis: University of Minnesota Press.
———. 1995. On a confusion about a function of consciousness. *Behavioral and Brain Sciences*, 18 (2): 227–247.
Boden, Margaret. 1977. *Artificial intelligence and natural man*. New York: Branch Line.
Bommasani, Rishi, Drew A. Hudson, et al. 2021. On the opportunities and risks of foundation models. *arXiv:abs/2108.07258* [cs.LG].
Boolos, G. S., J. P. Burgess, and R. C. Jeffrey. 2007. *Computability and logic*. Cambridge: Cambridge University Press.
Borghini, Andrea, and Neil E. Williams. 2008. A dispositional theory of possibility. *Dialectica* 61: 21–41.
Bostrom, Nick. 2003. *Superintelligence: paths, dangers, strategies*. London: Oxford University Press.

———. 2013. Why I want to be a posthuman when I grow up. In *The transhumanist reader*, edited by Max More and Natasha Vita-More, 28–53. Oxford: Wiley-Blackwell.

Boyd, Robert, and Peter J. Richerson. 1996. Why culture is common, but cultural evolution is rare. *Proceedings of the British Academy: Evolution of Social Behaviour Patterns in Primates and Man* 88: 77–93.

Boyle, Evan A., Yand I. Li, and Jonathan K. Pritchard. 2017. An expanded view of complex traits: from polygenic to omnigenic. *Cell* 169: 1177–1186.

Bringer, Eran, Abraham Israeli, et al. 2019. Osprey: weak supervision of imbalanced extraction problems without code. In *Proceedings of the 3rd international workshop on data management for end-to-end machine learning*, 1–11. https://doi.org/10.1145/3329486.3329492.

Bringsjord, Selmer. 2015. A refutation of Searle on Bostrom (re: malicious machines) and Floridi (re: information). *APA Newsletter on Philosophy and Computation* 15 (1): 7–9.

Brogaard, Berit. 2017. The publicity of meaning and the perceptual approach to speech comprehension. *ProtoSociology* 34: 144–162.

———. 2019. Seeing and hearing meanings: a non-inferential approach to speech comprehension. In *Inference and consciousness*, edited by Timothy Chan and Anders Nes, 99–124. London: Routledge.

Brooks, Rodney A. 1991. Intelligence without representation. *Artificial Intelligence* 47 (1–3): 139–159.

Brown, Noam, and Tuomas Sandholm. 2019. Superhuman AI for multiplayer poker. *Science* 365 (6456): 885–890.

Brown, Tom B., Benjamin Pickman Mann, et al. 2020. Language models are few-shot learners. *arXiv abs/2005.14165*.

Brundage, Miles. 2014. Limitations and risks of machine ethics. *Journal of Experimental & Theoretical Artificial Intelligence* 26 (3): 355–372.

Bühler, Karl. 1927. *Die Krise der Psychologie*. Jena: Gustav Fischer.

———. 1990. *Theory of language: the representational function of language*. Amsterdam: John Benjamins Publishing Company.

Bulgakov, Mikhail. 1967. *The master and Margarita*. New York: Grove Press.

Cabessa, Jérémie, and Hava Siegelmann. 2014. The super-Turing computational power of plastic recurrent neural networks. *International Journal of Neural Systems* 24: 1450029.

Cantwell Smith, Brian. 2019. *The promise of artificial intelligence: reckoning and judgment*. Cambridge, MA: MIT Press.

Carey, Susan, and Fei Xu. 2001. Infants' knowledge of objects: beyond object files and object tracking. *Cognition* 80: 179–213.

Cavalli-Sforza, Luigi Luca. 2000. *Genes, peoples, and languages*. New York: Farrar, Straus & Giroux.

Chaitanyaa, Lakshmi, Krystal Breslinb, et al. 2018. The HIrisPlex-S system for eye, hair and skin colour prediction from DNA: introduction and forensic developmental validation. *Forensic Science International: Genetics* 35: 125–135.

Chalmers, David J. 1996. *The conscious mind: in search of a fundamental theory*. Oxford: Oxford University Press.

———. 2010. The singularity: a philosophical analysis. *Journal of Consciousness Studies* 17: 7–65.

———. 2012. The singularity: a reply to commentators. *Journal of Consciousness Studies*: 141–167.

———. 2016. The singularity: a philosophical analysis. In *The singularity: could artificial intelligence really out-think us (and would we want it to)?*, edited by Uziel Awret, 12–88. Exeter: Imprint Academic.

Chan, Ronald Ping Man, Karl A. Stol, and C. Roger Halkyard. 2013. Review of modelling and control of two-wheeled robots. *Annual Reviews in Control* 37 (1): 89–103.

Chapman, Jeremy R., David Kasmier, et al. 2021. Conceptual Spaces For Space Event Characterization Via Hard And Soft Data Fusion. In *American Institute of Aeronautics and Astronautics (AIAA) Scitech Forum*, 11–15. https://doi.org/10.2514/6.2021-1163.

Chatterjee, Deen K. 2003. Moral distance: introduction. *The Monist*: 327–332.

Chen, Ritchie, Felicity Gore, et al. 2020. Deep brain optogenetics without intracranial surgery. *Nature Biotechnology*: 1–4.

Chollet, François. 2017. *Deep learning with Python*. Shelter Island, NY: Manning Publications Company.

Chu, Dominique, Roger Strand, and Ragnar Fjelland. 2003. Theories of complexity. *Complexity* 8 (3): 19–30.

Church, Alonzo. 1936. A note on the Entscheidungsproblem. *Journal of Symbolic Logic* 1: 40–41.

Churchland, Paul M. 1981. Eliminative materialism and the propositional attitudes. *The Journal of Philosophy* 78: 67–90.

Clark, Andy. 2013. Re-inventing ourselves: the plasticity of embodiment. In *The transhumanist reader*, edited by Max More and Natasha Vita-More, 111–127. Oxford: Wiley-Blackwell.

Clarke, Edmund M., Orna Grumberg, et al. 1999. State space reduction using partial order techniques. *International Journal on Software Tools for Technology Transfer* 2 (3): 279–287.

Cohen, Michael K., Badri N. Vellambi, and Marcus Hutter. 2019. Asymptotically unambitious artificial general intelligence. *CoRR abs/1905.12186*.

Coleman, Jonathan R. I., Julien Bryois, et al. 2019. Biological annotation of genetic loci associated with intelligence in a meta-analysis of 87,740 individuals. *Molecular Psychiatry* 24 (2): 182–197.

Conerton, Paul. 1979. *How societies remember*. New York: Cambridge University Press.

Conrad, Rolf. 1999. Contribution of hydrogen to methane production and control of hydrogen concentrations in methanogenic soils and sediments. *FEMS Microbiology Ecology* 28: 193–202.

Cosmides, Leda, and John Tooby. 2005. Neurocognitive adaptations designed for social exchange. In *Handbook of evolutionary psychology*, edited by D. M. Buss, 584–627. Hoboken, NJ: Wiley.

Cowell, Robert G., A. P. Dawid, et al. 2007. *Probabilistic networks and expert systems*. Berlin: Springer.

Crandall, Richard E. 1996. *Topics in advanced scientific computation*. Chapter on Nonlinear and Complex Systems. Berlin: Springer.

Crosby, Matthew, Benjamin Beyret, and Marta Halina. 2019. The animal-AI Olympics. *Nature Machine Intelligence* 1 (257).

Damasio, Antonio R. 1999. *The feeling of what happens: body and emotion in the making of consciousness*. Boston, MA: Houghton Mifflin Harcourt.

D'Amour, Alexander, Katherine Heller, et al. 2020. Underspecification presents challenges for credibility in modern machine learning. *arXiv, eprint: 1906.01563*.

Darwiche, Adnan. 2018. Human-level intelligence or animal-like abilities? *Communications of the ACM* 61 (10): 56–67.
Darwin, Charles. 1872. *The expression of emotions in man and animals*. London: John Murray.
Dasgupta, Sakyasingha, and Takayuki Osogami. 2017. Nonlinear dynamic Boltzmann machines for time-series prediction. In *Proceedings of the 31st AAAI Conference on Artificial Intelligence*, 1833–1839. https://ojs.aaai.org/index.php/AAAI/article/view/10806.
Davidson, Donald. 1970. Mental events. In *Experience and theory*, edited by L. Foster and J. W. Swanson, 207–224. Oxford: Clarendon Press.
———. 1987. Knowing one's own mind. *Proceedings and Addresses of the American Philosophical Association* 60: 441–458.
———. 2009. *Truth and predication*. Cambridge, MA: Harvard University Press.
Davis, Martin. 2004. The myth of hypercomputation. In *Alan Turing: life and legacy of a great thinker*, edited by Christof Teuscher, 195–211. Heidelberg: Springer.
Davis, Martin, Yuri Matijasevic, and Julia Robinson. 1976. Hilbert's tenth problem. Diophantine equations: positive aspects of a negative solution. *Proceedings of Symposia in Pure Mathematics* 28: 323–378.
Davis, Zachary. 2017. Max Scheler and pragmatism. In *Pragmatic perspectives in phenomenology*, edited by O. Švec and Jakub Čapek, 158–172. New York: Routledge.
Deamer, David. 2005. A giant step towards artificial life? *Trends in Biotechnology* 23 (7): 336–338.
De Caro, Mario. 2015. Realism, common sense, and science. *The Monist* 98 (2): 197–214.
Degenaar, Jan, and J. Kevin O'Regan. 2015. Sensorimotor theory of consciousness. *Scholarpedia* 10: 4952.
Dennett, Daniel C. 2018. Facing up to the hard question of consciousness. *Philosophical Transactions of the Royal Society B: Biological Sciences* 373.
De Soto, Hernando. 2000. *The mystery of capital: why capitalism triumphs in the West and fails everywhere else*. New York: Civitas Books.
Dignum, Virginia. 2018. Ethics in artificial intelligence: introduction to the special issue. *Ethics and Information Technology* 20 (1): 1–3.
Drace, Sasa. 2013. Evidence for the role of affect in mood congruent recall of autobiographic memories. *Motivation and Emotion* 37: 623–628.
Dreyfus, Hubert L. 1992. *What computers still can't do: a critique of artificial reason*. Cambridge, MA: MIT Press.
Dreyfus, Hubert L., Stuart E. Dreyfus, and Tom Athanasiou. 2000. *Mind over machine*. New York: Simon/Schuster.
Dubhashi, Devdatt, and Shalom Lappin. 2017. AI dangers: imagined and real. *Communications of the ACM* 60 (2): 43–45.
Eden, Amnon H., and James H. Moor, editors. 2012. *Singularity hypotheses: a scientific and philosophical assessment*. Dordrecht: Springer.
Efron, Bradley. 1979. Bootstrap methods: another look at the jackknife. *The Annals of Statistics* 7 (1): 1–26.
Einstein, Albert. 1905. Über die von der molekularkinetischen Theorie der Wärme geforderte Bewegung von in ruhenden Flüssigkeiten suspendierten Teilchen. *Annalen der Physik* 322 (8): 549–560.
Eisenstein, Elizabeth L. 1980. *The printing press as an agent of change*. Cambridge: Cambridge University Press.
Ekbia, H. R. 2008. *Artificial dreams*. Cambridge: Cambridge University Press.

Elman, Jeffrey L., Elizabeth A. Bates, et al. 1996. *Rethinking innateness: a connectionist perspective on development*. Cambridge, MA: MIT Press.

Enderton, Herbert B. 2010. *Computability theory: an introduction to recursion theory*. Cambridge, MA: Academic Press.

Eysenck, Michael W., and Christine Eysenck. 2021. *AI vs Humans*. Abingdon: Routledge.

Falkovich, Gregory. 2011. *Fluid mechanics*. Cambridge: Cambridge University Press.

Falkovich, Gregory, and Katepalli R. Sreenivasan. 2006. Lessons from hydrodynamic turbulence. *Physics Today* 59 (4): 43.

Fernández-Villaverde, Jesús. 2020. *Simple rules for a complex world with artificial intelligence*. https://economics.sas.upenn.edu/pier/working-paper/2020/simple-rules-complex-world-artificial-intelligence.

Fetzer, Anita. 2017. Context. In *The Oxford handbook of pragmatics*, edited by Yan Huang, 259–276. London: Oxford University Press.

Feynman, Richard P., Robert B. Leighton, and Matthew Sands. 2010. *The Feynman lectures on physics (1964)*. Boston, MA: Addison-Wesley.

Fieguth, Paul. 2017. Complex systems. In *An introduction to complex systems*, 245–269. Berlin: Springer.

Fjelland, Ragnar. 2020. Why general artificial intelligence will not be realized. *Humanities and Social Sciences Communications* 7 (1): 1–9.

Fodor, Jerry A. 1981. The mind-body problem. *Scientific American* 244 (1): 114–123.

Fodor, Jerry A. 2005. Reply to Steven Pinker 'So how does the mind work?' *Mind and Language* 20 (1): 25–32.

Fodor, Jerry A., and Zenon W. Pylyshyn. 1988. Connectionism and cognitive architecture: a critical analysis. *Cognition* 28 (1–2): 3–71.

Ford, Martin. 2018. *Architects of intelligence: the truth about AI from the people building it*. Birmingham: Packt Publishing Ltd.

Forguson, Lynd. 1989. *Common sense*. London: Routledge.

Forguson, Lynd, and Alison Gopnik. 1988. The ontogeny of common sense. In *Developing theories of mind*, 226–243. London and New York: Cambridge University Press.

Frankfurt, Harry G. 1958. Peirce's notion of abduction. *The Journal of Philosophy* 55 (14): 593–597.

———. 1971. Freedom of the will and the concept of a person. *Journal of Philosophy* 68 (1): 5–20.

Freitas, Robert A. 2009. Welcome to the future of medicine. In *Studies in health technology and informatics*, edited by Renata G. Bushko, 149:251–256. Amsterdam, NL: IOS Press.

Friston, Karl. 2018. Does predictive coding have a future? *Nature Neuroscience* 21 (8): 1019–1021.

Fuxjager, Matthew J., and Barney A. Schlinger. 2015. Perspectives on the evolution of animal dancing: a case study of manakins. *Current Opinion in Behavioral Sciences* 6: 7–12.

Gabriel, Iason. 2020. Artificial intelligence, values, and alignment. *Minds and Machines* 30 (3): 411–437.

Gamut, L. T. F. 1991a. *Logic, language and meaning*. Vol. 1. Chicago and London: The University of Chicago Press.

———. 1991b. *Logic, language and meaning*. Vol. 2. Chicago and London: The University of Chicago Press.

Gando, A., Y. Gando, et al. 2011. Partial radiogenic heat model for Earth revealed by geoneutrino measurements. *Nature Geoscience* 4 (9): 647.

Gao, Jianfeng, Michel Galley, and Lihong Li. 2018. Neural approaches to conversational AI. *arXiv abs/1809.08267*.
Garson, James. 2018. Connectionism. In *The Stanford encyclopedia of philosophy*, Spring 2018, https://plato.stanford.edu/entries/connectionism/.
Gavaldà, Ricard, and Hava T. Siegelmann. 1999. Discontinuities in recurrent neural networks. *Neural Computation* 11 (3): 715–745.
Gavrilets, Sergey, and Peter J. Richerson. 2017. Collective action and the evolution of social norm internalization. *Proceedings of the National Academy of Sciences* 114 (23): 6068–6073.
Gehlen, Arnold. 1988. *Man: his nature and place in the world [1940]*. New York: Columbia University Press.
———. 1993 (1940). *Der Mensch. Seine Natur und seine Stellung in der Welt*. Frankfurt am Main: Vittorio Klostermann.
Gelman, Susan A., and Henry M. Wellman. 1991. Insides and essences: early understandings of the non-obvious. *Cognition* 38 (3): 213–244.
Ghazvininejad, Marjan, Chris Brockett, et al. 2017. A knowledge-grounded neural conversation model. *arXiv abs/1702.01932*.
Gibson, James J. 1963. The useful dimensions of sensitivity. *American Psychologist* 18 (1): 1–15.
———. 1966. *The senses considered as perceptual systems*. Boston, MA: Houghton Mifflin.
———. 2015. *An ecological theory of perception (1979)*. Boston, MA: Houghton Miflin.
Gilman, Sander L., Carole Blair, and David J. Parent. 1990. *Friedrich Nietzsche on rhetoric and language*. Oxford: Oxford University Press.
Goebel, Randy, Ajay Chander, Katharina Holzinger, et al. 2018. Explainable AI: the New 42? In *Machine learning and knowledge extraction*. Lecture notes in computer science. 11015, edited by A. Holzinger, P. Kieseberg, et al., 295–303. Berlin: Springer.
Goertzel, Ben, and Cassio Pennachin, editors. 2007a. *Artificial general intelligence*. Berlin and Heidelberg: Springer-Verlag.
———. 2007b. The Novamente artificial intelligence engine. In *Artificial general intelligence*, edited by Ben Goertzel and Cassio Pennachin, 76–129. Berlin and Heidelberg: Springer-Verlag.
Gómez-Vilda, Pedro, A. R. M. Londral, et al. 2013. Characterization of speech from amyotrophic lateral sclerosis by neuromorphic processing. In *Natural and artificial models in computation and biology (IWINAC 2013)*, edited by J. M. Ferrández-Vicente, J. R. Álvarez Sánchez, et al., Berlin/Heidelberg: Springer.
Goodfellow, Ian J., Yoshua Bengio, et al. 2014. Generative adversarial networks. *arXiv abs/1406.2661*.
Goodfellow, Ian J., Yoshua Bengio, and Aaron Courville. 2016. *Deep learning*. Cambridge, MA: MIT Press.
Gopnik, Alison, and Andrew N. Meltzoff. 1997. *Words, thoughts, and theories*. Cambridge, MA: MIT Press.
Goriounova, Natalia A., and Huibert D. Mansvelder. 2019. Genes, cells and brain areas of intelligence. *Frontiers in Human Neuroscience* 13: 44.
Görlach, Manfred. 1996. And is it english? *English World-Wide* 17 (2): 153–174.
Gottfredson, Linda S. 1997. Mainstream science on intelligence. *Intelligence* 24: 13–23.
Graves, Alex, Greg Wayne, and Ivo Danihelka. 2014. Neural Turing machines. *arXiv, eprint: 1410.5401*.
Green, Patrick A., Nicholas C. Brandley, and Stephen Nowicki. 2020. Categorical perception in animal communication and decision-making. *Behavioral Ecology* 31 (4): 859–867.

Grice, H. Paul. 1957. Meaning. *The Philosophical Review* 66: 377–388.

———. 1989. Logic and conversation. In *Studies in the way of words*, 22–40. Cambridge, MA: Harvard University Press.

Gunter, Pete A. Y. 1991. Bergson and non-linear non-equilibrium thermodynamics: an application of method. *Revue Internationale de Philosophie* 45 (177): 108–121.

Haack, Susan. 2011. *Defending science–within reason: between scientism and cynicism*. Prometheus Books.

Hagendorff, Thilo. 2020. The ethics of AI ethics: an evaluation of guidelines. *Minds and Machines* 30 (1): 99–120.

Hampshire, Stuart. 1959. *Thought and action*. London: University of Notre Dame Press.

Hanks, William. 1996. Language form and communicative practices. In *Rethinking linguistic relativity*, edited by J. J. Gumpertz and S. C. Levinson. Cambridge, MA: Cambridge University Press.

Harré, Rom, and Edward H. Madden. 1975. *Causal powers: theory of natural necessity*. Oxford: Blackwell Publishers.

Hartmann, Nicolai. 2014. *Ethics (3 volumes) [1949]*. London: Routledge.

Hastie, Trevor, Robert Tibshirani, and Jerome Friedman. 2008. *The elements of statistical learning*. 2nd ed. Berlin: Springer.

Hastings, J., W. Ceusters, et al. 2011. Dispositions and processes in the Emotion Ontology. In *Proceedings of the 2nd international conference on biomedical ontology*, 71–78, http://ceur-ws.org/Vol-833/paper10.pdf.

Haugeland, John. 1985. *Artificial intelligence: the very idea*. Cambridge, MA: MIT Press.

———. 1993. Mind embodied and embedded. In *Mind and cognition: 1993 International Symposium*, edited by Yu-Houng H. Houng and J. Ho, 233–267. Taipei: Academica Sinica.

Hayek, Friedrich August von. 1937. Economics and knowledge. *Economica* 4 (13): 33–54.

———. 1945. The use of knowledge in society. *The American Economic Review* 35 (4): 519–530.

———. 1952. *The sensory order. An inquiry into the foundations of theoretical psychology*. Chicao, IL: Chicago University Press.

———. 1967. Notes on the evolution of systems of rules of conduct. *Studies in Philosophy, Politics and Economics*: 66–81.

———. 1996. *Studies in philosophy, politics and economics*. New York: Touchstone.

———. 2014a. *The market and other orders*. Edited by Bruce Caldwell. Chicago: University of Chicago Press.

———. 2014b. The pretence of knowledge. In *The market and other orders*, edited by Bruce Caldwell, 362–372. Chicago: University of Chicago Press.

Hayes, P. J. 1985. The second naive physics manifesto. In *Formal theories of the commonsense world*, edited by J. R. Hobbs and R. C. Moore. Norwood, NJ: Ablex Publishing.

Heft, Harry. 2001. *Ecological psychology in context: James Gibson, Roger Barker, and the legacy of William James's radical empiricism*. Mahwah, NJ: Lawrence Erlbaum.

———. 2017. Perceptual information of an entirely different order: the cultural environment in The senses considered as perceptual systems. *Ecological Psychology* 29: 122–145.

Heineman, George T., Gary Pollice, and Stanley Selkow. 2008. *Algorithms in a nutshell*. Sebastopol, CA: O'Reilly.

Hempel, Carl. 1969. Reduction: ontological and linguistic facets. In *Philosophy, science, and method: essays in honor of Ernest Nagel*, edited by M. White, S. Morgenbesser, and P. Suppes. New York: St Martin's Press.

Hertz, Heinrich. 1899. *The principles of mechanics presented in a new form*. London: Macmillian/Company.

Herzig, Andreas, Laurent Perrussel, et al. 2016. Refinement of intentions. In *Logics in artificial intelligence*, edited by Loizos Michael and Antonis Kakas, 558–563. Cham: Springer International Publishing. ISBN: 978-3-319-48758-8.

Hesse, Mary. 1963. *Models and analogies in science*. London: Sheed/Ward.

———. 1980. *Revolutions and reconstructions in the philosophy of science*. Brighton, Sussex: The Harvester Press.

Hibbard, Bill. 2012. Model-based utility functions. *Journal of Artificial General Intelligence* 3 (1): 1–24.

Hirschberg, Julia, and Christopher D. Manning. 2015. Advances in natural language processing. *Science* 349: 261–266.

Hobaiter, Catherine, and Richard W. Byrne. 2014. The meanings of chimpanzee gestures. *Current Biology* 24: 1596–1600.

Hochreiter, Sepp, and Jürgen Schmidhuber. 1997. Long short-term memory. *Neural Computation* 9 (8): 1735–1780.

Hohwy, Jakob. 2013. *The predictive mind*. Oxford: Oxford University Press.

Holton, Robert, and Bryan S. Turner. 2010. *Max Weber on economy and society*. London and New York: Routledge.

Horgan, John G., Max Taylor, et al. 2017. From cubs to lions: a six stage model of child socialization into the Islamic State. *Studies in Conflict & Terrorism* 40 (7): 645–664.

Hornik, Kurt. 1991. Approximation capabilities of multilayer feedforward networks. *Neural Networks* 4 (2): 251–257.

Horton, Robin. 1982. Tradition and modernity revisited. In *Rationality and relativism*, edited by Martin Hollis and Steven Lukes, 201–260. Cambridge, MA: MIT Press.

Hu, Zicheng, Alice Tang, et al. 2020. A robust and interpretable, end-to-end deep learning model for cytometry data. *Proceedings of the National Academy of Sciences* 117 (35): 21373–21380.

Huang, Yan. 2017. Implicature. In *The Oxford handbook of pragmatics*, edited by Yan Huang, 155–179. London: Oxford University Press.

Humphries, Nicolas E., Daniel W. Fuller, et al. 2010. Environmental context explains Lévy and Brownian movement patterns of marine predators. *Nature* 465 (7301): 1066–1069.

Husserl, Edmund. 1989. *The crisis of European sciences and transcendental phenomenology: an introduction to phenomenological philosophy [1936]*. Evanston, IL: Northwestern University Press.

———. 2000. *Logical Investigations [1901]*. Abingdon: Routledge.

Hutchinson, G Evelyn. 1957. *A treatise on limnology. vol 1: geography, physics and chemistry*. New York: John Wiley & Sons.

Hutchison, Clyde A., Ray-Yuan Chuang, et al. 2016. Design and synthesis of a minimal bacterial genome. *Science* 351 (6280).

Hutter, Marcus. 2012. Can intelligence explode? *Journal of Consciousness Studies* 19 (1–2): 143–166.

Hwangbo, Jemin, Joonho Lee, et al. 2019. Learning agile and dynamic motor skills for legged robots. *Science Robotics* 4 (26).

Ingarden, Roman. 1973. *The literary work of art. Investigations on the borderlines of ontology, logic and the theory of literature*. Evanston, IL: Northwestern University Press.

———. 1983. *Man and value*. Munich: Philosophia.

———. 1986. *The work of music and the problem of its identity*. Berkeley, CA: University of California Press.

———. 2013. *Controversy over the existence of the world*. Vol. I. Frankfurt a. M.: Peter Lang Edition.

———. 2019. *Controversy over the existence of the world*. Vol. II. Frankfurt a. M.: Peter Lang Edition.
Jackson, Pete. 1998. *Introduction to expert systems*. Boston, MA: Addison Wesley.
Jacob, Pierre. 2008. What do mirror neurons contribute to human social cognition? *Mind and Language* 23: 190–223.
Jaderberg, Max, Wojciech M. Czarnecki, and Iain Dunning. 2019. Human-level performance in first-person multiplayer games with population-based deep reinforcement learning. *Science* 364: 859–865.
Jeamblanc, Monique, Marc Yor, and Marc Chesney. 2009. *Mathematical methods for financial markets*. Berlin and New York: Springer.
Jelbert, Sarah A., Alex H. Taylor, et al. 2014. Using the Aesop's fable paradigm to investigate causal understanding of water displacement by New Caledonian crows. *PLoS ONE* 9 (3): e92895.
Jensen, Arthur R. 1998. *The g factor: the science of mental ability*. Westport, CT: Green- wood.
Jo, Jason, and Yoshua Bengio. 2017. Measuring the tendency of CNNs to learn surface statistical regularities. *arXiv abs/1711.11561*.
Johansson, Ingvar. 1998. Pattern as an ontological category. In *Formal ontology in information systems*, edited by N. Guarino, 86–94. Amsterdam, NL: IOS Press.
———. 2012. *Ontological investigations*. Frankfurt am Main: de Gruyter.
Jumper, John, Richard Evans, et al. 2020. High accuracy protein structure prediction using deep learning. In *Critical assessment of techniques for protein structure prediction (CASP-14)*, edited by John Moult, 22. https://predictioncenter.org/casp14/.
Kandel, Eric, John D. Koester, et al. 2021. *Principles of neural science*. New York: McGraw Hill.
Kant, Immanuel. 1991. *The metaphysics of morals (part 1): the philosophy of law–an exposition of the fundamental principles of jurisprudence as the science of right (1797)*. Cambridge: Cambridge University Press.
———. 1998. *Groundwork of the metaphysics of morals [1795]*. Cambridge: Cambridge University Press.
———. 2000. *Critique of the power of judgment*. The Cambridge Edition of the Works of Immanuel Kant. Cambridge: Cambridge University Press.
Karras, Tero, Samuli Laine, and Timo Aila. 2018. A style-based generator architecture for Generative Adversarial Networks. *arXiv abs/1812.04948*.
Karray, Mohamed, Neil Otte, et al. 2021. The Industrial Ontologies Foundry (IOF) perspectives. *International conference on interoperability for enterprise systems and applications*. Tarbes, France: IOF–Achieving Data Interoperability Workshop.
Katzen, Abraham, Hui-Kuan Chung, et al. 2021. The nematode worm C. elegans chooses between bacterial foods exactly as if maximizing economic utility. *bioRxiv, 2021.04.25.441352*.
Keil, Frank C. 1989. *Concepts, kinds and cognitive development*. Cambridge, MA: MIT Press.
———. 1994. Explanation, association, and the acquisition of word meaning. *Lingua* 92 (1–4): 169–196.
Kempes, Christopher P., Geoffrey B. West, and Mimi Koehl. 2019. The scales that limit: the physical boundaries of evolution. *Frontiers in Ecology and Evolution* 7: 242.
Kim, In-Kyeong, and Elizabeth S. Spelke. 1999. Perception and understanding of effects of gravity and inertia on object motion. *Developmental Science* 2 (3): 339–362.
Kim, Jaegwon. 1984. Concepts of supervenience. *Philosophy and Phenomenological Research* 45 (2): 153–176.
King, Julia, Michele Insanally, et al. 2015. Rodent auditory perception: critical band limitations and plasticity. *Neuroscience* 296: 55–65.

Klenke, Achim. 2013. *Probability theory: a comprehensive course*. 2nd ed. New York and Berlin: Springer.
Kogo, Naoki, and Raymond van Ee. 2014. *Neural mechanisms of figure-ground organization: border-ownership, competition and perceptual switching*, 352–372. Oxford: Oxford Handbook of Perceptual Organization.
Kolmogorov, A. N. 1941a. Dissipation of energy in the locally isotropic turbulence. *Doklady Akademii Nauk SSSR* 31: 538–540.
———. 1941b. The local structure of turbulence in incompressible viscous fluid for very large Reynolds numbers. *Doklady Akademii Nauk SSSR* 30: 301–305.
Kross, E., A. Duckworth, et al. 2011. The effect of self-distancing on adaptive versus maladaptive self-reflection in children. *Emotion* 11: 1032–1039.
Kurzweil, Ray. 2005. *The singularity is near*. New York: Viking Press.
Kwiatkowski, Tom, Jennimaria Palomaki, et al. 2019. Natural questions: a benchmark for question answering research. *Transactions of the Association for Computational Linguistics* 7: 453–466.
Ladyman, James, James Lambert, and Karoline Wiesner. 2013. What is a complex system? *European Journal for Philosophy of Science* 3 (1): 33–67.
Ladyman, James, Stuart Presnell, et al. 2007. The connection between logical and thermodynamic irreversibility. *Studies in History and Philosophy of Science* 38 (1): 58–79.
Lai, Guokun, Wei-Cheng Chang, et al. 2017. Modeling long- and short-term temporal patterns with Deep Neural Networks. *arXiv abs/1703.07015*.
La Mettrie, Julien Offray de. 1748. *L'homme machine*. Leiden: Elie Luzac.
Landauer, Rolf. 1961. Irreversibility and heat generation in the computing process. *IBM Journal of Research and Development* 5 (3): 183–191.
Landgrebe, Jobst. 2022. Certifiable AI. *Applied Science* 12 (3): 1050. https://doi.org/10.3390/app12031050.
Landgrebe, Jobst, and Barry Smith. 2021. Making AI meaningful again. *Synthese* 198: 2061–2081. https://doi.org/10.1007/s11229-019-02192-y.
La Porta, A., G. A. Voth, et al. 2001. Fluid particle accelerations in fully developed turbulence. *Nature* 409: 1017–1019.
Lapuschkin, Sebastian, Stephan Wäldchen, et al. 2019. Unmasking clever Hans predictors and assessing what machines really learn. *Nature Communications* 10 (1): 1–8.
Larsen, Rasmus Rosenberg. 2020. Psychopathy as moral blindness: a qualifying exploration of the blindness-analogy in psychopathy theory and research. *Philosophical Explorations* 23 (3): 214–233.
Larson, Erik J. 2021. *The myth of artificial intelligence: why computers can't think the way we do*. Cambridge, MA: Harvard University Press.
Latrémouille, Christian, Alain Carpentier, et al. 2018. A bioprosthetic total artificial heart for end-stage heart failure: results from a pilot study. *The Journal of Heart and Lung Transplantation* 37 (1): 33–37.
Lau, Ellen F., Colin Phillips, and David Poeppel. 2008. A cortical network for semantics: (de)constructing the n400. *Nature Reviews Neuroscience* 9: 920–933.
LeCun, Yann. 2015. *Facebook AI director Yann Lecun on his quest to unleash deep learning and make machines smarter*. https://spectrum.ieee.org/automaton/artificial-intelligence/machine-learning/facebook-ai-director-yann-lecun-on-deep-learning..
Leff, Harvey, and Andrew F. Rex. 2002. *Maxwell's demon 2–entropy, classical and quantum information, computing*. London: IOP Publishing.
Legg, Shane, and Marcus Hutter. 2007. Universal intelligence: a definition of machine intelligence. *Minds and Machines* 17: 391–444.

Leike, Jan, David Krueger, et al. 2018. Scalable agent alignment via reward modeling: a research direction. *arXiv abs/1811.07871*.
Lepore, Ernie, and Matthew Stone. 2018. Pejorative tone. In *Bad words: philosophical perspectives on slurs*, edited by David Sosa, 134–153. Oxford: Oxford University Press.
Levesque, Henri J. 2014. On our best behaviour. *Artificial Intelligence* 213: 27–35.
Levinson, Stephen C. 1983. Deixis in pragmatics. In *Pragmatics*, 54–96. Cambridge, MA: Cambridge University Press.
Lewis, David. 1979. Scorekeeping in a language game. In *Semantics from different points of view*, 172–187. Berlin: Springer.
Li, Bian, Michaela Fooksa, et al. 2018. Finding the needle in the haystack: towards solving the protein-folding problem computationally. *Critical Reviews in Biochemistry and Molecular Biology* 53: 1–28.
Li, Jiwei, Will Monroe, et al. 2016. Deep reinforcement learning for dialogue generation. *CoRR abs/1606.01541*.
Li, Michael. 2018. *An introduction to mathematical modeling of infectious diseases*. Berlin: Springer.
Li, Zongyi, Nikola Kovachki, et al. 2020. Fourier neural operator for parametric partial differential equations. *arXiv, eprint: 2010.08895*.
Lin, Stephanie, Jacob Hilton, and Owain Evans. 2021. TruthfulQA: measuring how models mimic human falsehoods. *arXiv: 2109.07958*.
Loebner, Sebastian. 2013. *Understanding semantics*. New York: Routledge.
Lorini, Giuseppe. 2018. Animal norms: an investigation of normativity in the non-human social world. *Law, Culture and the Humanities*. Los Angeles: SAGE Publications, https://doi.org/10.1177/1743872118800008.
Lotze, Hermann. 1841. *Metaphysik*. Leipzig: Weidmann'sche Buchhandlung.
Lovelace, Ada, and Luigi Menabrea. 1843. Sketch of the Analytical Engine invented by Charles Babbage esq. In *Scientific memoirs. Selected from the Transactions of Foreign Academies of Science and Learned Societies and from Foreign Journals, 3*, edited by Richard Taylor. London, 666–690.
Lowe, E. Jonathan. 2005. How are ordinary objects possible? *The Monist* 88 (4): 510–533.
Lucas, John R. 1961. Minds, machines and Gödel. *Philosophy*: 112–127.
———. 2003. The Gödelian argument: turn over the page. *Etica e Politica* 5 (1): 1.
Lucas, Peter, and Linda Van Der Gaag. 1991. *Principles of expert systems*. Wokingham: Addison-Wesley.
Luo, Huaishao, Lei Ji, et al. 2020a. UniVL: a unified video and language pre-training model for multimodal understanding and generation. *arXiv: 2002.06353*.
Luo, Yuan, Alal Eran, et al. 2020b. A multidimensional precision medicine approach identifies an autism subtype characterized by dyslipidemia. *Nature Medicine* 26 (9): 1375–1379.
Lyons, John. 1977. Deixis, space and time. In *Semantics*, 636–724. Cambridge: Cambridge University Press.
Mackie, John L. 1977. *Inventing right and wrong*. London: Penguin.
Maier, John. 2020. Abilities. In *The Stanford encyclopedia of philosophy*, Winter 2020, https://plato.stanford.edu/entries/abilities/.
Manning, Christopher D., and Hinrich Schütze. 1999. *Foundations of statistical natural language processing*. Cambridge, MA: MIT Press.
Manolio, Teri A., Francis S. Collins, et al. 2009. Finding the missing heritability of complex diseases. *Nature* 461: 747–753.
Marcus, Gary. 2018. Deep learning: a critical appraisal. *arXiv 1801.00631*.
Marcus, Gary, and Ernest Davis. 2019. *Rebooting AI: building artificial intelligence we can trust*. New York: Vintage.

———. 2020. *GPT-3, Bloviator: openAI's language generator has no idea what it's talking about.* https://www.technologyreview.com/2020/08/22/1007539/gpt3-openai-language-generator-artificial-intelligence-ai-opinion/.

———. 2021. Has AI found a new foundation? *The Gradient.* https://thegradient.pub/has-ai-found-a-new-foundation.

Margolin, Emmanuel A., Richard Strasser, et al. 2020. Engineering the plant secretory pathway for the production of next-generation pharmaceuticals. *Trends in Biotechnology* 28: 1034–1044.

Marshak, Alexander, and Anthony Davis. 2005. *3D radiative transfer in cloudy atmospheres.* Berlin: Springer.

Mathew, Sarah, and Robert Boyd. 2011. Punishment sustains large-scale cooperation in prestate warfare. *PNAS* 108 (28): 11375–11380.

Matthiessen, Christian M., and Abhishek K. Kashyap. 2014. The construal of space in different registers: an exploratory study. *Language Sciences* 45: 1–27.

McCann, Bryan, James Bradbury, et al. 2017. Learned in translation: contextualized word vectors. *arXiv abs/1708.00107.*

McCauley, Joseph L. 1993. *Chaos, dynamics, and fractals: an algorithmic approach to deterministic chaos.* Cambridge: Cambridge University Press.

———. 2009. *Dynamics of markets: the new financial economics.* 2nd ed. Cambridge: Cambridge University Press.

McCulloch, Warren S., and Walter Pitts. 1943. A logical calculus of the ideas immanent in nervous activity. *The Bulletin of Mathematical Biophysics* 5 (4): 115–133.

McDermott, Drew. 1976. Artificial intelligence meets natural stupidity. *ACM Sigart Bulletin,* 57: 4–9.

McFadden, Daniel. 1963. Constant elasticity of substitution production functions. *The Review of Economic Studies* 30 (2): 73–83.

McLaughlin, Brian, and Karen Bennett. 2018. Supervenience. In *The Stanford encyclopedia of philosophy,* Winter 2018, https://plato.stanford.edu/entries/supervenience/.

McShane, Marjorie, and Sergei Nirenburg. 2021. *Linguistics for the age of AI.* Cambridge, MA: MIT Press.

Medin, Doug, and Brian H. Ross. January 1989. The specific character of abstract thought: categorization, problem solving, and induction. *Advances in the Psychology of Human Intelligence* 5: 189–223.

Meibauer, Jörg. 2001. *Pragmatik.* Tübingen: Stauffenburg.

Merkle, Ralph C. 2013. Uploading. In *The transhumanist reader,* edited by Max More and Natasha Vita-More, 157–164. Oxford: Wiley-Blackwell.

Merleau-Ponty, Maurice. 2012. *Phenomenology of perception [1945].* London: Routledge.

Merrell, Eric, David Limbaugh, et al. 2021. *Capabilities.* https://philpapers.org/rec/MERC-14.

Milkowski, Marcin. 2013. *Explaining the computational mind.* Cambridge, MA: MIT Press.

Mill, John S. 1863. *Utilitarianism.* London: Parker, Son/Bourn.

Millikan, Ruth Garrett. 2018. Biosemantics and words that don't represent. *Theoria* 84 (3): 229–241.

Mills, John A. 2012. Behaviorism. In *Encyclopedia of the history of psychological theories,* edited by Robert W. Rieber, 98–110. New York: Springer.

Milton, Katharine. 2000. Quo vadis? Tactics of food search and group movement in pri- mates and other animals. In *On the move: how and why animals travel in groups,* edited by Sue Boinski and Paul A. Graber, 375–418. Chicago: Chicago University Press.

Min, Erxue, Xifeng Guo, et al. 2018. A survey of clustering with deep learning: from the perspective of network architecture. *IEEE Access* 6: 39501–39514.

Minsky, Marvin L. 1991. Logical versus analogical or symbolic versus connectionist or neat versus scruffy. *AI Magazine* 12 (2): 34–34.

Mises, Ludwig von. 1936. *Socialism: an economic and sociological analysis*. London: Jonathan Cape.

Mitchell, Melanie. 2009. *Complexity: a guided tour*. Oxford: Oxford University Press.

Moor, James. August 2006. The nature, importance, and difficulty of machine ethics. *IEEE Intelligent Systems* 21: 18–21.

———. 2009. Four kinds of ethical robots. *Philosophy Now* 72.

Moortgat, Michael. 1997. Categorial type logics. In *Handbook of logic and language*, edited by J. van Benthem and A. ter Meulen. London: Elsevier.

Moosavi-Dezfooli, Seyed-Mohsen, Alhussein Fawzi, et al. 2016. Universal adversarial perturbations. *CoRR abs/1610.08401*.

Mora, Peter T. 1963. Urge and molecular biology. *Nature (Berlin)* 199 (4890): 212–219.

Morgenstern, Martin. 1997. *Nicolai Hartmann zur Einführung*. Hamburg: Junius-Verlag.

Mouritsen, Henrik, Dominik Heyers, and Onur Güntürkün. 2016. The neural basis of long-distance navigation in birds. *Annual Review of Physiology* 78: 133–154.

Muehlhauser, Luke. 2013. What is AGI? https://intelligence.org/2013/08/11/what-isagi/.

Muehlhauser, Luke, and Louie Helm. 2012a. The singularity and machine ethics. In *Singularity hypotheses: a scientific and philosophical assessment*, edited by Amnon H. Eden and James H. Moor, 101–125. Dordrecht: Springer.

Muehlhauser, Luke, and Anna Salamon. 2012b. Intelligence explosion: evidence and import. In *Singularity hypotheses: a scientific and philosophical assessment*, edited by Amnon H. Eden and James H. Moor, 15–40. Dordrecht: Springer.

Müller, Stefan. 2016. *Grammatical theory: from transformational grammar to constraint-based approaches*. Berlin: Language Science Press.

Mulligan, Kevin. 1987. Promisings and other social acts: their constituents and structure. In *Speech act and Sachverhalt. Reinach and the foundations of realist phenomenology*, edited by Kevin Mulligan. New York: Springer.

———. 1995. Perception. In *The Cambridge companion to Husserl*, edited by David Woodruff Smith and Barry Smith. Cambridge: Cambridge University Press.

———. 1998. From appropriate emotions to values. *The Monist* 81 (1): 161–188.

———. 2018. How to marry phenomenology and pragmatism. Scheler's proposal. In *Pragmatism and the European traditions*, edited by Maria Baghramian and Sarin Marchetti, 37–64. London: Routledge.

Mulligan, Kevin, Peter Simons, and Barry Smith. 2006. What's wrong with contemporary philosophy? *Topoi* 25 (1–2): 63–67.

Nagel, Thomas. 1975. What is it like to be a bat? *The Philosophical Review* 83 (4): 435–450.

Nandakumaran, A. K., and P. S. Datti. 2020. *Partial differential equations: classical theory with a modern touch*. Cambridge, MA: Cambridge University Press.

Neil, Daniel, Michael Pfeiffer, and Shih-Chii Liu. 2016. Phased LSTM: accelerating recurrent network training for long or event-based sequences. *arXiv abs/1610.09513*.

Newell, Allen, and Herbert A. Simon. 1976. Computer science as empirical inquiry: symbols and search. *Communications of the ACM* 19 (3): 113–126.

Newman, Mark E. J. 2005. Power laws, Pareto distributions and Zipf's law. *Contemporary Physics* 46 (5): 323–351.

Nielsen, Michael, and Isaac Chuang. 2010. *Quantum computation and quantum information*. New York: Cambridge University Press.

Nienhuys-Cheng, Shan-Hwei, and Ronald de Wolf. 2008. *Foundations of inductive logic programming*. Berlin: Springer.

Nietzsche, Friedrich. 1980. Über Wahrheit und Lüge im aussermoralischen Sinne. In *Friedrich Nietzsche: sämtliche Werke*, edited by Giorgio Colli and Mazzino Montinari. Vol. 1. Berlin: de Gruyter.

Nozick, Robert. 1985. Interpersonal utility theory. *Social Choice and Welfare (Berlin)* 3 (2): 161–179.

Nyíri, Kristóf. 2014. Image and time in the theory of gestures. In *Meaning and motoricity: essays on image and time*. Frankfurt a. M.: Peter Lang.

Oare, Steve. June 17, 2018. Practical brass physics to improve your teaching and playing. *Kansas Music Review*.

Ochando, Jordi, Farideh Ordikhani, et al. 2020. Tolerogenic dendritic cells in organ transplantation. *Transplant International* 33 (2): 113–127.

O'Regan, J. Kevin, and Alva Noë. 2001. A sensorimotor account of vision and visual consciousness. *Behavioral and Brain Sciences* 24: 939–1031.

O'Shaughnessy, Brian. 1980. *The will: a dual aspect theory*. 2 vols. Cambridge: Cambridge University Press.

Osoba, Osonde A., Benjamin Boudreaux, and Douglas Yeung. 2020. Steps towards value-aligned systems. In *Proceedings of the AAAI/ACM conference on AI, ethics, and society*, 332–336, https://dl.acm.org/doi/10.1145/3375627.3375872.

Ouimet, Kirk. 2020. *The universe function*. https://kirkouimet.medium.com/the-universe-function-92012c0c67c5.

Parsons, Talcott. 1949. *The structure of social action [1937]*. New York: Free Press.

———. 1951. *The social system*. London: Routledge.

———. 1968. Social interaction. In *International encyclopedia of the social sciences*, edited by David L. Sills, 429–440. New York: Macmillan.

———. 1971. *The system of modern societies*. Englewood Cliffs, NJ: Prentice-Hall.

Parzen, Emanuel. 2015. *Stochastic processes*. Mineola, NY: Courier Dover Publications.

Pautz, Adam, and Daniel Stoljar, editors. 2019. Poise, dispositions, and access consciousness: reply to Daniel Stoljar. In *Blockheads! Essays on Ned Block's philosophy of mind and consciousness*, 537–544. New York: MIT Press.

Pavone, Arianna, and Alessio Plebe. 2021. How neurons in deep models relate with neurons in the brain. *Algorithms* 14 (9): 272.

Pearl, Judea. 2020. The limitations of opaque learning machines. In *Possible minds: twenty-five ways of looking at AI*, edited by John Brockman, 13–19. New York: Penguin Books.

Pearl, Leavitt J. 2018. Popitz's imaginative variation on power as model for critical phenomenology. *Human Studies* 41 (3): 475–483.

Peirce, Charles Sanders. 1935. Some amazing mazes. In *Collected papers of Charles Sanders Peirce*, edited by Charles Hartshorne and Paul Weiss. Cambridge, MA: Harvard University Press.

Pennachin, Cassio, and Ben Goertzel. 2007. Contemporary approaches to artificial general intelligence. In *Artificial general intelligence*, edited by Ben Goertzel and Cassio Pennachin, 1–30. Berlin and Heidelberg: Springer-Verlag.

Penrose, Roger. 1994a. Mathematical intelligence. In *What is intelligence?*, edited by Jean Khalfa, 107–136. Cambridge: Cambridge University Press.

———. 1994b. *Shadows of the mind*. Oxford: Oxford University Press.

Percival, Steven L., Sladjana Malic, et al. 2011. Introduction to biofilms. In *Biofilms and veterinary medicine*, 41–68. Berlin: Springer.

Perko, Lawrence. 2013. *Differential equations and dynamical systems*. 3rd ed. Berlin: Springer.

Petitot, Jean, and Barry Smith. 1990. New foundations for qualitative physics. In *Evolving knowledge in natural science and artificial intelligence*, edited by J. E. Tiles, G. T. McKee, and C. G. Dean, 231–249. London: Pitman Publishing.

Piccinini, Gualtiero. 2003. Alan Turing and the mathematical objection. *Minds and Machines* 13: 23–48.

———. 2015. *Physical computation: a mechanistic account*. Oxford: Oxford University Press.

———. 2017. Computation in physical systems. In *Stanford encyclopedia of philosophy*, Summer 2017 Edition, Edward N. Zalta (ed.), https://plato.stanford.edu/archives/sum2017/entries/computation-physicalsystems/.

Pierson, Hugh O. 2012. *Handbook of carbon, graphite, diamonds and fullerenes: processing, properties and applications*. Norwich, NY: William Andrew.

Pinker, Steven. 2020. Tech prophecy and the underappreciated causal power of ideas. In *Possible minds: twenty-five ways of looking at AI*, edited by John Brockman. New York: Penguin Books.

Popitz, Heinrich. 2017a. *Phenomena of power*. New York: Columbia University Press.

———. 2017b. Social norms. *Genocide Studies and Prevention: An International Journal* 11: 3–12.

Prigogine, Ilya. 1955. *Introduction to thermodynamics of irreversible processes*. New York: Interscience Publishers.

Prigogine, Ilya, and René Lefever. 1973. Theory of dissipative structures. In *Synergetics*, edited by H. Haken, 124–135. Wiesbaden: Vieweg+Teubner Verlag.

Purcell, Edward M. 1977. Life at low Reynolds number. *American Journal of Physics* 45: 3–11.

Putnam, Hillary. 1975. The meaning of "meaning". *Minnesota Studies in the Philosophy of Science* 7: 131–193.

Quine, Willard Van Orman. 1969. Ontological relativity. In *Ontological relativity and other essays*, 26–68. New York: Columbia University Press.

Rabinowitz, Neil C., Frank Perbet, et al. 2018. Machine theory of mind. *CoRR abs/1802.07740*.

Radford, Alec, Jeffrey Wu, et al. 2018. Language models are unsupervised multitask learners. *Technical report*. https://paperswithcode.com/paper/language-models-are-unsupervised-multitask.

Rajpurkar, Pranav, Jian Zhang, et al. November 2016. SQuAD: 100,000+ questions for machine comprehension of text. In *Proceedings of the 2016 conference on empirical methods in natural language processing*, 2383–2392. Austin, TX: Association for Computational Linguistics.

Ramesh, Aditya, Mikhail Pavlov, et al. 2021. Zero-shot text-to-image generation. *arXiv: 2102.12092*.

Ramsey, Frank Plumpton. 1931. *The foundations of mathematics and other logical essays*. London: K. Paul, Trench, Trubner & Company, Limited.

Ramsey, William. 2019. Eliminative materialism. In *Stanford encyclopedia of philosophy*, https://plato.stanford.edu/entries/materialism-eliminative/.

Rao, Rajesh P. N., and Dana H. Ballard. 1999. Predictive coding in the visual cortex: a functional interpretation of some extra-classical receptive-field effects. *Nature Neuroscience* 2 (1): 79–87.

Reich, Wendelin. 2010. Three problems of intersubjectivity—and one solution. *Sociological Theory* 28 (1): 40–63.

Reinach, Adolf. 1969. Concerning phenomenology. *The Personalist* 50 (2): 194–221.

———. 1989. *Sämtliche Werke: textkritische Ausgabe in 2 Bänden*. Edited by Karl Schuhmann and Barry Smith. Munich: Philosophia.

———. 2012. *The a priori foundations of the civil law [1913]*. Edited by John F. Crosby. Frankfurt am Main: ontos Verlag.
Rescorla, Michael. 2020. The computational theory of mind. In *The Stanford encyclopedia of philosophy*, Winter 2020, https://plato.stanford.edu/entries/computational-mind/.
Richerson, Peter, and Robert Boyd. 2005. *Not by genes alone: how culture transformed human evolution*. Chicago, IL: Chicago University Press.
Roberts, David, Drake Morgan, and Yu Liu. 2007. How to make a rat addicted to cocaine. *Progress in Neuro-Psychopharmacology and Biological Psychiatry* 31: 1614–1624.
Roberts, Larry S., John Janovy, and Steve Nadler. 2013. *Foundations of parasitology*. New York: McGraw-Hill.
Robinson, A., and A. Voronkov. 2001. *Handbook of automated reasoning*. Cambridge, MA: Elsevier Science.
Robinson, William. 2019. Epiphenomenalism. In *Stanford encyclopedia of philosophy*, https://stanford.library.sydney.edu.au/entries/epiphenomenalism/.
Rojas, Raúl. 1997. Konrad Zuse's legacy: the architecture of the Z1 and Z3. *IEEE Annals of the History of Computing* 19 (2): 5–16.
Rosch, Eleanor. 1975. Cognitive representation of semantic categories. *Journal of Experimental Psychology* 104: 192–233.
Rose, Michael C. 2013. Immortalist fictions and strategies. In *The transhumanist reader*, edited by Max More and Natasha Vita-More, 196–204. Oxford: Wiley-Blackwell.
Rothblatt, Martine. 2013. Mind is deeper than matter. In *The transhumanist reader*, edited by Max More and Natasha Vita-More, 317–326. Oxford: Wiley-Blackwell.
Rothschild, Daniel, and Seth Yalcin. 2017. On the dynamics of conversation. *Noûs* 51 (1): 24–48.
Russell, Bertrand. 1938. *Power: a new social analysis*. New York: Routledge.
Sacks, Harvey, Emanuel Schegloff, and Gail Jefferson. 1974. A simplest systematics for the organization of turn-taking for conversation. *Language* 50: 696–735.
Sandberg, Anders. 2013. Feasibility of whole brain emulation. In *Theory and philosophy of artificial intelligence*, edited by Vincent C. Müller, 251–264. Berlin: Springer.
Schaeffer, Jonathan, Neil Burch, et al. 2007. Checkers is solved. *Science* 317 (5844): 1518–1522.
Schaffer, Jonathan. 2015. What not to multiply without necessity. *Australasian Journal of Philosophy* 93 (4): 644–664.
———. 2021. Ground functionalism. In *Oxford Studies in the Philosophy of Mind*, 171–207. Oxford: Oxford University Press.
Schegloff, Emanuel. 2000. Overlapping talk and the organization of turn-taking for conversation. *Language in Society* 29 (1): 1–63.
———. 2017. Conversation analysis. In *The Oxford handbook of pragmatics*, edited by Yan Huang, 435–449. London: Oxford University Press.
Scheler, Max. 1961. *Man's place in nature*. New York: The Noonday Press.
———. 1973. *Formalism in ethics and non-formal ethics of values*. Evanston: Northwestern University Press.
———. 2008. *The nature of sympathy*. Piscataway, NJ: Transaction Publishers.
Schlossberger, Matthias. 2016. The varieties of togetherness: Scheler on collective affective intentionality. In *The phenomenological approach to social reality. History, concepts, problems*, edited by Alessandro Salice and Hans B. Schmid, 173–195. Berlin: Springer.
Schmidhuber, Jürgen. 1990. Making the world differentiable: on using self-supervised fully recurrent neural networks for dynamic reinforcement learning and planning in non-stationary environments. *Technical report*. TU Munich.

———. 2007. Gödel machines: fully self-referential optimal universal self-improvers. In *Artificial general intelligence*, edited by Ben Goertzel and Cassio Pennachin, 199–226. Berlin and Heidelberg: Springer-Verlag.

———. 2012. Philosophers and futurists, catch up. *Journal of Consciousness Studies* 19 (1–2): 173–182.

Schmidt, Karen L., and Jeffrey Cohn. 2001. Human facial expressions as adaptations: evolutionary questions in facial expression research. *American Journal of Physical Anthropology* Suppl 33: 3–24.

Schoggen, Phil. 1989. *Behavior settings: a revision and extension of Roger G. Barker's ecological psychology*. Standford, CA: Stanford University Press.

Schopenhauer, Artur. 1986. *Die Welt als Wille und Vorstellung*. Frankfurt am Main: Suhrkamp.

Schuhmann, Karl, and Barry Smith. 1987. Questions: an essay in Daubertian phenomenology. *Philosophy and Phenomenological Research* 47: 353–384.

———. 1990. Elements of speech act theory in the work of Thomas Reid. *History of Philosophy Quarterly* 7: 47–66.

Schuster, Heinz G., and Wolfram Just. 2005. *Deterministic chaos*. 4th ed. New York: Wiley VCH.

Schwab, Klaus. 2017. *The fourth industrial revolution*. New York: Penguin Books.

Searle, John R. 1969. *Speech acts. An essay in the philosophy of language*. Cambridge, MA: Cambridge University Press.

———. 1975. A taxonomy of illocutionary acts. In *Language, mind and knowledge*, edited by K. Gunderson, 344–369. Minneapolis: University of Minnesota Press.

———. 1978. Literal meaning. *Erkenntnis* 13 (1): 207–228.

———. 1980. Minds, brains, and programs. *Behavioral and Brain Sciences* 3: 417–457.

———. 1983. *Intentionality: an essay in the philosophy of mind*. Cambridge, MA: Cambridge University Press.

———. 1990. Collective intentions and actions. In *Intentions in communication*, edited by Philip R. Cohen, Jerry Morgan, and Martha Pollack, 401–415. Cambridge, MA: MIT Press.

———. 1992. *The rediscovery of the mind*. Cambridge, MA: MIT Press.

———. 1995. *The construction of social reality*. New York: Simon/Schuster.

———. 1998. How to study consciousness scientifically. *Brain Research Reviews* 26: 379–387.

———. 2002. Why I am not a property dualist. *Journal of Consciousness Studies* 9 (12): 57–64.

———. October 2014. What your computer can't know. *New York Review of Books*.

Seirin-Lee, Sungrim, T. Sukekawa, et al. 2020. Transitions to slow or fast diffusions provide a general property for in-phase or anti-phase polarity in a cell. *Journal of Mathematical Biology* 80 (6): 1885.

Sellars, Wilfrid. 1963. Philosophy and the scientific image of man. In *Science, perception and reality*, 1–40. New York: Humanities Press.

Shapiro, Scott J. 2014. Massively shared agency. In *Rational and social agency: the philosophy of Michael Bratman*, 257–293. Oxford: Oxford University Press.

Sidnell, J., and N. J. Enfield. 2017. Deixis and the interactional foundations of reference. In *The Oxford handbook of pragmatics*, edited by Yan Huang, 217–239. London: Oxford University Press.

Siegelmann, Hava T., and Eduardo D. Sontag. 1994. Analog computation via neural networks. *Theoretical Computer Science* 131: 331–360.

Silberstein, Michael, and Anthony Chemero. 2012. Complexity and extended phenomenological-cognitive systems. *Topics in Cognitive Science* 4 (1): 35–50.

Silver, David, Demis Hassabis, et al. 2016. Mastering the game of Go with deep neural networks and tree search. *Nature* 529 (7587): 484–489.

Silver, David, Thomas Hubert, et al. 2018. A general reinforcement learning algorithm that masters chess, shogi, and Go through self-play. *Science* 362 (6419): 1140–1144.

Smaili, Fatima Zohra, Xin Gao, and Robert Hoehndorf. 2019. Formal axioms in biomedical ontologies improve analysis and interpretation of associated data. *Bioinformatics* 36 (7): 2229–2236.

Smith, Adam. 1790. *Theory of moral sentiments, or an essay towards an analysis of the principles by which men naturally judge concerning the conduct and character.* 6th ed. The Strand, London: A. Strahan/T. Cadell.

Smith, Barry. 1990. Towards a history of speech act theory. In *Speech acts, meanings and intentions. Critical approaches to the philosophy of John R. Searle*, edited by A. Burkhardt, 29–61. Berlin: de Gruyter.

———. 1992. An essay on material necessity. *Canadian Journal of Philosophy*: 301–322.

———. 1994. Fiat objects. In *Parts and wholes: conceptual part-whole relations and formal mereology, 11th European conference on artificial intelligence*, edited by Nicola Guarino, Laure Vieu, and Simone Pribbenow, 14–22. Amsterdam: European Coordinating Committee for Artificial Intelligence.

———. 1995. Formal ontology, common sense, and cognitive science. *International Journal of Human-Computer Studies* 43 (5–6): 641–667.

———. 1997. Realistic phenomenology. In *Encyclopedia of phenomenology*, edited by Lester Embree, 586–590. Dordrecht/Boston/London: Kluwer Academic Publishers.

———. 1999. Truth and the visual field. In *Naturalizing phenomenology: issues in contemporary phenomenology and cognitive science*, edited by Jean Petitot, F. J. Varela, et al., 317–329. Stanford: Stanford University Press.

———. 2000. Objects and their environments: from Aristotle to ecological ontology. In *Life and motion of socio-economic units*, 84–102. London/New York: Taylor and Francis.

———. 2003. John Searle: from speech acts to social reality. In *John Searle*, edited by Barry Smith, 1–33. Cambridge: Cambridge University Press.

———. 2005. Against fantology. In *Experience and analysis*, edited by J. Marek and E. M. Reicher, 153–170. Vienna: ÖBV & HPT Verlag.

———. 2008. Searle and de Soto: the new ontology of the social world. In *The mystery of capital and the construction of social reality*, edited by Barry Smith, David Mark, and Isaac Ehrlich, 35–51. Chicago: Open Court.

———. 2013. Diagrams, documents, and the meshing of plans. In *How to do things with pictures: skill, practice, performance*, edited by András Benedek and Kristóf Nyíri, 165–179. Frankfurt a. M.: Peter Lang.

———. 2021. Making space: the natural, cultural, cognitive and social niches of human activity. *Cognitive Processing* 22 (1): 77–87.

Smith, Barry, Michael Ashburner, et al. 2007. The OBO foundry: coordinated evolution of ontologies to support biomedical data integration. *Nature Biotechnology* 25 (11): 1251–1255.

Smith, Barry, and Berit Brogaard. 2000. A unified theory of truth and reference. *Logique et Analyse*: 169/170, 49–93.

———. 2002. Quantum mereotopology. *Annals of Mathematics and Artificial Intelligence* 36 (1): 153–175.

Smith, Barry, and Roberto Casati. 1994. Naive physics: an essay in ontology. *Philosophical Psychology* 7 (2): 227–247.

Smith, Barry, and Werner Ceusters. 2010. Ontological realism: a methodology for coordinated evolution of scientific ontologies. *Applied Ontology* 5 (3–4): 139–188.

Smith, Barry, Olimpia Giuliana Loddo, and Giuseppe Lorini. 2020. On credentials. *Journal of Social Ontology* 6 (1): 47–67.

Smith, Barry, and Achille C. Varzi. 1999. The niche. *Noûs* 33 (2): 214–238.

———. 2002. Surrounding space. *Theory in Biosciences* 121 (2): 139–162.

Smolensky, Paul. 1990. Tensor product variable binding and the representation of symbolic structures in connectionist systems. *Artificial Intelligence* 46 (1): 159–216.

Solomon, Karen O., Doug Medin, and Elizabeth Lynch. 1999. Concepts do more than categorize. *Trends in Cognitive Sciences* 3: 99–105.

Spaulding, Shannon. 2013. Mirror neurons and social cognition. *Mind and Language* 28 (2): 233–257.

Spear, Andrew, Werner Ceusters, and Barry Smith. 2016. Functions in Basic Formal Ontology. *Applied Ontology* 11 (2): 103–128.

Spelke, Elizabeth S. 1990. Principles of object perception. *Cognitive Science* 14 (1): 29–56.

———. 2000. Core knowledge. *American Psychologist* 55 (11): 1233–1243.

Spelke, Elizabeth S., and Linda Hermer. 1996. Early cognitive development: objects and space. In *Perceptual and Cognitive Development*, 71–114. San Diego and London: Academic Press.

Spelke, Elizabeth S., and Katherine D. Kinzler. 2007. Core knowledge. *Developmental Science* 10 (1): 89–96.

Sperber, Dan, and Nicolas Claidière. 2008. Defining and explaining culture (comments on Richerson and Boyd, *Not by Genes Alone*). *Biology and Philosophy* 23 (2): 283–292.

Stalnaker, Robert. 2012. *Mere possibilities: metaphysical foundations of modal semantics*. Princeton, NJ: Princeton University Press.

Steele, David Ramsay. 2013. *From Marx to Mises: post-capitalist society and the challenge of economic calculation*. Chicago: Open Court.

Stern, William. 1920. *Die Intelligenz der Kinder und Jugendlichen und Methoden ihrer Untersuchung*. Leipzig: Barth.

Stevenson, Charles Leslie. 1938. Persuasive definitions. *Mind* 47 (187): 331–350.

Stivers, Tanya, N. J. Enfield, et al. 2009. Universals and cultural variation in turn-taking in conversation. *Proceedings of the National Academy of Sciences* 106 (26): 10587–10592.

Stoljar, Daniel. 2017. Physicalism. In *Stanford encyclopedia of philosophy*, https://plato.stanford.edu/entries/physicalism/.

Stooke, Adam, Anuj Mahajan, et al. 2021. Open-ended learning leads to generally capable agents. *CoRR abs/2107.12808*. https://arxiv.org/abs/2107.12808.

Strachan, Tom, and Andrew Read. 2018. *Human molecular genetics*. London: Chapman & Hall/CRC.

Strecker, Jonathan, Sara Jones, et al. 2019. Engineering of CRISPR-Cas12b for human genome editing. *Nature Communications* 10: 212.

Strickland, Eliza. 2019. *How IBM Watson overpromised and underdelivered on AI health care*. https://spectrum.ieee.org/biomedical/diagnostics/how-ibm-watson-overpromised-and-underdelivered-on-ai-health-care.

Strychalski, Elizabeth A., Clyde A. Hutchinson III, et al. 2016. Design and synthesis of a minimal bacterial genome. *Science* 351 (6280): aad6253.

Sutton, Richard S., and Andrew G. Barto. 2018. *Reinforcement learning: an introduction*. Cambridge, MA: The MIT Press.

Swat, Maciej J., Pierre Grenon, and Sarala Wimalaratne. 2016. ProbOnto: ontology and knowledge base of probability distributions. *Bioinformatics* 32 (17): 2719–2721.

Syropoulos, Apostolos. 2008. *Hypercomputation. Computing beyond the Church-Turing barrier*. Boston, MA: Springer.

Talmy, Leonard. 2018. *The targeting system of language*. Cambridge, MA: MIT Press.

———. 2021. Structure within morphemic meaning. *Cognitive Semantics* 7 (2).

Tam, Vivian, Nikunj Patel, et al. 2019. Benefits and limitations of genome-wide association studies. *Nature Reviews Genetics* 20: 467–486.

Taylor, Charles. 1985. The concept of a person. In *Philosophical papers, Volume 1: human agency and language*, Cambridge: Cambridge University Press. 97–114.

Thomsen, Erik, and Barry Smith. 2018. Ontology-based fusion of sensor data and natural language. *Applied Ontology* 13: 295–333.

Thurner, Stefan, Peter Klimek, and Rudolf Hanel. 2018. *Introduction to the theory of complex systems*. Oxford: Oxford University Press.

Turing, Alan. 1937. On computable numbers, with an application to the Entscheidungsproblem. *Proceedings of the London Mathematical Society* 42 (1): 230–265.

———. 1950. Computing machinery and intelligence. *Mind* LIX: 433–460.

———. 1951. *Can digital computers think?* http://www.turingarchive.org/browse.php/B/5.

———. 1952. The chemical basis of morphogenesis. *Philosophical Transactions of the Royal Society of London Series B* 237 (641): 37–72.

Valiant, Leslie G. 1984. A theory of the learnable. *Communications of the ACM* 27 (11): 1134–1142.

Vallor, Shannon. 2016. *Technology and the virtues: a philosophical guide to a future worth wanting*. Oxford: Oxford University Press.

Vanderstraeten, Raf. 2002. Parsons, Luhmann and the theorem of double contingency. *Journal of Classical Sociology* 2 (1): 77–92.

Vaswani, Ashish, Noam Shazeer, et al. 2017. Attention is all you need. *arXiv abs/1706.03762*.

Verschueren, Jef. 1999. *Understanding pragmatics*. London and New York: Arnold.

Vetter, Barbara. 2020. Perceiving potentiality: a metaphysics for affordances. *Topoi* 39 (5): 1177–1191.

Vinge, Vernor. 1993. *The coming technological singularity*. https://edoras.sdsu.edu/~vinge/misc/singularity.html.

———. 2013. Technological singularity. In *The transhumanist reader*, edited by Max More and Natasha Vita-More, 365–375. Oxford: Wiley-Blackwell.

Vogt, Lars, Peter Grobe, et al. 2012. Fiat or bona fide boundary—a matter of granular perspective. *PLoS ONE* 7 (12): e48603.

Wallach, Wendell, and Colin Allen. 2008. *Moral machines: teaching robots right from wrong*. Oxford: Oxford University Press.

Walsh, Toby. 2017. The singularity may never be near. *AI Magazine* 38 (3): 58–62.

Wang, Chaoyue, Chang Xu, et al. 2019. Evolutionary generative adversarial networks. *IEEE Transactions on Evolutionary Computation* 23 (6): 921–934.

Warwick, Kevin, and Huma Shah. 2016. Can machines think? A report on Turing test experiments at the Royal Society. *Journal of Experimental & Theoretical Artificial Intelligence* 28 (6): 989–1007.

Weber, Max. 1976. *Wirtschaft und Gesellschaft*. Tübingen: Mohr Siebeck.

———. 1988. *Gesammelte Aufsätze zur Wissenschaftslehre*. Tübingen: J.C.B. Mohr.

Weinstein, Michael, and Jürgen Schmidhuber. 2017. Von Menschen, Stachelschweinen und Robotern. *Schweizer Monat Dossier: Big Data und KI*. https://schweizermonat.ch/von-menschen-stachelschweinen-und-robotern/

Werner, Konrad. 2020. Enactment and construction of the cognitive niche: toward an ontology of the mind-world connection. *Synthese* 197 (3): 1313–1341.

Werner, Sven. 2017. International review of district heating and cooling. *Energy* 137: 617–631.

Whitehead, Alfred North. 1911. *An introduction to mathematics*. London: Williams/Norgate.

Wiles, Andrew John. 1995. Modular elliptic curves and Fermat's last theorem. *Annals of Mathematics* 141 (3): 443–551.

Williams, Bernard. 1985. *Ethics and the limits of philosophy*. Cambridge, MA: Harvard University Press.

Williamson, Timothy. 2005. Contextualism, subject-sensitive invariantism and knowledge of knowledge. *The Philosophical Quarterly* 55 (219): 213–235.

Wilson, Edward O. 2000. *Sociobiology: the new synthesis*. Cambridge, MA: Harvard University Press.

Wimsatt, William C. 1994. The ontology of complex systems: levels of organization, perspectives, and causal thickets. *Canadian Journal of Philosophy* 24 (Sup 1): 207–274.

Wisnewski, Jeremy. 2019. Affordances, embodiment, and moral perception: a sketch of a moral theory. *Philosophy in the Contemporary World* 25 (1): 35–48.

Wittgenstein, Ludwig. 2003. *Philosophical investigations: the German text, with a revised English translation*. Malden, MA: Blackwell.

Wojtyła, Karol. 1979. *Primat des Geistes: Philosophische Schriften*. Degerloch, Stuttgart: Seewald Verlag.

Wolpert, David H., and William G. Macready. 1997. No free lunch theorems for optimization. *IEEE Transactions on Evolutionary Computation* 1 (1): 67–82.

Wu, Jiayan, Jingfa Xiao, et al. 2014. Ribogenomics: the science and knowledge of RNA. *Genomics, Proteomics & Bioinformatics* 12 (2): 57–63.

Yudkowsky, Eliezer. 2001a. *Coherent extrapolated volition*. San Francisco: The Singularity Institute.

———. 2001b. *Creating friendly AI 1.0: the analysis and design of benevolent goal architectures*. San Francisco: The Singularity Institute.

———. 2008a. Artificial intelligence as a positive and negative factor in global risk. In *Global catastrophic risks*, edited by Nick Bostrom and Milan M. Cirkovic, 308–345. New York: Oxford University Press.

———. 2008b. *Efficient cross-domain optimization*. https://www.lesswrong.com/posts/yLeEPFnnB9wE7KLx2/efficient-cross-%20domain-optimization.

Zaibert, Leo. 2018. *Rethinking punishment*. Cambridge: Cambridge University Press.

Zhou, Li, Jianfeng Gao, et al. 2020. The design and implementation of XiaoIce, an empathetic social chatbot. *Computational Linguistics* 46 (1): 53–93.

Ziv Konzelmann, Anita. 2013. Introduction. In *Institutions, emotions, and group agents: contributions to social ontology*, edited by Anita Ziv Konzelmann and Hans Bernhard Schmid, 1–15. Berlin: Springer.

INDEX

Page numbers in **bold** indicate Glossary entries.

abduction, 29
adaptation, 40, 44, 45, 47, 127, 151, **304**
affordance, 16, 46
   moral, 278
agent, 49, 50, 58, 59, 60, 61, 91, 109, 150, 174, 245, 251, 252, 254
   autonomous, 275
   ethical, 2, 251, 252, 254, 257
   superintelligent, 274
AGI, *see* general artificial intelligence
AI ethics, 2, 90, 99, 101, 102, 250, 251
AI explosion, 272
AI winter, 10, 288
Alexander, Samuel, 27
algorithm, 50, 58, 62, 110
   computable, 18, 109, 115
   optimisation, 12, 114, 147, 165, **304**
   stochastic, 146
ambiguity, 232
analytic philosophy, 5, 7, 77, 277
anisotropy, 138, 183, **304**
Anscombe, G. M. E., 66, 71
Aristotle, 65, 134, 175, 196
artefact, 36, 38, 45, 110, 125, 131, 188
artificial general intelligence, *see* general artificial intelligence
artificial intelligence, *see* AI winter, *see* general artificial intelligence, *see* narrow AI, *see* symbolic (logic-based) AI

   connectionist, 148
   in biology and medicine, 297
   limits of, 13, 48, 243, 298
   narrow, 161, 288, 296, 301
   symbolic, 12
   without representation, 293
artificial life, 198, 280, 281, 282
   using engineered bacteria, 282
ATP, 129, 135, 196, 197, 282
Austin, J. L., 6, 7, 65, 76

Babbage, Charles, 60
Barker, Roger, 7, 77, 228
Basic Formal Ontology (BFO), 38, 127
Bergson, Henri, 125
Block, Ned, 27, 210, 211
Boden, Margaret, 286
Boltzmann, Ludwig, 125, 159, 187
Bostrom, Nick, 3, 48, 260, 261, 264, 266, 268, 269–271, 274, 287
   on quantum computers, 264
Boyd, Robert, 43, 45, 46
brain emulation, 195, 199
brain enhancement, 8, 13, 202, 268
brain, imaging, 267
Brehm, Alfred, 111
Bringsjord, Selmer, 210, 213
Brooks, Rodney, 59, 293, 294
Brownian motion, 132, 163, 164, 208
Bühler, Karl, 65, 68

Index

cancer, 129, 135, 140, 154
capability, 37, 38, 42, 118, 278, **304**
　linguistic, 63, 66, 67, 72, 73, 76, 88, 217, 220, 221, 243
　mental, 42, 205, 253, 262, 272
　social, 91–93, 101, 106, 245, 249, 253
categories, 6, 46, 48, 67, 70, 147, 203
causality, *see* interactions
Chalmers, David, 5, 28, 195, 196, 197, 199, 201, 202, 203, 211, 212, 272
chaos, 136, 137, 139, 140, 204, 226, **304**
　deterministic, 124, 137, 189, 226, 290, **304**
chatbot, 64, 114, 125, 150, 151, 213, 218, 227, 237, 238, 241
　state of the art, 237, 238, 239
Chinese Room argument, 210, 266
Chollet, Franois, 16, 168, 299
Church, Alonzo, 11, 12, 115
Churchland, Paul, 27
cognitive enhancement, 268
common sense, 3, 34, 65, 70, 111, 118, 214, 229, 232, 241, 299
community, 91, 92, 93, **304**
complex traits, 141
compositional AI, 291, 292
computability, 12, 114, 115, 116, 122, 149, 161, 190
computation, **304**
computer
　as driven device, 134, 204, 206
　definition of, 89
connectionism, 12
conscience, 249
consciousness, 4, 11, 206, 210, 212, **305**
　definition, 205
consciousness, flow of, 135, 220
context, 7, 70, 72, 88, 123, 225, 231, 240
　horizon, 78, 79, 84, 91, 230
　of a conversation, 64, 75, 76, 77, 78, 81, 82, 85, 88, 218, 223, 225, 227, 229, 230, 231, 233, 234,
　social, 79, 96, 128, 248, 249
context-dependent, 139, 151, 226, 228, 235, 238, 242
context-free, 137, 242, 289
conversation, 63, 64, 65, 66, 67, 69, 71, 73, 74, 76, 150, 159, 164, 164, 229, 233
creativity, 16, 43, 45, 48, 125, 170, 209, 215, 233, 243, 300
culture, 40, 41, 43, 45, 47, 71, 91, 96, 203, 214, 243, **305**

cumulative cultural evolution, 45, 46
cyborgs, 271, 282

data, explicit vs. implicit, 236
data, synthetic, 10, 169, 180, **305**
Davidson, Donald, 32, 33
Davis, Ernest, 177, 299
Davis, Martin, 264
decidability, 115, 116, 117, 167, 190, 231
deep neural network (dNN), 57, 145, 147, 165, 238
Dennett, Daniel, 212
Descartes, Ren, 262
dialect, 66, 73, 86, 86, 222
digital immortality, 260, 285, 286
disposition, 37, 38, 39, 68, 72, 76, 128, 130, 175, 204, 211, 278, 279, **305**
distribution, 144, 152, 164
　'data without regular distribution', 88, 150, 151, 164, 173, 233, 235
　Bernoulli, 144, 145
　from non-ergodic process, 150
　Gaussian, 144, 145, 163
　multivariate, 118, 145, 151, 152, 165, 170, **305**
　non-parametric, 145, 152, 165, 170
　parametric, 144, 145, 152
　representative, 164
　training, 146
　univariate, 144
double contingency, 93, 96
Dreyfus, Hubert, 67
drivenness, *see also* human excess drive, 132, 133, 135, 135, 138, 166, 183, 196, 197, 197, 203, **305**
　accidental, 136, 204
　animate, **305**
　artificial, 147, **305**
　essential, 135, 197
　natural, **305**

economic calculation argument, 157
element (of a system), 3, 29, 111, 117, 118, 122, 127, 128, 129, 130, 131, 132, 144, 145, 149, 183, **306**
element types, 117, 122, 126, 128, 134
emanation, 4, 23, 24, 28, 30, 31, 34, 58, 59, 61, 109, 118, 119, 152, 164, 166, 170, 175, 186, 206, 209, 219, 220, 247, 257, 268, 279, **306**
embodied cognition, 214
emotion, perception of, 95
emotions, 70, 75

perception of, 93, 94, 95, 247
emulation, 112, 114, 124, 204, 210, 226, 245, **306**
  dialogue, 227, 237
  of brain, 189, 195, 196, 199, 265, 266
  of consciousness, 12, 210, 212
  of morality, 101, 250
energy, 129, 132, 133, 134, 136, 183, 204
engineering, 112, 121
entelechy, 134
entropy, 125, 134, 136, 186, 187, **306**
  negative, 135, 205
entropy model, 181, 186
environment, 7, 40, 44, 45, 46, 123, 137, **306**
  controlled, 178
  versus environment description, 49, 51
epidemiology, 162
equilibrium, 125, 132, 133, 187
ergodicity, 127, 138, 145, 151, 183, 186, **306**
Ersatz-definition, 59, 203, 213, 265, 287
event, erratic, **306**
evolution, **306**
evolution argument for the possibility of AGI, 200, 201
evolutionary process models, 185
explainability, 166
explanation, 7, 158
  causal, 111, 143, 158
explicit network, 185
extended Newtonian mathematics, 258

face-to-face interaction, 83, 94, 228, 229
Fermi's paradox, 14
Feynman, Richard, 182
fiat entity, 118
Fodor, Jerry, 26, 293
folk psychology, 3, 29
force
  homogeneous, 122
  isotropic, 122
force overlay, 130, 138, 224
foundation models, 177
Fourier transformation, 32
Fourier, Joseph, 121
Frankfurt, Harry, 17, 278
Frege, Gottlob, 6, 100
function (mathematics), **306**
function (of a system or an artefact), 35, 70, 130, **306**
function, recursive (computer science), **306**

functional, 146, 148, 166, 291

games, 9, 55, 146, 152, 174
Gehlen, Arnold, 6, 39, 41, 66, 69, 215
general artificial intelligence, 10, 13, 91, 101, 115, 124, 126, 159, 196
genetic engineering, 270, 284
genetics, 155, 156, 267
geometry, 104
gestures, 66, 69, 86
Gibson, J. J., 7, 52, 53, 94, 247, 293
goals, *see* intentions 275
Gottfredson, Linda, 37
GPT-3, 166, 177, 240, 241
granular partition, 28, 30, 35, 117, 118, 122, 127, 140
  temporal, 29
Grice, Paul, 66, 76, 83
GWAS, 141, 141
Gödel's theorem, 208
Gödel, Kurt, 58, 190

habitat, 44, 45
halting problem, 115
Harré, Rom, 37
Hartmann, Nicolai, 6, 100–104
Haugeland, John, 161, 299
Hayek, Friedrich August von, 40, 157
Hayes, Patrick, 299
Heisenberg, Werner, 182
Hertz, Heinrich, 110
Higgs boson, 110
Horton, Robin, 3, 214
human excess drive, 39, 40, 135
human intelligence, 16, 18
human mind-body continuum, 23, 28–30, 35, 124, 141, 260–262, 266, 268
human neurocognitive system, xi, 128, 135
Husserl, Edmund, 5, 45, 47, 78, 94
Hutter, Marcus, 49, 263, 275
hypercomputation, 116, 263, 264, 265

identity, 39, 78, 278, **307**
image recognition, 219, 265
immortality, 260, 285
immunology, 155
Ingarden, Roman, 6, 86, 127
insects, 293, 295
instinct, 40, 42–44, 67, 298, **307**
institution, 79, 91, 92, 97
intelligence, 14, 37, **307**
  as mental capability, 38

human, 1, 17, 24, 41, 45, 190
   Hutter definition, 49, 50, 51
   machine, 14, 17, 49, 51, 60, *see also* useful machine intelligence
   objectifying, 45, 46, 47, 61, 67, 71, 262, **307**
   primal, 41, 51, **307**
intentions, 38, 39, 40, 42, 43, 47, 68, 72, 74, 76, 83, 85, 86, 88, 89, 95, 135, 148, 203, 227, 275, 276, **307**
interaction types, 117, 128, 129, 137, 139, 185, 186
   variable, 149
interactions, 111, 164, 299
   fundamental, 3, 28, 29, 122, 131
   social, 93, 105
interpretation, *see* machine interpretation
intersubjectivity, 94–96, 247, 249, **307**
   definition, 95
introspection, 28, 29
irreversibility, 134, 138, 139, 183
isotropy, **307**

Kant, Immanuel, 158
Kim, Jaegwon, 31
Kolmogorov complexity function, 50
Kolmogorov, Andrey, xii, 183, 301
Kurzweil, Ray, 1

La Mettrie, Julien Offray de, 26, 263
language
   aggregate of capabilities, 73, 221
   evolution of, 43, 66, 149, 223
   invented, 223, 236
law, 65, 72, 91, 96, 97, 248, 249, 250, 296
laws of physics, 3, 24, 29, 30, 32, 35, 121, 129, 137
   language dependent view of, 33
Leibniz, Gottfried Wilhelm, 120
Leonardo da Vinci, 182
Lewis, David, 78
life, *see also* artificial life, 135, 135, 135, 200, 281
logic system, 116, 122, 123, 126, 128, 129, 130, 132, 148, 152
   used as approximate model of complex system, 161, 177
logic, first-order, 116, 117, 231
longevity, 284, 285
Lorentz force, 112
Lorenz, Konrad, 65

loss function, 17, 62, 147, 149, 179, 257, **307**
Lotze, Herrmann, 100
Lovelace, Ada, 60
Lucas, John R., 190, 208

machine, 26
   definition, 196, 197
machine language interpretation, 218, 221, 229, 230
machine language production, 219, 227, 231
machine learning, **308**
macrostate, 132, 187
macrostate (thermodynamics), **308**
Marcus, Gary, 177, 241, 298
Markov model, 127, 161, 164
Markov property, 16, 81, 136, 149, 164, 175, 186, 234, 239
mathematics, *see* Newtonian mathematics, extended
   technically useful applied mathematics, 123
Maxwell equations, 112, 121
measurement, 23, 117, 118, 144, 145
measurement error, 124, 189, **308**
medicine, 124, 142, 154, 297
mental process, 4, 23, 24, 29, 30, 32
microstate, 132, 187, 189
microstate (thermodynamics), **308**
military applications of AI, 296, 297
Mill, John Stuart, 99, 100, 253
mind-body continuum, **308**
mind-body problem, 23, 266, see also human mind-body continuum
   naturalistic dualism, 28
   reductive physicalism, 25
   type-type identity theory, 26
Minsky, Marvin, 12
Mises, Ludwig von, 157
model, 109, 146
   adequate, 110, 112, 119, 123, 124, 152, 153, 159, **308**
   approximately predictive, 112, 113, 179
   classification, 147, 290
   complex system, 162
   conditioning, 177, 240
   descriptive, 35, 111, 143, 153
   economic, 157, 158
   entropy, 187
   entropy model, 181, 186
   exact, 112, 119, 124, 150, 158
   explicit, 114, 114, 160, 190
   explicit (mathematics), **308**

financial, 160, 163
graph-based, 144, 185
hyperparameters of, 148
implicit, 114, 161, 165, 166, 179, 190
implicit (machine learning), **308**
mathematical, 110, 112, 119, 122, 132, 139, 151, 159, 165
parameter-greedy, 186
parameterisation, 147, 151
parametric, **308**
partial, 113, 153, 161, **309**
physical, **309**
predictive, 110, 112, 113, 139, 153
regression, 147, 148, 161, 188
stochastic, 112, 144, 146, 147, 148, 151, 163, 177, 188, **309**
types of, 160
symbolic, **309**
synoptic, 8, 112, 113, 153, 186, **309**
system, 221, 222, 223
types of, 123, 124
validity of, 110, 122, 129
model (science), **308**
model underspecification, 160
model-induced escape, 172, 178
monism
anomalous, 32, 33
materialistic, 25, 28
mechanical, 26
nomological, 29
types of, 25, 111, 112
Moor, James H., 251, 252
morality, *see* values
no machine model of, 250
multiple realisability, 30, 31, 266

n-body problem, 9, 68, 158, 162, 188, 189
nanotechnology, 283
narrow AI, 12, 17, 61, 161, 171, 179
nave physics, 111, 299
neural machine translation, 146, 147
neural network, 12
LSTM, 58, 171
neurons, 25, 128, 131, 156, 168
Newell, Allen, 299
Newton's laws, 111, 120, 189
Newton, Isaac, xii, 120
Newtonian mathematics, extended, 113, 119, 149, 152, 188, 190, 198, **309**
no free lunch theorem, 16, 170, 171, 288
nominalism, 34
non-Mendelian inheritance, 141, 284

norm
behavioural, 248
legal, 97, 106, 248
moral, 92, 98, 103, 246, 251, 278
social, 90, 93, 95-98, 239, 240, 300, **309**

objectification, **309**
observation, 23, 29, 144
observation (physics), **309**
observer-dependent, 11, 206, 207
ontology, *see also* common sense 4, 5, 27, 38, 206
AI uses, 297
social, 7, 65, 90
operator, *see also* functional, 146, 291
operator (functional analysis), **309**
over-fitting, 142, 170

parameterisation (statistical learning), **309**
partition, granular, 4, 29, **310**
patents, 300
Pearl, Judea, 15, 299
Peirce, Charles Sanders, 17, 53, 215
Penrose, Roger, 190, 208
person, 38, 93, 260
as source of ethical behaviour, 103, 277
definition, 286
digitally cloned, 260
pharmacology, 154, 155
phase space, 132, 145, 151, 224, **310**
Pinker, Steven, 15
planning, 40, 41, 42, 45, 46, 64, 71, 76, 210
poker, 174
Popitz, Heinrich, 81, 97, 279
Popper, Karl, 65
power, 80, 81, 97, 106, 279
prediction, 110, 111, 116, 120, 122
almost exact, 113, 119, 122
exact, 119, 123, 157, **310**
prediction (mathematics), **310**
Prigogine, Ilya, 125
primary theory, 3, 118, 214, 277
prior knowledge, 241, 291, 299
probability, conditioned, **310**
process model (engineering), **310**
protein phosphorylation, 128, 162, 198, 267
Putnam, Hilary, 67, 85, 232

qualitative physics, 111
quantum computer, 264
quantum computers, 264
Quine, W. V. O., 37

Ramseyfication, 27
realism, 3
    common-sense, 3
    scientific, 3
realism, ontological, 3
realist phenomenology, school of, 5, 102, 127
recursive function, 115, 116, 122, 146
Reinach, Adolf, 6, 65, 97, 102
reinforcement learning, 10, 173, 174, 175, 238, 274
    applied to social dialogue, 239
reliability, 112, 121, 123, 179
reproduction, 38, 39, 67, 135, 143, 270, 285
    with machines, 260
reward, 49, 50, 57, 99, 275
reward trace, 55, 150
Richerson, Peter J., 43, 45, 46
robots, 49, 63, 210, 280, 290, 293
Rosenblatt, Frank, 188
Rothblatt, Martine, 260
Russell, Bertrand, 39

sample, 144
    representative, 145, 150–152
    training, 88, 146, 148, 150–152, 179, 180
Sartre, Jean-Paul, 94
scaling, 181, 182, 301
scallop theorem, 283
Scheler, Max, 6, 41, 51, 65, 69, 91, 93, 95, 100, 102, 104, 205, 261, 263, 277
Schmidhuber, Jrgen, 2, 50, 58, 165, 166, 272, 274, 275
Schopenhauer, Arthur, 71
Schrdinger equation, 123
Schtz, Alfred, 94
Searle, John R., 6, 7, 11, 27, 39, 45, 65, 205, 206, 207, 209, 210, 212, 266
selection, 109, 117, 200, 201
self-driving cars, 123, 178, 292
sensorimotor activity, 69, 292
sensorimotor perception, 53, 101
sensors, 51, 52, 54, 123
service industries, 295
Shannon, Claude, 186
Simon, Herbert A., 299
simulation, 14, 114, 265, **310**
singularity (mathematics) **310**
Singularity, the, 1, 2, 9, 14, 16, 260, 274

situation, **310**
Smith, Adam, 100, 106
Smolensky, Paul, 12
social fact, 34
social norm
    definition, 95
socialisation, 86, 91, 92, **311**
society, 16, 77, 91, 92, 248
solar system, 116, 118, 122, 140
speech
    acts, 6, 7, 65
    as sensorimotor activity, 54, 69
Spelke, Kim, 46, 70
Sperber, Dan, 43
Spinoza, 135
state, 206, **311**
state variable, 132, 224, **311**
steam engine, 133, 134, 136, 137, 204
Stein, Edith, 6
Stern, William, 37, 41
stochastic process, **311**
superintelligence, 1, 261, 263, 268, 270
supervenience, 28, 31
supervised learning, 147, 238
survival, 38, 39, 67, 135
symbolic (logic-based) AI, x
symbolic AI, 61
synthetic training data, *see* data, synthetic
system, **311**
    biological, 125, 129, 130, 135
    boundary, 117, 122, 127, 136, 137, 162, 226
    chemical, 132
    climate system, 132, 150, 153
    complex, 89, 116, 123, 124, 125, 126, 128, 178, **311**
    animate, 143
    evolutionary character of, 126, 127, 128, 138, 178
    context-dependent, 139, 151, 162
    context-free, 123, 128, 137
    dissipative, 133, 134, 183
    driven, 132 *see also* drivenness 197
        animate, 134, 143, 197
        inanimate, 134, 136, 197
    ecological, 36, 89
    ergodic, **311**
    hybrid, 123, 289
    interactions, 117, 122, 127
    logic, *see also* logic system, **312**
    non-driven, 133
    non-ergodic, **312**
    organic, 8, 123

outcome, 117, 118, 119
  philosophical theories of, 126, 127
  relatively isolated, 127
  state of, 130, 131
  traffic, 178, 178, 292
system (information theory), **311**
system of systems, 118, 124

Talmy, Len, 83, 225
technosphere, 41, 43, 47, 121
thermodynamics, 125, 134
thinking, categorical, 46, **312**
Thomas Reid, 65
training sample, 62, 166, 179, 234, 254
transfer learning, 177
transhumanism, 9, 259, 282
turbulence, 136, 140, 182, 183, 283, 301
Turing machine, 12, 114, 115
  niversal, 207
  universal, 207
Turing test, 78, 88, 217
Turing, Alan, 11, 45, 60, 111, 115
Turing-computable, **312**

unsupervised learning, 142, 176
useful machine intelligence, 13, 57, 60, 63
utilitarianism, 99, 102
utility function, 49, 50‑55, 56, 58, 59, 62, 159, 252

vagueness, 73, 78, 220
value blindness, 102
value ethics, 100, 101, 102

value feelings, 100, 104, 278
values, 92, 92, 100, 253
  demand character, 101, 103
  moral, 102
  space of, 102, 104
variable, 35, 116, 144, 145
  random, 50, 144, 163
variance, 66, 141, 144, 174, 237, **312**
  genetic, 141, 200
  linguistic, 66, 72, 73, 76, 88
vector, **312**
vector space, 145, 147, 149, **312**
virology, 154, 197
von Neumann, John, 12, 207

Walsh, Toby, 14
Weber, Max, 91, 122
Whitehead, Alfred North, 67
whole brain emulation, *see* emulation
Wiener process models, 163
will, 203, 260, 275
  act of, 249, 278
  effectivity, 278
  extrapolation of, 276
  no machine will, 205, 279
  person as source of, 277
Winograd Challenge, 232
Wittgenstein, Ludwig, 66
Wojtyła, Karol, 6

Yudkowsky, Eliezer, 48, 58, 59, 276, 277, 279, 280
zombies, 211, 212

Printed in Great Britain
by Amazon